# STUDIES ON VOLTAIRE AND THE EIGHTEENTH CENTURY

## 259

General editor

PROFESSOR H. T. MASON

Department of French
University of Bristol
Bristol BS8 1TE

RUTH WHELAN

# The Anatomy of superstition: a study of the historical theory and practice of Pierre Bayle

THE  VOLTAIRE  FOUNDATION

AT THE TAYLOR INSTITUTION, OXFORD

1989

© *1989 University of Oxford*

ISSN 0435-2866

ISBN 0 7294 0372 6

*British Library cataloguing in publication data*

Whelan, Ruth
The Anatomy of superstition: a study of the
historical theory and practice of Pierre Bayle.
— (Studies on Voltaire and the eighteenth century,
ISSN 0435-2866; 259)
1. French philosophy. Bayle, Pierre; 1647-1706
I. Title  II. Series
194
ISBN 0-7294-0372-6

*Printed in England at The Alden Press, Oxford*

*For Muriel and Charles*

# Contents

Acknowledgements ix

Abbreviations xi

Introduction 1

I. Prologue: the objectivity of the historian
  1. Agreda 9
  2. Nestorius 31

II. The historian as moralist
  3. 'La racine du mal': the psychology of total depravity and the psychology of the historian 59
  4. Godliness and good learning: the ethics of the Republic of Letters 87

III. History, criticism and faith
  5. 'Les têtes de l'Hydre': theological method and historical method 119
  6. The Ariadne's thread: Bayle and Scripture 146

IV. Theology and history
  7. 'Le doigt de Dieu' and 'le théâtre du monde': the philosophy of history 183
  8. 'Le rire des honnêtes gens': historical iconoclasm: conclusion 233

Appendices 241
  Appendix I. Nestorius: the background 243
  Appendix II. Biblical articles in the *Dictionnaire* 248
  Appendix III. The lives of the popes 249

Bibliography 251

Index 263

# Acknowledgements

My research was funded by Trinity College Dublin, the French government, the International Federation of University Women (Winifred Cullis Grant) and the Collège de France. The Ecole normale supérieure provided me with accommodation for three years in Paris. Many friends gave moral and financial support: Paul Brennan, Sue Brown, Virginia Davis, Susan Leonard, Muriel McCarthy, Larry Scott, John Woodeson, and my parents.

The librarians of the Department of Early Printed Books, the Berkeley and Lecky libraries of Trinity College Dublin, Muriel McCarthy of Archbishop Marsh's Library Dublin, the librarians of the National Library of Ireland, the Queen's University Belfast, the University Library Maynooth, the Cashel Diocesan Library, the Bodleian and Taylorian libraries in Oxford, the British Library, the Royal Library in the Hague, the Bibliothèques nationale and Mazarine, the Bibliothèque de la Société de l'histoire du protestantisme and the libraries of the Ecole normale supérieure in Paris have been unfailingly courteous and helpful.

Many colleagues and friends have read the manuscript of this book, in some cases reading several drafts. Haydn Mason, Harry Bracken, Walter Rex and Muriel and Charles McCarthy commented helpfully on the final draft. From Roger Little I have received inestimable help and encouragement. Roger Zuber, Elisabeth Labrousse and Jean-Paul Pittion were generous with their time and scholarship at every stage in the preparation. To them I am especially grateful.

Ruth Whelan
Trinity College Dublin

# Abbreviations

## 1. Bayle's works

| | |
|---|---|
| *APD* | *Addition aux Pensées diverses* |
| *Avis* | *Avis important aux refugiez sur leur prochain retour en France* |
| *CG* | *Critique générale de l'Histoire du calvinisme de M. Maimbourg* |
| *CP* | *Commentaire philosophique sur ces paroles de Jésus-Christ 'Contrains-les d'entrer'* |
| *CPD* | *Continuation des Pensées diverses* |
| *NLC* | *Nouvelles lettres de l'auteur de la Critique générale* |
| *NRL* | *Nouvelles de la République des lettres* |
| *OD* | *Œuvres diverses*: Bayle's collected works, in 4 volumes. There were two editions, the second (1737) is here designated *OD*; references are to volume and page numbers; the pages are in double columns. |
| *PD* | *Pensées diverses sur la comète* |
| *Projet* | *Projet […] d'un dictionnaire critique* |
| *RQP* | *Réponse aux questions d'un provincial* |

## 2. Other

| | |
|---|---|
| *BHR* | *Bibliothèque d'humanisme et de renaissance* |
| *BSHP* | *Bulletin de la Société de l'histoire du protestantisme* |
| *BU* | *Bibliothèque universelle* |
| *DTC* | *Dictionnaire de théologie catholique* |
| *HOS* | *Histoire des ouvrages des savants* |
| *JS* | *Journal des savants* |
| *PMLA* | *Publications of the Modern Languages Association* |
| *RHLF* | *Revue d'histoire littéraire de la France* |

# Introduction

Soleo enim et in aliena castra transire, non tamquam transfuga sed tamquam explorator.

Seneca, *Ad Lucilium*, Ep.II

Il y a si peu d'Histoires où la vérité paroisse à nu, & sans les fausses couleurs que l'Historien trouve propres à le décharger de quelque chagrin ou de quelque mécontentement, ou à l'armer de quelque trait de critique contre des personnes vivantes. Il les fait venir sur son chemin en traitant l'Histoire des Indes. Tous les Lecteurs ne devinent pas à qui il en veut; mais il y en a qui le devinent, & il sçait bien qu'il y en aura qui le feront.

Bayle, 'Remond', in *Dictionnaire*[1]

PIERRE Bayle belongs to that *fin de siècle* generation of scholars and writers – inheritors of traditions and forerunners of innovations – so aptly designated the generation of 'la crise de la conscience européenne'.[2] His contemporaries differed, however, in their assessment of his work. While some, anticipating modern critics, saw him as a sceptic and saboteur of traditions, others were more struck by his scholarship and the encyclopedic nature of his reading. In 1690, Bayle springs spontaneously to the mind of Antoine Furetière: seeking to define the word 'littérature' in his *Dictionnaire universel*, he places his learned friend in a pantheon of post-Renaissance scholars, Scaliger, Saumaise, Lipse, Casaubon and Grotius, as a further and living example of 'gens de grande littérature, d'une profonde littérature'.[3] In this view Bayle re-incarnates the Renaissance author: his writings feed on his reading of literature – ancient, modern and in all its forms. Now, Furetière's definition isolates two of his friend's characteristics which are often neglected.[4] Bayle is first and foremost a reader, secondly an antiquarian: his gaze is turned upon the past.[5]

Neglect of Bayle's indisputably *erudite* intellectual temperament is one of the root causes, in our opinion, of the indecision typifying interpretations of his

1. 'Remond', footnote D, in *Dictionnaire historique et critique* (Rotterdam 1720). All references are to this edition.
2. Cf. Paul Hazard, *La Crise de la conscience européenne 1680-1715* (Paris 1935). References are to the English translation: *The European mind 1680-1715*, trans. J. Lewis May (Harmondsworth 1973), unless otherwise stated.
3. Antoine Furetière, 'Littérature', in *Dictionnaire universel* (La Haye 1690); cf. Marc Fumaroli, *L'Age de l'éloquence* (Genève 1980), p.24ff., for the significance of Furetière's explanation of the word.
4. Bayle wrote the preface to Furetière's *Dictionnaire*.
5. See chapter 4 below, especially p.115-16.

thought. Three hundred years of debate illustrate that the often obscure scholarship of the *Dictionnaire historique et critique* defied even the next wave of writers.[6] The apparent similarities of language, irony and ideas, their enthusiasm to 'écraser l'infâme' blinded eighteenth-century writers to the vast unshared territory dividing humanist curiosity from Enlightened endeavour. Like Seneca of old, Bayle enters the enemy camp as a scout but his forays for information were read as the activities of a traitor. The plight of the modern critic is even more acute, separated not by time alone but by centuries of culture from a writer 'd'une profonde littérature'. Rather than look at Bayle through the eyes of Voltaire, the critic must seek to don as spectacles those books and that past so familiar to the *philosophe* of Rotterdam. Pondering his writings in the light of what he read will not resurrect the 'real Bayle' but it may contribute to the rediscovery of a forgotten Bayle.

Any study of Bayle through his sources must, however, avoid the methodological errors of many historians of ideas devoted to the understanding of Renaissance, classical and Enlightenment thinkers. Ernst Cassirer's distinction of the 'deeper strata' of Enlightenment philosophy from the 'lengthwise' or chronological consideration it normally receives is important and, applied to the subject in hand, calls for a study of Bayle's thought as it evolves in reaction to the books of his choice.[7] This book is designed, then, not only to identify the unperceived threads, the genesis and maturation of a thought, but also to capture in action the psychological and intellectual alchemy[8] whereby a diversity of traditions and ideological systems are soldered together into a trenchant and uncompromisingly honest philosophy, impatient with the errors and slovenly apprehensions of other thinkers, past and present. The method is that of the 'dynamics of

6. See chapter 6 below, p.175-79.
7. As early as 1932, Ernst Cassirer maintained that 'We gain no access to the deeper strata of the philosophy of the Enlightenment if, like most historians of the period, we merely consider this philosophy lengthwise, that is, if we just string its various intellectual formulations along the thread of time and study them chronologically' (*The Philosophy of the Enlightenment*, trans. Fritz C. A. Koelln and James P. Pettegrove, Boston 1966, p.viii). He called instead for a study of the fundamental intellectual forces of eighteenth-century philosophy in action and 'in the constantly evolving process of thought'. A similar point is made in Elisabeth Labrousse, *Bayle* (Past Masters) (Oxford, New York 1983), p.11-12, 88 and 90. This method, used by Elisabeth Labrousse (*Pierre Bayle*, vol.i: *Du pays de Foix à la cité d'Erasme*; vol.ii: *Hétérodoxie et rigorisme*, La Haye 1963-1964) and Walter Rex (*Essays on Pierre Bayle and religious controversy*, The Hague 1965), is that of this book which, broadly speaking within the same school of thought, is more particularly devoted to the study of Bayle through the dynamics of reception of his sources.
8. The phrase occurs in Noémi Hepp, 'Quelques aspects de l'antiquité grecque dans la pensée française du XVIIe siècle', *XVIIe siècle* 131 (1981), p.118, and is taken here to mean the intellectual and psychological forces peculiar to an individual author, which transform his reading and meditations thereon into a fresh and individual intellectual artefact.

reception',[9] and together with the identification of certain intellectual distortions resulting from Bayle's reading, the conflicts inseparable from a thought which grows *de seconde main*,[10] and the political and historical circumstances acting as catalysts to his work, it yields new insight into the crisis of the European conscience at the close of the *grand siècle*. Bayle, a herald of the Enlightenment, may have inadvertently contributed to the secularisation of European thought, but he himself – like so many of his contemporaries – is caught in the cross-current of debates which are essentially theological.

To rediscover the antiquarian and bookish side to Bayle's nature is not to neglect the Protestant flavour of his thought. The author as reader brings to the books of his choice a set of values and preconceived ideas which focus his primarily antiquarian gaze. Contrary to received opinion,[11] the selections and quotations liberally displayed throughout Bayle's works are made neither innocently nor naively. History, the subject of this study, is chosen as an area where the source and attitudes to it eloquently demonstrate the dialectic between the ideal of objectivity, for which Bayle is renowned, and the conceptual reconstruction of the past inseparable from his and any scholarly endeavours.[12] The Prologue (chapters 1 and 2) selects two articles from the *Dictionnaire* to form a cross-section of his work which, by a process of contextualisation and exegesis, reveal the committed nature of the entries. The critique of superstition, as Jurieu was later to observe, may be 'à la mode',[13] but Bayle is far from Spinozist in his acerbic iconoclasm. Agreda, the Spanish mystic, and the recent interest in her writings personify and revitalise, to his mind, the reasons for the continuing separation of the Calvinists from Rome. Nestorius, a much maligned 'heretic', is, on the contrary, rehabilitated. The procedure may smack of the *libertins érudits* but its purpose, drawing on the image of the fourth-century thinker current at the time, is to highlight the politicisation of religion. As a Protestant *avant la lettre*, Nestorius embodies the creation of schism and heresy, not by the protestors and the critics but by the dominant political party who, resistant to criticism, condemn and force the dissenters from the Church.

9. On the theory of this, see H. Jauss, *Pour une esthétique de la réception*, trans. Claude Maillard et Jean Starobinski (Paris 1978).

10. Cf. Antoine Compagnon, *La Seconde main, ou le travail de la citation* (Paris 1979).

11. Richard H. Popkin (Pierre Bayle, *Historical and critical dictionary*, selections, Indianapolis, New York, Kansas City 1965, p.xliv) is not alone in the belief that Bayle uses his sources with scrupulous accuracy (see below p.184-85). While our author's obsession with accuracy of reference is not to be disputed, as this study will show, he knowingly selects biased sources and 'doctors' those available to him.

12. See below, p.183-232, and Donald R. Kelley, *Foundations of modern historical scholarship* (New York, London 1970).

13. [Pierre Jurieu], *Le Philosophe de Rotterdam accusé, atteint et convaincu* (Amsterdam 1706), p.21; the passage is quoted below, p.9.

3

The second section (chapters 3 and 4) reveals the author struggling with the bias of history, as exemplified by the propagandist activities of Louis Maimbourg. His portrait of the Jesuit in action foreshadows the reading grid later used in the *Dictionnaire* to filter history of its impurities. Maimbourg is also the centre of moral reflections in which the psychology and epistemology of the historian are related to the plight of man since the Fall. The consideration of error yields to the pursuit of truth, as Bayle, in tones reminiscent of Christian humanism and Stoicism, details his ideals for scholarship, wistfully thought to be the common currency of the Republic of Letters. Ideal history, the chimera of his humanist forebears, is the combined result of asceticism and research, moderation in all things with the exception of the *libido sciendi*.

Theology and scholarship are in a dialectical relationship in Bayle's thought and form the focal point of section three (chapters 5 and 6). Chapter five traces the origin of the historico-critical method, which gave the name to the *Dictionnaire*, to a Calvinist theological method. Emphasis, here, is on Bayle's maturing judgement. As his reading advances in scope and depth, a method conceived in religious controversy is transformed via sceptical and critical humanism into a more broadly based scholarly tool, devoted to the eradication of error and superstitious history. The relationship is reversed in the chapter on Scripture. A theology of Holy Writ – derived from a Calvinist background and education – encounters and rejects, albeit haltingly and with compromise, the more liberal and humanist biblical criticism of a Richard Simon. It is here and in the final section that the fundamental ambivalence of Bayle's thought emerges.

Caught, in his attitude to Simon and in his philosophy of history (chapter 7), between his humanist yearnings and his theological convictions, he on occasion attempts to hold together two mutually exclusive positions. Historical causation in the areas of ethics, politics and religion becomes the scene of a *va et vient* between anthropocentric and theocentric forces and, as with Scripture, Bayle is incapable of deciding between them. This *oui et non* to reason, this simultaneous acceptance of and apparent indifference to faith lend that peculiarly perplexing flavour to Bayle's work. The critic watching the tensions develop, attempting to seize them in all their inconsistencies is, perhaps, in a more privileged position than Bayle's immediate successors. He is that perceptive reader sought by the *philosophe* of Rotterdam – often unsuccessfully – all his life.[14] One who, by

14. Bayle began sending his manuscripts and published works to friends for comment as early as 1681 (to Minutoli, 1 January 1681, *OD*, iv.601-602; see Elisabeth Labrousse, *Inventaire critique de la correspondance de Pierre Bayle*, Paris 1961, p.105, no 172), when he pleaded with Minutoli 'n'oubliez pas l'anatomie des deux Pieces sur le *Maréchal de Luxembourg*'. (This work was published as an appendix in Edmond Lacoste, *Bayle, nouvelliste et critique littéraire*, Paris 1929, p.33-66.) He

anatomical dissection and historical reconstruction, perceives the targets of his author's writings, the conflicts he resolved and those unreconciled which he handed to the ensuing generation of writers.

continued the practice thereafter. Jurieu might be considered an unsuccessful if half-perceptive reader of the *Pensées diverses* (see below, p.187-90) and it is not unlikely that the remark in the article 'Remond' (quoted above, p.1, n.1), an article added to the second edition of the *magnum opus* is, in part, an invitation to its readers to be discerning towards the author, himself aware of the biases and *bêtes noires* written into the *Dictionnaire*.

# I. Prologue:
# the objectivity of the historian

# 1. Agreda

Apres que les Superstitions 'ont esté détruites par la tres-profonde humilité de Jesus-Christ, par la Predication des Apostres, & par la Foy des Martyrs qui sont morts pour la verité, & qui vivent avec la verité', ainsi que l'asseure saint Augustin: il y a sujet de s'estonner qu'elles soient aussi répandües dans le Christianisme, qui est une Religion toute de sainteté & de verité, que nous les y voïons aujourd'hui avec douleur.

Jean-Baptiste Thiers, *Traité des superstitions*[1]

C'est une chose qui devient fort à la mode: Dans tous les siécles précedens il y a eu des erreurs populaires qui ne faisoient aucun mal; même il y en a eu, dont les Chrétiens ont fait un bon usage: Mais dans nôtre siécle des gens pour paroître habiles ont découvert ces petites erreurs, les ont refutées avec un grand appareil de litterature, de témoignages & de citations: qu'est-il arrivé de-là? C'est que plusieurs personnes ont été induites à douter des faits les plus certains favorables au Christianisme.

Pierre Jurieu, *Le Philosophe de Rotterdam*[2]

PIERRE Bayle, a Huguenot writer living in exile in Holland, is surely the most misunderstood writer of his age. Both his contemporary and later readers have widely diverged as to his real intentions. His literary output – in the form of religious controversy, literary journalism, philosophical and theological reflections and historical research – was enormous. He was, however, chiefly remembered in the eighteenth century for his *Dictionnaire historique et critique*,[3] a biographical dictionary which, on its vast procession from 'Aaron' to 'Zuylichem', provided over two thousand articles on both ancient and contemporary philosophers, biblical heroes and heroines, Roman Catholic saints, Protestant leaders,

1. Jean-Baptiste Thiers, *Traité des superstitions selon l'Ecriture sainte, les decrets des conciles, et les sentimens des saints peres, et des theologiens* (Paris 1679), Preface, aiir. Thiers is associated by Bayle wth Jean de Launoy and 'quelques autres [qui] ont écrit contre les fausses traditions, ou contre le culte des fausses reliques, ou contre les dévotions indiscrétes pour la sainte Vierge' (*CPD*, §CXXXI, *OD*, iii.372b-73a). On the significance of this association see below, p.119ff.

2. p.20-21. Jurieu himself was one of the most vigorous critics of pagan and Roman Catholic superstition (see below, p.26). The change in tone may be attributed to his involvement with the Cévenne prophets and his insight and fears as a pastor concerning the shift away from popular devotion. The perception of the shift as a deliberate sabotage of religious values in general is, however, highly questionable.

3. Eighteenth-century authors were also greatly taken with the famous paradox of the virtuous atheist and immoral idolater (first proposed in the *Pensées diverses* (1682-1683) and continued and modified in the *Continuation des pensées diverses* (1704)) and the arguments for toleration (*Commentaire philosophique*, 1686). See Pierre Rétat, *Le Dictionnaire de Bayle et la lutte philosophique au XVIIIe siècle* (Paris 1971), p.15-60, 153-214, 353-441, and H. T. Mason, *Pierre Bayle and Voltaire* (Oxford 1963), p.78-103, 133-38.

9

prophets and pseudo-prophets, popes, courtesans, theologians and Early Church Fathers. The work held spellbound its eighteenth-century detractors and admirers and fascinated some of the first minds of that century: among others, Leibniz, Voltaire, Frederick the Great, archbishop William King, bishop Berkeley, Shaftesbury, Jonathan Swift and David Hume. The *Encyclopédie* (1751-1772), under the direction of Diderot and d'Alembert, and Voltaire's *Dictionnaire philosophique* (1764) owe much in both ideology and form to the earlier work.[4] In fact, Bayle's *Dictionnaire* has more than once been described both as the Bible of the eighteenth century and the Arsenal of the Enlightenment.[5] How, it must be asked, can a work disparagingly designated by its author 'un Ouvrage sec & ennuiant de sa nature'[6] be one of the most exciting works of an age?[7]

The answer lies in the fact that, despite the apparent objectivity and impersonality of its erudite presentation, the *Dictionnaire* is much more than a purveyor of interesting and alphabetical facts. Behind Bayle's deceptively antiseptic text, with its forbidding folio columns of footnotes and footnotes on footnotes, there lurks both a selectivity and a committed writer. Selectivity is seen in the choice of articles.[8] On important figures such as Plato, Cicero, Horace, Aquinas, Montaigne,[9] Gassendi, Richelieu, Corneille, and Servetus the author wrote no articles, while obscure figures such as Jean Fernel, Armand de Gontaut, Pierre Jarrige, the Parthenai women, Quellenec, Barbarus, Golius, and Zuerius receive fairly substantial entries. Moreover, these articles – apparently collected at random – are loosely but definitely connected by a marvellous succession of themes, to which Bayle turns and returns: religious intolerance, superstition, prophecy, the masculine fears of castration and impotency, the necessity for historical accuracy, the possibility of finding certitude in any of the human sciences, the power which women wield through sex, the relationship between reason and faith, the influence of the Fall on human nature and all human activity and the consequent necessity of submission to the biblical revelation in every area of life. The obsessional preoccupation with these themes together with a personal commitment to many of them, has fascinated readers of the

4. Rétat, p.215-71, 353-441 and *passim*; Mason, p.16-17, 144-45.

5. For example, Emile Faguet, 'Pierre Bayle', in *Dix-huitième siècle: études littéraires* (Paris 1890), i.1. Paul Dibon, 'Redécouverte de Bayle', in P. Dibon and others, *Pierre Bayle, le philosophe de Rotterdam* (Paris 1959), p.viii.

6. *Projet et fragments d'un dictionaire critique* (1692), §v, in *Dictionnaire*, iv.2979.

7. Popkin, in Pierre Bayle, *Historical and critical dictionary*, p.xi, poses a similar question.

8. This selectivity may be partially accidental; see below, p.184-85.

9. It seems certain that Bayle had planned an article on Montaigne; references to footnotes O and F of an entry 'Montaigne' occur in the 'Observation générale' to the *Eclaircissemens*, at marginal notes 2 and 3, *Dictionnaire*, iv.2986.

*Dictionnaire* and related works over the centuries. Nonetheless, these self-same themes have posed problems for the critics. For there is more than one Bayle.[10]

To some, such as his contemporary and erstwhile benefactor Pierre Jurieu, he is a menace to true religion, a secret atheist and worse who advances theological, political and philosophical theories subversive of traditional values.[11] To others, less emotional and more sympathetic – such as Voltaire – he is a free-thinker who jettisoned the binding orthodoxies of the seventeenth century, a herald of the negative and critical thought of the Enlightenment.[12] This view of Bayle as a 'philosophe avant la lettre' (Dibon, p.viii) has won the approval of some highly subtle critics in the twentieth century. Howard Robinson (1931)[13] and Paul Hazard (1935) agree that Bayle's thought is inimical to the prevailing orthodoxies. His scepticism with respect to religious belief, precipitated by his double conversion, develops gradually thereafter, only to culminate in total scepticism.[14] The *Pensées diverses sur la comète* constitute an attack on religious belief in general, stemming from a repugnance to the miraculous. This distaste for the supernatural recurs in the *Dictionnaire*, where the critique of paranormal phenomena among the pagans reverberates onto Christianity, forming a 'slant-wise' attack on biblical miracles.[15] Consideration of the work of the *libertins érudits* led René Pintard (1943) and Pierre Rétat (1980) to identify – and quite rightly so – the libertine and heterodox elements in Bayle's thought, nourished from youth on the books of these ideological non-conformists.[16] In a study,

---

10. For a more complete survey of critical positions on Bayle, consult W. H. Barber, 'Bayle: faith and reason', in *The French mind: studies in honour of Gustav Rudler*, ed. W. Moore, R. Sutherland, E. Starkie (Oxford 1952), p.109-25; Dibon, p.vii-xvii; Rex, *Essays*, p.ix-xv; Karl C. Sandberg, *At the crossroads of faith and reason: an essay on Pierre Bayle* (Tucson 1966), p.8-16; Raymond Vancourt, 'La religion de Bayle', *Critique* (October 1960), p.879-92.

11. 'Ceux qui ne se laisseront pas ouvrir les yeux sur [l'athéisme de Bayle] [...] sont des aveugles volontaires'; 'les Ecrits de Vaninus athée, [...] ceux de Hobbes, et enfin ceux de Spinosa et de tous les Spinosistes, n'approchent pas du poison des Ecrits de nôtre Philosophe' ([Jurieu], *Le Philosophe*, p.47, 135).

12. Mason, p.25-54; Rétat, p.215ff.

13. Howard Robinson, *Bayle the sceptic* (Columbia 1931).

14. Hazard, p.124, 134-35, 139. According to Hazard, however, although Bayle's position necessarily led to 'absolute scepticism', he held himself from the brink by an effort of will, convinced he had a 'mission to fulfil' in the eradication of error (p.139). See below, p.179 and note 116; Robinson, p.3, 11-13, 243 and *passim*.

15. The phrase is Robinson's, p.172, see also 3, 11, 13, 20, 25-26, 161, 171-74, 214-15; Hazard, p.129-30, 136, 188.

16. René Pintard, *Le Libertinage érudit dans la première moitié du XVIIe siècle* (Paris 1943), i.572-75. Since the publication of Elisabeth Labrousse's two-volume study, however, Pintard has changed his mind ('Les problèmes de l'histoire du libertinage, notes et réflexions', *XVIIe siècle*, 127 (1980), p.131-61). Rétat, unwilling in 1971 to challenge Labrousse's interpretation (*Le Dictionnaire de Bayle*, p.10, note 10), has since espoused Pintard's former position ('Libertinage et hétérodoxie: Pierre Bayle', *XVIIe siècle* 127 (1980), p.197-211).

meticulous in its comparison of Bayle with contemporary thinkers, Gianfranco Cantelli (1969) concludes from the divergences observed, that Bayle uses but abuses the positions of Christian thinkers in his day. To him, the *philosophe* of Rotterdam is both a 'miscredente e ateo', immersed in a 'radicale scetticismo'.[17] Ciro Senofonte (1978) challenges his compatriot's position, arguing instead for an evolution in Bayle's thought. The Calvinism of his youth is steadily impregnated with rationalism and a 'purificazione del cristianesimo', terminating in a pre-Enlightenment deism.[18] Crowning this school, Gianni Paganini (1980), in a tightly reasoned study, pinpoints Bayle's systematic pilfering of Renaissance rationalistic philosophy and his deadly up-dating of its dialectic between reason and faith. To him, Bayle is not a sceptic only, he is also a first-rate metaphysician.[19]

To another school of critics, the eighteenth-century Bayle is a 'déraciné malgré lui' (Dibon, p.viii) who must be replaced within the trends of his own time – Protestant, Cartesian and erudite – if he is to be properly understood. Sainte-Beuve was the first (1835) to affirm that the author of the *Dictionnaire* 'était religieux'.[20] Deprived of youthful proselytising zeal by his double conversion, he retains nonetheless a submission to the dictates of Providence; while often couched philosophically, it stems from a sincerity of belief (i.366-67, 377-78). Cornelia Serrurier (1912) sees Bayle's work as that of a moralist, more interested in man's relations to his fellows than in his attitude to the Divinity. His reflection on the corruption of human nature leads him ineluctably to conclude the perdition of mankind apart from divine grace. Far from undermining the biblical revelation, the *philosophe* of Rotterdam portrays reason as an errant instrument when it disrespects the authority of Scripture. His thought only makes sense then, 'à condition de le classer parmi les croyants: [...] il est un calviniste froid mais sincère'.[21] W. H. Barber (1952) extends this line of interpretation from the conception of human nature to the conception of history; both, according to him, are 'not only profoundly Christian but essentially Calvinist. It is, therefore, above all as a Protestant [...] that Bayle must he studied if a full understanding of his outlook and significance is to be reached' (p.115, 125). The three masterly studies of Elisabeth Labrousse (1963 and

17. Gianfranco Cantelli, *Teologia e ateismo: saggio sul pensiero filosofico e religioso di Pierre Bayle* (Firenze 1969), p.vi and *passim*.

18. Ciro Senofonte, *Pierre Bayle dal Calvinismo all'Illuminismo* (Napoli 1978), p.255, and *passim*.

19. Gianni Paganini, *Analisi della fede e critica della ragione nella filosofia di Pierre Bayle* (Firenze 1980), *passim*.

20. C.-A. Sainte-Beuve, 'Du génie critique et de Bayle', in *Portraits littéraires* (Paris 1862-1864), i.377.

21. Cornelia Serrurier, *Pierre Bayle en Hollande: étude historique et critique* (Apeldoorn 1912), p.94, 109, 191, 201, 207.

1964) and Walter Rex (1965) answer this call to arms. To the former, Bayle is undoubtedly sceptical – no system of thought could conceal its flaws from so piercing a scrutiny – but his scepticism is limited. His attacks on clerics and theologians might have seemed to undermine the creeds they represented but 'c'est au nom du Christianisme de droit qu'il condamne le Christianisme de fait'. Moreover, his rigoristic morality is the antithesis of the external moral conformity of the sceptics. Only by replacing our author 'dans le contexte huguenot qui a présidé à sa formation et dans celui du Refuge au sein duquel s'est épanouie sa maturité' may the apparent contradictions in his thought be resolved.[22] The exegetical study of the latter reveals these contradictory trends at work – superstition and verity, revolution and monarchy – he notes also the compatibility of Cartesianism and Calvinism in Bayle's writings. In fact, according to Walter Rex, Bayle's thought is dominated by the somewhat fluid orthodox Calvinism of the last quarter of the seventeenth century: 'Bayle not only reflects a minority problem, he speaks for an age.'[23] The age of which he is the voice – with its sixteenth-century echoes – forms the concern of Jacques Solé who, in a series of articles (1968-1977) recreates the vast pageant of our author's *Weltanschauung* and its place within Protestant historiography. To him the author of the *Dictionnaire*, a second and less biased Jean Claude,[24] 'a tenu à rendre au protestantisme le service que Bossuet avait apporté au catholicisme par son *Histoire des Variations*: faire rejaillir le mérite de l'objectivité de l'historien sur la confession à laquelle il appartient'.[25] To the metaphysician and sceptic is added a Bayle concerned both for scholarship and his communion.

For all their diversity, these often conflicting interpretations have three things in common. Firstly, all agree to a meaning behind the words in Bayle's writings. Secondly, none would dispute that this hidden meaning is frequently subversive. To some it is subversive of Christianity, to others only of institutionalised

22. Labrousse, *Pierre Bayle*, ii.593, 605, 609.
23. Rex, *Essays*, p.xiii, and *passim*.
24. Jean Claude (1619-1687) served the Reformed church at Charenton (Paris) until the Revocation. He was one of the leading lights among the Huguenots in the latter half of the century and was particularly prized for his *Defense de la Réformation* (1673), a polemical and historical work (cf. Eugène Haag & Emile Haag, *La France protestante*, Paris, Genève 1846-1859, iii.473a-481b). Solé's link between Bayle and Claude is particularly astute, since the latter is one of our author's heroes ('Claude', footnote B).
25. Jacques Solé, 'Religion et méthode critique dans le *Dictionnaire* de Bayle', in *Religion, érudition et critique à la fin du XVIIe siècle et au début du XVIIIe* (Paris 1968), p.116; see also 'Religion et vision historiographique dans le *Dictionnaire* de Bayle', in *Religion, érudition*, p.119-200; 'Religion et conception du monde dans le *Dictionnaire* de Bayle', in *BSHPF.* 117 (1971), p.545-81; 118 (1972), p.483-509; *Bayle polémiste* (extraits du *Dictionnaire historique et critique*) (Paris 1972); 'Pierre Bayle, historien de la réforme', in *Historiographie de la Réforme*, ed. Philippe Joutard (Paris, Neuchâtel, Montréal 1977), p.71-80.

religion and particularly paganism and Roman Catholicism. Thirdly, both schools of thought affirm, whether directly or indirectly, that presuppositions concealed from the reader affect the way Bayle writes history. If he is an atheist or a free-thinker then he denies or erases the intervention of a personal God in human affairs. If he is a Calvinist then he accepts – albeit with reservations – the control of history by divine Providence. While some critics, however, have considered Bayle's historical theory,[26] none has examined what actually happens when he investigates the past.[27] An exegetical discussion of the article 'Agreda', selected for its acerbic iconoclasm, is here presented as a test case of this historical practice. A reconstruction of her biography and ideas, as available to Bayle, yields to contextualisation. Here, combining the author of the *Dictionnaire*'s citation of sources and cross references with their resonances to the intellectual and political history of French Calvinism in the preceding twenty years, the study attempts to seize the subterranean meaning of the entry in the *Dictionnaire*. The chapter considers afresh the perplexities facing the critic who hasards an interpretation of this most complex of authors. In his amusing if unfair attack on the Spanish nun, does he pick up the gauntlet of Protestant anatomies of superstition[28] or anticipate the 'slantwise' assaults of a Voltaire? Is he, as Jurieu and others would hold, using erudition and satire to induce unbelief or – and this is our opinion – is his voice, despite its Protestantism, one of many in a generation grieved at the obfuscation of Christianity by error and superstition?

Maria de Coronel was born in Castille in the village of Agreda – from which she took her name – on 2 April 1602. At the age of eight she took a vow of chastity and nine years later in January 1619, three months before her seventeenth birthday, she, together with her mother and sister, entered the convent of the Immaculate Conception, founded by her family in the village of her birth.[29] On 2 September she was allowed to take her final religious vows, and

---

26. Labrousse, *Pierre Bayle*, ii.3-102, 449-96; Robinson, p.41ff.

27. Rex, *Essays*, p.197ff., investigates the historical background and the political concerns embedded in the article 'David'; F. R. Knetsch, 'Le jugement de Bayle sur Comenius', *Bulletin de la commission de l'histoire des églises wallonnes* 6, 4 (1969-1971), p.83-96, provides a similar article on Bayle's personal concerns in the article 'Comenius'. Neither draws conclusions for our author's historical practice. This study has as its purpose an analysis both of the 'conceptual basis of the historian's quest' (Kelley, p.4) and the manner in which these ideological preoccupations affect and are written into history.

28. Pierre Du Moulin, *Nouveauté du papisme opposée à l'antiquité du vrai christianisme* (Sedan 1627); and his *Anatomie de la messe* (Genève 1636); *Deuxième partie de l'Anatomie de la messe* (Sedan 1639); cf. Rex, *Essays*, p.3-29.

29. Cf. the article 'Agreda' in A. Vacant and E. Mangenot (ed.), *Dictionnaire de théologie catholique* (Paris 1903-1950), i.627 (hereafter *DTC*), and Bayle 'Agreda', *in corp*. The article first appeared in the second edition (1702).

in 1627, was constrained by a papal bull to accept the position of Mother Superior, a position she retained until the end of her life. Under her leadership the convent reached a very high level of spiritual and material development. She had it rebuilt, together with a beautiful chapel, outside the city walls and it became known throughout Spain as a centre of the most fervent spirituality.[30]

Although she wrote six devotional works, two of which were published,[31] she became famous for her mystical visions contained in *La Mistica ciudad de Dios*.[32] The work, as its full title indicates, is a detailed history of the mother of Jesus, based on private revelations granted to the Spanish mystic. It opens by detailing the manner in which these revelations were imparted. Raised by divine grace to a state of mystical contemplation, Maria was prepared by six angels and later two more for entry into the divine presence. There she saw the Virgin as the Apocalypse is said to describe her[33] and was commanded to contemplate and record. The history proper starts with an account of the creation of the world, in which the Virgin played a prominent part.[34] The story of the miraculous annunciation of the birth of the Virgin to her parents, saints Anne and Joachim, is then given, followed by an account of the many supernatural events of her childhood. Her importance was attested by the several transportations to heaven enjoyed at this time; as also by the 930 angels assigned by God to protect and aid her on earth and to act as her ambassadors to heaven. Her failure to speak immediately after her birth did not result from human inability but a sovereign decision of her own. A child prodigy, she swept the house before the age of three, a task facilitated by angelic intervention.[35] The narrative rests on certain

30. 'Agreda', *DTC*, i.627.

31. See *DTC*, i.627-28, for a complete bibliography.

32. *Mistica ciudad de Dios, milagro de su omnipotencia y abismo de la gracia: historia divina y vida de la virgen madre de Dios, reyna y señora nuestra Maria santissima, restauradora de la culpa de Eva y medianera de la gracia, manifestada en estos ultimos siglos por la misma señora a su esclava sor Maria de Jesus, abbadesa de el convento de la Immaculada Concepcion de la villa de Agreda de la provincia de Burgos, para nueva luz de el mundo, alegria de la iglesia catolica y confianza de los mortales* (Madrid 1670) (DTC, i.628).

33. Apocalypse, xii.1ff.; xxi.1ff.; cf. *JS*, lundi 16 janvier 1696; on the theological implications of this, see 'Immaculée conception', *DTC*, vii.866-71. The perspective adopted in this short account of the life and works of Agreda is that of Bayle's contemporaries; on the bias in his sources, consult below, p.17-18.

34. The argument is based on a private interpretation of Proverbs, viii.14ff; cf. *JS*, *idem*, p.30, and lundi 26 novembre 1696, p.378; Bayle, 'Agreda', footnote B, first reflection *in fine*. For the private revelations of the Spanish mystic, consult Marie d'Agreda, *La Mystique Cité de Dieu*, trans. Thomas Croset (Marseille 1695), p.1-2, 16-17, 29, 32, 43, 45, 243ff., 258ff., and Jacques Le Brun, *La Spiritualité de Bossuet* (Paris 1972), p.640, n.95.

35. *HOS*, septembre, octobre, novembre 1696, p.140-41. Bayle, 'Agreda', footnote A; distortion of *La Mystique Cité* is to be expected from the Protestant journalist Henri Basnage de Beauval. Paul Hoffer, *La Dévotion à Marie au déclin du XVIIe siècle: autour du jansénisme et des 'Avis salutaires de la B. V. Marie à ses dévots indiscrets'* (Paris 1938), p.261, holds that Agreda was unfairly treated. Cf. Le

theological assumptions. Espousing a Scotist theology, it teaches both implicitly and explicitly the doctrine of the Immaculate Conception. Moreover, the application of certain biblical passages – often given a Messianic interpretation – to the Virgin, seems to confirm her as co-mediator with Christ.[36]

The work, from its publication in Madrid in 1670, divided public opinion. Despite the reticences of the Holy See, it became a best-seller among the Franciscans and those devoted to Mary (Le Brun, p.629). For, as Bossuet later disparagingly observed, it recounts episodes over which the Gospels discreetly draw a veil.[37] A translation into French, begun by Pierre Grenier, *conseiller* to the Parliament at Bordeaux and a supporter of devotion to the Virgin, was later abandoned (Le Brun, p.629-30). In 1695, however, encouraged by the Franciscans, Thomas Croset's translation *La Mystique Cité de Dieu* was published in Marseille, bearing a permission to print signed by J. I. de Foresta-Colongue, vicar general to the city.[38] The times were inauspicious. The book appeared not only at a period of hostility to the Franciscans but also at the height of the disputes concerning quietism.[39] Its mystical nature, compromising in itself at such a time, appeared more heterodox in the light of the support given it by many implicated in the debate (Le Brun, p.631-32). Bossuet, heavily involved in the opposition to quietism and whose Augustinianism and personal affiliations fostered a hostility to the Franciscans and their translation, organised a pressure group, demanding the censure of the ill-fated work (Le Brun, p.633ff.). The Franciscans themselves did not remain idle as the stormy encounter in the theological faculty at the Sorbonne illustrates.

In May 1696,[40] six doctors of the Sorbonne were nominated to test the orthodoxy of *La Mystique Cité*. The choice of P. Guischard, Claude Le Feuvre, P. Chaussemer, Jean Saussoy, Nicolas Gobillon and Thomas Roulland, who all shared a Thomist theology and sympathy with the bishop of Meaux, is the result

---

Brun, *La Spiritualité*, p.629, n.2.

36. The Scotist implications are evident in *La Mystique Cité* (p.48, 61, 64, 66, 70, 78ff., 287, 288-89) and known to Bayle via *JS*, lundi 26 novembre 1696, p.378-79; Bayle, 'Agreda', footnote B, first reflection. Le Brun, p.637, 640 and n.98. Contemporaries were hostile to the work's support for the Immaculate Conception because the doctrine had not yet been ratified by the church (Le Brun, p.630, and *DTC*, vii.1119-79).

37. J.-B. Bossuet, *Remarques sur le livre intitulé: La Mystique Cité de Dieu*, in *Œuvres* (Versailles 1815-1819), xxx.640, and below, p.28; Le Brun, p.641.

38. Le Brun, p.631. According to Le Brun, this permission compromised the *Mystique Cité* since the Jansenists and the 'anti-mystics' alike were hostile to the vicar general.

39. Not only was the book translated by a Franciscan, Agreda herself belonged to a female Franciscan order (Le Brun, p.630-31). The mystical nature of the work inevitably led to the connection with quietism (p.629). For the reaction to quietism, see Leszek Kolakowski, *Chrétiens sans Eglise: la conscience religieuse et le lien confessionnel au XVIIe siècle* (Paris 1969), p.492ff.

40. 'Agreda', *DTC.*, i.629.

of pressure from the latter and guaranteed a censorship board by definition hostile to the book (Le Brun, p.635). On Monday 2 July of the same year, they reported and censured nineteen propositions deemed 'téméraires, scandaleuses et qui offensoient les oreilles chastes'.[41] Contrary to normal practice, their statement was printed and distributed to the other members of the Faculty, who were to meet and discuss the document twelve days later, Saturday 14 July.[42] Meanwhile, those sympathetic to Agreda assembled a party of like-minded men in order to resist the official condemnation of the book, felt to be imminent. The papal nuncio – at the instigation of the Franciscans – had earlier tried and failed to prevent the preliminary censure.[43] At this point, the Franciscan Méron declared himself in possession of two papal briefs forbidding the Sorbonne to proceed.[44] The two briefs were, however, proven bogus and, once discovered, Méron was forced to retract and leave Paris in disgrace.[45] The Sorbonne met as planned, then, on 14 July and thereafter 29 times before they finally decided (17 September) to condemn the work. The delay was caused by the intrigues and counter-plots mounted by the two sides, intrigues, moreover, publicly denounced in a number of pamphlets and picked up by some of the learned journals.[46] Nonetheless, the party inspired by Bossuet carried the day: *La Mystique Cité* was condemned by the Theological Faculty by a majority of 50 votes and the decision was ratified on 1 October of that year.[47]

The account of the episode given in the *Dictionnaire* is based on three main sources: the anonymous pamphlet *L'Affaire de Marie d'Agreda et la maniere dont on a cabalé en Sorbonne sa condamnation* (Cologne 1697) and the articles published in the *Journal des savants* and the *Histoire des ouvrages des savants* respectively.[48] All three are *a priori* hostile to the work of the Spanish mystic. The first, written by Méron, is slanderous in its attempt to vindicate his own and his party's

41. Le Brun, p.636; 'Agreda', footnote C; *JS*, lundi 26 novembre 1696, p.379.

42. Le Brun, p.636; Bayle, 'Agreda', footnote C; Bossuet, letter LXI of the *Lettres sur l'affaire du quiétisme*, in *Œuvres*, xl.205.

43. Bossuet, letters LXVI, LXVII, LXIX, LXX, xl.211-27.

44. The anonymous pamphlet *L'Affaire de Marie d'Agreda*, cited above, is attributed by the card-index of the Bibliothèque nationale to Méron. Le Brun notes another attribution (p.638, n.73). If the pamphlet was written by Méron, a Franciscan, then the hostility to Bossuet and the moderate party therein is a further example of the split between popular and more severe devotion at the end of the century (see below, p.27-28).

45. Bossuet, letter LXI, xl.205-206.

46. For a list of the pamphlets, see Le Brun, p.636-37, notes 59 and 60.

47. Le Brun, p.639; 'Agreda', in *DTC*, i.629; Bayle, 'Agreda', footnote C; Bossuet, letter LXXI, xl.228; Hoffer, p.251-61.

48. I have been unable to consult this pamphlet since the only extant copy (to my knowledge) has been misplaced by the Bibliothèque nationale. My knowledge of its contents comes from Bayle, 'Agreda', and Le Brun, p.636-37. The articles in the *JS* are cited above, notes 33 and 36, and the *HOS*, above, note 35.

defeat.[49] The articles in the *Journal* express that distaste for the devotions of the *peuple* – and by extension Maria de Agreda – so common among the intellectuals of the day.[50] The third, composed by Henri Basnage, a Huguenot also in exile, reflects the contempt for 'Roman idolatry' shared by generations of Protestants.[51] The selection may result from mere paucity of sources but, given both Bayle's critical acumen and methodology,[52] the ingenuous credulity evinced here is nothing if not roguishly knowing. In fact, with that allusiveness which has so tortured his critics, he himself points to the subversive intentions of the entry:

Bien a valu à la Religion Chrétienne, que les Celsus, & les Porphyres, n'aient pas pu la combatre par les armes que de tels Ecrits infinis en nombre peuvent fournir aujourd'hui. Que n'eût point dit en ce tems-là contre l'Eglise un Auteur Païen, qui auroit eu la véhémence & le caractere d'Arnobe? Si Henri Etienne, & Philippe de Marnix, revenoient au monde, quels suplémens ne feroient-ils point par la mystique Cité de nôtre Marie d'Agreda: l'un à son Apologie d'Herodote, l'autre à son Tableau des différens de la Religion?[53]

The reference to the pagan philosophers, celebrated for their hostility to Christianity and its miracles,[54] might suggest a Voltairian reading were it not followed by the allusion to the two sixteenth-century Calvinist polemicists, famed for their derision of Roman Catholicism.[55] Moreover, these authors are consistently associated in Bayle's work with a use of comedy as a polemical

49. Above, n.44, and Le Brun, p.636.

50. Jacques Le Brun, 'Critique des abus et signifiance des pratiques (la controverse Leibniz-Bossuet)', in *Theoria cum praxi*, Akten des III. internationalen Leibnizkongresses, 1977 (Wiesbaden 1980), p.247-57.

51. Rex, *Essays*, p.3-29, and below, p.119ff. and 183ff. It is not unlikely that Bayle's attention was drawn to the 'affaire Agreda' by Basnage de Beauval, author of the *HOS*, with whom he was in close contact.

52. Below, p.119ff. Hostility to Agreda is evident in the articles in the *JS*, lundi 16 janvier 1696, p.30; lundi 26 novembre 1696, p.377.

53. 'Agreda', footnote B, reflection III.

54. Celsus was a second-century eclectic Platonist whose hostility to Christianity is known only through the fragments of the *Alethes logos* (*The True doctrine*), preserved in Origen's *Contra Celsum*. Porphyry (AD *c.*233-304) was well known as a violent opponent of Christianity and defender of paganism, as the surviving fragments of his fifteen-book *Kata Christianos* (*Against the Christians*) indicate. The weight of the two thinkers' attacks fell on the miraculous nature of Christianity and their method was one of burlesque satire. Arnobius, born in the third century AD, was a Christian apologist and in his *Disputationum adversus gentes* he defends Christianity by demonstrating the ridiculous inconsistencies of paganism.

55. Henri Estienne (1528-1598), *Introduction au Traité de la conformité des merveilles anciennes avec les modernes, ou traité préparatif à l'apologie pour Hérodote* (1566); Philippe de Marnix (1538-1598), *Tableau de la différence entre la religion chrétienne et le papisme* (1599); both satirise Catholicism via its similarities with paganism.

tool.[56] In other words, the *philosophe* of Rotterdam not only places the article within a tradition of religious controversy, he also alerts the reader to the caricatural nature of the entry. Hints are provided as to the significance of the caricature.

Theological concerns are to the fore in the opening footnotes to the article. Firstly, a series of abusive epithets indicates the presence of that hostility to 'mystiquerie' characteristic of intellectuals, Jansenists and advocates of a more severe devotion in the *grand siècle*.[57] The mystical insights of the Spanish nun are dismissed as the 'folies' and 'imaginations' of a 'cerveau malade de dévotion'.[58] Cross-references and resonances to other entries and works suggest that, if not an impostor, Agreda at least suffered delusions of grandeur and vanity: yet another victim of the all-pervasive 'passions humaines'.[59] In other words, the Spanish mystic is one more test-case of Bayle's psychopathology of religion, said to have inspired the eighteenth-century confrontation with the gods.[60] Psychopathology and Augustinian theology are, however, indissociable, as is implied by the running commentary in the article 'Nestorius'[61] on the development of popular devotions. Echoing the earlier analysis in the *Pensées diverses*, Bayle contrasts the brief duration of moral reform – 'un état contraire aux inclinations de la nature'[62] – with the untrammelled growth of devotion to the Virgin:

D'où il faut conclure que l'innovation introduite dans le Christianisme, quand on y a établi le culte de la Sainte Vierge trois ou quatre cens ans plus ou moins après l'Ascension de Jesus-Christ, a été favorisée par les dispositions naturelles & machinales de l'homme, puis qu'elle a fait des progrès continuels & prodigieux, & qu'elle subsiste encore aujourd'hui avec tout autant de force qu'elle en a jamais eu. On ne comprend pas que si elle n'avoit point trouvé de très grandes convenances dans les passions humaines, elle eût pu tant prospérer destituée qu'elle étoit de l'apui de l'Ecriture, & de la bonne tradition.[63]

56. 'Sainte-Aldegonde', footnote G, and 'Viret', footnotes C and D; for a near contemporary opinion of Estienne's *Apologie*, see Sallengre, *Mémoires de littérature* (La Haye 1715-1717), i.38-58; see below, p.233-40.

57. Le Brun, 'Critique des abus', p.247-57, and Rex, *Essays*, p.145.

58. 'Agreda', footnotes A and B.

59. 'Nestorius', footnote N, and the cross-references from this to other articles; 'Borri', footnote B.

60. Frank E. Manuel, *The Eighteenth century confronts the gods* (Cambridge, Mass. 1959), p.34-40. Manuel fails to perceive the theological basis of this psychopathology in Bayle's case, as indeed that of so many Augustinians of the day: cf. Bernard Tocanne, *L'Idée de nature en France dans la seconde moitié du XVIIe siècle* (Paris 1978), p.182ff.

61. The footnote N to the entry 'Nestorius' was added in 1702 and we may conjecture that it was written at about the same time as 'Agreda'. The two articles are linked by cross-reference.

62. Below, p.223-24 for the place of this position in Bayle's wider historiographical vision.

63. 'Nestorius', footnote N; below, p.122ff. and 214ff.

Not only is the author a tributary of the Huguenot Jacques Basnage's *Histoire de l'Eglise*;[64] in this statement, he also applies to mariology the methodological principles prevalent in the religious controversy of the time (below, p.121ff). That is to say, the spurious nature – from the Protestant point of view – of devotion to the Virgin is highlighted by its opposition to Scripture and the tradition of the Early Church, considered normative; a position reinforced in our article by references to the Spanish nun's abuse of Holy Writ.[65] Moreover, the success of this apocryphal tradition is attributed to its flattery of fallen instincts, the driving force of 'le génie grossier des peuples' ('Nestorius', footnote N).

Calvinist sensibilities join Calvinist methodology in the second theological observation. Following a list of the propositions to be censured in the work – its propagation of the doctrine of the Immaculate Conception and view of Mary as Mediatrix – the *philosophe* of Rotterdam, with all the penetration of his Jesuit formation,[66] focusses on the barbarity of the Scholastic theology with which it is informed. Scholastics, he muses, designate by the 'mots barbares d'*aseitas* & d'*abalieitas*'[67] the essential differences between the Divinity and humanity. The former indicates that God 'n'a rien qui vienne d'ailleurs' and the latter that 'les créatures n'ont rien qui ne procede d'ailleurs'; together they force the conclusion that all the divine attributes, with the exception of *aseitas*, may be communicated to created beings ('Agreda', footnote B). Drawing out the logical consequences of Agreda's revelations, he adds:

Si donc Dieu a conféré effectivement à la Sainte Vierge tout ce qu'il a pu lui conférer, il s'ensuit, selon les dogmes de l'Ecôle, dont la Sœur Marie de Jesus faisoit grand cas, que la Sainte Vierge a éxisté de tout tems, qu'elle peut tout, qu'elle sait tout, qu'elle remplit tous les lieux, & qu'à tous égards elle est infinie. [...] cela étant, ne doit-on pas s'étonner, que la Sorbonne ait seulement dit, que 'cette proposition est fausse, téméraire & contraire à la doctrine de l'Evangile'? Une telle censure ne sent-elle pas la molesse?

The shocked tones of the author's reproof to the Theological Faculty are the fruit of his convictions. As the quotation from the book of Proverbs – 'Par moi règnent les Rois ...'[68] – which follows the observation – implies, he is horrified

64. Jacques Basnage, *Histoire de l'Eglise, depuis Jésus-Christ jusqu'à present* (Rotterdam 1699), vol.ii, bk.xviii. ch.10, p.1070-81.
65. 'Agreda', marginal note 13; Bossuet makes a similar point, *Remarques sur le livre*, in *Œuvres*, xxx.637-38; Le Brun, *La Spiritualité*, p.630, 641-42.
66. Labrousse, *Pierre Bayle*, i.50ff. It must not be forgotten that Bayle abandoned Roman Catholicism after eighteen months because of its *criterium veritatis* and materialistic theology – both at issue in the article 'Agreda'.
67. 'Agreda', footnote B, reflection I; cf. Bossuet, *Remarques sur le livre*, xxx.639ff., although the author does not draw the same polemical conclusions as Bayle.
68. Proverbs, viii.15; the passage is traditionally applied to the Word and its application to the Virgin – a created being – provokes the charge of materialism. Bayle is quoting from the *JS*, lundi

by the application to a creature of attributes, according to the Scripture, exclusive to the Creator. Behind this in turn lies not only the implacable opposition to 'metaphysical materialism' of the Cartesian[69] but also the unremitting critique of theological materialism – to the Calvinist mind, inseparable from Roman Catholicism.[70] At this point, however, the article, a worthy successor to its heritage of anatomies of superstition, switches to the more sordid aspects of the 'affaire d'Agreda'.

Abandoning his periodical sources in favour of the anonymous pamphlet, Bayle selects two stories, which in any but an iconoclastic article he would dismiss as an unfounded slander (below, p.90-94, 134ff.). The first spotlights the personal enmity between the translator, Thomas Croset, and the bishop of Saint-Pons, Percin de Montgaillard, a good friend to Bossuet.[71] Without a grain of criticism, Bayle, quoting his source let it be noted, leads his reader to believe that the bishop's opposition to the work was the result of injured vanity; Croset had spread malicious rumours, following Montgaillard's interference in his career.[72] The second attributes a venal motivation to the same bishop. Noting the loss made by his printer – also that of Croset – over the paltry sales of his books, the pamphleteer suggests he sought the condemnation of *La Mystique Cité* in order to make the price soar, thereby compensating his printer. Bossuet and other prelates were annexed to this personal vendetta and the 'intrigue', 'cabale', and 'brigues' continued throughout the hearing in the Sorbonne.[73] Moreover, the Franciscans emerge from the entry's image of the hearing, if not whitewashed, at least less maligned. They *supplicated* the Faculty not to indulge in precipitate condemnations. They declared their *willingness to desist* in their support for the work, if it *in any way injured* the rights of the Gallican church.[74] Finally, they expressed their opposition *in writing* to the condemnation, once it was published, before finally withdrawing.[75] The author of the *Dictionnaire* is

26 novembre 1696, p.378, which evinces a similar horror: 'La Faculté [de Théologie de Paris] déclare au contraire que les paroles du 8. chapitre des Proverbes ne se doivent entendre à la lettre que de la Sagesse incréée ou incarnée, & que la proposition tirée du livre de la Religieuse Espagnole est fausse & téméraire.'

69. Labrousse, *Bayle* (Past Masters), p.68.

70. On the association of Cartesianism and Calvinism in the critique of Catholic 'materialism', see below, p.133-34, and Rex, *Essays*, p.77ff. [Pierre Jurieu], *Examen de l'eucharistie de l'Eglise romaine* (Rotterdam 1686), p.321-95, also focusses on the idolatrous and ridiculous nature of Scholastic theology, albeit without Bayle's urbanity.

71. Le Brun, *La Spiritualité*, p.631.

72. 'Agreda', footnote C, quoting from *L'Affaire de Marie d'Agreda*, p.13ff.

73. *Idem*, quoting from *L'Affaire*, p.30ff. The case of Agreda typifies, to Bayle's mind, the politicisation of ecclesiastical decisions. *CPD*, §§xxvII, xxIX, *OD*, iii.226-28, 230-31, cites the article as an illustration of politics in the censure of P. Le Comte.

74. Hoffer, p.251-61, discusses the Gallican dimension to the affair.

75. 'Agreda', footnote C, quoting *L'Affaire*, p.37ff.

no friend to the Franciscans. They not only uphold, to his mind, a materialistic theology, they also embody all the 'superstitions monacales' summed up in his pejorative 'moinerie'.[76] Not only that, the articles in the *Journal des savants* make the theological dimension to the case quite clear. Intrigues acknowledged, the Roman Catholic prelates were no less grieved than the Protestant writers by the 'culte immoderé, superstitieux, & faux' recommended in *La Mystique Cité*.[77] So, while satisfying the exigencies of objectivity, inasmuch as he cites his source and allows the reader to form his own judgement as to its bias (below, p.102-103, 233-40), Bayle is nonetheless using it as a tool to debunk the censure of Agreda's book.

His reasons are given in footnote D to the article. First, he notes, as Henri Basnage had observed before him, the careful prefatorial statement to the printed censure. According to the prelates, the condemnation in no way diminished legitimate devotion to the Virgin, still honoured for her Immaculate Conception and as the Mother of God and intercessor of the faithful.[78] This is forthwith interpreted by our author as a lack of courage:

Cela montre, que l'on n'eut pas le courage de publier la censure de la Faculté, sans y joindre des préservatifs; & par là, nous pouvons conoître à quels périls on s'expose, quand on desapprouve les erreurs les plus palpables qui amplifient les honneurs de la Sainte Vierge. On s'expose, non seulement à l'indignation des peuples; mais aussi, à celle des Moines, & de plusieurs autres Ecclésiastiques. On cherche donc des moiens de parer le coup par des préfaces étudiées. Quelle servitude! & qu'elle fait voir que le mal est incurable! [... L'Eglise] ne peut souffrir, ni le mal, ni le remede.[79]

The intention is clear. As so often in the *Dictionnaire*, the author seizes upon a conflict within the Catholic church in order to reverse the accusations brought by Bossuet against the Protestants. Rome, too, has her variations and disputes.[80] The remark, however, also has deeper resonances. Not only is the church resistant to reform – a standard Protestant argument[81] – the resistance also

76. 'François (d'Assise)', and below, n.82.
77. *JS*, lundi 26 novembre 1696, p.378.
78. *JS*, lundi 26 novembre 1696, p.377; cf. *HOS*, septembre, octobre, novembre (1696), p.140, while the 'slant' of the article is similar to that adopted later by Bayle, it shows none of the latter's intellectual force or satirical verve.
79. 'Agreda', footnote D; below, p.214ff.
80. On the *Dictionnaire* as a reversal of Catholic ecclesiastical historiography, below, p.214ff.; on the variations of Rome, 'Daillé', *in corp.*; the notion is present in Jean Claude, *La Défense de la Réformation* (Quevilly, Rouen 1673), p.19.
81. Philippe Du Plessis Mornay, *Le Mystère d'iniquité c'est à dire l'histoire de la papauté par quels progrez elle est montée à ce comble, & quelles oppositions les gens de bien lui ont faict de temps en temps* (Saumur 1611), *passim*, and Johannes Henricus Heidegger, *Historia papatus, novissimo historiae Lutheranismi et Calvinismi, fabro ... reposita acc. Fr. Guicciardini Historia papatus* (Amstelodami 1684), *passim*. Both works are drawn upon in the *Dictionnaire* (below, p.224-26). The notion, moreover, that Rome resists reformation and persecutes reformers is at least as old as Flaccius Illyricus's

comes from the majority of her members, from all levels: the *peuples* and the *moines*[82] and the *ecclésiastiques*. The cabals necessary to the condemnation of *La Mystique Cité* are, therefore, attributed to this minority/majority split in public opinion. There would have been no need to 'cabaler' if 'les esprits n'eussent été dans un endurcissement prodigieux'. Nor would prefatory 'adoucissemens' have been required ('Agreda', footnote D). These are more than ivory-tower reflections on the degeneration of Roman Catholicism.

The entry and the related article 'Nestorius' contain deliberate echoes both to a controversy which shook French Calvinism in the years before the Revocation and to Bayle's own intervention in that debate. A comment on the astounding development of popular devotions over the centuries indicates those the author has in mind when talking of a conflict between a majority and a minority:

le culte de la Sainte Vierge est monté à des excès si énormes, & s'y maintient si hautement, que les Jansénistes, qui ont voulu donner des avis sur ce sujet, n'y ont rien gagné; & pour un homme qui se conforme à leurs modifications, il y en a deux mille au pied de la lettre qui suivent le Pere Crasset. Considérez, je vous prie, les obstacles que l'on a trouvez en Sorbonne, quand on y a censuré le Livre d'une Religieuse Espagnole.[83]

The references to Adam Widenfeldt's *Monita salutaria B. V. Mariae ad cultores suos indiscretos* (1673)[84] and Jean Crasset's *La Veritable devotion envers la S. Vierge etablie et defendue* (1679)[85] are symbolic of movements, on the one hand of criticism and on the other of defence of mariology, within Roman Catholicism in the decade prior to the Revocation. The former appeared anonymously in Ghent but quickly developed notoriety and, indeed, support among the Jansenists and more moderate Catholics – among them Bossuet – in France (Hoffer, p.183ff.). Upbraiding the 'dévots indiscrets' for their credulous belief in apocryphal tales and excessive encomia of Mary, it recommends as an alternative to

---

*Catalogus testium veritatis* (1556) and the *Centuries de Magdebourg*; cf. Claude-Gilbert Dubois, *La Conception de l'histoire en France au XVIe siècle (1560-1610)* (Paris 1977), p.36ff., and *passim*.

82. On the synonymy *peuple-moine*, see below, p.65, 95-97, 119ff.; Jean-Pierre Beaujot, 'Du syntagme "erreur populaire" et de ses ambiguïtés chez Pierre Bayle', in *Beiträge zur Analyse des sozialen Wortschatzes*, ed. Ulrich Ricken (Halle 1976/1977), p.59-70.

83. 'Nestorius', footnote N, added in 1702.

84. The Liège edition (1674) of the *Monita* appears as an appendix to Melchior Leydecker, *Historia Jansenismi libri VI* (Trajecti ad Rhenum 1695), p.631-40, which is the edition used here. On this, Hoffer, p.140ff.

85. Paris 1679. The unpaginated Preface opens with a reference to the *Monita*, '[qui] détourne quantité de gens de [la] devotion', and reveals that the work is intended to counteract the pernicious effect of the *Monita*. On Crasset, see H.-M. Baron (S.J.), 'Le P. Jean Crasset (1618-1692), le jansénisme et la dévotion à la Sainte-Vierge', *Bulletin de la Société française d'études mariales* 3 (1937), p.137-67, and 'L'offensive janséniste contre Crasset', *B.S.F.E.M.* 4 (1938), p.175-82; Hoffer, p.241ff.

'superstitious devotion', a life of true repentance and good works.[86] The latter, concerned by the reduction in mariological practices, attempts to reinstate the devotion in what has been described as 'un des plus beaux livres de mariologie du XVIIe siècle' (Hoffer, p.243, 27). When the *Monita* was placed on the Index in June 1674 (Hoffer, p.172ff.), Jansenists and moderates alike sprang to its defence, declaring it a corrective to popular errors and a means of divesting the Protestants of the accusations of idolatry brought against Rome. Here is the key to the author of the *Dictionnaire*'s evocation of the conflict.[87]

The *Monita* forms part of the eirenic movement in Europe and more particularly in France, devoted to the re-unification of the churches in the second half of the seventeenth century.[88] The debates within the respective confessions over predestination, grace and free will had not only fostered a greater mutual understanding,[89] they also caused a shift in the Protestant reading of the reasons for the original separation from Rome. Justification by faith, no longer a primary cause in the thought of Pierre Jurieu, for example, yields to an emphasis on the *idolatry* of Catholicism, whose resistance to reform drove the protesters from the church.[90] In reply, moderate Catholics – of whom Bossuet is the voice in his *Exposition de la doctrine de l'église catholique* (1671) – stressed all the doctrines held in common by the churches.[91] Particular attention was paid to the devotion to Mary and the saints, which the bishop of Meaux divests of its apparent idolatry by arguing that it 'se rapporte nécessairement à Dieu'.[92] The intention is clearly that of dispossessing the Protestants of their reasons for a continued separate existence. Huguenot opposition to the *Exposition* was rife from the first edition (Orcibal, p.34). But in the wake of mass conversions and increased political oppression, voices of protest were raised with renewed vigour: the *Exposition* was decried as one of the 'pernicieuses méthodes [...] inventées [...]

86. *Monita*, in Leydecker, p.631-33; Hoffer, p.137-38.

87. The conception of ecclesiastical history as one of degeneration met with opposition is a commonplace of Reformed historiography; see above, n.81, and below, p.214ff., for its place in Bayle's wider historiographical vision.

88. Hoffer, p.157ff., and Jean Orcibal, *Louis XIV et les protestants* (Paris 1951), p.29ff.; M. Tabaraud, *Histoire critique des projets formés depuis trois cents ans pour la réunion des communions chrétiennes* (Paris 1824), p.132ff.

89. Alfred Rébelliau, *Bossuet, historien du protestantisme: étude sur 'l'Histoire des Variations' et sur la controverse au dix-septième siècle* (Paris 1903), p.17.

90. [Pierre Jurieu], *La Politique du clergé de France* (Cologne 1681), p.195; *Preservatif contre le changement de religion* (La Haye [1682]), p.52ff., 97ff., 135ff.; *Abbregé de l'histoire du Concile de Trente* (Genève 1682), *passim*; *Le Janseniste convaincu de vaine sophistiquerie* (Amsterdam 1683), p.14, 32, 35-36; *Lettres pastorales: addressées aux fideles de France qui gemissent sous la captivité de Babylon*, 4th edition (Rotterdam 1687-1689), letter XI (1 February 1689), p.85a; letter XIV (15 March 1689), p.105aff. and *passim*.

91. Works cited in note 88 above.

92. *Exposition*, in *Œuvres*, xviii.78; Le Brun, 'Critique des abus', p.247-57.

pour dorer la pillule qu'on vouloit nous faire avaler'.[93] The literature of religious controversy, in the few tense years before the Revocation, testifies, however, to the predominance of one polemical argument over all others.

In what might be seen as a last-ditch stand, a bevy of writers and pastors appeal to the faithful to remain firm in their Protestant convictions and their separation from an idolatrous communion.[94] The proof of its idolatry comes not only from 'la pratique [...] de toute l'Eglise Romaine'[95] but also from the publications of its clerics, foremost among them Abelly and Crasset.[96] Bayle later has this to say in the entry given to the former ('Abelly' (Louis), *in corp.*):

Il a fait [...] un Livre [...] sur la *Tradition de l'Eglise touchant le Culte de la Sainte Vierge*. Ce dernier Ouvrage, imprimé pour la seconde fois à Paris, l'An 1675, fit un grand Plaisir aux Protestans, parce qu'il leur fournit de bonnes Armes contre les Convertisseurs, qui vouloient leur faire accroire, que s'il y avoit quelque chose d'excessif dans cette espece de Dévotion, ce n'étoit que des Pensées Monacales, ou des Abus que les Evêques corrigeoient journellement. Ce même Livre servit à ceux de la Religion contre celui de Mr. l'Evêque de Condom, intitulé [*Exposition de la Doctrine de l'Eglise Catholique*]. En effet, Mr. Abelly se rendit le Protecteur des Pensées les plus outrées concernant la Dévotion envers la Vierge Marie. C'étoit ruiner les Efforts de l'autre Prélat, & les Vues de ceux qui ont publié ou aprouvé les *Avis salutaires de la Sainte Vierge à ses Dévots indiscrets*.

93. [Jean Graverol], *Instructions pour les Nicodémites* (1687) (Amsterdam 1700), p.121; cf. Elie Benoist, *Histoire de l'Edit de Nantes* (Delft 1693-1695), iv.556.

94. For example Graverol, p.122; Jurieu, *Préservatif*, p.31.

95. The quotation is from Jean Le Clerc, *BU* (1688), vol.xi, art.x, 'Livres concernant l'Exposition de la doctrine de M. de Meaux', p.438-99. The following remark generalises the proof from Catholic superstition, indicating its widespread nature: 'Les Protestans accusent l'Eglise Romaine d'Idolâtrie, & d'avoir recours à d'autres Sauveurs que Jesus-Christ. Les Adoucisseurs se recrient là dessus comme sur une calomnie atroce, & soûtiennent qu'on ne doit rendre qu'à Dieu seul un culte religieux, & que nous ne sommes sauvez que par les merites de Jesus-Christ. Les Réformez leur montrent qu'ils invoquent les Saints, & qu'ils leur rendent, aussi bien qu'à la Croix, aux Images, aux Reliques, un culte tout semblable à celui par lequel les Payens vénéroient les Démons ou les Heros, les Dieux Inférieurs, leurs statuës & leurs Idoles: Qu'ils croient satisfaire la Justice divine par des satisfactions, des Indulgences, des Vœux, des Pelerinages: Que, selon eux, le merite de ces actions, & ceux de leurs Saints, joints aux merites de Jesus-Christ, procurent la reconciliation des pecheurs avec Dieu. Ils leur prouvent que ce sont-là les Doctrines qu'enseignent leurs Théologiens, leurs Papes, leurs Conciles; non seulement dans les gros volumes, qui ne sont faits que pour les Savans, mais aussi dans les Catechismes, dans les heures, & les autres Livres de Dévotion à l'usage du peuple. Ils ajoûtent que c'est la pratique, non seulement de quelques Laïques, & de quelques Moines ignorans & superstitieux; mais de toute l'Eglise Romaine, dans ses Rituels, ses Breviaires, ses Missels, & autres Offices publiques; qu'elle n'a jamais condamné aucun de ceux qui poussent la superstition jusqu'à l'excès, que les Adoucisseurs semblent blamer; mais que bien loin qu'elle ait envie de réformer ces abus, elle persecute ceux qu'on soupçonne avoir quelque dessein de les abolir, comme les Jansenistes & Quietistes' (p.484-85). Cf. [Marc Antoine de La Bastide], *Réponse au livre de monsieur l'evesque de Condom* (Rouen 1672), p.3ff.; Jurieu, *La Politique*, p.109-11.

96. Jurieu, *La Politique*, p.111-13; *Préservatif*, p.59-60; *Le Janséniste convaincu*, p.57-58, 76ff.; xve *Lettre pastorale* (1 April 1689), p.115bff.; [La Bastide], *Seconde réponse à monsieur de Condom* (n.p. 1680), p.79ff., and Hoffer, p.229ff.

25

The statement elevates the use of Crasset and Abelly into a polemical method employed in the propaganda warfare of the time. That is to say, the superstition of a majority – public acclaim of Abelly and Crasset attests to numbers – is opposed to the opinions of a minority, thereby exposed as unrepresentative of Roman Catholicism as a whole. A similar if more brilliant method had been implemented by Bayle in the earlier *Pensées diverses* (1682-1683). There, vividly describing the superstition of paganism and linking it to Roman Catholicism,[97] he alleges Bossuet's recently published *Discours sur l'histoire universelle* (1681) as proof that the public practice of the majority and not the private sentiments of a minority of philosophers must form the standard by which paganism is to be judged. A footnote links the argument to the recent opposition to the *Exposition*.[98] The article 'Agreda' then, given all its resonances, is to be read as a renewed counter-attack on Catholic claims to be free of superstition and a 'slantwise' defence of Huguenot political and religious rights to a separate existence. The 'obstacles qu'on a trouvez en Sorbonne' to the censure of *La Mystique Cité* are proof positive that the moderates continue in a minority. Roman Catholicism, as at the time of the Reformation, can suffer neither its ills nor their remedies.

The entry, added to the second edition of the *magnum opus* (1702), was written at least ten years after the Revocation.[99] It is, however, more than an anachronistic reaction to earlier debates. Many Huguenots, according to Jean Le Clerc, converted under pressure because they trusted 'des promesses générales de Réformation', which at the time he wrote (1688) 'n'avoient pas une ombre de sincerité'.[100] The persistent idolatry of the Catholic church is the subject of many of Jurieu's *Lettres pastorales*[101] and so vigorous were his accusations that Bossuet stated his justification anew in an *Avertissement aux Protestants sur le reproche de l'idôlatrie* (1691). Affirming the same doctrinal interpretation

97. Rex, *Essays*, p.30ff.; below, p.122ff, and 214-18.

98. *PD*, §CXXVIII, *OD*, *OD*, iii.82a-83a; *APD*, iii.162a, reveals that this polemical thrust was recognised by Bayle's contemporaries. Among them was William Wake, *An exposition of the doctrine of the Church of England, in the several articles proposed by monsieur de Meaux* (London 1686), p.xv-xviii.

99. The information for the article 'Agreda' became available in January and November 1696, too late for the first edition. The letter 'A' came off the presses with the first volume in folio in 1695 (Labrousse, *Pierre Bayle*, i.245). The article was written, then, some time in the period 1696-1701, at the same time as footnote N to 'Nestorius', to which 'Agreda' is linked at marginal note 36.

100. Le Clerc, 'Livres concernant l'exposition', p.452-53: 'Outre le bruit d'un accommodement des deux Religions, qu'on semoit depuis plusieurs années parmi le peuple, & dont on avoit fait dresser divers plans à quelques Ministres; M. de Meaux & ses imitateurs laissoient échapper de temps à autre des promesses générales de Réformation, pourvû qu'on vouloit se rëunir. [...] il paroît maintenant qu'il n'y avoit pas une ombre de sincerité dans toutes les avances que les Cath[oliques] Rom[ains] faisoient' (p.452-53).

101. See n.90 above.

of the alleged superstition, he maintains 'qu'assurément il n'y eut jamais d'idolâtrie plus innocente et plus pieuse que la nôtre'.[102] This tone is continued in 1693 by Adrien Baillet in his *De la devotion à la Sainte Vierge*; written in the spirit of Widenfeldt's work, it resuscitated the controversy surrounding the *Monita*.[103] These re-invigorated disputes are present in the final admonition to our entry ('Agreda', footnote D, *in fine*):

Finissons par dire, que si la Faculté de Théologie de Paris a espéré que sa censure ôteroit du chemin de ceux qu'on nomme Nouveaux Réünis une pierre d'achopement, elle s'est trompée: car, les opositions, qu'il lui a falu surmonter dans son propre Corps; & le mécontentement, qui a éclaté après la publication de la censure; ont beaucoup plus scandalisé les Réünis, que la censure n'auroit pu les édifier.

The indignant comment testifies to Bayle's persistence in the belief that superstition, despite prefatorial palliatives, always has the upper hand (see below, p.142-45, 214ff.). The urbanity with which this more than bookish intellectual expresses his contempt for the ineptitude[104] and *mauvaise foi* of the moderate party, in its attempted reforms, should not blind the reader to the true target of the article. A token of solidarity with those still in France, seduced by unfulfilled promises, it bears within it the history, the tragedy and the consequent bitterness of French Protestants towards the end of the *grand siècle*.

Curiously, however, this hostility to the moderates for political reasons masks a more profound theological unity. For the *philosophe* of Rotterdam's critique of the 'fables', 'rêveries', and 'visions' of Agreda's work[105] ricochets in the writings of contemporary Catholic intellectuals.[106] Not only that, his horror at the mystic's abuse of Scripture and the temerity with which she and others

102. Bossuet, *Avertissement sur l'idolâtrie*, in *Œuvres*, xxi.239.
103. Adrien Baillet, *De la devotion à la Sainte Vierge et du culte qui lui est dû* (Paris 1696, nouvelle édition). The unpaginated preface reveals its proselytising intentions directed at the Huguenots. Basnage de Beauval annexes Baillet to the Protestant critique of Roman superstition (*HOS*, décembre 1693, janvier, février 1694, art.II, p.165ff.). Cf. Hoffer, p.254ff.
104. Bayle's earlier and transitory conversion to Catholicism is proof, according to Rex, of 'how strongly he had felt the pull toward Christian unity' (*Essays*, p.177). This desire for unity expresses itself in the *Dictionnaire* in hostility to sectarianism ('Mammilaires') and sympathy towards those of eirenic spirit ('Erasme'). In theory, then, Bayle might have favoured the *projets de réunion* were it not for the bad faith and Machiavellianism they subsequently were proven to harbour. He is scathing in his articles on those who weld politics and religion together in an onslaught against freedom of conscience (*CP*, 'Milletiere' and 'Rotan'). His indignation may also stem from disappointment: the oppressive and deceitful measures taken against the Huguenots made true Christian unity even more of a chimera than it had been at the time of Erasmus.
105. 'Agreda', footnotes A and D. On the wider significance of this lexis in Bayle's work, below, p.70-72, 126-28.
106. Thiers, *Traité des superstitions, passim*; Bossuet, *Remarques sur le livre*, in *Œuvres*, xxx.637-40; Hoffer, p.37ff., notes the conflict within Roman Catholicism between a more rationalistic and a more devotional approach to doctrine and worship; Le Brun, *La Spiritualité*, p.641, and 'Critique des abus', p.247-57.

'nous donnent comme révélé ce qu'ils ont apris par la lecture'[107] merely echoes the fears of her co-religionaries, who perceive the work as a self-styled 'cinquième Evangile'.[108] The vigorous iconoclasm of the *Dictionnaire* is reproduced, then, in mirror image by Bossuet (*Remarques sur le livre*, xxx.640):

On ne voit rien, dans la manière dont parlent à chaque page Dieu, la Sainte Vierge et les anges, qui ressente la majesté des paroles que l'Ecriture leur attribue. Tout y est d'une fade et languissante longueur; et néanmoins cet ouvrage se fera lire par les esprits foibles, comme un roman d'ailleurs assez bien tissu, et assez élégamment écrit; et ils préféreront la lecture à celle de l'Evangile, parce qu'il contente la curiosité que l'Evangile veut au contraire amortir; et l'histoire de l'Evangile ne leur paroîtra qu'un très-petit abrégé de celle-ci.

A similar opposition is present, in this case, between the linguistic majesty of Scripture[109] and the verbal insipidity of Agreda; the divinity of biblical truth and the 'romanesque' flavour of *La Mystique Cité*. Moreover, a deeper dichotomy – one evident throughout this transitional generation – informs the opposition. As both Bossuet and Bayle's notion of the *peuple* as a source of the work's popularity indicates, the critique of religious abuses in the second half of the century is founded on 'la coupure opérée dans le sujet de la religion entre un "peuple" et des "doctes", coupure de nature intellectuelle et sociale, mais non plus théologique (élus-réprouvés) ou ecclésiologique (clercs-laïcs)'.[110] That is to say, long before the Enlightenment proper, a division in mentalities is obvious, a division placing a small group of 'éclairés' in conflict with the opinions or devotions of the majority. Forgetting momentarily our author's Calvinist tones, the critique of the Spanish mystic becomes one more expression of the dismay of a 'docte-laïc', when faced with the predominance of popular error in Western Christendom.[111] The case of Agreda makes it no less clear, however, that this conflict of mentalities is not between secretly atheistic subversives and theological traditionalists but between two religious perceptions and traditions. Nonetheless, as is implied by the fall in devotional and the rise in critical publications at the end of the century,[112] this dichotomy *unwittingly* induces

107. 'Agreda', footnote B, fourth reflection.
108. Le Brun, *La Spiritualité*, p.637 and n.61.
109. On Bossuet's notion of the 'éloquence' particular to Scripture, Le Brun, *La Spiritualité*, p.641-42.
110. Le Brun, 'Critique des abus', p.255; *La Spiritualité*, p.642.
111. Bayle is here in the company of a host of scholars, Antoine Arnauld, Jean de Launoy, Richard Simon, Jean-Baptiste Thiers, and Bossuet himself, some of whom are his intellectual heroes. See below, p.119ff.
112. Henri-Jean Martin, *Livre, pouvoirs et société à Paris au XVIIe siècle (1598-1701)* (Genève 1969), ii.797.

'cette terrible cure d'amaigrissement'[113] and purge of popular culture necessary to the dawn of the *siècle des Lumières*.

At one moment in the entry, however, Bayle's voice seems to mimic that of Porphyry and Celsus (see above, p.18). In tones simultaneously evocative of libertines and Enlightened thinkers, he espouses the imposture theory of the origin of religion (Manuel, p.7, 35), in order to explain the rise of hagiography and popular devotion. Priestly guile, he muses, may be identified as one of the causes of superstition ('Nestorius', footnote N):

Les Moines & les Curez, s'étant aperçus que la dévotion pour la Sainte Vierge étoit un grand revenu à leurs Cloîtres, & à leurs Eglises, & qu'elle croissoit à proportion que les peuples se persuadoient plus fortement le crédit & la bonté de cette Reine du monde, travaillérent avec toute leur industrie à augmenter l'idée de ce crédit, & de cette inclination bien faisante.

The success of Agreda and those like her is attributed, then, to a mixture of credulity and malice, weakness and venality.[114] The propensity of post-lapsarian human nature to swallow myth and fables (see below, p.81ff.) is cunningly exploited by clerics, eager to reap the pecuniary fruits of men's foibles. The overall anti-Catholic bias of the article together with the reference to 'Moines & Curez' imply, however, that the remark is made more in an Erasmian than a Voltairian spirit,[115] an implication reinforced by the evangelical alternative of a clergy forbidden 'de recevoir ni sou ni maille d'aucun dévot'[116] proposed by the author as a curb on priestly venality. Such is the fundamental ambiguity and allusiveness of Bayle's writings, however, that only by a process of exegesis and contextualisation does a theme shared by free-thinkers throughout the ages resound through the centuries in Calvinist tones.

Given the dialectic of theology and history in the work of the *philosophe* of Rotterdam (see below, p.119ff.), the entry 'Agreda' conceals yet another level of 'meaning behind the words'. The significance of the lexis 'fables', 'romans', 'rêveries', and 'visions' for our author's methodology will be explored at a later stage (below p.70-72, 119ff.). Suffice it to say here that, in the inimitable terms of Elisabeth Labrousse, the article forms a 'test-tube' of the development of historical error.[117] The conception of *La Mystique Cité* as an apocryphal Scripture

113. Roger Zuber, 'Guez de Belzac et les deux Antiquités', *XVIIe siècle* 131 (1981), p.135.

114. See below, p.220ff. The position is found in Gabriel Naudé, *Science des princes, ou considér-ations politiques sur les coups d'état* (n.p. 1752), i.111ff., ii.36ff. This is a reprint of the 1673 edition in two volumes, which is that cited by Bayle in the *Dictionnaire*; cf. 'Hadrien VI', footnote G.

115. On Bayle and Erasmus, see below, p.1228-30, 236.

116. 'Nestorius', footnote N; Bayle cherishes an ideal of an ascetic clergy, of which Calvin is the archetype ('Calvin', footnote Z).

117. This dimension to the article 'Agreda' was suggested by Elisabeth Labrousse during a discussion of one of the earlier drafts of this chapter.

permits an opposition between the spurious and the true source of both religious and historical truth.[118] At this point, Bayle's conviction that not only superstition but apocryphal history gains the upper hand (below, p.120-21, p.142ff.) triggers off a historical reflection on the proliferation of hagiography. To priestly guile is added, then, an argument reminiscent of contemporary debates concerning the relative merits of 'histoire éloquente' and 'histoire savante' (below, p.55ff.). Attempting to explain Agreda's, to his mind, exaggerated encomia of Mary as co-ruler with Christ, he alludes to the natural propensity of rhetoric to become increasingly inflated ('Nestorius', footnote N):

> Les Prédicateurs se servirent de toutes les hyperboles, & de toutes les figures que la Rhétorique peut fournir. Les Légendaires ramassérent toutes sortes de miracles: les Poëtes se mirent de la partie; on établit des prix annuels pour ceux qui feroient un plus beau Poëme à la loüange de la Mere de Dieu. Ce qui fut d'abord une saillie d'Orateur, ou un enthousiasme de Poëte, devint ensuite un aphorisme de dévotion. ...[ Ces Maximes ne sont] plus un simple essort de Rhétoricien qui s'échauffe en chaire; [elles sont] passée[s] dans les Livres que l'on met entre les mains des dévots.

Just as in history, rhetoric is seen not as the slave but the master of truth (below, p.68). To the bombastic rhetoric of the preacher is added the slovenly research or even inventions of the collector of legends,[119] and this falsely started tradition, codified in print, is fed as gospel to the 'imagination des peuples'.[120] The hypothesis, no matter how vain,[121] finds its parallel in Bayle's conception of the development of spurious historical traditions (below, p.126-28). That is to say, the article 'Agreda', properly conceived, is not only the work of a polemicist, it is also that of an advocate of critical history. As such, it takes its place within the exemplary scholarship of the *Dictionnaire*, designed to eradicate human error of all kinds (below, p.119ff., 233-40). It is this generalisation of the target of the article which, in our opinion, led to the misreading of Bayle by the next wave of writers. Once the particular political and ideological context is forgotten, the use of the Spanish mystic to criticise superstition and error on a wider scale brings the *magnum opus* surprisingly close to the propaganda activities of those determined to 'écraser l'infâme'. The bridge between the two mentalities extends even further in the case of Nestorius, a *cause célèbre*, to which we now turn.

118. 'Agreda', footnote B, reflection four; Michael Geddes, *The Life of Maria de Jesus of Agreda: a late famous Spanish nun* in *Miscellaneous tracts* (London 1705-1709), iii.63-64, makes a similar generalisation.

119. 'Bezanites', footnote B.

120. 'Nestorius', footnote N.

121. This and the 'imposture theory' of the origin of religion, by which it is inspired, is an inadequate explanation of the rise of superstition and hagiography. Bayle seems aware of its inadequacy. Cf. Manuel, p.35.

# 2. Nestorius

Combien ces opinions communes que j'entreprends de combattre & renverser sont enracinees dans la fantaisie de quelques Historiens [...] lesquels
n'estans d'une complexion assez forte & bien temperee pour resister à la
contagion des Erreurs populaires & communes, se sont laissez gaigner
facilement à la persuasion de toutes ces calomnies, qui se maintiennent
aujourd'huy contre l'innocence & la bonne vie de ceux que la seule
consideration de leur merite estoit plus que suffisante de delivrer de ce
soupçon.

Gabriel Naudé, *Apologie pour tous les grands personnages* [1]

[Nestorius] prend place dans cette longue galerie d'hérésiarques ou d'athées
qui peuple le *Dictionnaire*; Bayle est non seulement heureux de parler avec
objectivité de ces hommes que Moreri avait condamnés ou passés sous
silence; en brossant leur biographie, il a souvent l'occasion de flétrir la
persécution et le fanatisme.

Alain Niderst, in *Dictionnaire* (Sélections) [2]

IN the 1690s, the normally dissenting voices of Bossuet and Jurieu unite in
a duet of protest against a 'heresy' apparently decimating their respective
communions. The writings of leading intellectuals – Louis-Ellies Du Pin, a
Catholic ecclesiastical historian, and Elie Saurin, a Protestant theologian and
*érudit* – testify to a rehabilitation of Nestorius, whose opinions were deemed
heretical by the third ecumenical council at Ephesus in 431. [3] Two features are
noted by the respective guardians of orthodoxy. On the one hand, a sympathetic

---

1. Gabriel Naudé, *Apologie pour tous les grands personnages qui ont esté faussement soupçonnez de
Magie* (Paris 1625), 'Preface', ã iiii. For Naudé, cf. Pintard, *Le Libertinage*, i.463ff.; for his influence
on Bayle, see below, p.132ff.
2. Pierre Bayle, *Dictionnaire historique et critique* (Sélections), ed. Alain Niderst (Paris 1974),
p.109.
3. Louis-Ellies Du Pin, *Nouvelle bibliotheque des auteurs ecclesiastiques* (vols 1-3, Paris 1686-1689;
vols 4-6, Mons 1691-1692); the history of the council of Ephesus is in vol.iv (actually tom.iii, part
II) p.41aff. Elie Saurin, *Apologie pour le sieur Saurin* [...] *contre les acusations de M. Jurieu* (Utrecht
1692), p.78-92; *Examen de la théologie de M. Jurieu* (La Haye 1694), ii.795ff.; on Saurin, consult
Jacques-Georges de Chauffepié, *Nouveau dictionnaire historique et critique pour servir de supplément
ou de continuation au Dictionnaire historique et critique de M. Pierre Bayle* (Amsterdam, La Haye 1750-
1756), vol.iv, 'Saurin', and especially footnote G. For a short account of the Nestorian heresy and
the council of Ephesus, consult Appendix I. This short narrative is not designed as a 'normative'
history of the episode, it merely reconstructs it from the sources available to Bayle (see Du Pin,
and Louis Doucin, S.J., *Histoire du nestorianisme*, La Haye 1698) and is proposed as a *résumé* of the
data available to him at the time of composition.

treatment of the heretic becomes an index of secret Socinian loyalties.[4] On the other, the consequent revision of the history of the council reveals libertine or latitudinarian tendencies.[5] Vociferous protests of innocence from the historian and the *érudit* were to no avail: the former agreed to revise his history, the latter succeeded in clearing himself of the accusations but received neither satisfaction nor apology from his accuser.[6] While neither side is innocent of animosity,[7] the conflict is more ideological than personal. Both of the authors draw on traditions sympathetic to Nestorius within their respective confessions, traditions in opposition not only to the received reading of the episode but, in the Catholic's case, to the seat of authority within the church (see below, p.42-43). The article 'Nestorius', written on 10 February 1696,[8] sides with the heresiarch and his defenders. No slavish imitation, however, the entry constitutes a dynamic reutilisation of both the recent sympathetic account *and* the ideology by which it is informed. On first reading, the resulting narrative may appear Socinian or even libertine in tendency. On closer inspection, it testifies to the presence in the *Dictionnaire* of a historical typology, created to answer the preoccupations and defend the rights of a persecuted minority.

The text of the article and the related footnote A evince a sympathy to Nestorius's christology, the kernel of the dispute between the heresiarch and his accuser St Cyril of Alexandria. The former had protested against the title *theotokos* (God-bearer) attributed to the mother of Christ, on the grounds that it undermines the impassibility of the Deity: God, by definition, cannot be born, suffer or die. The latter, however, saw the criticism as subversive of the hypostatic union of the divine and human natures in the Christ and read Nestorius's alternative doctrine of a *moral* union between the two natures – those of the Word and the man – as a renewal of the Samosatian heresy of the

4. J.-B. Bossuet, *Mémoire de ce qui est à corriger dans la Nouvelle bibliothèque des auteurs ecclésiastiques de M. Dupin*, in *Œuvres*, xxx.581-88; Pierre Jurieu, *La Religion du latitudinaire, avec l'Apologie pour la Sainte Trinité, appellée l'heresie des trois dieux* (Rotterdam 1696), p.291 and *passim*.

5. J.-B. Bossuet, *Remarques sur l'histoire des conciles d'Ephèse et de Chalcédoine, de M. Dupin*, in *Œuvres*, xxx.544-45; Jurieu, *La Religion du latitudinaire*, p.292ff. Bossuet and Jurieu may have been wrong to argue that Du Pin and Saurin were in fact sympathetic to Socinianism. None the less, a sympathetic treatment of Nestorius is indicative of a shift in the *understanding* of christological doctrine which heralds eighteenth-century attitudes to the supernatural. See below, p.34-35.

6. Bossuet's correspondence testifies to dialogues between the two thinkers, dialogues which ended in Du Pin's agreement to revise his history. Letters xxv-xxxiv, in *Lettres diverses*, in *Œuvres*, xlii.653-69; cf. François de Harlay, *The Condemnation of monsieur Dupin, his History of ecclesiastical authors, by the archbishop of Paris; as also his own Retractation, translated out of French* (London 1696), *passim*. Bayle, 'Nestorius', footnote H, and Chauffepié, footnote G, give accounts of the Saurin-Jurieu conflict.

7. The sources cited in n.6 above testify to the personal animosities which clouded the ideological issues.

8. The article is dated by Bayle in marginal note (a) of 'Nestorius'.

two *persons* in the Christ, tantamount to a denial of divinity (see Appendix 1). Bayle's cautious textual assertion that 'il y a des gens qui prétendent que le sens auquel [Nestorius] rejettoit cette épithete est raisonnable & orthodoxe' is defended in the footnote with copious but slightly distorted quotations from Du Pin's *Nouvelle bibliothèque des auteurs ecclésiastiques*.[9] The first of these, in summarising Nestorius's hostility to Cyril's doctrine, seen as a revitalisation of the Arian and Apollinarian heresies, omits an introductory passage present in the original source: 'Comme Saint Cyrille avoit mandé à Nestorius que ses Ecrits avoient été portez à Rome, & qu'on ne les y avoit pas reçûs favorablement, Nestorius crût devoir écrire là-dessus à Saint Celestin.'[10] The calculated omission neglects Du Pin's awareness of the heterodox implications of Nestorius's position, heterodoxy to which Rome was alerted, before the arrival of the heresiarch's letters to Pope Celestine.[11] In other words, the persuasion of the heretic's innocence, found in the text, is based on a knowing reorganisation of the source, effected to suit our author's preconceptions. The second quotation is even more telling.

Nestorius had expounded his notion of the incarnation in the second of two letters replying to missives from Cyril (Appendix 1). The Catholic historian provides a summary of the exposition, which reappears in a clipped form in the *Dictionnaire*. The passage in angled brackets is missing from the footnote:

⟨Cette lettre [de Cyrille] fit éclater entierement la dispute. Nestorius s'en trouva fort offensé & y fit réponse, en accusant Saint Cyrille, de donner un mauvais sens aux paroles du Concile de Nicée & d'avancer plusieurs erreurs. Il dit qu'il explique mal le Concile de Nicée, parce que ce Concile ne dit pas du Verbe qu'il soit né, qu'il ait souffert, & qu'il soit mort, mais de nôtre Seigneur Jesus-Christ Fils unique de Dieu; termes qui conviennent également à l'humanité et à la divinité.⟩ Il loüé Saint Cyrille d'avoir reconnu la distinction des deux natures en Jesus-Christ; mais il l'accuse de ruiner dans la suite cette verité, & de rendre la divinité passible & mortelle. Il avoüé que les deux natures sont unies, mais il soûtient qu'on ne peut pas à cause de cette union attribuer à l'une des deux des qualitez qui n'appartiennent qu'à l'autre, & il pretend que toutes les fois que l'Ecriture Sainte parle de la passion & de la mort de Jesus-Christ, elle l'attribuë à la nature humaine, & jamais à la divinité.[12]

The dismissal of papal disapproval in the first omission – apparently a mere Protestant tic – is informed, then, by a profound accord between Bayle and the heresiarch. A similar concern for divine impassibility is evident, together with

9. A full reference is given in note 3, above. Bayle is using the Dutch edition whose pagination is identical to that cited here.
10. Du Pin, iv.286b; compare with Bayle, 'Nestorius', footnote A.
11. See Appendix 1. Du Pin is mistaken in his chronology of the epistolary exchange. The error is not noted by Bayle.
12. Du Pin, iv.287b; Bayle, 'Nestorius', footnote A.

a recognition of Nestorius's appreciation of the two *natures* in the incarnate Word. More disquieting, however, is the removal of the latter's eccentric interpretation of the Nicene creed. For his refusal to attribute human suffering to the Word has at heart the doctrine of moral rather than hypostatic union. If both natures retain their essential properties, then it is legitimate to speak of the afflictions of the Christ from which the Divinity is exempt. Consequently, the excision of the fundamental opposition between this and the conception enshrined in the Creed seems to imply a subversion, on Bayle's part, of doctrinal traditions, a subversion possibly inspired by Socinian sympathies.

A final set of quotations contrasts the position espoused by Nestorius with that upheld by St Cyril. Again, the passage is dexterously truncated to portray the former in a more favourable light:

⟨La doctrine, ou plûtôt l'heresie de Nestorius, est de croire, que le Verbe de Dieu ayant prévû, que celui qui naîtroit de Marie, seroit saint & grand, l'a à cause de cela choisi pour le faire naître d'une Vierge, & lui a donné des graces, par lesquelles il a merité d'être appellé le Fils de Dieu, le Seigneur & le Christ; que c'est ce qui l'a fait mourir pour nous, & qu'il l'a ensuite ressuscité;⟩ que ce Verbe s'est incarné, ⟨parce qu'il a toûjours été avec cet homme, comme il a aussi été avec les Prophetes, mais d'une maniere plus particuliere. Que Nestorius avouë qu'il a été avec lui⟩ dans le ventre de la Vierge mais qu'il n'avouë pas qu'il soit Dieu naturellement; ⟨mais qu'il dit qu'il a été ainsi appellé à cause de la bonne volonté que Dieu a euë pour lui,⟩ & que c'est l'homme qui est mort, & qui est ressuscité. ⟨Voilà de quelle maniere Saint Cyrille expose la doctrine de Nestorius; & voici comme il explique la sienne.⟩ Nous confessons que le Verbe de Dieu est immortel, & la vie même; mais nous croyons qu'il s'est fait chair, & que s'étant uni avec une chair animée d'une ame raisonnable, il a souffert en sa chair, comme il est dit dans l'Ecriture; & parce que son corps a souffert, on dit qu'il a aussi souffert, quoi-qu'il soit d'une nature impassible; & parce que son corps est ressuscité, on dit qu'il est ressuscité. Mais Nestorius n'est pas de cet avis: car il dit que c'est l'homme qui est ressuscité, & que c'est le corps de l'homme qui nous est proposé dans les saints Mysteres. Nous croyons au contraire, que c'est la chair & le sang du Verbe qui vivifie toutes choses.[13]

The deliberate neglect of the heterodox implications of Nestorius's doctrine is here at its most radical. The heresiarch's denial of the absolute continuity between the Word before and the Christ after the incarnation is omitted, as is the emphasis on *sunapheia* (conjunction) rather than hypostasis, to indicate the manner in which the two natures were united. Moreover, absent also is the notion of the Christ not as God but as *theophoros* (God-bearing), in whom the Divinity dwelt in a similar if more intense way to the indwelling of the prophets (Appendix I). Instead, the heresiarch appears to hold in tension the paradoxical doctrine of St Cyril, whereby the Word, once 'enfleshed', suffered the indignities

13. Du Pin, iv.288b-89a; Bayle, 'Nestorius', footnote A.

inseparable from the human condition. Thus, the two-fold conclusion, drawn by the *philosophe* of Rotterdam at this point, becomes ineluctable. Firstly, and keenly perceptive, comes the assertion that 'il n'y avoit qu'une Dispute de mots entre eux; [...] la Dispute ne rouloit point sur la chose même'.[14] In other words, a wedge is driven between Nestorianism and Nestorius: verbal rather than ideological differences led to the attribution to the heresiarch of a heresy he did not maintain. Secondly and necessarily, a Nestorius proven innocent of heterodoxy is immediately transformed into a victim of oppression. His verbal reinterpretation of the incarnation, rejected by the self-acclaimed orthodoxy of St Cyril, is the sole cause of his supposed heresy. In a word, not heretical *per se*, the heresiarch is so considered by those wedded to a different terminology. The rehabilitation, then, is complete. Partiality, however, not 'objectivity' motivates this espousal of the cause of the persecuted individual. The article hints at the reasons behind this partial reconstruction.

The accord between the fifth-century thinker and Bayle resides on both a philosophical and a theological basis. In the first place, siding with Nestorius, Bayle maintains that the epithet 'Mère de Dieu' may be rejected without impingement on the doctrine of the hypostatic union. For

Il est très possible qu'un Ange soit uni à un corps humain au moment de la conception, de telle sorte que cet Ange & ce corps humain fissent un homme, tout de même que le corps & l'ame d'Adam en faisoient un. La femme qui concevroit, & qui nourriroit dans son sein le corps auquel cet Ange seroit uni, seroit bien la Mere de la personne qui resulteroit de l'union hypostatique de cet Ange avec ce corps; mais elle ne seroit point la mere de l'Ange. Nous ne pourrions pas même dire qu'Eve ait été la mere de l'ame d'Abel, quoi qu'elle fût la mere d'Abel. Disons la même chose de la sainte Vierge; elle est la Mere de Jesus-Christ, mais non pas du Verbe, qui en s'unissant avec un corps a formé un tout qu'on apelle Jesus-Christ.[15]

Cartesian dualism with its related difficulties and not Socinian subversion is concealed in this commentary. To the *philosophe* of Rotterdam, the mind-matter distinction of Descartes constitutes an irrefragable metaphysical truth,[16] a truth, moreover, rendering the hypostatic union problematical. If the interaction between immaterial mind and material extension is difficult to define,[17] then the relationship between an immaterial Deity and a material body in the incarnation also defies comprehension. Thus, while it is clear from this article

14. 'Nestorius', footnote A; the position, in a more nuanced form, reappears in modern analyses of the episode; cf. Henry Chadwick, *The Early Church* (1967) (Harmondsworth 1978), p.195-205.
15. 'Nestorius', footnote A.
16. Labrousse, *Pierre Bayle*, ii.175ff.
17. Descartes solved the difficulty to his own satisfaction by using the pineal gland, which lies at the base of the brain, as the centre for the interaction of the mind and body. Cf. Descartes, *Les Passions de l'âme*, §§XXX-XXXIV, ed. Geneviève Rodis-Lewis (Paris 1970), p.88-92.

and other assertions that Bayle doubts neither the incarnation nor hypostasis,[18] his refusal to countenance a fusion between the two natures – divine and human – in the Christ, testifies to a Cartesian reinterpretation of the doctrine, closing the gap between his position and that of the fifth-century thinker. Just as the hypothetical angel and the soul are distinct from corporeal man, so the Word must be held to indwell but remain separate from the man Jesus. Of necessity and 'dans un sens de rigueur' ('Nestorius', footnote A) – the qualification is important for its philosophical connotations – Mary did not bring forth God. The harmonious understanding between the two thinkers is informed, however, by a second and deeper cause.

A concern for divine impassibility, as we have seen, links the reinterpretation of the incarnation present in the thought of the heresiarch and his latest defender. As St Cyril's summary of the two positions (above, p.34) implies, the understanding of hypostasis in turn yields to a conception of 'les saints Mysteres' and, notable among them, the eucharist. Cyril's doctrine leads inevitably to transubstantiation: the flesh and blood of the Word are proposed in the sacramental elements. Just as the immutable Word appropriates a human nature which becomes *im*personal, allowing Divinity to be incarnate or 'enfleshed', so – according to Bayle – in the Catholic eucharist, God 'se met à la place d'une substance anéantie sans remplir cette place'.[19] The Cartesian critique of the Cyrillian incarnation bears within it, then, the Protestant-Cartesian antipathy to Catholic eucharistic doctrine. Bayle's repudiation of the fusion of the divine and human natures in the Christ is paralleled in his rejection of a dogma whereby 'un Dieu infini, immense, spirituel [...] a un corps comme vous, & comme moi'.[20] This antipathy to philosophical and theological materialism, a

18. For example, 'Pyrrhon', footnote B, reflection III. It is interesting that for Bayle, as for Amyraut before him (Rex, *Essays*, p.103), the incarnation and the hypostatic union are Christian mysteries, by definition against reason. The position adopted in 'Nestorius' is indicative, then, of the tensions between reason and faith in his thought.

19. *CG*, letter XXVIII, §xvii, *OD*, ii.134a. That is to say, the Cartesian distinction of substance and mode, rendering impossible the Aristotelian distinction of essence and attribute, necessary to transubstantiation, also makes difficult an Aristotelian understanding of the incarnation. (See above, p.20-21, and below, p.133-34.) Interesting to note, the incarnation and the distinction *de fait* and *de droit* are also at issue in this chapter of the *Critique générale* (see below, p.46ff.).

20. *CG*, *loc. cit.*; Saurin (*Apologie pour le sieur Saurin*, p.79) espouses a similar understanding of the Nestorian position, arguing for its greater conformity to the Protestant conception of the Christian mysteries (see below, p.43-44). This is one of the many sources which undoubtedly suggested the reading of the episode in the *Dictionnaire* ('Nestorius', footnote H). Charles Drelincourt, *Replique aux responses de monsieur Camus evesque de Belley* (Charenton 1645), is an eloquent testimony both to the accusations of Nestorianism brought against the Protestants (the pamphlet is an indignant rejection of the charges) and to those of Protestant ambivalence to the *theotokos*. While Drelincourt accepts the term because it expresses a theological truth *implicit* in Scripture ('nous ne faisons point de difficulté de dire avec les Anciens que la Vierge Marie est Mere de Dieu. Car celui qu'elle a engendré est Dieu sur toutes choses benit eternellement', p.294), he none the less has

leitmotiv of our author's work, momentarily peers out from behind the commentary in footnote A:

Ce n'est donc point une preuve qu'on rejette le dogme de l'union hypostatique, que de dire que la sainte Vierge doit être nommée la Mere de Jesus-Christ, mais non pas la Mere de Dieu: c'est seulement une preuve que l'on préfere le langage éxact des Philosophes au langage populaire, & aux synecdoches des Rhétoriciens.

The observation echoes the article 'Agreda', to which it is explicitly linked,[21] revitalising the opposition between the *éclairés* and the *peuple*, the philosopher and the rhetorician so fundamental to the *Dictionnaire*.[22] That is to say, Nestorius is not only proven innocent, he is embraced as one of a select group of thinkers whose piercing critique subverts the perennial drift of human nature towards error and superstition (below, p.214ff.). It is hardly surprising, then, that this and similar entries contributed to the eighteenth-century image of our author as a *philosophe avant la lettre*. The article, nonetheless, has other and more far-reaching theological implications.

An analysis of the council of Ephesus is provided in footnotes B and C, again liberally bestrewn with citations from Du Pin's history. The notes form a running commentary on the textual affirmation that 'on ne vit jamais un Jugement plus précipité, ni plus suspect de passion, que celui [...] contre Nestorius'. The 'irrégularitez' of the measures against the heresiarch are the focal point of the first remark. The Catholic historian had listed seven possible objections against the ecumenicity of the council. The assembly, 'tumultuaire & precipitée', favoured the Cyrillian doctrine as a result of 'passion' and 'brigue'.[23] St Cyril's

pastoral and philosophical reserves. His pastoral concern is focused on the inability of the *peuple* to conceive the correct limitations of the title. For some, he argues, 'ne comprennent pas à l'abord qu'elle n'est point sa Mere entant qu'il est Dieu: Mais par une pensée confuse ils s'imaginent qu'elle est proprement Mere de sa Divinité comme de son humanité' (p.297). This critique of a potentially materialistic theology, which reappears in the *Dictionnaire*, is also at the heart of his philosophical concerns: 'C'est fort bien dit que la Saincte Vierge est *Mere de Dieu*. Mais c'est fort mal dit *qu'elle est Mere de la Divinité* ou *de la Divine Majesté*. En termes de Philosophie on diroit que la Proposition est veritable, *In concreto* & non pas *in abstracto*' (p.299, italics in original). The work was read by Bayle and cited in 'Nestorius', footnote P. We may conclude, then, that, from the first edition, the link Nestorianism-Protestantism was firmly established in our author's mind, the reference to Drelincourt, added to the second edition, reinforces the earlier reading, challenged after the appearance of the first edition (see below, p.46). Baillet, among the Catholics (*De la devotion*, p.[aviir] and 3-4), accepts the link Protestant-Nestorian and reads the Nestorian heresy as a *mariological* rather than a christological dispute. Bayle and Saurin's positions are more nuanced but similar in their perspective.

21. 'Agreda', marginal note 36. The concerns of the article are similar, not only the reiterated critique of materialism but also a mutual concern with excessive devotion to Mary: 'Nestorius', footnote N.

22. See above, p.27-28; 'Nestorius', footnote N; and below, p.119ff.

23. Du Pin, p.320b; cited 'Nestorius', footnote B.

presidency as a cleric subverted the secular authority of the imperial convocation and officers, sent to preside.[24] Nestorius, seconded not only by his supporters but also by unaligned prelates, protested against convening the council prior to the arrival of the Orientals.[25] The heresiarch declared his intention to appear before the assembled prelates once the Antiochenes had arrived.[26] St Cyril neglected to await the arrival of the papal legates and the Western bishops.[27] The assembly was comprised of prelates devoted to its president and his cause.[28] Finally, Cyril – Nestorius's enemy – 'a tout fait & tout reglé dans le concile'.[29] All factors, together with the 'précipitation' of the proceedings,[30] indicate that the patriarch of Alexandria was motivated by 'passion'.[31] Evidently pleased by the account, Bayle underscores three of the most important accusations ('Nestorius', footnote B):

On n'emploia qu'une séance à citer Nestorius, à éxaminer ses Ecrits, & ceux de Cyrille, à ouïr des témoins, à le déposer. Celui qui présidoit à cette Assemblée étoit St. Cyrille, la partie adverse de Nestorius. Il fit commencer le Concile sans attendre les Evêques d'Orient, ni les Légats du Saint Siege [...] Tout cela témoigne que l'Empereur n'écrivit pas à Cyrille sans conoissance de cause qu'"il le consideroit comme l'auteur de ce trouble'.

The critique, presupposing Nestorius's innocence, is designed to explain his otherwise unfathomable condemnation. Emphasis, as in the original source, is placed on the superior political judgement and 'clout' of the patriarch of Alexandria. In other words, the maligned thinker – who did not receive a fair hearing – was condemned not for heresy but because he was outmanoeuvred. The comment finishes with a neat reversal of the received reading of the episode. Cyril, not Nestorius, becomes the cause of the civil and ecclesiastical disturbances consequent on the trial ('Nestorius', footnote B). Following a rhythm by now familiar, the author of the *Dictionnaire* turns next to the more shameful side of the affair.

John of Antioch, a Nestorian sympathiser – continues Bayle, drawing on Du Pin – arrived some days after the Cyrillian council and hastily held a clandestine meeting wherein Cyril, in turn, was condemned and deposed.[32] The Emperor, informed of the conflict, received deputations from both sides. The Orientals by letter and in the person of count Candidian outlined the injustice meted out

24. Du Pin, p.320b; cited in 'Nestorius', footnote B.
25. Du Pin, p.320b; cf.p.293; cited in 'Nestorius', footnote B.
26. Du Pin, p.321a; cited in 'Nestorius', footnote B.
27. Du Pin, p.293; cited in 'Nestorius', footnote B.
28. Du Pin, p.320b; cited in 'Nestorius', footnote B.
29. Du Pin, p.320b; cited in 'Nestorius', footnote B.
30. Du Pin, p.320b; cited in 'Nestorius', footnote B.
31. Du Pin, p.321a-b; 'Nestorius', and footnote B; cf. Saurin, *Apologie pour le sieur Saurin*, p.82.
32. Du Pin, p.296a-b; summarised in 'Nestorius', footnote C.

to their party. At first sympathetic, the Emperor was later persuaded by the three bishops sent by Cyril and by the intervention of his doctor to uphold the decision of the council.[33] Finally, torn between the two sides, he declared Cyril and Nestorius deposed and communicated his decree to both parties (Du Pin, p.302a-b). The Antiochenes acquiesced but the Cyrillians protested and the disturbances were renewed. Deputations again arrived at the imperial household, now at Chalcedon, and the Orientals again won the initial advantage. None the less, a judicious distribution of bribes, this time to one of the Emperor's preferred eunuchs, turned the tide in favour of Cyril (Du Pin, p.303a-304a). Bayle terminates the narrative with a cynical observation. Du Pin had argued that the allegations of bribery were brought by one of Cyril's enemies – a factor casting doubt on their veracity ('Nestorius', footnote C):

Je le veux; mais quelle meilleure raison donneroit-t-on du promt changement de l'Empereur? Il reconoissoit pour orthodoxes les Evêques de chaque parti, & cependant il prononce que 'Nestorius avoit été justement deposé' [...] il prononce, dis-je, cela peu après avoir paru favorable aux Orientaux qui s'étoient soumis à ses ordres; pendant que le parti de Cyrille avoit hautement refusé de s'y soumettre. Cette procédure sent fort l'effet de l'argent distribué par St. Cyrille aux Conseillers de l'Empereur: & voilà comment en quelques rencontres on est orthodoxe ou hérétique, selon qu'on a, ou que l'on n'a pas des sommes d'argent à faire donner.

Jurieu may well be right in his accusation of latitudinarianism: the remark is worthy of Gabriel Naudé in its detection of the *arcana imperiorum*, the 'fraudes & stratagèmes'[34] behind ecclesiastical decrees. To the charges of irregularity and injustice, then, is joined that of corruption: heresy and orthodoxy depend not on dogma but on *politique* and *intrigue*.

Curiously, however, the ecclesiastical historian on whom Bayle draws had provided a step-by-step reply to each of these protestations. Cyril was the delegated representative of the Roman See and rightfully presided over the council (Du Pin, p.290a). The protesting bishops (p.293b-294, 322a) were in attendance when the assembly was convened. The prelates awaited the Orientals for some days and deliberations only began at the latter's request, communicated by messenger. The charges of precipitation were invalid for three reasons. Firstly, Nestorius had already been judged and the council met not to consider but to execute judgement (p.289). Secondly, despite the heresiarch's promise to appear after the arrival of the Antiochenes, the assembly still acted rightfully in citing him three times and condemning him by default (p.322b). Thirdly, the session, lasting from early morning till late at night, could hardly be termed brief (p.322b-323a). Finally, to the charge of bias in the composition of the

33. Du Pin, p.301a-b; summarised, with a citation, in 'Nestorius', footnote C.
34. Naudé, *Science des princes*, i.13, 361ff., and above, p.29; below, p.220ff.

council, Du Pin replied by naming several oriental bishops present, concluding that, by definition, men of God would not conspire against justice and innocence. Moreover, the description of the consultations with the Emperor in the *Nouvelle bibliotheque* not only indicates that bribery was employed by the Antiochenes but also refers, on occasion, to the 'modestie' and calm characteristic of Cyril's party.[35] As manifold entries in the *Dictionnaire* intimate, the *philosophe* of Rotterdam normally takes account of the *pour* and *contre* of historical evidence (below p.119ff.) and, following critical examination, either decides in favour of one position or suspends his judgement. Here, however, he is dismissive of Du Pin's affirmations: 'Mr. du Pin n'a rien oublié pour répondre à ces Objections; mais la matiere lui a été si peu favorable, qu'on peut dire que ses Réponses sont la foiblesse elle-même' ('Nestorius', footnote B). Clearly, the attitude results from a determination to present Nestorius as the personification of 'innocence oprimée'[36] and not from a consideration of historical data. The entry, therefore, not only challenges Bayle's reputation for impartiality and objectivity, it also catches him *en flagrant délit*, committing the kind of historical *fraude pieuse* he attacks so penetratingly elsewhere in the *magnum opus* (see below, p.59ff., 119ff.). The reasons behind the words, however, far from whimsical or latitudinarian, are both scholarly and firmly theological.

The acclaim visited on Du Pin by journalists in the years 1686-1691[37] – keenly followed by the author of the *Dictionnaire*[38] – was overshadowed in the 1690s by noises rumoured abroad that his research gave expression to some of the most dangerous heresies. Bossuet was the first to question the doctrine of original sin implicit in the *Nouvelle bibliotheque* and eventually a memoir was presented to the Sorbonne, accusing its author of Socinianism, disrespect for the Church Fathers and 'd'avoir donné prise aux Heretiques, en parlant du culte des Images comme d'une chose indifferente, & inconnuë dans les premiers siecles'.[39] To the charge of favouring a Protestant reading of ecclesiastical

---

35. Du Pin, p.304a-b, 323a; Du Pin none the less remarks that St Cyril '[se laissa] emporter à la chaleur de la dispute' (p.324b).

36. The phrase is Saurin's (*Apologie pour le sieur Saurin*, p.80).

37. *BU* (1686), iii.38-76; (1688), viii.335-66; *HOS*, septembre, octobre, novembre 1687, p.279-303; mars, avril, mai 1691, p.291-309; septembre, octobre, novembre 1691, p.47-59; *JS*, 3 June 1686, p.116-19; 22 December 1687, p.69-72; 18 & 25 October 1688, p.276-84; 13 March 1690, p.92-95; 26 February 1691, & 5 March 1691, p.60-70; *NRL*, juin 1686, art.IV, *OD*, i.574a-76b.

38. Bayle took all these periodicals, and reference is made to the *HOS* in 'Nestorius', footnote L. As the later works indicate, our author was an avid reader of such sources, from which he derived much of his impressive bibliographical knowledge and, in later years, his acquaintance with many books he no longer had the enthusiasm to read.

39. Basnage de Beauval gives an account of the dispute in *HOS*, septembre, octobre, novembre 1692, p.140-43. The quotation is from p.142.

history – a fact which did not escape the Huguenot journalists[40] – was added, as the review by Basnage de Beauval reveals, that of Nestorianism.[41] The dual indictmeeent was taken up early in 1692 in two memoirs, circulated by Bossuet, the first of which dwells on the overall heretical implications of the history. The bishop of Meaux defends, among others, the doctrine of purgatory, the Apocrypha, the celibacy of the clergy and the veneration of saints, relics and images against Du Pin's contention that they are absent from the doctrine and practice of the Church in the first three centuries.[42] The second concentrates on the reading of the councils of Ephesus and Chalcedon given by Du Pin and focuses on his apparent sympathy to Nestorius. His account of the heresy receives a two-fold criticism. Firstly, according to Du Pin, the heresiarch opposed 'quelques expressions reçues dans l'Eglise': he subverted an ecclesiastical tradition and not a fundamental christological doctrine.[43] Secondly, Du Pin thought the term 'mother of God' was *possible* rather than necessary to christology (Bossuet, *Remarques*, xxx.58off.). Bossuet, in reply, painstakingly argues that Nestorius had undermined *biblical* christology and that the *theotokos* is abandoned only at the risk of orthodoxy.[44] The image of the council of Ephesus is the object of an equally sharp critique. Du Pin's answers to objections against its ecumenicity are dismissed as feeble by his critic: 'il n'y a personne qui nnn'ait ressenti qu'il poussoit bien plus fortement l'attaque que la défense' (Bossuet, *Remarques*, xxx.553). Emendations are suggested. Cyril is categorically the lawful representative of the pope and in no way undermined imperial authority (p.537-38). The council was decidedly not precipitate: the infirmity of the prelates and insanitary conditions at Ephesus rendered the convocation imperative (p.561). The bribery employed by both parties was only an indirect cause of a condemnation resulting from generalised hostility to Nestorian doctrine (p.549-51). In other words, the criticisms and the suggested amendments all highlight *inherent* weaknesses in the historian's account; weaknesses, moreover, diffused by the periodicals[45] and later turned to advantage by the ever-sensitive Bayle. The

40. The advantage to be drawn from Du Pin's history was noted by all the Protestant journalists cited in note 37 above. The accusation is reiterated in Bossuet's *Mémoire* and *Remarques*, xxx.475-640, *passim*, esp. p.478 and 516, who points to the periodicals' use of Du Pin as an index of the dangers of the historian's work (*Mémoire*, p.517).

41. *HOS*, septembre, octobre, novembre 1692, p.141-42.

42. Bossuet, *Mémoire*, xxx.475-518, *passim*. The bishop of Meaux's remarks are known to Bayle only through Basnage de Beauval's articles; these are sufficient, however, to alert our author to the fatal flaws of the *Nouvelle bibliothèque*.

43. Bossuet, *Remarques*, xxx.579.

44. Bossuet, *Remarques*, xxx.579; cf. *Mémoire*, xxx.581ff.

45. Basnage de Beauval summarises Du Pin's retractions in *HOS*, mars, avril, mai 1693, p.526-28; cited by Bayle, 'Nestorius', marginal note (70).

conflict between the two Catholics, ostensibly erudite, also reposes on ideological issues.

Du Pin's history presents a two-fold challenge to the seat of authority within the Church, a challenge disclosing important nuances between his own and Bossuet's position. Theoretically, accord and not dissent should characterise the two writers' reading of ecclesiastical history. In the first place, Du Pin's conclusion that purgatory and the veneration of saints, relics and images are inimical to the Early Church is the fruit not only of hypercriticism but of a 'jansénisant' hostility to popular error.[46] That is to say, both writers figure among the *éclairés* striving in the latter half of the century – by instruction or erudition (below, p.119ff.) – to rid Catholicism of its superstitions (above, p.27-28). The bishop of Meaux, however, for all his emphasis on the purity of Catholic worship (above, p.24-25), stops short of reading his convictions *back into* history.[47] For so to do is to undermine the *antiquitas* of Catholic doctrine, one of the criteria of truth of his Church (below, p.119ff., 214ff.). Thus, in a climate of renewed tension between Roman and reformed communions, it was imperative to deprive Huguenots – overjoyed to find support for their confession in a Catholic historian – of the advantage to be reaped from Du Pin's imprudence. In the second place Bossuet, himself a convinced Gallican,[48] detects a latent and displeasing Gallicanism in the *Nouvelle bibliotheque*. Du Pin's stress on St Cyril's subversion of imperial power was tantamount to support for the supreme power of the monarch in the convocation of ecumenical councils and church synods.[49] Ever sensitive to nuance, the bishop of Meaux maintains: 'S'il ne faut pas flatter Rome, il ne faut pas non plus lui rendre odieuse, aussi bien qu'aux autres catholiques, l'ancienne doctrine de France, en ôtant du pape ce qui lui appartient légitimement, et en outrant tout contre lui.'[50]

The observation, true to its author's interpretation of the Gallican position,[51] is also made with one eye on the Protestants. The *Remarques* display a concern lest Du Pin's image of the assembly at Ephesus become a generalised attack on conciliar authority. *Réformés* and libertines alike, he muses, 'regardent les conciles comme des assemblées purement humaines, où l'on suit les mouvemens

46. Jacques Le Brun alerted me to Du Pin's Jansenist sympathies during a presentation of this study to his seminar in the Hautes Etudes (IVe section), 28 May 1983.

47. Aimé-Georges Martimort, *Le Gallicanisme de Bossuet* (Paris 1953), p.199, sees this intellectual caution as fundamental to Bossuet's temperament. On conviction as a prism for history, see below, p.59ff. and 183ff.; Dubois, *La Conception, passim*; and Kelley, *Foundations, passim*.

48. Martimort, *passim*, and by the same author, *Le Gallicanisme* (Paris 1973), p.79-103.

49. Bossuet, *Remarques*, xxx.546.

50. Quoted by Martimort, *Le Gallicanisme de Bossuet*, p.645; for Bossuet's attitude to Du Pin, see Martimort, p.199, n.2.

51. Martimort, p.644-45, for the nuances in Bossuet's Gallicanism.

que donnent les Cours et des raisons politiques'.[52] His fears are realised in the *Dictionnaire*.

Bayle's one-sided reading of the council of Ephesus depends, then, on a sophisticated appreciation of the advantages to be drawn from a historian at variance with his own communion. Far from a *fraude pieuse*, on Bossuet's admission, the account is capable of being substantiated by the original source. It is probable that Bayle was inspired by the similar, albeit less brillant use of Du Pin by Huguenot journalists in their reviews of the *Nouvelle bibliothèque*.[53] Like Le Clerc and Basnage before him, the *philosophe* of Rotterdam draws from the test-case of Ephesus general conclusions subversive of Catholic ecclesiastical authority:

Que n'a-t-on une Histoire de ce Concile par un Fra-Paolo! [...] Car il ne faut pas s'imaginer, que sous prétexte que dans les autres Conciles on n'a point usé d'une aussi grande précipitation, que le fut celle de Cyrille dans celui d'Ephese, les passions & les cabales y aient eu moins de part. Il est bien nécessaire que le St. Esprit préside dans ces Assemblées, car sans cela tout seroit perdu. Cette assistance extraordinaire, & beaucoup plus forte que la générale, doit nous rassûrer, & nous persuader fermement que le St. Esprit a fait son œuvre au milieu des déréglemens de la créature, & que des ténébres des passions il a tiré la lumiere de sa vérité, non pas dans tous les Conciles, mais dans quelques-uns.[54]

The passing reference to Paolo Sarpi's *Istoria del concilio tridentino* is symbolic not only of a political reading of ecclesiastical history (below, p.224) but of the consistent Protestant use of such studies in the polemical war against Rome. Louis-Ellies Du Pin is annexed, as are so many Catholic critics (below, p.119ff.), to a self-consciously Protestant historiography. His research becomes a proof that Rome, having strayed from veracity, turns dissenters into heretics by superiority of numbers and political machinations.

The allusion to the council of Trent evokes, however, a more immediate *arrière-plan* to Bayle's rehabilitation of Nestorius. According to the bishop of Meaux, Nestorius is a particular favourite of Protestant writers: 'M. DuPin n'ignore pas combien cet hérésiarque a de défenseurs parmi les Protestants.'[55] The remark constitutes an indirect reference to a pre-existent shift in the reading of the episode, present in the *Lettres pastorales* of Pierre Jurieu (letter XVI, 15 April 1687, p.129ff.). In his propaganda warfare against Bossuet's *Exposition*, Jurieu not only adduces the conflict between Jansenist and *dévot outré*

---

52. Bossuet, *Remarques*, xxx.545.

53. References given above, n.37, 39, 45.

54. 'Nestorius', footnote B. Jacques Basnage, *Histoire de l'Eglise*, vol.i, part II, bk.x, ch.4, p.508-10, concentrates on the *passion* and *cabales* of the council of Ephesus and questions its infallibility on that basis.

55. Bossuet, *Remarques*, xxx.544.

as proof of Catholic idolatry,[56] he also provides a popularised ecclesiastical history[57] in which the Nestorian heresy plays a key role. While stating his repugnance to Nestorius's doctrine of two persons in the Christ, Jurieu sees the opposition to the heresiarch as a trigger of superstition:

> Le zele malentendu pour la Vierge commença à l'occasion de l'heresie de Nestorius qui [...] ne trouvoit pas bon qu'on appellast la Vierge *Theotocos*, Mere de Dieu [...] Pour s'opposer à cela on tomba dans d'autres excés, & on commença à donner à la Vierge des tîtres grands & magnifiques. [...] Nous ne nions pas [...] que la Sainte Vierge ne puisse dans un bon sens étre appellée *Mere de Dieu*, puis qu'elle est Mere de Jesus-Christ qui est Dieu. Mais ce fut pourtant aux Docteurs du cinquiéme siecle une temerité malheureuse d'innover dans les termes. [...] Cyrille d'Alexandrie [...] est assurement l'un des premiers qui a donné occasion au culte religieux de la Vierge. Car en se voulant s'opposer à Nestorius, lequel ne vouloit pas qu'on appellast Marie, la *Mere de Dieu*, il passe dans un autre excés, & pousse aussi loin comme il peut les loüanges de la Vierge Marie.[58]

The reconstruction provides a distant echo to the entry in the *Dictionnaire*, inasmuch as the patriarch of Alexandria is more culpable than the heresiarch. The latter's heresy may be repugned but, bearing in mind Cyril's supposed rhetorical development of eulogistic epithets, the heretic begins to be welcomed as a distant *testes veritatis* of Protestant doctrine.[59] This breach in the received reading is capitalised upon by Elie Saurin – nearer in his perception to the *philosophe* of Rotterdam – to whom Nestorius seems 'plus ortodoxe que Cyrille; parce que la doctrine du premier me [paraît] plus conforme à la nôtre que celle du dernier'.[60] With the advent of Du Pin's history, the periodicals run by Huguenots testify to a further *glissement*: the 'heretic' recognised two *natures* in the Christ and his opposition to the *theotokos* and subsequent defeat reveal the superstition and corruption of a politically superior but erroneous Church, personified in St Cyril.[61] At the time of composition of the article 'Nestorius', then, Bayle could and did both substantiate his own reading of the episode and draw freely on a Huguenot reconstruction wherein Nestorius had already become a Protestant *avant la lettre*. The entry, however, is more than a mirror image – albeit with panache – of stock Protestant positions.

The author of the *Dictionnaire*'s perception of Nestorius as a critic of material-

---

56. See above, ch. 1, nn.90 and 96.
57. The popularised history starts with the fifth lettre pastorale, 1 October 1686 and continues thereafter, interspersed with a commentary on contemporary events, particularly recent miracles and prophecies.
58. XVIe lettre pastorale, 15 April 1687, p.130a, p.131b.
59. On the notion of the *testes veritatis*, see above, ch.1, n.81, and below, p.214ff.
60. Saurin, *Apologie pour le sieur Saurin*, p.78.
61. *HOS*, mars, avril, mai 1691, p.300-307; septembre, octobre, novembre 1692, p.141-42.

istic theology also bears within it a conception of the episode as an unwitting contributor to superstition, to be found in the thought of Pierre Jurieu. In a remark heavy with allegiance to the Reformation and disappointment at its partial failure (below, p.228-30), Bayle observes:

Or, voici comment je croi que par accident, les Disputes de Nestorius & de Cyrille ont augmenté sur la terre les honneurs de la Ste. Vierge. Le titre de Mere de Dieu contesté pendant quelque tems, & enfin victorieux, & confirmé par les Canons des Conciles, fit plus d'impression qu'il n'en faisoit: il devint une grande affaire; le parti vaincu fut regardé comme impie, le parti vainqueur se regarda donc comme le patron de la piété; on aima sa victoire, on fortifia cette partie de la foi, comme une breche d'où l'ennemi avoit été repoussé, & où il pourroit donner un nouvel assaut. Parcourez l'Histoire de l'Eglise, vous verrez que dans tous les Siecles les Disputes qui n'ont pas été victorieuses, n'ont servi qu'à redoubler les abus.[62]

The tone of defeat, the fruit of long years of historical reflection together with recent experience and observation of the persecution of the *réformés*, intimates a psychological, as strong as the intellectual, bond between Bayle and the fifth-century thinker. Nestorius, innocent of heresy, concerned for reform, is a *type* of the experience of reformers through the ages: not only anathematised and oppressed, he also involuntarily contributes – here the pertinence of the *affaire Agreda* should be noted – to a further degeneration in doctrine and devotion.[63] This self-identification with a thinker from the past is more sophisticated than its echo to Jurieu might imply. For, challenged by Doucin's *Histoire du nestorianisme* (1698),[64] Bayle defends the stance of his article in the second edition with the celebrated distinction between matters of doctrine (*question de droit*) and matters of fact (*question de fait*).[65] Papal and conciliar authority – as the Jansenists had striven to prove[66] – governed only the first, since infallibility in matters of fact lies beyond human capacities.[67] In other words, the distinction

62. 'Nestorius', footnote M; cf. *BU* (1691), xi.27, *in fine*.

63. 'Luther', footnote CC, cross-reference from 'Nestorius', marginal note (80); see below, p.214ff.

64. Reference given, n.3, above; Doucin is aware of the contemporary resurgence of 'Nestorianism', which he attributes to 'la pretenduë Reforme' and 'la fatale liberté qu'elle a donnée à chacun de se rendre l'arbitre de sa creance' (p.4). The history, then, as with all readings of the Nestorian controversy in the *grand siècle*, has a contemporary thrust, here the eradication of contemporary Nestorianism-Jansenism-Protestantism.

65. 'Nestorius', footnote O; the distinction of *fait* and *droit* is applied to the case of Nestorius by Saurin (*Apologie pour le sieur Saurin*, p.78), from whom Bayle may have taken the idea for his article.

66. G. Gerberon, *Histoire generale du jansenisme* (Amsterdam 1700), gives a detailed account of seventeenth-century Jansenism, listing and frequently identifying authors of the vast pamphlet warfare. I used this work as a guide through the development of the *distinction de fait et de droit* and on occasion of the Jansenist use of Nestorius (esp. i.300ff., ii.133ff., iii.3-171); see also Augustin Gazier, *Histoire générale du mouvement janséniste* (Paris 1922); the edition of Pascal's *Provinciales* by Louis Cognet (Paris 1983) provides a more concise history of the debates (p.i-lxxxv).

67. Gerberon, iii.4-5; Bayle, 'Nestorius', footnote O.

covers Bayle against charges of Socinianism and Nestorianism: repudiating heresy (*question de droit*), he none the less refuses to attribute Nestorianism to Nestorius (*question de fait*). The argument not only sets up a chain of associations between Jansenism and Protestantism, it also hints at a deeper and more contemporary reading of the case.

The presentation of the case of Nestorius given by Du Pin, a Jansenist sympathiser, represents a second and perhaps unconscious stage in the utilisation of Nestorianism in defence of Jansenism. In the years following the publication of Jansenius's *Augustinus* (1640), opposition to its supporters centred on five propositions extrapolated from the work and deemed heretical. Associates of Port-Royal were asked to sign a formulary repudiating the five propositions.[68] In self-defence, the admirers of the *Augustinus* repeatedly agreed to sign the formulary, provided their signature meant only a condemnation of the five propositions, certainly heretical (*question de droit*), and did not signify that the said propositions were present in Jansenius's text (*question de fait*).[69] As harassment

68. Gerberon, i.301ff.; Cognet, p.vii-xviii.

69. The distinction developed gradually throughout a succession of pamphlets. The Papal Bull *Cum occasione* (31 May 1653) condemned the five propositions and implicated Jansenius as their source. A new stage in the controversy was introduced by the refusal of absolution in the confessional to Roger Du Plessis, marquis de Liancourt, duke of Rocheguyon and pair de France, unless he severed his ties with Port-Royal. Antoine Arnauld's pamphlet, *Lettre d'un docteur de Sorbonne à une personne de condition* (24 February 1655) (in *Œuvres*, ed. Bellegarde and Hautefage, Paris, Lausanne 1774-1782, xix.311-34), employs the distinction implicitly and applies it to a contemporary dissenter, the duke, and, by extension, the Jansenists: they condemn the five propositions (*question de droit*) but deny that they themselves are heretics (*question de fait*) (cf. esp., p.324-25, a vociferous denunciation of those who *create* heretics by their 'zele inconsidéré'). The distinction becomes explicit in a pamphlet the following year, directed against Annat: *Seconde lettre* [...] *à un duc et pair de France* (10 July 1655) (in *Œuvres*, xix.337-558), where Arnauld distinguishes between 'la foi catholique' and 'ce point de fait' (p.455), namely, the attribution of a heresy, repugned as such, to a given individual. The distinction, moreover, is generalised by a wealth of examples drawn from ecclesiastical history, among them third- and fourth-generation Nestorianism (p.457ff.). Pascal's *Les Provinciales* (1656) (esp. letters 1-3 and 17-18, p.3-52 and 327-80) popularised the distinction and drew opposition from the Assembly of the Clergy in the guise of a formulary, again attributing the propositions to Jansenius, ratified by a Papal Constitution (16 October 1656). The 'grande persécution de 1661' (Gazier, i.113) stemmed from the resolution – initiated by a decision of the Assembly of the Clergy (1 February 1661) and ratified by a royal decree (13 May 1661) – to oblige the signature of the formulary (Gerberon, ii.481ff.). A new and important stage in the use both of the distinction of *fait* and *droit* and of Nestorianism was introduced at that point by Henry Arnauld, bishop of Anger, in his reply to the royal decree (6 July 1661). He challenges 'le fait de Jansénius' by arguing for the possibility of the existence of a heresy, without the support of any known heretics, and cites the accusations of Apollinarianism against St Cyril and of Nestorianism against John of Antioch; both are presumed free of heresy. (The letter was attributed to Antoine Arnauld and is reprinted in the *Œuvres*, xxii.610-13.) That is to say, it is now first-generation Nestorianism which becomes a heresy without heretics and, furthermore, the episode has been raised to the level of an *exemplum*, containing instruction relevant to contemporary controversies. The argument was overturned by an anonymous pamphlet, *Réflexions sur la Lettre d'un évêque* ([1661?]): here John of Antioch, it is argued, a disciple of Nestorius, denied the attribution of the Nestorian heresy to

became more generalised, Arnauld and Nicole spearheaded a pamphlet warfare in two stages, to affirm their innocence and defend their rights.[70] The first stage affirms their unimpeached Catholicism, despite their distinction between

Nestorius. That is to say, John of Antioch becomes a Jansenist *avant la lettre* who was later forced, by the combined authority of Church and State, to renounce his distinction; he admitted that Nestorius taught the Nestorian heresy. (Summarised in the 'Préface historique et critique' to Arnauld's *Œuvres*, xxi.XLIV.) The contribution to the image of Nestorius in the *grand siècle* is important. For the first time, the *distinction de fait et de droit* is applied to the heretic himself and, following this view of John of Antioch's position, it becomes possible to conceive the Nestorian heresy bereft of a heresiarch, Nestorius. Not only that, the image here is also raised to the level of an *exemplum*, this time to encourage Church and State to unite against the Jansenists. The dangers of this most recent use of Nestorius were forthwith appreciated and rejected by Arnauld in two pamphlets: *Avis sur un autre libelle, contre la Lettre de monseigneur l'évêque d'Angers au roi* (1661) (in *Œuvres*, xxi.399-400) and *Eclaircissement sur le différent entre Jean d'Antioche & S. Cyrille, dont il est parlé dans la Lettre de M. l'Evêque d'Angers au roi du 6 juillet 1661* (1661) (in *Œuvres*, xxi.349-74). Both deny that 'le fait de Nestorius' (*Avis*, p.399) was ever in question and distinguish the case of Jansenius from that of the heresiarch by drawing on the pre-established parallel Calvin-Nestorius (see above, n.20) 'une dispute de doctrine' where 'le fait n'est point contesté' (*Eclaircissement*, p.357). That is to say, while Church and State legitimately joined forces against those two heresiarchs, requiring believers to anathematise a doctrine indisputably held by the maligned thinkers, they may not do so in the case of the Jansenists, for whom 'le fait de Jansénius' is still in doubt. The defence of Jansenism depends on the separation of their cause from that of all other 'heresies'; Bayle's defence of Protestantism will repose on the creation of a parallel between Jansenism and other carefully selected heresies. From 1664 to 1668, a series of pamphlets was written to defend the nuns of Port-Royal in their refusal to sign a formulary stating that Jansenius's meaning had been heretical. The anonymous *Remède contre les scrupules qui empêchent la signature du formulaire* (1664) and the *Lettre au R.P. Annat, jésuite, sur ses remèdes contre les Scrupules* (1664) (cf. Gerberon, iii.103) add little but proof of the vulgarisation of the link Calvin-Nestorius and the distinction of Jansenius from both. For, while no detailed discussion of ecclesiastical history is provided, the latter is again likened to fourth-generation Nestorians, wrongfully accused of Nestorianism, and the Catholic Church is accused of the *creation* of schism. The same year saw the first of a series of letters, attributed to Nicole (Gazier, i.163), given the suggestive title l'*Heresie imaginaire*, the fifth of which (3 February 1665), in its discussion of the grounds for excommunication, imposes a slightly altered perspective on the case of Nestorius. Some believers in John of Antioch's patriarchate, suspected of sympathy to Nestorius, were about to be forced by Maxim, a zealous deacon, to retract, when the patriarch intervened. Those who were Nestorians were not to be tolerated, while those who repugned the doctrine but refused to attribute it to Nestorius were to be left in peace (p.15-16). The *distinction de fait et de droit* is not only again applied to first-generation Nestorians, it is now the basis of an argument for toleration. It is as yet impossible to establish whether or not Bayle read all these pamphlets as they appeared, or later had access to them. None the less, the upheaval associated with the Jansenists was keenly followed by contemporary Protestants (see below, p.49-50) and, as Doucin's *Histoire du nestorianisme* indicates (esp. bk.VI and p.552-53), leading thinkers were not only acquainted with many of the pamphlets, they also appreciated their significance for a more generalised reading of ecclesiastical history. In a word, acquaintance with the pamphlets was hardly necessary, since the application of the *fait* and *droit* to Nestorius or his followers, the use of the episode as an *exemplum* and as an argument either against or for toleration are, as it were, in the air.

70. Gerberon, *passim*, names all the pamphlets. It is perhaps artificial to separate the two phases of the campaign, since the defence of the Jansenist conscience and the arguments from ecclesiastical history are interdependent from the beginning. None the less, as the conflict proceeds, the argument from ecclesiastical history achieves greater importance and popularisation.

doctrine and fact. The Catholic faith, asserts Arnauld, depends on Scripture and tradition and not on attributions of doctrines to Jansenius or any other thinker. Thus, *questions de fait* do not constitute 'un légitime sujet de tenir des personnes, qui sont très-catholiques & très-attachées à la communion de l'Eglise, pour hérétiques & corrompues dans la foi'.[71] The statement is tantamount to a defence of the rights of the erring conscience: apparent support of a heresy, as in the case of Port-Royal, may result only from a misguided – from the viewpoint of the accuser – intellectual apprehension of available data. The second stage applies the argument to test-cases from ecclesiastical history, foremost among them second- and third-generation Nestorianism (cf. note 69, above). When asked by the Emperor Justinian to sign a formulary testifying to the presence of Nestorianism in the writings of Theodore of Mopsueta, Theodoret of Cyrus and Ibas of Edessa, clerics, had refused, maintaining that the heresy, detestable in itself (*question de droit*), was absent from the arraigned works (*question de fait*) (Arnauld, p.46off.). Arnauld seizes the example, transforming it into a precedent for his own party's behaviour (p.463):

sans perdre le titre de Catholique, on peut quelquefois avoir des raisons considérables pour ne pas demeurer d'accord, dans une question de fait, de ce qui aura été clairement & manifestement déterminé, par la plus grande & la plus infaillible autorité qui soit dans l'Eglise, qui est celle d'un Concile œcuménique, où le Pape préside par ses Légats [...] l'Eglise ne prétend point être infaillible dans les choses qui sont de fait, qui peuvent souvent n'être pas examinées avec assez de soin dans ces saintes assemblées, ou être altérées par des préjugés & des bruits publics.

At this point, the distinction of *fait* and *droit* becomes a reading grid, through which selected episodes of ecclesiastical history may be filtered. A history read through Jansenist spectacles testifies to the orthodoxy of their position: 'sans perdre le titre de Catholique', they may legitimately condemn heresy while not finding it in the *Augustinus*. It may be Arnauld's intention merely to people his defence with Jansenists *avant la lettre* but, as Doucin – citing Du Pin as an example – was later to point out, the procedure is capable of generalisation. Nestorians aside, Nestorius himself and any heresiarch whatsoever can capitalise on the distinction, 'sur tout dans des matieres aussi délicates qu'on a vu qu'etoit celle du Nestorianisme, & que le sont toutes les autres qui ont fourni la matiere des hérésies' (Doucin, p.553). Doucin argues from experience. In the years preceding the Revocation, Bayle and other writers appropriated the distinction of *fait* and *droit*, applying it to the plight of the *réformés*.[72] The article 'Nestorius', then, in its refusal to attribute Nestorianism to Nestorius and its acceptance of

71. Antoine Arnauld, *Seconde lettre* [...] *à un duc et pair de France*, in *Œuvres*, xix.455.
72. Cf. my paper 'D'une hérésie à l'autre: Bayle et la querelle des jansénistes dans la pensée protestante d'avant la Révocation', in preparation.

the heretic as a Protestant *avant la lettre*, both consciously takes advantage of the Jansenist reading grid and – by deliberate echo to the polemical literature of the early 1680s – defends the rights of the erring *Protestant* conscience. The argument has three phases, the third of which appears in the footnotes to 'Nestorius'.

In the first place, Bayle is not alone in his acceptance of the association between Jansenism and Calvinism in matters pertaining to predestination and free will. Initiated by the enemies of Port-Royal as an iconoclastic tool, the link is a common-place of reformed polemics, designed to shelter the *réformés* under the shadow of a party, once deemed heretical but reconciled to the Church since 1669.[73] The presentation in the *magnum opus* of the Jansenist repudiation of Calvinist affiliations as an 'artifice' and a 'distinction mal fondée [...] afin d'éviter les fâcheuses suites que l'on prévoioit, si l'on demeuroit d'accord de quelque conformité [...] avec les Calvinistes' ('Jansenius', footnote H) has at heart, then, a psychological and ideological self-identification designed to defend the Reformation against charges of schism. If the Augustinianism of the Jansenists did not suffice to make them heretics, then why are the *réformés* not acceptable, given their adherence to the theologian of Hippo? The question, for all its naivety, is reiterated obsessively and in a variety of forms in the years prior to the Revocation (above, n.72). Bayle picks it up in the *Critique générale* (1683), initiating a new phase in the self-identification.

Accepting idolatry as the cause of separation from Rome,[74] our author transforms the Jansenists into a precedent for a continued separate existence and a plea for toleration in the face of increasing persecution. The crux of Catholic superstition, as always, is the *hoc est corpus meum*, the basis of the doctrine of transubstantiation. Catholics, argues Bayle, maintain that the words must be read literally, while Protestants hold to a figurative sense. The Catholic contention is in turn founded on its claim to infallibility: the words support transubstantiation because it has pleased an infallible Church 'de choisir, entre les diverses explications qui leur pouvoient être données, celle qui enferme la transsubstantiation' (*CG*, lettre xxviii, p.138b). The choice of a meaning appropriate to the words is, however, a *question de fait* and, beckoning to the Jansenists, Bayle observes:

[L'Eglise] avouë de bonne foi que toute question, où il s'agit du sens d'un Auteur, est une question de fait, & qu'elle n'a point reçu de Dieu le privilége de l'infaillibilité pour decider que Jansénius, par exemple, a dit dans une telle page une telle ou une telle chose. Elle doit donc convenir que quand il s'agit de déterminer le sens d'un verset de

---

73. Gerberon, i.19ff.; I. Bourlon, *Entre cousins germains: controverse entre les jansénistes et les calvinistes* (Arras, Paris n.d.), *passim*.
74. See above, p.24-26; *CG*, lettre xxviii, §xvii, *OD*, ii.134a.

l'Ecriture, c'est une véritable question de fait, pour laquelle Dieu ne lui a point accordé la grace d'être infaillible.[75]

The Protestants, then, like the Jansenists before and the Nestorius of the *Dictionnaire* afterwards, are mistakenly thought to be heretics. They are guilty not of heretical convictions (*question de droit*) but of a misguided – from the Catholic viewpoint – interpretation of a scriptural passage (*question de fait*). The distinction leads naturally to an allusion to the constraint of the Protestant conscience rife at the time. Thus, pleading for an opportunity for the Huguenots to examine the matter more carefully, Bayle adds that, if convinced, they will embrace the doctrine; if not, 'nous demandons la même grace que les Jansénistes ont obtenuë, qui est que nous ne soyons pas obligez de croire qu'un tel Livre dit cela, quoi que l'Eglise l'assure' (p.138b). There can be no doubt that the plea is rhetorical: the hostility to the Catholic eucharist is so ingrained – as Bayle knew from personal experience (see above, ch.1, n.66) – as to be ineradicable. Consequently, the identification with the Jansenists, by emphasising the *bonne foi* of the Huguenots, open to instruction, rejects persecution and defends their right to adhere to their convictions. The *Dictionnaire*, in its echo of these early phases of the argument, will add a new dimension: the bitterness of a writer, whose labour for toleration, in the light of ensuing circumstances, was so much labour in vain.

The article 'Nestorius', then, written eleven years after the Revocation, casts an acerbic backward glance on the fate of the 'petit troupeau', whose rights Bayle strove so passionately to defend in the *Commentaire philosophique*. The reformed/Jansenist distinction between *fait* and *droit* transmutes the heresiarch into an early adherent of Protestant antipathy to superstition and a fifth-century supporter of a figurative interpretation of the Christian mysteries. The allusion to the council of Trent elevates the entry into a typology of the creation of schism, not by the dissenters, innocent of heresy, but by a numerically and politically superior group, mistakenly convinced of its own orthodoxy. In the third phase of the demonstration Bayle, this time by a reversal of the arguments of Louis Thomassin's *Traité de l'unité de l'Eglise* (1686-1688),[76] sounds the causes of the apparent rout of his confession which, unlike the Jansenists, became an object of generalised intolerance. Thomassin's work constitutes a further example of a polemical use of history to substantiate ideology, here the ideology of oppression. A compilation of edicts and political measures employed 'pour ramener à l'unité de l'Eglise ceux qui s'en étoient separez' (Thomassin,

75. *CG*, letter xxix, §vii, *OD*, ii.138a-b.
76. Louis Thomassin, *Traité de l'unité de l'Eglise, et des moyens que les princes chrestiens ont employez, pour y faire rentrer ceux qui en estoient separez* (Paris 1686-1688); cited in 'Nestorius', footnote E.

i.78), the study – hailed by Catholic and satirised by Protestant journalists, our author among them[77] – is 'une Apologie indirecte des moïens dont on s'est servi en France, pour y ruiner le parti des Protestans'.[78] The Nestorian sect figures in the demonstration and its success in the Orient is attributed to the tolerance of Mohammedan monarchs – according to Thomassin – culpable for their neglect of the 'lois sévéres' of the Christian emperors, by which Providence maintained religious orthodoxy and unity in the West (Thomassin, i.368ff.). Thomassin, consistent with his beliefs, adduces the unity and universality of western Christendom, achieved by secular means, as proof of its veracity (i.100ff.). The *philosophe* of Rotterdam, arguing from Nestorianism by cross-reference to the article 'Mahomet', presents this politically contrived unity as a sign of the error of the Church of Rome (see below, p.214ff.)

Presupposing the falsehood of Islam, then, and maintaining that toleration is inconsistent with its precepts,[79] Bayle perceives the intolerant measures of Christian monarchs as an adoption of 'voies Mahométanes',[80] equally at variance with the spirit of the Gospel.[81] That is to say, the undeniable 'étendue'[82] or universality of Islam finds its parallel in the universality of Catholicism and both, by inference, are erroneous religions. Once proven erroneous, however, the origin of their universality becomes problematic and, in his answer to the dilemma, Bayle simultaneously links the case of the Jansenists and the plight of the Protestants ('Mahomet', footnote N):

[Mahomet prit le parti de contraindre par les armes à se soumettre à sa Religion]. Il ne faut point chercher ailleurs la cause de ses progrès; nous l'avons ici toute entière. [...] comment résister à des armées conquérantes qui éxigent des signatures? Interrogez les Dragons de France, qui servirent à ce métier l'an 1685: ils vous répondront qu'ils se font forts de faire signer l'Alcoran à toute la terre, pourvu qu'on leur donne le tems de faire valoir la Maxime, *compelle intrare, contrain les d'entrer.*

The ubiquity of Islam and Catholicism and the latter's recent domination in France result, then, from the use of arms to coerce belief. The reference to a 'formulaire', endorsed under pressure, echoes and reverses the case of the

---

77. *JS*, 5 August 1686, p.186-88, opens the article as follows: 'Jamais Ouvrage ne fut plus propre que celui-ci pour le tems où nous sommes, que l'on peut regarder comme le comble de la gloire du Roi. Sa lecture doit achever de convaincre les *nouveaux Catholiques*, & le peu de P.R. qui restent encore dans le Royaume, qu'il n'y a rien de plus juste que la conduite qu'on a tenue à leur égard, & confondre en même tems les Protestants étrangers qui ne cessent de la rendre odieuse par leurs écrits pleins d'emportemens & de calomnies' (p.186). *HOS*, septembre-novembre 1687, p.18off.; *NRL*, art.v, novembre 1686, *OD* i.688a-90b.

78. *NRL*, art.v, novembre 1686, *OD* i.688a; ref. *HOS*, septembre-novembre 1687, p.180.

79. 'Nestorius', footnote E; 'Mahomet', footnotes N and AA.

80. 'Nestorius', footnote E; 'Mahomet', footnote P.

81. 'Mahomet', footnotes O and P; 'Nestorius', footnote E; see below, p.214ff.

82. 'Mahomet', footnote N; cf. 'Nestorius', footnote E.

Jansenists: the Huguenots, unable to hide behind the distinction of *fait* and *droit*, were constrained to sign away their religious freedom. The argument testifies to an unshakable allegiance to the Reformation, despite its reduced numbers and apparent defeat under the reign of Louis XIV. For if violence, common to Mecca and Rome and contrary to the Gospel, is the cause of *multitudo*, then persecution and minority become signs of the true Church (see below, p.214ff.). The link with Nestorius is more complex if no less present.

The *Commentaire philosophique*, to which the above quotation alludes, has at heart the conviction that coercion in religion is contrary to the 'Morale de Jesus-Christ' (see below, p.165ff.) The conviction reposes in turn on a revision of the myth of the primitive Church, common to the thinkers of the day (see below, p.123, 124ff.). The divine origin of Christianity, to Bayle's mind, is attested by its initial conquering of the world by peaceful means ('Mahomet', footnote O):

L'Evangile prêché par des gens sans nom, sans étude, sans éloquence, cruellement persécutez & destituez de tous les apuis humains, ne laissa pas de s'établir en peu de tems par toute la terre. C'est un fait que personne ne peut nier, & qui prouve clairement que c'est l'Ouvrage de Dieu. [...] la Religion Chrétienne s'est établie sans le secours du bras séculier, [...] la Religion de Mahomet s'est établie par voie de conquête [...] Bien nous en prend d'avoir les trois prémiers Siecles du Christianisme à couvert du parallêle; car sans cela ce seroit une folie que de reprocher aux Mahométans la violence qu'ils ont emploiée pour la propagation de l'Alcoran: ils nous feroient bientôt taire [...].

The *notae* or signs of the Early Church in the first three centuries are, therefore, its modest origins, its experience of persecution, its ubiquity and toleration.[83] As the continuation of the comment and Thomassin's study reveal, after 300 AD the Christian Church – not unlike the Mohammedans – increasingly applied to secular powers to consolidate or extend her influence. The trial of Nestorius is a case in point. Innocent of heresy – like the Jansenists and the Protestants – he was made a heretic and persecuted by Christians,[84] by virtue of Cyril's corrupt manipulation of the emperor Theodosius. Here the utilisation of Du Pin achieves its greatest force: his Gallicanism is reversed against the all-Catholic France of Louis XIV. The Catholic historian had stressed the necessity of imperial intervention to curb ecclesiastical disturbances: Bayle, employing the emphasis, abuses its import. Theodosius, the tool of the clergy in the person of Cyril,[85] and, by implication, the French monarch become 'Christian-Mohammeds': more intolerant than the prophet of Islam, they pervert the spirit

83. See below, p.214ff., for the wider historiographical context of these ideas.
84. The persecution of Nestorius is stressed in footnotes D and E.
85. The Protestants in the Revocation era consistently attribute their difficulties not to the monarch but to the clergy, of which he is seen to be the tool: see below, p.80.

of the Gospel, oppress and persecute witnesses to the truth throughout the ages.

The article 'Nestorius', as we have seen, depends on a complex web of associations and echoes derived from some of the 'best-sellers' in Bayle's day. Not only that, the *glissements* in the reading of the episode were themselves vulgarised by the periodicals on which Bayle also draws. In other words, positing a hypothetical 'common reader' in the last quarter of the century, it may be argued that an appreciation of the true targets of the entry reposes on a complicity between author and public, a complicity, moreover, fully exploited in the *Dictionnaire*. This shared perspective renders the article and many others both abstruse and apparently similar to the methods and ideologies of the philosophers of the next century.[86] By definition, the common reader in the eighteenth century no longer possesses the tools and concepts necessary to the author-reader complicity. Consequently, many of the entries become generalised; Bayle's sympathy to 'heretics and deviants of all kinds' (Mandrou, p.291) takes on the guise of a pre-Enlightenment thought and a 'method for attacking accepted ideas and established dogmas, protected by stern institutions'. The task of scholarship, then, is one of restoration: the rediscovery of an essentially *religious* context, in which Bayle strives, albeit in vain, to inform and influence a public opinion hostile to his co-religionaries.

The article, however, contains a second and more generalised typology – opposed to that of Nestorius – which bridges the divide between classical and Enlightenment thought. Delighted by Du Pin's pejorative image of St Cyril as a corrupt and impassioned cleric, Bayle elevates the patriarch of Alexandria into an archetype of ecclesiastical politics. The generalisation is effected by reference in the footnotes to two contemporary accusations of Nestorianism, the one brought by Jurieu against Elie Saurin ('Nestorius', footnote H), the other by the Jesuits against the Oratorians at Mons (footnote G). Selectivity is again in evidence: Bayle takes his information from sources defending the respective victims.[87] Not only that, the episodes are presented in such a way as to echo and conform to the *pattern* of the original episode. In every case, a fellow-believer is denounced for a heresy, of which he is innocent, by an 'Accusateur' ('Nestorius', *in corp.*) not himself devoid of heterodox tinctures.[88] The latter

86. The similarities are noted by Robert Mandrou, *From humanism to science, 1480-1700*, trans. Brian Pierce (Harmondsworth 1978), p.291, and Rex, *Essays*, p.168.
87. The information for the case against Saurin is taken from the latter's *Apologie pour le sieur Saurin* and, for the Oratorians, from Antoine Arnauld, *Difficultés proposées à M. Steyaert docteur et professeur en théologie de la Faculté de Louvain* (1691) (in *Œuvres*, viii.469-553).
88. Saurin (*Examen de la théologie*, p.869) and Arnauld (*Difficultés*, in *Œuvres*, viii.498-513) strive to prove on the one hand Jurieu guilty of the heresy he detects in others and on the other the Jesuits guilty of calumny.

makes unfaithful extracts from his fellow's works, offering them as representative to a council, synod or jury who then comes to a decision on that basis ('Nestorius', footnotes G and H). The accuser is invariably impassioned and resorts to cavils and machinations both to avoid his own and precipitate his opponent's condemnation.[89] Finally, while the spectators and judges frequently appreciate the injustice of the proceedings, they rarely take preventive measures. The pattern evokes the following observation ('Nestorius', footnote I):

Voilà le portrait d'une infinité de gens. Ils conoissent le tort d'un Accusateur; ils le détestent; ils en diront à l'oreille de leurs amis tout le mal imaginable; mais s'il peut nuire & déservir, ils se gardent bien, étant ses Juges, de prononcer rien qui le flétrisse. Ils ont mille tours de souplesse pour esquiver, & pour laisser dans les afaires mille plis, & mille entortillemens. Ce qui montre que l'ascendant du crédit sur la Justice est un mal presque incurable dans le genre humain; c'cst cc qui fera que les personnes puissantes ne craindront jamais de semer des calomnies utiles.

Cyril, Jurieu and the Jesuits, aided in their denunciations by the implicit collaboration of the silent majority, become types of the persecutor. Their authority substantiates their calumnies and all conspire in favour of another seemingly perennial drift in man's nature: the predominance of injustice and oppression in the course of human history.[90] While the criticism functions by opposition to the evangelical ideal contained in the revised biography of Nestorius, its universality and trans-confessionalism are worthy of the Enlightenment. Here and in the final stages of the entry, Bayle indeed becomes the herald of a new age.

The *philosophe* of Rotterdam's utilisation of Louis-Ellies Du Pin's history of the council of Ephesus is more than a penetrating appreciation of the polemical advantages it offers. The article, in the first edition, testifies to a profound respect for the writer's courageous acceptance of the role of a 'Historien équitable' ('Nestorius', *in corp.* and footnote L). Challenged by Doucin (see above, p.45) in the interval, however, the second edition both reiterates the stance of the first and refuses to accept Du Pin's amended version of the story. The refusal, inseparable from Bayle's conviction of Nestorius's innocence, is also based on his perception of the cause of the historian's retractions. Two are alleged, the first of which is retained. People withdraw earlier opinions either 'dans la peur d'être oprimez' ('Nestorius', footnote O) or because they subsequently recognise a mistake. The first is more probable, muses Bayle, since Du Pin evidently appreciated that 'il est du devoir d'un bon Catholique Romain d'aquiescer, [...] sans donner lieu à de malheureuses & très dangereuses

---

89. 'Nestorius', footnotes G and H; cf. Chauffepié, *Nouveau dictionnaire*, 'Saurin', footnote G; Arnauld, *Difficultés, passim.*

90. 'Manichéens', footnote D; see below, p.214ff.

distinctions du fait & du droit'. In other words, authority was brought to bear on verity but its triumph in Du Pin's recantation cannot replace the undeniable accuracy of his first account. The original version is to be preferred for its equity; in the second Du Pin, an earlier defender of innocence, becomes one more tool of ecclesiastical politics, motivated by instincts of self-preservation. The argument touches on one of the fundamental concerns of the *Dictionnaire*: the transformation of history into a vehicle of oppression (see below, p.235), as the related article 'Rodon' reveals. Rodon,[91] an early seventeenth-century defender of Nestorius, is acclaimed by Bayle ('Rodon', footnote B). For

Sans doute il n'a prétendu que chagriner les Papistes, & leur faire honte de l'opression où ils tiennent la mémoire des innocens, tandis qu'ils élevent jusques aux nues un Hérétique qui eut pour lui le bras séculier, la faveur de l'Empereur, & la cabale prédominante d'un Concile. Si l'on vouloit même pousser un peu loin la charité, l'on assûreroit qu'il n'eut point d'autre motif que de secourir l'innocence, en faisant paroître que c'est à tort que Nestorius est regardé comme un Hérétique.

To the hostility to St Cyril – here at its most radical – is joined an antagonism to a propaganda machine, capable of influencing the opinions of succeeding generations. Here Bayle, despite his Protestantism, simultaneously joins hands with Gabriel Naudé[92] and Voltaire: he, like them, espouses deviancy to subvert the 'stern institutions' of an inherently unjust society. The opposition of propaganda to equity in the historical enterprise is not, however, without resonances of the recent experiences of the Huguenots. They too fell victim to a propaganda warfare diffused through so-called histories. In his resistance to oppressive ideologies, Bayle may be subsequently aligned with free-thinkers but his anatomy of the mentality of the oppressor belongs firmly to the Augustinian *siècle de Louis XIV*. This is the topic of our next chapter.

91. François La Planche, *L'Evidence du Dieu chrétien* (Strasbourg 1983), p.45-48, for an analysis of some of Rodon's work.
92. He joins Naudé only in the *Apologie pour tous les grands personnages*, designed to defend the reputations of scholars and famous men, wrongfully, to its author's mind accused of magic. Naudé, however, as we shall see (below, p.144, 231-32) favours propaganda and even calumny, especially in the quelling of Protestantism; at this point, Bayle and he part company.

# II. The historian as moralist

# 3. 'La racine du mal':[1] the psychology of total depravity and the psychology of the historian

> Il n'est d'ailleurs pas vraisemblable que dans la foule innombrable des historiens nous ne puissions trouver personne qui ne doive son inspiration à une instance ou à un intérêt, à une animosité ou à quelque autre passion. Le prudent lecteur de l'histoire tiendra donc un juste milieu entre ces deux défauts, dont l'un provient de la vanité et l'autre de la sottise; il se contentera de faire un choix minutieux pour ne conserver que les meilleures sources, et de ne porter sur les faits le moindre jugement avant d'être bien au courant des mœurs et du génie de l'historien.
>
> Jean Bodin, *Methodus ad facilem historiarum cognitionem*[2]

> Ce n'est pas seulement dans les sciences qu'il est difficile de distinguer la vérité de l'erreur, mais aussi dans la plupart des sujets dont les hommes parlent, & des affaires qu'ils traitent. Il y a presque par-tout des routes différentes, les unes vraies, les autres fausses; c'est à la raison d'en faire le choix. Ceux qui choisissent bien, sont ceux qui ont l'esprit juste; ceux qui prennent le mauvais parti, sont ceux qui ont l'esprit faux, & c'est la premiere & la plus importante différence qu'on peut mettre entre les qualités de l'esprit des hommes.
>
> Arnauld and Nicole, *La Logique de Port-Royal*[3]

IT is hardly surprising that the first published statement of that historical pyrrhonism, for which Bayle was later to become famous,[4] occurs in the *Critique générale de l'Histoire du calvinisme de M. Maimbourg*,[5] a work which, read in its wider context, was one of almost one hundred books and pamphlets in the

---

1. The phrase is Bayle's, in 'Launoi, (Jean de)', footnote I.

2. Jean Bodin, *Methodus ad facilem historiarum cognitionem* (Parisiis 1566); nouvelle édition et traduction par Pierre Mesnard, in *Œuvres philosophiques*, Corpus général des philosophes français, v, iii (Paris 1951), p.294. A similar position is in evidence in François La Mothe Le Vayer, *Du peu de certitude qu'il y a dans l'histoire*, in *Œuvres* (Paris 1669), xiii.430, 433. La Mothe Le Vayer follows Bodin quite closely in this and other works. On Bodin and Renaissance historiography, cf. Dubois, *passim*, and George Huppert, *The Idea of perfect history: historical erudition and historical philosophy in Renaissance France* (Urbana, Chicago, London 1970), *passim*.

3. Antoine Arnauld and Pierre Nicole, *La Logique ou l'art de penser* (Paris 1970), p.35. For convenience reference is also made to the pagination in *Œuvres*, vol.xli-xlii, p.105.

4. Pierre de Crousaz, *Examen du pyrrhonisme ancien et moderne* (La Haye 1733), *passim*; Robinson, *Bayle the sceptic*, *passim*; A. D. Momigliano, *Studies in historiography* (London 1966), p.10.

5. It was published by Wolfgang in Amsterdam but appeared under the false rubric Villefranche, Pierre le Blanc, 1682; see Labrousse, *Pierre Bayle*, i.180-83; *CG*, letter I, §iv; letter II, §iii, *OD*, ii.11a, 13a.

Revocation era, touching on the Reformation and its history.[6] As has been noted by Alfred Rébelliau,[7] an increasing lassitude with the purely doctrinal aspects of religious controversy between the Catholic and Protestant communions yielded a new interest in ecclesiastical history: each confession strove to prove its legitimacy and antiquity from the Fathers and the history of the Early Church. With the publication in 1671 of Nicole's *Prejugez legitimes contre les calvinistes*, the field of interest was concentrated more particularly on the legitimacy and necessity of the Reformation and the divine vocation of the Reformers.[8] Reply and counter-reply followed and throughout the period the charge of sedition was added to that of schism, launched against the *réformés* (Perry, p.6-7):

Reaching into the Protestant past, Catholic polemicists reminded their readers of every action the Protestants had cause to regret, of every crime the Protestants, guilty or not, had ever been charged with. They accused the Reformed of having caused the schism in the Church. They painted vivid pictures of the violence of the Reformation, and charged the Reformed with having brought about the French civil wars. Finally, the Catholics told the Reformed that they were not, and indeed never had been, true Frenchmen, since they had never been integrated into French society.

However, as Protestant controversists hastened to point out, these vivid pictures painted by Catholic polemicists were merely one possible (and by no means true) reading of the history of the Reformation and the French civil wars. In fact, Protestant writers took it upon themselves to prove the divine vocation of the Reformers[9] and the innocence of the *réformés*, where the political unrest of the sixteenth century was concerned.[10] Thus, the very nature of the exchange between Bayle and Maimbourg – a Protestant critique of a Catholic reading of Reformation history – explains why the former should doubt the possibility of historical certitude. Generalising from the variant readings of the same historical events rife in the controversy of the time, he concludes that the interpretation of the Reformation and the ensuing events depends more on ideological conviction than on historical research. He continues by admitting: 'je vous avouë que je ne lis presque jamais les Historiens dans la vuë de m'instruire des choses qui se sont passées, mais seulement pour savoir ce que l'on dit dans chaque

6. Elisabeth Israels Perry, *From theology to history: French religious controversy and the Revocation of the Edict of Nantes* (The Hague 1973), p.7.

7. Rébelliau, p.1-93, *passim*; Remi Snoeks, *L'Argument de tradition dans la controverse eucharistique entre catholiques et réformés français au XVIIe siècle* (Louvain 1951), *passim*; Bayle, *NRL*, septembre 1686, cat.IV, *OD*, i.652b.

8. Pierre Nicole, *Prejugez legitimes contre les calvinistes* (Paris 1671), chs.4-9, p.76-197; Perry, p.8-10.

9. Jean Claude, *La Défense de la Réformation*, parts 1, 2, 3; [Jean Graverol], *L'Eglise protestante justifiée par l'Eglise romaine* (Genève 1682), p.71ff.; Perry, p.8-10.

10. Perry, p.8-10.

Nation & dans chaque parti, sur les choses qui se sont passées.'[11] Consequently, for the author of the *Critique générale*, the recent concentration on Reformation history had resulted not in a greater clarification and comprehension of the events but in a lamentable partiality. The chief value of the 'histories' lay in the insight they gave into the thought-processes of the various parties engaged in the political and religious conflict.

It was dangerous, however, to argue, at a time when the Protestants were defending their right to exist, that historical pyrrhonism necessarily results from the partiality of contemporary accounts of the Reformation. The danger lies in the *de facto* dismissal of all Protestant replies to Maimbourg and like historians. For Bayle does not omit his co-religionaries from his musings (*CG*, letter I, §iv, p.11a):

si d'un côté le bon sens veut que je me défie d'un Historien Huguenot, & que je le soupçonne, ou de n'avoir pas pénétré les pernicieux desseins de son parti, faute de discernement, & à cause des préjugez qui l'aveuglent, ou de les avoir dissimulez afin de sauver l'honneur de sa Religion; de l'autre côté le même bon sens veut aussi, que je me défie d'un Historien de la Communion Romaine, & que je le soupçonne, ou d'avoir malicieusement tû certaines circonstances qui serviroient à la justification des Huguenots, ou de leur avoir imputé faussement des choses qui les rendent haïssables, ou d'avoir crû par des jugemens préoccupez, que tout ce qui se faisoit dans son parti étoit légitime, & qu'au contraire ceux qu'il regardoit comme Hérétiques, n'étoient animez que d'un esprit de rage, de fureur, & d'impiété.

Anticipating the *prise de position* in the article 'Nestorius', *all* confessional and ideological history is called into question. Bayle's refusal to spare Protestant narratives, however, deprives his co-religionaries of the possibility of proving, from *their* reading of history, the loyalism of their politics and the divinity of their religion, innocent of both subversion and schism. Paradoxically, this apparent despair concerning the possibility of historical certitude is the fellow of a continuing practice of history in the *Critique générale* and the *Dictionnaire*. Not only that but, as we have seen in the case-studies of 'Agreda' and 'Nestorius' and as many entries on heroes of the civil wars indicate, Bayle continues both to present his own alternative readings of certain controversial events and to filter from existing accounts of the civil wars a – to his mind – legitimate account of the incidents. Necessarily, then, the dismissal of confessional and ideological history is merely a first step to a more radical approach, capable of establishing historical composition on a more secure basis.

While those of Bayle's contemporaries who replied to Maimbourg refuted

---

11. *CG*, letter I, §iv, *OD*, ii.10b; cf. La Mothe Le Vayer, *Discours de l'histoire, où est examinée celle de Prudence de Sandoval*, in *Œuvres*, ii.225.

him point by point,[12] the author of the *Critique générale* – possibly influenced by sceptical humanism[13] – switches the attention, particularly in the first five letters, from the *témoignage* to the *témoin*.[14] This in his opinion is the most effective way of undermining the *Histoire du calvinisme*:

La passion est toute visible dans le Livre dont il s'agit: un Historien passioné n'est guere croyable: j'ai fait voir que Monsieur Maimbourg a eu des raisons très-fortes & très-particulieres, de nous trouver coupables, & de nous dénigrer prodigieusement: il est facile à un habile homme d'empoisonner les faits les plus innocens. Que voulez-vous davantage pour ne vous soucier pas que l'Histoire des Calvinistes, composée par le Jésuite Maimbourg, les charge d'injures & d'infamies?[15]

That is to say, Bayle first goes to the root of the problem. On the grounds that a writer's handling of factual material provides his readers not simply with a narrative of events but also with a 'portrait de son cœur',[16] he links Maimbourg's reading of Calvinism to his personality, psychology and motives in writing. The questionable image of the Jesuit yielded by this investigation allows Bayle on the one hand to conclude that his 'history' necessarily distorts the events, and on the other to dismiss the *récit* as a typical expression of a given personality and set of interests, rather than a considered treatment of the facts.

The procedure, however, is not original. Quite apart from its place in humanist historiography,[17] it had been used four years before the *Critique générale* by Antoine Arnauld and Pierre Nicole in their joint *Defense de la traduction du Nouveau Testament imprimé à Mons*,[18] a work used in the fourth letter of the *Critique*. Consequently, its importance for Bayle's view of history lies in its

12. For a list of these replies, see the entry 'Maimbourg' in *DTC*, ix.1659-60.

13. Bodin, *Methodus, passim*, and La Mothe Le Vayer, in his writings on history, both approach the problem of historical composition from the viewpoint of the frailty of human nature and the historian's personality.

14. This procedure is consistent with Bayle's overall historical methodology: see Elisabeth Labrousse, 'La méthode critique chez Pierre Bayle et l'histoire', *Revue internationale de philosophie de Bruxelles* 11 (1957), p.450-66; reprinted in E. Labrousse, *Notes sur Bayle* (Paris 1987).

15. *CG*, letter I, §iv, *OD*, ii.11a-b.

16. The notion that a writer draws a self-portrait by the way he handles his facts is stated for the first time in the *Additions aux pensées diverses*, where Bayle undermines Jurieu's accusations (see Labrousse, *Pierre Bayle*, i.226ff.) by questioning the minister's reliability as a witness. His unreliability is established by the appeal to the negative self-portrait which emerges from his arguments against Bayle (*APD*, *OD*, iii.177-79; cf. 'Mahomet II', footnote K), The procedure is practised, however, right from the early works and continues throughout the *Dictionnaire*.

17. Labrousse, 'La méthode', p.452.

18. *Defense de la traduction du Nouveau Testament imprimé à Mons contre les sermons du P. Meinbourg* [sic] *jésuite* (Cologne 1668), p.5ff. The original edition of this work is cited here, since it is the one used by Bayle in the *Critique*. For convenience, however, the pagination of the reprint in the *Œuvres*, vol.v-vi (the *Defense* is in tom.vi, p.551-784) is cited on each occasion in brackets. Here, p.553ff.

generalisation. That is to say, while the critique of Maimbourg is *ad hominem*, once linked to the biographies and discourses on historians elsewhere in Bayle's work it appears to form part of a 'blue-print' of the bad historian. The generalisation is effected through the opposition of *bon sens* to *passion*, an opposition evocative not merely of Cartesianism, [19] but also of the debate between 'histoire éloquente' and 'histoire savante' dividing the aesthetic theorists of the day. [20] Moreover, while our author's analysis owes much to the Stoical reading-grid of La Mothe Le Vayer, [21] the conception of the historian as a victim of his passions represents an extension of an Augustino-Calvinist anthropology into historical composition. And, as we shall see, this notion of the Republic of Letters as subject to a dialectical interplay between 'historiens passionés' and 'historiens éclairés' is but one more manifestation of the inseparability of theology and history in the scholarship of the *philosophe* of Rotterdam. Firstly, however, let us consider the portrait of the bad historian which emerges from the critique of Louis Maimbourg.

One of the focal points of attention in the *Critique générale* is the thirty years spent by the Jesuit as a preacher, a factor constituting 'un préjugé qu'il n'est pas profondément savant' [22] and therefore unfit to compose history. The test-case and explanation of the – for Bayle – prejudicial effect of preaching is Maimbourg's reaction to the publication by Port-Royal of *Le Nouveau Testament de Notre-Seigneur Jesus-Christ, traduit en français, selon l'édition vulgate, avec les différences du grec*, which appeared at Mons – hence the more popular name, 'la Version de Mons' – in 1667. Initially, the translation was a great success: five editions appeared in that same year and another four the year after. [23] Opposition, however, was strong and Louis Maimbourg preached a series of sermons against the translation on 28 August and 4 September 1667, in the Jesuit church in the rue Saint-Antoine in Paris. [24] The sermons have not survived. None the less, extracts sent at the time to Arnaud and Nicole, forming the basis of the *Défense*,

19. Descartes, *Les Passions de l'âme*, p.29ff.

20. Fumaroli, *L'Age de l'éloquence*, p.585ff.; Gilles Declercq, 'Un adepte de l'histoire éloquente, le père Maimbourg, S. J.', *XVIIe siècle* 143 (1984), p.130.

21. Cf. Julien-Eymard d'Angers, 'Stoïcisme et "Libertinage" dans l'œuvre de François La Mothe Le Vayer', in *Recherches sur le stoïcisme au XVIe et XVIIe siècles*, ed. L. Antoine (Hildesheim, New York 1976), p.481-506.

22. *CG*, letter IV, §iii, *OD*, ii.20a. The reference to Maimbourg's Jesuit education is not innocent, since it contains an allusion to a school of Jesuit rhetoric totally at variance with Bayle's idea of the good historian: cf. Fumaroli, p.179ff.; below, p.66ff.

23. F. Vigoureux, *Dictionnaire de la Bible* (Paris 1926-1928), ii.368, col.2; cf. Richard Simon, *Histoire critique des versions du Nouveau Testament* (Rotterdam 1690), ch.35, p.396; 'Préface historique & critique', in Arnauld, *Œuvres*, vol.v/vi, p.v-vi.

24. Moréri, *Grand dictionnaire historique* (Paris 1759), vii.91a; 'Préface historique & critique', in Arnauld, *Œuvres*, vol.v/vi, p.vi-vii.

facilitate a reconstruction of the two accusations which constitute for Bayle a significant insight into the Jesuit's abilities as a historian.

Maimbourg argues in an exaggerated but half-perceptive way that the alterations to the text of the Vulgate in the Mons translation – a clearer rendering of the original Greek, according to the Jansenists – encouraged both Protestant doctrine and moral licentiousness. Thus,

les Auteurs de cette traduction sont d'intelligence avec Genéve; [...] ils ont eu pour but d'y faire glisser le venin des erreurs Calvinistes; [...] ils ont voulu aneantir un des Sacremens de l'Eglise, détruire la coopération du libre arbitre avec la grace, ruiner la Primauté de saint Pierre, abolir l'invocation des saints, oster aux Catholiques une des plus fortes preuves de la presence réelle de Jesus-Christ dans l'Eucharistie [...][25]

The exaggeration in the Jesuit's accusations – commonplace in the association of Jansenism and Protestantism (above, p.49-50) – is perhaps obvious. It is instructive, none the less, to compare his assertion with the scholarly criticisms of the translation, later made by Richard Simon. The latter, no friend to Port-Royal,[26] carefully traces the similarities between the 'Version de Mons' and those translations of Scripture published by Protestants, notably Theodore de Bèze.[27] He refrains, however, from claiming that the Jansenists had intended to favour reformed doctrine. Maimbourg's accusation, then, constitutes a half-truth. Instead of limiting himself to the affinities between Jansenist and Calvinist translations, he exaggerates the similarities to form a caricature: the Port-Royal translators are painted as undercover agents for Geneva.

The second accusation is as distorted as the first: the Jansenists are accused of promoting, by deliberate mistranslation, the vices of incontinence and fornication. There are two disputed passages. Firstly, the verses in St Paul's epistle to the Galatians, where the apostle lists the fruit of the Spirit (v.22). The translators had construed the Vulgate's *continentia* as 'temperance' in French and Maimbourg maintains that, properly understood, 'la temperance ne regarde que le boire & le manger'.[28] The Jesuit's intention in restricting the meaning is, according to the authors of the *Défense*, to prove 'par ses paroles & par ses gestes qu'on avoit esté bien aise de se servir de ce mot pour ne pas défendre l'incontinence'.[29] Furthermore, asserts Maimbourg, the translators deliberately omitted the word 'fornication' from the title of the fourth chapter of the first

25. *Defense*, part I, p.31 (*Œuvres*, vol.v/vi, p.578).

26. Paul Auvray, *Richard Simon* (Paris 1974), p.107-108.

27. Simon, *Histoire critique des versions*, ch.36, p.441b-44a; cf. also his *Histoire critique des principaux commentateurs du Nouveau Testament* (Rotterdam 1693), chs.59 and 60, p.891-926, a work which Bayle will later cite frequently in the *Dictionnaire*, e.g. 'Mariana', marginal note 91.

28. *Defense*, part III, p.157 (*Œuvres*, vol.v/vi, p.656; the disputed translation is included in this volume (p.388b) which reprints the *Nouveau Testament* of Mons).

29. *Defense*, part III, p.52 (*Œuvres*, vol.v/vi, p.653).

epistle to the Corinthians, despite the fact that the vice is censured therein. They thereby, he continues, limited the import of the chapter to the virtue of 'user saintement du mariage'. The consequence of the omission is then drawn in the most heinous terms: it constitutes 'un piege qu'on tendoit aux jeunes gens débauchez, qui tireront delà une consequence, que la fornication n'est defenduë qu'aux personnes mariées, & partant que ce n'est pas un peché mortel à ceux qui ne le sont pas'.[30] Not only is the logic faulty, the dispute a mere cavil about words, but the accusations, *topoi* of historical iconoclasm ('Bezanites', footnote A), are also based on half-truths. It is clear from Simon's analysis of some of the variants from the Vulgate in the Mons translation that the Jansenists had *intended* to alter the Latin text. Their purpose, however, was to make Scripture more widely available to the ordinary people, that it might act as a corrective rather than a corrupting influence.[31] Moreover, the charge of corruption of the young is dismissed as nonsense by the authors of the *Défense* and Bayle after them, given the reputation of Port-Royal for moral rigorism.[32]

To the author of the *Critique générale*, these accusations are nothing short of calumny, and he proves his assertion by appealing to the widespread popularity and approbation given to the Mons translation:

Car non-seulement les Apologies de la Version de Mons, ausquel je n'ai pas ouï dire que les Jesuites ayent repliqué, ont justifié clairement, que tous les passages attaquez par leur Prédicateur, étoient conformes aux Versions, & aux explications d'un grand nombre de Jésuites, ou d'autres Théologiens reconnus très-orthodoxes dans l'Eglise Romaine: mais aussi la permission que le Roi & les Prélats du Royaume accorderent peu après d'imprimer, de vendre, de lire cette Version, est une preuve manifeste, que les erreurs dont elle avoit été accusée, sont des calomnies très-malicieuses.[33]

The argument is similar to that put forward by the authors of the *Défense*[34] and is used as a foil by Bayle, who favours the translation (below, p.152), against the condemnations the 'Version de Mons' was soon to receive.[35] More important to our subject, however, is the significance for Bayle of Maimbourg's judgement of the translation, once compared with the widespread approbation it received. It proves, according to the *philosophe* of Rotterdam, that the Jesuit was only half-

---

30. *Defense*, part III, p.153 (*Œuvres*, p.653-54). For the disputed passage, see the same volume, p.332a-334b.

31. *Defense*, p.3-32 (*Œuvres*, vol.v/vi, p.xiii-xxxii).

32. *Defense*, p.3-32, *CG*, letter IV, §§v & vi, *OD*, ii.22a-b, 24b-25a.

33. *CG*, letter IV, §v, *OD*, ii.21b.

34. *Defense*, p.8, and Simon, *Histoire critique des versions*, ch.35, p.396b.

35. The translation was condemned on 18 November 1668 by Hardouin de Perefixe, archbishop of Paris, and later by Popes Clement IX (1668) and Innocent XI (1679) ('Préface historique & critique', in *Œuvres*, vol.v/vi, p.i-x). Bayle chooses to ignore the papal condemnations, arguing only that the universal approbation the translation received undermines the validity of the condemnation by the bishops of the kingdom.

informed when preaching against the Jansenists. Consequently, his first concern was not that of clarifying the facts of the situation:

Il faut donc conclure que toutes ses clameurs partoient d'un principe de malignité. Il savoit que rien n'étoit plus capable d'exposer les Ecclésiastiques de Port-Royal à l'exécration publique, que de les faire passer pour des disciples de Calvin; c'est pourquoi il faisoit son fort de cette accusation-là.[36]

That is to say, Maimbourg's self-emancipation from the facts of the case was undertaken for its polemical advantages. It facilitated the creation of a negative image of the Jansenists, the better to sway public opinion.

The significance of this cameo of Maimbourg's activity as a preacher[37] for his work as a historian lies in Bayle's conception of the role of rhetoric and imagination in historical composition. Moreover, his attitude to the Jesuit bears within it the opposition, at least as old as the sixteenth century, between 'historiographie sénéquiste' and 'histoire cicéronianiste'.[38] So, like Bodin before him (*Methodus*, p.300), Bayle, favourable to the former, none the less displays a certain ambivalence to Maimbourg's publicly acclaimed eloquent narratives.[39] His 'maniere d'écrire' is 'libre, animée, brillante, & pleine de divers agrémens' and, although diffuse, his style has 'du brillant, & sur tout beaucoup de vivacité'.[40] These superior gifts of eloquence and vivacity are responsible, according to Bayle, for the great success of the Jesuit's histories.[41] As he was later to observe in the *Continuation des Pensées diverses*, if used within certain limits, oratorical skills are a positive embellishment to the historical narrative (*CPD*, §II, *OD*, iii.191b):

pour des esprits supérieurs qui se rendent maîtres de leur sujet, & de leurs forces, & qui entendent le réglement des limites, rien ne peut être plus avantageux quand ils écrivent une histoire, que de s'être bien nourris du suc de la poëtique, & de l'éloquence

36. *CG*, letter IV, §v, *OD*, ii.21b.
37. The picture of Maimbourg's preaching abilities painted by the authors of the *Defense* ('Avertissement', p.6-9; *Œuvres*, vol.v/vi, p.554-56), as also by Bayle ('Maimbourg', footnote C), is something of a caricature, if we are to trust the Jesuit's extant sermons as representative of his skills (*Sermons pour le Caresme où toutes les parties de chaque évangile sont comprises et rapportées à un point principal*, Paris 1672). However, given that a contemporary eye-witness, Godefroi Hermant, mentions the 'comédie' which Maimbourg 'ne laissait pas de jouer' and refers to his 'sermons scandaleux' (*Mémoires de Godefroi Hermant*, ed. A. Gazier, Paris 1905-1910, iv.316-23, 348-50), we may conclude that the conflict is between those who advocate a more severe eloquence and those favouring the dramatisation of religious and other truths.
38. Declercq, p.129-30; Fumaroli, p.392ff.
39. The ambivalence is most obvious later in the *Dictionnaire* 'Maimbourg', footnote D, where the tension is between the Jesuit's attractive style and his lack of accuracy.
40. *CG*, letter IV, §i, *OD*, ii.19a-b.
41. *NRL*, avril 1684, art.III, *OD*, i.27a; *NLC*, 'Avis au lecteur', *OD*, ii.163a; Bayle is not insensible to Maimbourg's rhetoric and before it was used against the Protestants he seems to have taken pleasure in the slightly malicious bent of the histories: to Minutoli, 1 January 1680, *OD*, iv.578b.

des Orateurs. C'est par-là qu'ils peuvent donner à leur style cette majesté, & cette sublimité dont il a besoin, & faire des descriptions si animées que les Lecteurs se croyent presque transportez à la vûë des événemens.

The comment is preceded by a reference to the doubts of his imaginary interlocutor concerning the influence of preaching and rhetoric on history. Bayle's hypothetical interlocutor opposes the 'style concis' to the 'style de déclamateur', giving his support to the former. Here, however, Bayle attempts a reconciliation of the two. Rhetoric is acceptable only within the limits of well informed and erudite history ('maîtres de leur sujet'), a position holding in tension the aesthetic criterion of *vraisemblance* and *vérité* (Declercq, p.121). The emphasis is on the dramatisation of scholarship. Properly used, rhetoric so enlivens the facts of history that they become a vivid recreation of the events described, making the reader feel like an eye-witness.[42] In this case, rhetoric is the maidservant of history: far from going beyond the facts, it serves them. Imagination revivifies erudition, it does not escape from its control.[43]

As Bayle's reflections elsewhere indicate, however, it is the cavalier attitude of the orator to factual data which he most fears. Here the ambivalence towards Maimbourg comes into play, in the form of an opposition between the *bon sens* of the philosopher and the passion of the *rhéteur*. The comment occurs during the controversy with Pierre Jurieu concerning the thesis of the virtuous atheist.[44] The minister had been scandalised by our author's paradox and the latter is in turn shocked that Jurieu should wish him to hide a historical fact capable of demonstration. Look elsewhere, he retorts, for someone willing to suppress historical data:

vous chercherez, s'il vous plaît, ailleurs que parmi des Professeurs en Philosophie, les gens que vous souhaitez. Adressez-vous à des Professeurs de Rhétorique, cherchez des Orateurs, des Déclamateurs; ces Messieurs-là ne se soucient guere d'éclairer l'esprit; ils se contentent de persuader par l'entremise des passions; ils vont droit au cœur, & non pas droit à l'entendement; ils tâchent d'exciter l'amour, la haine, la colere; ils ne montrent les objets que d'un côté, les uns seulement du côté du mal, les autres seulement du côté du bien, ils outrent, ils exténuënt, ils déguisent, ils supriment selon l'interêt de la cause.[45]

The commentary picks up the 'anti-cicéronianisme' present not only in Bayle's work[46] but also in the contemporary aesthetic theory of those devoted to the

---

42. Declercq, p.127, who argues that Maimbourg's position on rhetoric is very near to that of classical tragedy.
43. *CPD*, §ii, *OD*, iii.192a-b.
44. Labrousse, *Pierre Bayle*, i.226ff.
45. *APD*, *OD*, iii.178a; cf. *NLC*, letter xx, §§i-vi, *OD* ii.297a-301b.
46. Cf. 'Erasme', footnote I.

Senecan and more severe Augustinian eloquence.[47] On the one hand, the task of the philosopher and, by extension, the historian is to enlighten the mind by – in the words of Jean Bodin – 'la narration exacte des actions passées' (*Methodus*, p.287). On the other, the purpose of the orator is to convince and to move the heart and passions. The hostility Bayle evinces at this point is typical of an Augustino-Cartesian suspicion of these essentially depraved organs of perception.[48] For if persuasion is the object, then the orator is seen to bypass the mind, subordinating the facts to his persuasive intention. Hence, intentionally or unintentionally, he creates a certain *image* of the events, truncating or suppressing as it suits his purpose. So, in oratory, history or fact becomes the maidservant of the cause espoused by the orator.[49]

As we have seen in the case of the translation of Mons, Maimbourg was true to his calling as a preacher and orator. The Jansenists, at the expense of the facts, are presented in such a way as to do them most harm in the public eye. Even more important, however, is the indication that the Jesuit carried into the composition of the *Histoire du calvinisme* the techniques acquired as a preacher. The historian's style which, generally speaking, the author of the *Critique générale* finds so animated, when writing about the Protestants, becomes a 'style impetueux'.[50] Moreover, a violent style was deliberately chosen by Maimbourg as a more effective means of persuasion: 'pour faire plus d'impression sur les Lecteurs, il s'est chargé d'un grand nombre d'épithetes diffamatoires, & de descriptions violentes qu'il a répétées mille & mille fois'.[51] One of the essential features of 'histoire éloquente' is emphasised here: the predominance of hyperbole as a narrative mode (Declercq, p.127). Furthermore, the Jesuit exhibited a cavalier attitude to the facts: suppressing, overemphasising, rearranging at will.[52] In other words, he is faithful to his own conception of history: for Maimbourg 'le fait devient exemplaire et la narration démonstrative' (Declercq, p.128). Finally, his intention, like that of the orator, was the creation of a certain image of the Calvinists: 'un portrait [...] hideux de la conduite de nos Prédécesseurs', in order 'de nous charger de la haine & de l'exécration publique'.[53] The technique is that of 'le portrait à clé' (Declercq, p.122). It is

47. Fumaroli, p.70ff. and 116ff., and below, p.106ff.
48. The suspicion of the passions is common to Cartesians and Augustinians of the day (Tocanne, p.182ff.). For Descartes, however, the passions are not necessarily a depraved organ of perception or motivation (*Les Passions de l'âme*, §§LIII-LVIII, p.108-11); to Cartesianism, then, is joined the pessimism of an Augustinian anthropology (below, p.82-83).
49. 'Cimon', footnote D; Naudé, also following Bodin, opposes history to poetry/embellishment (*Apologie*, p.12).
50. *CG*, letter I, §i, *OD*, ii.7a.
51. *CG* letter I, §ii, *OD*, ii.10a.
52. *CG*, letter I, §ii, *OD*, ii.10a.
53. *CG*, letter I, §ii. *OD*, ii.10a.

therefore hardly suprising that Bayle declares the *Histoire du calvinisme* worthy of a 'jeune Déclamateur qui s'exerce sur les lieux communs de l'Invective':[54] the espousal of historical eloquence has transformed the *récit* into a historical satire, the literary counterpart of panegyrics and hagiography (Declercq, p.121). Anticipating the *Dictionnaire*, Bayle finishes by presenting the Jesuit as a kind of outlaw from the Republic of Letters; his techniques, far from serving history, amount to a *'Filouterie* [exercée] sur les monumens Historiques'.[55]

While the critique of the Jesuit's transferral of oratorical techniques into history is *ad hominem* – it depends on the analysis of his previous preaching activity – it is clear from the context that Maimbourg represents a *type* of the historian. The author of the history of Calvinism is one for whom the defence of a cause, be it political, religious or personal, is more important than a dispassionate elucidation of the facts. With textual resonances to Bodin's *Methodus* (p.295), Bayle compares this type of historian to a lawyer who creates a different story from the same facts, depending on whether he acts for the defence or the prosecution:

il n'y a point de fait qui entre les mains de deux habiles Avocats appointez contraires, ne prennent des formes toutes différentes. Un Historien comme Tacite, qui agiroit de mauvaise foi, feroit une vie de Louis XIV. peu glorieuse, sur les mêmes faits qui porteront au souverain degré de la Gloire le nom de ce grand Monarque; & l'on peut dire qu'à l'égard de la réputation, toute la destinée des Princes est entre les mains des Historiens.[56]

The mention of Tacitus signifies a school of historiography whose concentration on the private details of the lives of public figures frequently constitutes historical iconoclasm (see below, p.205ff.). Two kinds of rhetorical history are envisaged: that of the panegyrist and that of the detractor, and the *Histoire du calvinisme* belongs to the latter. The remark yields the key to the article 'Nestorius'. The heresiarch, to Bayle's mind, was the object of the calumnies of St Cyril which, owing to the latter's superior political muscle, were handed down in history to posterity. Hence Nestorius and many others are the victims of the eloquent historian, endowed like Maimbourg with superior imagination, 'pour tourner les choses en cent manieres adroites & agréables',[57] and with 'une bonne dose

---

54. *CG*, letter I. §ii, *OD*, ii.9a.
55. *CG*, letter I, §ii, *OD*, ii.10a.
56. *CG*, letter I, §ii, *OD*, ii.10a; *RQP*, §XXII, *OD*, iii.538b-39a. According to Perry (p.14-15) the names both of Maimbourg and of Varillas were synonymous with bad history in the latter half of the *grand siècle*. Bayle's portrait of the former Jesuit's talents was undoubtedly of major importance in the formation of this public opinion.
57. *CG*, letter IV, *OD*, ii.19b. The distrust of imagination is based on the notion of its unreliability: 'L'imagination n'est pas un dépositaire bien fidele de ce que les sens lui confient; elle brouille étrangement les especes: peu de gens rapportent les choses toutes telles qu'ils les ont vûës, ou

de rhétorique [qui] donne du relief aux circonstances avantageuses, & fait disparoître celles qui ne le sont pas'.[58] The reputation of public figures is most certainly in the hands of the historian. In the *Critique générale* and later the *Dictionnaire*, Bayle takes the part of the denigrated and the oppressed, determined to redress the imbalance created in the 'monumens Historiques' by the techniques of historians who mould and shape the facts to their own ends.

Like La Mothe Le Vayer before him, Bayle's conception of 'histoire éloquente' either as satire or as panegyric leads to a consideration of the place of the supernatural in the historical *récit*.[59] Maimbourg is not criticised in this instance, for his histories evince a certain scepticism towards tales of the paranormal. The terms used to describe the Jesuit's cavalier attitude reveal, however, the existence of a more reprehensible one. While he is 'cavalier' and 'raisonnable', other historians show 'crédulité' and are termed 'superstitieux'.[60] The credulous approach, according to Bayle, again echoing Le Vayer, is in evidence in the works of the Spanish historians Luis de Avila and Sandoval. Their descriptions of Charles V's celebrated victory over the duke of Saxony in 1547 include an allusion to the miraculous assistance given to the Spanish monarch (*PD*, §XCVI, *OD*, iii.64a):

Non contens d'avoir dit qu'un aigle vola doucement durant quelque tems sur l'Infanterie Espagnole, pendant qu'elle passoit l'Elbe sur un pont de bateaux, & qu'un grand loup, qui étoit sorti d'une forêt prochaine fut tué par les soldats qui étoient déja passez; ils ont assûré fort sérieusement, que le Soleil s'arrêta tout court, pour donner aux Impériaux le loisir de remporter une pleine victoire: ce qui est un renouvellement de l'un des plus grands miracles que Dieu ait faits pour établir son peuple dans le païs de Canaan.

The kernel of the criticism lies in the biblical allusion. The miracles performed in Canaan were tokens of special divine favour to a chosen people. In other words, Bayle detects a latent nationalism in the Spanish historians' 'affectation':[61] it suggests that Spain, like Israel, is an object of God's electing love. The comment provokes an interesting association of ideas. The censured historians are compared to the 'Sophistes de la Grece', who earned a living by forging

---

entenduës; ils confondent les noms, les lieux, & les tems & plusieurs autres circonstances, & ils croient néanmoins rapporter la vérité' (*RQP*, §XXIV, *OD*, iii.544a; cf. also *RQP*, §XXXIV, *OD*, iii.559b, where the power of the imagination over 'le corps & l'ame' is seen as 'despotique'. *NLC*, letter II, §ii, *OD* ii.167, presents the force of the imagination as one of the causes of error.)

58. *RQP*, §XVII, *OD*, iii.528b.

59. La Mothe Le Vayer, *Discours de l'histoire, où est examinée celle de Prudence de Sandoval*, in *Œuvres*, ii.167ff.

60. *CG*, letter IV, §iii, *OD*, ii.19b; cf. *PD*, §§XCVI, XCVII, *OD*, iii.64a-66a.

61. The position is in La Mothe Le Vayer, *Discours de l'histoire*, in *Œuvres*, ii.169ff., from which Bayle borrows almost verbatim.

'déclamations' and 'panégyriques' non pas sur les Mémoires qu'on leur fournis-
soit, mais sur les idées qu'ils se formoient eux-mêmes de tout ce qui se peut
paroître le plus admirable'. That is to say, the historian unduly given to such
tales is mastered by 'imaginations hyperboliques'[62] and not by his source.
Moreover, the critique thrusts more deeply at the aesthetic criteria of Ciceronian
history. Its preference for *vraisemblance* deprives it of an 'éthique de la vérité'
(Declercq, p.121), alone capable of purging history of these 'alimens spirituels
si corrompus'.[63]

A parallel exists at this point between nationalistic and ecclesiastical usage of
the miraculous. Hagiography, like its secular counterpart, is a declamation on
a theme, embellished by tales of the paranormal (*PD*, §v, *OD*, iii.11a):

Quel desordre ne voit-on pas dans ces grands & immenses volumes, qui contiennent les
Annales de tous les différens Ordres de nos Moines, où il semble qu'on ait pris plaisir
d'entasser sans jugement et par la seule envie de satisfaire l'émulation ou plûtôt la
jalousie, que ces Sociétez ont les unes contre les autres, tout ce que l'on peut concevoir
de miracles chymériques?

The observation might be a running commentary on the article 'Agreda' and
provides further insight into the position adopted therein. The Spanish mystic's
history of the Virgin is but one example of the widespread practice of essentially
superstitious historians. Spurious miracles, hagiographical *topoi* are part of a
rhetoric of persuasion, inimical to history conceived as truth about the past. Just
as the entry devoted to the Spanish nun reposes on the oppostion *peuple/docte*,
so 'histoire éloquente' is presented as a transfer of popular attitudes into the
written medium (*PD*, v, *OD*, iii.10b):

il paroît dans la plûpart [des Historiens] une si grande envie de raporter tous les miracles
& toutes les visions, que la crédulité des peuples a autorisées, qu'il ne seroit pas de la
prudence de croire tout ce qu'ils nous débitent en ce genre-là.

Once the historian is emancipated from the source, his authorities are those of
the credulous masses. Instead of instructing and informing popular opinion –
as Bayle attemps to do in 'Agreda' and 'Nestorius' – he becomes its voice. His
so-called histories are thereby deprived of credence: they are a further expression, albeit in the written medium, of the perennial 'erreur populaire' (see
below, p.119ff.)

This conception of the bad historian as a writer turned orator, and its
application to the case of the miraculous, reveals our author's concern for the

---

62. *PD*, §xcvii, *OD*, iii.64b.
63. The phrase is La Mothe Le Vayer's, *Jugement sur les anciens et principaux historiens*, in
*Œuvres*, iii.26. Cf. Fumaroli (p.392ff.), for an analysis of other reactions to the 'corruption of
eloquence'.

vulnerability of history. Its reliability depends on the disposition of its author. If he is prepared to place the task of elucidating the facts above all other preoccupations, then the narrative will attain a very high degree of accuracy. If, however, he has more of the disposition of the orator than of the historian, then the facts of history will be as clay in the potter's hand.[64] Moreover, this latter attitude makes the historian himself vulnerable: his cavalier attitude to the facts means that other factors are more likely to determine the way he writes, given that he does not consider himself bound by the sources available to him. It is time to examine some of these other factors and their determining influence on the bad historian's narrative.

The first and most deeply rooted of these forces is the influence of education on the way the historian perceives his facts. Maimbourg entered the Society of Jesus in 1626 at the age of sixteen, and only left it some fifty-five years later, by order of Pope Innocent XI, as a result of his Gallican sympathies.[65] Bayle alludes ironically to the enormous advantage of those fifty-five years to someone keen to paint a negative picture of the Calvinists.[66] For, as the author of the *Histoire du calvinisme* himself admits, the Jesuits are renowned for their hostility to the *réformés*: 'on n'a jamais accusez [... les Jésuites] d'estre trop indulgens & trop favorables aux Calvinistes'.[67] The implication is that gradually and unconsciously, through his formation in the Society, a certain amount of preconceived ideas became part of Maimbourg's conception of the Calvinists. His education, given its strong confessional overtones, made it impossible for him to perceive Calvinism as anything but a heresy, dangerous to Church and State. On taking his pen to write, he found his mind was already set – as a result of this *prévention*[68] – on a well-defined thought pattern. Its influence is threefold. Firstly, *prévention* makes neutrality impossible. This is why, argues Bayle later in the *Dictionnaire*, some have wished for a history of the Reformation, written by a historian with no confessional sympathies, such as Livy or Thucydides. However, the influence of prejudice is so subtle, he continues, that even in those ideal circumstances, it would make itself felt:

On souhaiteroit la plume de ces illustres Auteurs, non pas tant à cause de leur éloquence & de leur bon sens, qu'à cause qu'ils étoient Paiens, & qu'ils auroient pu être neutres entre les diverses Sectes du Christianisme, desorte qu'ils eussent décrit sans prévention & sans partialité le mal & le bien de la conduite des Papistes, des Luthériens, & des Calvinistes. Mais je ne sçai s'ils auroient pu se tenir dans une parfaite neutralité; car

---

64. The image used by Bayle is that of the bad historian as a kind of Procrustes; *CG*, letter v, §iii, *OD*, ii.28b.
65. Moréri, *Le Grand dictionnaire*, 'Maimbourg', vii.90b; *DTC*, ix.1655.
66. *CG*, letter I, §ii, *OD*, ii.8a.
67. Louis Maimbourg, *Histoire du calvinisme* (Paris 1682), p.150; *CG*, letter v, §iii, *OD*, ii.28b.
68. Cf. Labrousse, *Pierre Bayle*, ii.69ff.

comme le Papisme est plus conforme au Paganisme que la Religion Protestante, ils auroient pu se laisser préoccuper contre Luther & Calvin. Un Historien ne sçauroit être trop sur ses gardes, & il ne peut presque pas s'échaper des pieges de la prévention.[69]

The commentary reveals certain biases in Bayle's historiography: the similarity between paganism and Catholicism – a leitmotiv of his literary output – renders impossible the neutrality of the Ancient historians. While the remark is not unlike the earlier observations both of Jean Bodin (*Methodus*, p.312) and of La Mothe Le Vayer,[70] the *philosophe* of Rotterdam is more radical in his pessimistic scepticism. All three are suspicious of confessional historians, but Bayle alone sees no hope of complete dissociation from consciously and unconsciously acquired ideological assumptions.

What is true of religion is no less true of politics. A historian's political affiliations undoubtedly would affect the way he portrays social upheaval, were he to write about events far removed from his own time:

Suposez qu'un homme de notre Siecle fasse l'Histoire d'un Roi des Indes mort déthrôné depuis deux ou trois cens ans, vous croirez qu'aucun intérêt ne le pousse à user de mauvaise foi: cependant, si c'est un homme ennemi de la Monarchie, & aprobateur des Rebellions des sujets, il cherchera mille détours & mille déguisemens pour rendre odieuse la mémoire de ce Monarque, & pour justifier les guerres civiles qui le renversérent du thrône. Un Historien ennemi des Rebellions prendroit tout le contrepied de celui-là.[71]

The observation is undoubtedly stimulated by Bayle's perusal of sixteenth- and seventeenth-century histories of the civil wars in France. Republican Protestants like Agrippa d'Aubigné and Catholic *ligueurs* write in defence of the recourse to arms, while Jacques Auguste de Thou, a *politique*, retains a more balanced vision of both sides involved in the conflicts (Dubois, p.172-85). The issue was more recently re-opened in the *Refuge* by the politico-historical reflections of Jurieu[72] and Elie Benoît's *Histoire de l'Edit de Nantes*.[73] The critical distance established in the remark indicates not only a preference for de Thou but also the conviction that *prévention* – in the form of political ideologies – is *written into*

---

69. 'Remond', footnote D; cf. below, p.183ff.
70. La Mothe Le Vayer, *Discours de l'histoire*, in *Œuvres*, ii.224-25; *Du peu de certitude*, in *Œuvres*, xiii.436-37, where Bodin is specifically mentioned as the source.
71. 'Remond', footnote D; cf. 'Capriata', footnote C.
72. R. J. Howells, *Pierre Jurieu: antinomian radical* (Durham 1983), p.57-70, considers the division of opinion within the Refuge. On the politics of the Refuge, see Guy Howard Dodge, *The Political theory of the Huguenots of the Dispersion, with special reference to the thought and influence of Pierre Jurieu* (New York 1947), *passim*; Elisabeth Labrousse, 'The political ideas of the Huguenots of the Diaspora', in *Church, State and society under the Bourbon kings of France*, ed. Richard M. Golden (Kansas 1982), p.222-83; Herbert Schlossberg, 'Pierre Bayle and the politics of the Huguenot Diaspora', unpublished Ph.D. dissertation, University of Minnesota 1965, *passim*.
73. See Elisabeth Labrousse, 'Les guerres de religion vues par les huguenots du XVIIe siècle', in *Historiographie de la réforme*, p.37-44.

the narrative because of the historian's inability to perceive the validity of other positions.[74]

Secondly, the inability resulting from prejudice influences the way the historian reads his sources. Bayle chooses to express himself, in this instance, in Maimbourg's own words:

Il y a de grands hommes qui soit par préoccupation, soit par engagement, veulent absolument que certaines opinions, qu'ils sont fort résolus de soutenir, soient les véritables, avant que d'avoir examiné de sens rassis si elles le sont effectivement; ensuite ils tâchent toûjours de retourner du côté de leur sentiment, tout ce qu'ils lisent, au lieu de conformer de bonne foi leur sentiment à ce qu'ils trouvent.[75]

Anticipating his defence of toleration,[76] Bayle alludes here to the psychology of the act of reading.[77] A principle of selectivity is at work. The researcher starts with the conviction that he possesses the truth in the form of a preconceived religious or political ideology. Consequently, were he insatiable in his consultation of sources, the dynamics of reception are such that he retains as true only those facts favourable to his preconceptions. The historical fate of Nestorius and many others is sealed, then, by the predominance in historiography of pens wedded to the cause of successful or orthodox parties (see below, p.234-35).

Finally, selectivity also dictates the initial choice of sources. Bayle dismisses Florimond de Remond's proof texts as invalid, for 'Ses Citations valent peu de chose; car il allegue ou des gens de son Parti, & qui la plupart avoient eu des Démêlez personnels avec les Ministres, ou bien il allegue des Protestans selon qu'il avoit trouvé leurs Passages dans les Ecrits de ces gens-là' ('Remond', footnote D). That is to say, to the historian with confessional or ideological commitments, all the documents and argumentation of a writer with a different persuasion appear as mere chicanery. As a result of this distrust he quite naturally has recourse to the writings of his co-religionaries or compatriots: only there does he find that *évidence*[78] which seems to make their reading of history a true one. Such procedures of thought and research, however, form a vicious circle. The confessionally or ideologically biased historians to whom the researcher has recourse are *themselves* victims of *prévention*. The cumulative effect, therefore, is the creation of party-line histories whose image of the other is refracted through the subjective vision of the author or authors concerned. In

74. Naudé also notes a similar influence of *prévention*, in *Apologie*, p.18.
75. *CG*, letter v, §iii, *OD*, ii.28b. Louis Maimbourg, *Histoire de l'heresie des iconoclastes et de la translation de l'Empire aux François*, 2nd ed. (Paris 1679), i, p.aiiiir.
76. *NLC*, letter ix, *OD*, ii.217-28; *CP*, part ii, ch.9, *OD*, ii.427ff.
77. See above, p.3; below, p.150 and n.21.
78. *CP*, part ii, ch.1, *OD*, ii.396b; 'Papesse', footnote G; 'Roseo', *in corp.*; Labrousse, *Pierre Bayle*, ii.71ff.

a word, a historical tradition is created, oppressive inasmuch as it excludes the historical vision of individuals and minorities who are powerless to impose their point of view on the self-perpetuating majority.

The blinkering of intelligence by education and background is, however, to a large extent outside the historian's control. It only becomes reprehensible when it is combined with what Bayle terms false religious zeal (*CPD*, §xx, *OD*, iii.215a):

un désir ardent que leur secte soit triomphante, ou bien établie, & fort en état ou de subjuguer les autres, ou de se défendre contre elles. Ce zéle-là fait que des gens qui suivent très-mal la morale de l'Eglise, se batent comme des lions pour le temporel de la théorie, est un aussi grand obstacle à l'examen des raisons de chaque parti, que le vrai zéle.

The desire to triumph over the other party, be it political or religious, leads the historian to act in *mauvaise foi* and deliberately to alter and mould the facts to fit his preconceived ideas of right and truth. This change of *prévention* into *esprit de parti* and the consequent effect on the historical narrative do not happen without the complicity of the historian. The deliberate distortional intention, as the case of Maimbourg illustrates, results from the influence of the passions on the historian's judgement. The *démêlé* with the Jansenists is again used as an illustration.

The disputes between Jesuit and Jansenist came to an official end on 23 October 1668, when the King imposed silence on all those involved in the controversy. To Bayle's somewhat ironical turn of mind, the royal decision frustrated Maimbourg's unrelenting desire to denigrate the translators of the Mons New Testament. Consequently he turned to history for release and in the first of his works, the *Histoire de l'arianisme* (1673): 'Il se plaît à faire des peintures de l'Arianisme & des Ariens, où l'on puisse reconnoître le Jansenisme & les Jansenistes. Il fait ses réflexions & ses applications d'une maniere empoisonnée.'[79] Thus, the technique of the 'portrait à clé' is not only an instance of oratorical practice, it becomes a vehicle for the expression of venom. The Jesuit uses history to subvert the royal decree: the affinities created between ancient heresy and Jansenism, while not openly infringing the pacification, none the less decry, by association, the religious community at Port-Royal. The

---

79. *CG*, letter IV, §vi, *OD*, ii.23b. The Jesuit's sideways thrusts at the Jansenists were noted by Bayle as early as 1674: 'Au reste, on a remarqué que dans son histoire de l'*Arianisme*, il a fait glisser adroitement beaucoup de choses contre Mrs. de Port-Royal, ce qui n'a pas eu tout le bon effet, qu'il en attendoit peut-être; car ces voies obliques, ces attaques clandestines ont je ne sai quoi de choquant, même pour ceux qui observent la neutralité entre les *Jésuites* & les *Jansénistes*'. To Minutoli, 12 July 1674, in *OD* iv.581; Labrousse, *Inventaire*, p.82, no.54; cf. Ruth Elizabeth Cowdrick, *The Early reading of Pierre Bayle* (New York 1939), p.77, 200.

subversion has, according to Bayle, two psychological causes: the defeat and the humiliation Maimbourg suffered at the hands of the Jansenists.

In the first place comes the personal humiliation of being publicly proven wrong. The Jesuit used all his oratorical skills to prejudice the public against the Jansenists, on the grounds that they were dangerous heretics. The public approbation of the translation constitutes, to Bayle's mind, sufficient proof of the calumnious nature of the accusations. Hence, the Jesuit who, as a cleric, 'doit se piquer de conscience & de prudence' suffered a 'grande mortification' as a result of his calumny: his treatment of Port-Royal is not in conformity with his priestly office.[80] In the second place, to add insult to injury, Maimbourg's defeat was also that of his religious order, for the Jansenists proved themselves men of superior talent. Irony prevails, as Bayle adds that this was to subvert the claims of the Society of Jesus to intellectual hegemony, a most sensitive issue: 'Etre plus habile que les Jésuites; faire voir les foibles les plus honteux de cette Société; réfuter les Sermons du P. Maimbourg, comme des Ouvrages d'un petit apprentif; sont des crimes qui ne se pardonnent point.'[81] Bitterness results from public humiliation, and from bitterness grew 'une haine irréconciliable' against the Jansenists.[82] Personal animosity, complicated by party loyalties, yield a desire '[de se venger] des affronts que le Port-Royal lui avoit faits dans une juste défense'.[83] While the psychological analysis is simplistic, it serves to outline the function of history for Maimbourg. It becomes a release of passion, the 'passion de se venger',[84] and a compensation for wrongs suffered in the past. But, as in the case of Nestorius, Bayle's espousal of the cause of the Jansenists against the Jesuit is not altogether disinterested.

Generalising from one usage of the 'portrait à clé', the author of the *Critique générale* applies the analysis to the *Histoire du calvinisme*. If the Jesuit's motivation as a historian is to find in history a means of unleashing anger and animosity, then he could not avoid approaching the history of Protestantism in the same spirit: 'Jugez, Monsieur, s'il n'y a pas là dequoi être fait aux manieres emportées, & si le Pere Maimbourg qui regarde le Jansenisme comme une espece de Calvinisme, pouvoit manquer de venir à nous fort en colere.'[85] The affinity between Jansenism and Calvinism in Maimbourg's thought[86] means that he is

---

80. *CG*, letter IV, §v, *OD*, ii.21b. The rule for judging Maimbourg is that of decorum, see below, p.108, n.84.

81. *CG*, letter IV, §iv, *OD*, ii.20b; cf. letter I, §ii, *OD* ii.8b.

82. *CG*, letter I, §ii, *OD*, ii.8b.

83. *CG*, letter IV, §vi, *OD*, ii.23b.

84. *PD*, §clxxxi, *OD*, iii.116a-17a.

85. *CG*, letter I, §ii, *OD*, ii.8b.

86. The connection between Jansenism and Calvinism is a commonplace at the time (see above, p.49 and corresponding notes). Maimbourg uses it in reverse, the Calvinists become a *portrait à*

bound to use his latest history in the same way he used the previous ones. The Calvinists, becoming a 'portrait à rebours' (Declercq, p.122) of the *Port-Royalistes*, are painted negatively as a vehicle for revenge.

To the 'passion de se venger' is added a second unworthy motive – also contributing to the distorted picture of the Calvinists – that of ambition. Glossing Maimbourg's failure as a preacher, our author observes: 'La Fortune n'ayant pas secondé les bonnes intentions qu'il a toûjours euës, d'acquerir une glorieuse réputation, ni du côté de la Chaire, ni du côté de la Critique, ni du côté de la Controverse, il chercha un autre emploi à son esprit, & s'avisa de devenir Historien.'[87] The argument is unfair, since the Jesuit had acquired a widespread reputation for his preaching – albeit a somewhat dubious one.[88] As may be inferred from the critique of a similar restlessness in men of letters in the *Dictionnaire*,[89] Bayle is hinting that behind the chameleon nature of Maimbourg's career lies the determination to satisfy his ambition at any cost. When his dismissal from the Jesuits as a result of his Gallican sympathies earned him a royal pension of £3,000, Maimbourg also became historiographer to the Crown. The dangers of such a position are constantly outlined in the *magnum opus*.[90] It heralds the death of independence of judgement in a historian now answerable to a patron. The Jesuit's position is particularly vulnerable: his desire to succeed led to the adoption as his own of the prevailing official attitude to the Calvinists. His own hostility to the Huguenots is reinforced by the aim of the French court to 'ruiner le Calvinisme, en aussi peu de temps qu'il en mettoit à composer son Histoire'.[91] Hence, a pen 'hypothéquée au Roi par une grosse pension'[92] implies that Maimbourg becomes the official propagandist for the oppression of the Protestants: '[Maimbourg] a donc crû qu'il faloit préparer l'Apologie de toutes les violences que l'on employeroit pour venir à bout de ce grand dessein.'[93] His 'history' is but an oratorical *discours*. Like the lawyer before the court, he presents a *plaidoyer* in favour of the elimination of the Huguenots.

At this point, the analysis of *prévention* and its related vices is forcefully applied

rebours for the Jansenists.

87. *CG*, letter IV, §vi, *OD* ii.23b.

88. Alexander Chalmers, *The General biographical dictionary* (London 1812-1817), xxi.144, and above, note 37.

89. 'Accarisi (François)', footnote A; 'Alciat, (André)', footnotes G & N; 'Anaxagoras', footnote A; 'Decius', footnote B; 'Haillan', footnote M.

90. 'Baius', footnote A; 'Brun (Antoine le)', footnote G; 'Chigi (Fabio)', footnote D; 'Geldenhaur', footnotes K and R; 'Sabellicus', footnote H. Paul Jove, in the article of that name, is severely criticised for his venality and the effects it has on historical composition.

91. *CG*, letter I, §ii, *OD*, ii.9a.

92. *CG*, letter I, §ii, *OD*, ii.9b; cf. Naudé (*Apologie*, p.638-39), who also attributes historical error to ambition.

93. *CG*, letter I, §ii, *OD*, ii.9a.

to the *Histoire du calvinisme*. Its author's research techniques are, by definition, those of the propagandist and apologist (*CG*, letter I, §ii, *OD*, ii.9b-10a):

Il savoit, avant que de commencer son Histoire, qu'il nous faloit trouver coupables de mille séditions horribles. Plein de cet esprit il a feuilleté plusieurs Volumes; il a choisi certains faits qui lui ont paru favorables à ses fins, & sans se soucier beaucoup de l'ordre & de la véritable cause de ces faits, il leur a donné le commencement, le progrès, & le motif qui lui ont plû, de sorte qu'il nous a rendus tout aussi criminels qu'il a jugé à propos.

Maimbourg's brief to calumniate the Huguenots was, then, a determining influence on his research. The tenor of the 'history' decided in advance, the facts were subordinated to its apologetic purpose. His history of Calvinism may be dismissed as a work bereft not only of scholarship but also of that 'probité' (below, p.87ff.) necessary to historical composition.

The demonstration of the unreliability of the Jesuit's history through an exploration of his motivation and especially his venality is consistent with the distrust towards the venal historian expressed throughout the *magnum opus*. The venal historian writes to order, either in praise or denigration of his patrons and the events which concern them. Indeed, it is to venality that the two plagues of history, satire and flattery, are ascribed.[94] Not only the history of Calvinism, but history in general is vulnerable (*CG*, letter I, §ii, *OD*, ii.10a):

Il n'est rien de plus aisé, quand on a beaucoup d'esprit, & beaucoup d'expérience dans la profession d'Auteur, que de faire une Histoire Satyrique, composée des mêmes faits qui ont servi à faire un éloge. Deux lignes supprimées, ou *pour*, ou *contre*, dans l'exposition d'un fait, sont capables de faire paroître un homme, ou fort innocent, ou fort coupable: & comme par la seule transposition de quelques mots, on peut faire d'un discours fort saint, un discours impie; de même par la seule transposition de quelques circonstances, l'on peut faire de l'action du monde la plus criminelle, l'action la plus vertueuse. L'omission d'une circonstance, la supposition d'une autre, que l'on coule adroitement en cinq ou six mots; un je ne sai quel tour que l'on donne aux choses, changent entierement la qualité des actions.

Five techniques are noted: the suppression of key details, the transposition of key words and of key circumstances, the omission of crucial evidence and the supposition of alleged facts. All are present in the history of Calvinism, as the above version of Maimbourg at work indicates. The implication is clear. If such mishandling of sources can transform eulogy into satire, then the Jesuit's utilisation of such techniques suggests that his account of Calvinism is a 'through-the-looking-glass' *image* of the *réformés*. Anticipating the article 'Nestorius', Bayle indicates that the truth of the story lies in a *reversal* of the reading provided by the official historiographer.

94. 'Marillac, (Louis)', (2nd article), footnote A; *NLC*, letter III, §§ix, x, xi, *OD*, ii.182a-83b.

This conception of the facility with which 'histoire éloquente' becomes a satire, and the related notion of rhetorical history as a decadent form of 'histoire savante', has its roots in the conflicts of the 'âge de l'éloquence' to which Bayle belongs (Fumaroli, *passim*). Echoing the reaction to François Garasse's *Doctrine curieuse*[95] and its concept of 'la raillerie chrétienne' (Fumaroli, p.326ff.), Bayle adopts a severe, Augustinian moral attitude to certain kinds of satire.[96] In fact a synonymy exists between satire/*libelles diffamatoires* and *calomnie/médisance*, and these *genres* are in turn linked to the *passions* and irregular morality.[97] Undermining the 'véhémence inquisitoriale' (Fumaroli, p.327) of Garasse, the *philosophe* of Rotterdam portrays satire/*médisance* as a criminal act: 'Dans le fond, il y a des médisances qui sont aussi criminelles qu'un homicide, & qui partent d'un principe de haine si invétéré, que dans un sujet à bufle, ce seroient de bons coups de pistolet, & non pas de simples coups de langue.'[98] The attitude of the satirist is censured here. Hatred turns writing into as effective a means of expressing violence as murder. The link between the written word as an act of moral homicide and the wielding of arms with intent to kill leads to a slightly exaggerated notion of *libelles diffamatoires* as *more* reprehensible in the sight of God than acts of physical violence:

Quand je vois des gens d'Eglise se vanger de leurs ennemis, ou par des libelles diffamatoires, ou par des calomnies répanduës sécretement, je ne fais pas difficulté de dire, qu'il y a tel Gentilhomme, qui aïant estropié à coups de bâton un païsan, a moins offensé Dieu qu'ils ne l'offensent. Cette bile noire, & ce fiel qui se voïent dans toutes les pages de plusieurs Livres, plus facilement que ni le papier ni l'encre, supposent une disposition de cœur plus éloignée de la charité Chretienne, que ne le sont pas les violences d'un Cavalier qui bat son hôte, & qui jette ses meubles par la fenêtre. Mais l'Auteur n'a tué personne, ni cassé les bras à personne. Cela n'y fait rien, il n'est pas propre à cette sorte d'offense, il a d'autres armes offensives qu'il fait valoir.[99]

The indignation recalls the previous attitude to Maimbourg's calumnies of the Jansenists, seen as inimical to his priestly office. The remark, occurring in the *Pensées diverses*, stresses the inconsistency between faith and behaviour, one of

95. Fumaroli, p.325; cf. 'Garasse', who is one of the types of the unethical satirist in the *Dictionnaire*, as indeed for writers of a similar persuasion to Bayle's in matters of eloquence.
96. See below, p.107ff. According to Mary Claire Randolph ('Pierre Bayle's case agaist satire and satirists', *Notes and queries* 181 (6 December 1941), p.310-11), 'Satire has never had a more vigorously articulate enemy than Pierre Bayle' (p.310). Our author's conception of satire is, however, more subtle than Randolph leads us to believe. While that satire which is an expression of violence and passion is censured, Bayle admits and practises a kind of satire which does not infringe the ethical demands he makes on the man of letters (below, p.233-40).
97. *PD*, §CLXX, *OD*, iii.108b; *Dissertation sur les libelles diffamatoires*, in *Dictionnaire*, iv.2948-62, *passim*.
98. *PD*, §CLXX, *OD*, iii.108a.
99. *PD*, §CLXX, *OD*, iii.108a; cf. 'Bezanites', footnote B.

the targets of that work (see below, p.189ff.). Ecclesiastics, supposedly motivated by 'la charité chrétienne', give expression to their 'bile noire' in the 'fiel' of satire and are more culpable than the 'Cavalier' acting in accordance with the spirit of this world. The previous proofs of Maimbourg's desire for vengeance and the passing reference to his choleric temperament culminate here in a suggestion that the *Histoire du calvinisme* constitutes a satire morally reprehensible in its violence.

The *Critique générale* is not without an echo to this moralistic conception of the satirical mode. Two images are used to describe the Jesuit at work. Firstly,

je croi que c'eût été un spectacle bien divertissant, que de le voir occupé à composer ce dernier Ouvrage, dans cette Chambre à cheminée, qui avec une pension considérable a été, ou la récompense, ou l'acquisition de ses services. Il y a toutes les apparences du monde que le feu lui sortoit des yeux, qu'il faisoit toutes les grimaces d'un homme transporté de colere, & qu'il poussoit sa plume comme s'il eut voulu l'enfoncer dans le corps d'un Hérétique.[100]

The comparison of satire to an act of violence here achieves the level of a simile, wherein the pen is wielded as a sword. The second edition of the work omitted this image for a more forceful one: '[Maimbourg] s'étoit imaginé que sa plûme étoit devenuë l'épée de l'Ange exterminateur.'[101] The reference is biblical and refers to the Jesuit's conviction that he is God's divinely chosen instrument for the purge of the pernicious Calvinist heresy. In other words, given the tense political climate prior to the Revocation, the history of Calvinism is perceived as one more element in the oppressive measures taken against the Huguenots. Satirical history all too easily becomes an instrument of persecution.

The history itself, however, could not constitute a real persecution. It is rather the influence of its negative image of the Huguenots which Bayle most fears. An analogy is made between Maimbourg's history and the King's counsellors, always responsible in Protestant historiography before the Revocation for the oppression:[102]

Ce dessein [apologétique] lui a paru propre à deux usages: 1. à justifier la conduite que l'on tient en France à notre égard. 2. à donner une nouvelle vigueur au Roi & à ses Ministres, en cas qu'ils n'allassent pas aussi vîte que les Ecclésiastiques le souhaittent. Car c'est une chose étrange que les gens du monde, qui devroient être naturellement plus violens que les gens d'Eglise, sont néanmoins plus modérez dans les persécutions de Religion que les gens d'Eglise. Ce sont les gens d'Eglise qui animent les Rois & les Magistrats; qui leur mettent le fer à la main; qui se plaignent de leur molesse, dès qu'ils semblent moderer la rigueur des Ordonnances; & qui leur font craindre mille périls

100. *CG*, letter I, *OD* ii.8a, in a footnote; cf. *Avis important*, *OD*, ii.565b, 568a, 569b.
101. *CG*, letter I, *OD*, ii.8a.
102. Labrousse, *Pierre Bayle*, i.201.

chimériques, s'ils ne se défont pour une bonne fois de tous ceux qui ne suivent pas la Religion de l'Etat.[103]

History as propaganda forms a vicious circle. Ordered to write an *apologia* for the rigorous measures against the Protestants, Maimbourg and his *récit* move from instrument to instigator of persecution. The self-styled orthodoxy of the cleric, bereft of Christian charity like that of St Cyril in the Nestorian episode, brings its authority to bear on the mind of the King. The latter, innocent in absolutist historiography of the persecution, becomes in turn the tool of a clergy perpetuating its power and exclusive rights by a recourse to violence and, in the case of our Jesuit, the propaganda machine of bad history. It is this oppressive discourse, a decadent form of eloquence, that, in the *Critique générale* and the later *Dictionnaire*, Bayle seeks to defuse by an anatomy of its *supercheries* and superstitions and the mentality of which they are 'les fleurs du mal'.

Always the moralist, however, Bayle, influenced by Bodin and La Mothe Le Vayer, perceives historical 'bévues', whatever the cause, as 'un accident inseparable de nostre humanité'.[104] This is not to argue that the historian is always entirely responsible for the pernicious effect of the passions to which he is subject. For, not unlike Descartes, the 'passions de l'âme', to our author's mind, have both physiological and pyschological causes.[105] Maimbourg can hardly be blamed for his choleric temperament and *prévention*: both are the suspect fruits either of birth or of education.[106] None the less, the severity of Bayle's censure and the opposition of the Jesuit's motivations to those inspired by la 'charité chrétienne' imply that the *savant* is accountable for his collaboration with or control of his lower instincts. This position also contains seeds of *libertinage* and Cartesianism. La Mothe Le Vayer and Descartes, both sympathetic to neo-Stoicism,[107] advise study of the passions, that these 'forces seditieuses dans la Morale' might be tamed by 'la droite raison'.[108] On the one hand, the

---

103. *CG*, letter I, §ii, *OD*, ii.9b.

104. Bodin, *Methodus*, p.294 and *passim*. The phrase is La Mothe Le Vayer's in *La Promenade en neuf dialogues*, in *Œuvres*, xiii.61.

105. Descartes, *Les Passions de l'âme*, p.6; Labrousse, *Pierre Bayle*, ii.69ff.

106. Above, p.72ff.; Labrousse, *Pierre Bayle*, ii.69ff.

107. For La Mothe Le Vayer and Stoicism, see above, n.21. For Descartes and Stoicism, Julien-Eymard d'Angers, 'Sénèque, Epictète et le stoïcisme dans l'œuvre de René Descartes', in *Recherches sur le stoïcisme*, p.453-81.

108. Descartes, *Les Passions de l'âme*, §l, p.105-106; the phrase is La Mothe le Vayer's in *De la connoissance de soy-mesme*, in *Œuvres*, xiii.461. While Bayle is influenced by Stoicism (below, p.189ff.), his view of the passions differs from that of his two forebears. Neither Descartes nor La Mothe Le Vayer perceive the passions as a 'maladie de l'âme' (Descartes, *Les Passions*, p.14); in fact, according to Le Vayer 'les Passions ne sont que des inclinations indifferentes au bien ou au mal' (*De la connoissance*, p.460). Bayle, however, is unremitting in his suspicion of the passions as a corrupt force *within* the personality, while acknowledging their social utility. Cf. Jean Delvolvé, *Religion, critique et philosophie positive chez Pierre Bayle* (Paris 1906), p.96ff.; Labrousse, *Pierre Bayle*, ii.103ff.;

author of the *Dictionnaire*'s conception of the good historian (see below, p.87ff.) is undoubtedly affected by his own perusal of Stoical thinkers: '[un Historien] doit [...] se mettre le plus qu'il lui est possible dans l'état d'un Stoïcien qui n'est agité d'aucune passion' ('Usson', footnote F). On the other, the radical sceptical pessimism of his position (below, p.145) undermines the moral optimism of his celebrated forebears. Even the most ardent scholar cannot hope entirely to vanquish the sway of the passions and their contribution to a decadent historiography.[109] The reading-grid for the bad historian may often show characteristics of a libertine Cartesianism, but its underlying pessimism owes much, in the words of Elisabeth Labrousse, to 'l'influence de la psychologie janséniste des ruses de l'amour propre' and its related Augustinianism.[110]

The theological dimension to the critique of Maimbourg is present by implication in the opposition of the Jesuit's stated ideals to his unethical practice. The historian of Calvinism, to Bayle's mind, may be a dangerous propagandist but, in his own, he is 'sincere', a writer who, rejecting satire and panegyrics, wishes to 'rendre justice aux Hérétiques'.[111] This inconsistency between principles and practice – one of Bayle's *bêtes noires* – finds its parallel in the analysis of the psychology of human behaviour, first mooted in the *Pensées diverses sur la comète*. Noting the conflict in the personality when a human being is confronted with a decision as to a course of action, the author observes:

l'homme ne se détermine pas à une certaine action plûtôt qu'à une autre, par les connoissances générales qu'il a de ce qu'il doit faire, mais par le jugement particulier qu'il porte de chaque chose, lors qu'il est sur le point d'agir. Or ce jugement particulier peut bien être conforme aux idées générales que l'on a de ce qu'il doit faire, mais le plus souvent il ne l'est pas. Il s'accomode presque toûjours à la passion dominante du cœur, à la pente du tempérament, à la force des habitudes contractées, & au goût ou à la sensibilité que l'on a pour certains objets.[112]

The Jesuit had a general conception of historical equity but, in the act of writing, 'les idées générales' ceded to his passions, choleric temperament and the oratorical habits acquired as a preacher. Significantly, the Cartesian 'passions de l'*âme*' become, in our quotation, 'les passions du *cœur*'. As a later criticism of Jurieu – a type of Maimbourg – indicates, the use of history as a release of passion constitutes the imposition of a depraved and sinful sense on the historical *récit*.

Jurieu, in the *Esprit de Mr. Arnaud* (a late seventeenth-century equivalent of

below, p.193ff.
109. 'Remond', footnote D; below, p.183-84.
110. Labrousse, *Pierre Bayle*, ii.15; below, p.189ff.
111. Maimbourg, *Histoire du calvinisme*, p.335.
112. *PD*, §CXXXV, *OD*, iii.87a-b; cf. §CXXXVII, *OD*, iii.88a-89a.

Garasse's *Doctrine curieuse*), maintains that Grotius died an atheist.[113] Incensed by the accusation, not dissimilar to those brought by Jurieu against Bayle himself, the author of the *Dictionnaire* gives vent to his indignation:

Peut-on voir un aveuglement plus énorme? Ne faut-il pas avouër que l'envie de médire est de toutes les passions la plus capable de faire perdre de vue les idées du sens commun? [...] L'Accusateur [...] soutient clairement & nettement [que Grotius est mort athée], il faut donc qu'il le prouve [...] Or qui ne frémiroit d'horreur, en songeant qu'un homme, qui est mort de la maniere que Quistorpius l'a témoigné publiquement, est accusé d'être mort Athée? L'impudence d'un tel Calomniateur n'est-elle pas un prodige? Ne faut-il pas pour la croire en lisant son Livre, se représenter tout de nouveau ce que l'on a pu aprendre de l'infinie corruption du cœur humain & faire un acte de foi sur ces paroles de l'Ecriture, 'le cœur de l'homme est desesperement malin'?[114]

The passions blind the heart and the mind and provoke the supposition of facts, one of the characteristics of satire/*médisance*. The earlier opposition of *bons sens* and *passion*, *philosophe* and *rhéteur*, here carries the more forceful *corruption du cœur* in conflict with *les idées du sens commun*. That is to say, the scriptural revelation as to the cause of man's moral inconsistencies is vigorously applied to those of the man of learning. Satirical history is not merely decadent oratory, it is a depraved form of letters.

The problems attaching to historical composition are inseparable from those of the human predicament, which Bayle sums up, as had Pascal before him,[115] in terms of *contrariété*: 'la vie humaine n'est presque autre chose qu'un combat continuel des passions avec la conscience, dans lequel celle-ci est presque toûjours vaincue'.[116] In other words, Bayle's pessimistic attitude to the possibility of historical certitude is as *theological* as it is philosophical. His critique of Maimbourg is that of 'un pécheur qui constate les ravages du péché, bien plutôt que d'un homme compétent qui relève l'impéritie d'autrui'.[117]

Theological pessimism and historical scepticism find their unity in the *philosophe* of Rotterdam's understanding of the change effected by the Fall and original sin. A psychology of the soul is used to express metaphorically the radical reversal of mind and heart in the human personality ('Helene', footnote Y):

[Le vrai Systéme des Chrétiens] nous aprend que depuis que le prémier homme fut

113. [Pierre Jurieu], *L'Esprit de Mr. Arnaud, tiré de sa conduite, & des écrits de luy & de ses disciples, particulierement de l'Apologie pour les catholiques* (Deventer 1684), ii.308.
114. 'Grotius (Hugo)', footnote I; the Scriptural quotation is from Jeremiah xvii.9 and is a standard proof text for total depravity.
115. Pascal, *Pensées*, ed. Philippe Sellier, §151-64 (Paris 1976), p.83-92; on Bayle and Pascal, see Anthony McKenna, 'Pascal et Epicure: l'intervention de Pierre Bayle dans la controverse entre Antoine Arnauld et Malebranche', *XVIIe siècle* 137 (1982), p.421-28, esp. p.421, n.1.
116. 'Helene', footnote Y; cf. 'Ovide', footnote H.
117. Labrousse, *Pierre Bayle*, ii.36.

déchu de son état d'innocence, tous ses descendans ont été assujetis à une telle corruption, qu'à moins d'une grace surnaturelle ils sont nécessairement esclaves de l'iniquité, 'enclins à mal faire, inutiles à tout bien'. La Raison, la Philosophie, les idées de l'honnête, la connoissance du vrai intérêt de l'amour propre, tout cela est incapable de résister aux passions. L'Empire qui avoit été donné à la partie supérieure de l'ame sur l'inférieure a été ôté à l'homme depuis le péché d'Adam. C'est ainsi que les Théologiens expliquent le changement que ce péché a produit [...]

The conflict between the *corruption du cœur* and *les idées du sens commun* is the *natural* state of post-lapsarian man and by extension of the historian. On the one hand, pre-lapsarian man, in a state of innocence, lived according to the dictates of reason, or the higher part of the soul: 'l'âme', 'l'âme raisonnable', 'l'esprit'. On the other, after the Fall, man and his mind are controlled by the lower part of the soul: 'le corps', 'les sens', 'l'âme sensitive'. This Calvino-Augustinian[118] reinterpretation of Cartesian dualism (perhaps influenced in part by the *Logique de Port-Royal*) lies at the heart of the conception of the bad historian. Just as post-lapsarian man is incapable 'de résister aux passions', so the corrupt historian, of whom Maimbourg is a type, lives out in his decadent historiography the psychology of total depravity.

The extension of the effects of the Fall into the liberal arts is more radical, however, than even Jean Calvin's understanding of the effects of original sin. While the latter holds to the corruption of the entire personality at the Fall, he none the less exempts '[les] arts tant méchaniques que libéraux [... où] il apparoist qu'il y a quelque vertu en cest endroit de l'entendement humain'.[119] The extension of corruption to the historical disciplines may have come to Bayle via La Mothe Le Vayer. Both hold to an opposition between 'fables' and 'la vérité de l'Histoire'[120] and see some historian's indulgence in tales of the paranormal as the subjection of history to the popular mentality. The predilection for supernatural tales is linked by the earlier thinker to man's inclination to evil:

---

118. For Bayle's Augustinianism, see below, p.189ff. The Calvinism of the position is attested by the intertext of the quotation above. The phrase in inverted commas is drawn from the liturgy of the Reformed confession and recurs in *CPD*, §xxiii, glossed as follows: 'Les Chretiens, & surtout les Protestans, sont plus obligez que les autres à tirer cette derniere conclusion [i.e., the corruption of human nature], eux qui savent que le péché originel a corrompu la nature humaine, & qu'il l'infecte de telle sorte qu'il n'y reste rien d'entier. Les ténèbres obscurcissent l'entendement, la malice déprave la volonté' (*OD*, iii.220b). Bayle's *texte d'appui* in this later work is Charles Drelincourt, *Neuf dialogues contre les missionnaires sur le service des Eglises reformées* (Genève 1655), which defends the Reformed liturgy against charges of pessimism. The defence recognises the truth of the accusation but sees pessimism as the only legitimate interpretation of man's post-lapsarian state, as revealed in Scripture (p.1-28). Drelincourt's avowed source is Jean Calvin. Labrousse, *Bayle* (Past Masters), p.52, maintains that Bayle's view of the historian is inseparable from his Calvinism.

119. Calvin, *Institution de la religion chrestienne* (Paris 1859), vol.i, bk.2, ch.1, p.129b-30a.

120. La Mothe Le Vayer, *Discours de l'histoire*, in *Œuvres*, ii.158. Below, p.119ff.

'Comme l'on veut que nous aions tous une certaine inclination au mal, on a dit de mesme, que nous nous plaisions naturellement aux inventions fabuleuses' (La Mothe Le Vayer, *Discours de l'histoire*, p.162). The position reappears in Bayle's work as an analysis of child epistemology, paradigmatic of post-lapsarian epistemology:

L'esprit des enfans n'est pas mieux conditionné que leur cœur. Ils ne jugent des choses que selon le témoignage des sens: ils n'examinent rien, ils avalent les erreurs sans aucune défiance: ils croïent aveuglément tous les récits qu'on leur fait: les contes de peau d'âne, de ma mere l'oie, des fées, les traditions les plus fabuleuses, tout ce qui sent le prodige & le merveilleux, les histoires romanesques leur plaisent infiniment davantage que la simple & naïve vérité.[121]

Gullible credence is one more sign of a depraved intellect. Popular culture and popular belief, popular and superstitious histories are examples, in the written

---

121. *CPD*, §XXIII, *OD*, iii.220a. Our interpretation of the status of the child in Bayle's thought is somewhat different from that proposed by Elisabeth Labrousse. According to the latter (*Pierre Bayle*, ii.75-76) the child in his gullibility and credulity is 'non seulement innocent, mais bon, puisqu'il est conforme au Cinquième Commandement'. That is to say, the child is not to be held responsible for his ready acceptance of paranormal tales, since his acquiescence is but one expression of obedience to his parents to whom he is bound by the fifth commandment. In our opinion, however, the child in Bayle's thought, as in that of St Augustine (*De civitate Dei*, I, 3), is exemplary of post-lapsarian man prior to the influence of education and is part of our author's empirical demonstration of the effects of the Fall. Thus, the child, a picture of man since Adam's sin, is both guilty and morally responsible for his credulity, given the theological concept of immediate imputation. By immediate imputation is meant 'that in virtue of the union, federal and natural, between Adam and his posterity, his sin, although not their act, is so imputed to them that it is the judicial ground of the penalty threatened against him coming also upon them' (Charles Hodge, *Systematic theology* (Grand Rapids, Mich. 1979), ii.193; Hodge is a conservative evangelical and his interpretation of the Fall is similar to the Reformed tradition within which Bayle is working: see below, p.176). Given, then, that the child is part of Adam's posterity and that credulity is an expression of the effect of original sin, he is to be held responsible in the wider sense in which – before God – all mankind is responsible for his rebellion against the Deity.

This question of the status and function of the child in Bayle's thought is part, moreover, of a wider divergence of our analysis from that of Elisabeth Labrousse. To the latter, Bayle's perception of the child is part of a Cartesian epistemology: 'La méthode cartésienne [...] suppose [...] un discernement précis entre savoir objectif [...] et mémoire personelle; on peut donc le résumer en disant qu'elle nous demande de bâillonner l'enfant en nous, c'est-à-dire, de faire rigoureusement abstraction de toutes les notions *reçues* ou *apprises*, pour ne retenir que ce que nous avons *compris*, accueilli d'une manière réfléchie après examen' (*Pierre Bayle*, ii.69). The existence of Cartesian trends in Bayle's thought is undeniable. None the less, in the notion of the child and the concept of historical methodology (below, p.119ff.), Cartesianism does not constitute a final explanation of the intellectual and moral positions adopted by Bayle. That is to say, while Bayle shares with the Cartesians the notion that it is the unconsciously received ideas which must be examined and rejected (where necessary), the theological assumptions noted above, together with the moral and ethical context, whereby the 'homme bien éclairé' must not simply throw off his childhood but be an 'honnête homme' to boot (*CPD*, §XXIII, *OD*, iii.220b), imply that Cartesianism is but one of the modes used by Bayle to express intellectual and ethical positions inspired by his Augustino-Calvinist convictions.

medium, of a fatal flaw in the human personality. The oppositions *éclairé/supersti-tieux*, *peuple/docte* and *philosophe/rhéteur*, essential not only to 'Agreda' and 'Nestorius' but to the *Dictionnaire* as a whole (below, p.119ff.), repose on a more profound theological opposition between the elect and the reprobate. This theological opposition may be diluted and even secularised in the critique of Maimbourg but it is no less present. Its secularisation not only heralds the Enlightenment, it also permits the dialectic of the *Dictionnaire*. Consistently, the erring man of letters[122] and his decadent history are exposed by the erudite history and probity of those devoted to the ethics of the Republic of Letters. It is on this dialectic that the hope of history depends.

122. Cf., for example, the articles on or attitudes to the following: Bolsec, Garasse, Jurieu, Hall, Moréri, Remond, Varillas. Much could be said about the way Bayle's disputes with Jurieu function as catalysts to his position on satire and the ethics of writing in general but this is outside the scope of this study.

# 4. Godliness and good learning: the ethics of the Republic of Letters

> Mais comme il est très difficile d'être exempt de toute passion (bien que nous l'exigions comme une condition nécessaire chez notre historien idéal) il nous faudra tout d'abord nous garder d'acquiescer trop facilement à tout ce que l'écrivain nous dira de louable sur son compte, sur ses concitoyens, sur ses amis, et de déshonorant sur ses ennemis. Par contre nous regarderons comme extrêmement vraisemblable tout ce qui se rapportera aux exploits honorables et glorieux des ennemis. Quant au reste je récuse le jugement des familiers ou des adversaires et je réclame comme pour un arbitrage un tiers exempt de passion.
>
> Jean Bodin, *Methodus ad facilem historiarum cognitionem*, p.295

> On trouve en divers endroits de ce *Dictionaire* [de Mr. Bayle] plusieurs [...] remarques touchant le devoir d'un Historien.
>
> Basnage de Beauval, *Histoire des ouvrages des savants*[1]

THE notion of a fraternity of the learned, shared by Bayle with many of his contemporaries and humanist forebears,[2] is a welcome antidote to the pessimism of the critique of Maimbourg and like historians. Against his piercing analysis of religious prejudice, superstition, self-interest and ignorance as the common currency of the lettered, Bayle boldly presents the Republic of Letters as an ideal community where religious prejudice is to be remarkable for its absence and truth and reason are to be the foundation of all activity and interaction. In the preface to the *Nouvelles de la république des lettres*, dated March 1684,[3] while imploring his readers to forward their *éloges* of recently deceased men of letters, the author declares that

Nous n'examinerons point de quelle Religion ils auront été [...] il suffira qu'ils ayent été célébres par leur Science. Les Moines illustres de ce côté-là, n'obtiendront pas moins de justice qu'un autre Sçavant. Il ne s'agit point ici de Religion; il s'agit de Science: on doit donc mettre bas tous les termes qui divisent les hommes en differentes factions, & considerer seulement le point dans lequel ils se réünissent, qui est la qualité d'Homme illustre dans la République des Lettres. En ce sens-là tous les Sçavans se doivent regarder comme freres, ou comme d'aussi bonne maison les uns que les autres.[4]

---

1. *HOS*, septembre, octobre, novembre (1701), art.iii, p.477.
2. Jean Jehasse, *La Renaissance de la critique* (Saint-Etienne 1976), p.42, 49, 50, 60-61.
3. The March issue did not, however, appear until later in the spring (Labrousse, *Pierre Bayle*, i.190).
4. *NRL*, 'Préface', *OD*, i.2b. Cf. Ruth Whelan, 'Le *Dictionnaire* de Bayle: un cénacle livresque?', *Littérales* 1 (1986), p.37-51.

Given that religious allegiances are divisive, the emphasis is shifted from religion to learning. The validity of a scholar's work lies not in its confessional fidelity nor its furtherance of a sectarian cause but in its contribution to human knowledge. The Republic of Letters thereby becomes a community where unity is possible because of this laicisation of the value system: 'Science' is the foundation, the fraternal bond and final end of its membership.[5]

Later in the *Dictionnaire*, its author returns to this notion of a community united by its devotion to learning and extends its significance ('Catius', footnote D):

[La République des Lettres] est un état extrémement libre. On n'y reconoit que l'empire de la vérité & de la raison; & sous leurs auspices on fait la guerre innocemment à qui que ce soit. Les amis s'y doivent tenir en garde contre leurs amis, les peres contre leurs enfans, les beaux-peres contre leurs gendres [...] Chacun y est tout ensemble souverain & justiciable de chacun. Les loix de la société n'ont pas fait de préjudice à l'indépendance de l'état de nature, par raport à l'erreur & à l'ignorance: tous les particuliers ont à cet égard le droit du glaive, & le peuvent éxercer sans en demander la permission à ceux qui gouvernent.

The activity of the Republic of Letters has a double objective: the pursuit of truth, from which 'Science' is inseparable, and the critique and exclusion of ignorance. Three consequences – reminiscent of the humanist reaction to Ciceronian eloquence (Fumaroli, p.427ff.) – result from this two-fold purpose. Firstly, given that reason is presented as the faculty proper to the learned enterprise, affectivity and imagination are necessarily excluded. Secondly, all hierarchies are dissolved by the common purpose, fame is held as nothing if the scholar is mistaken: every *savant* is subject to the correction of his fellows. Thirdly, echoing Bodin (*Methodus*, p.295), in the interests of truth, sentimental ties are resolutely laid aside: neither kinship nor friendship is to impede the double objective of this fraternity.[6] A note of impersonal objectivity is struck in Bayle's ideal; religious convictions, imagination and personal involvement have no place in the learned enterprise.

The ideal is utterly antithetical to the historical practice personified by Maimbourg. In a later reflection on a historian of the same family, Florimond de Remond,[7] Bayle emphasises this antithesis, implying at the same time a means of controlling the corrupt historical activity of such writers:

5. This ideal has strong echoes from the Renaissance: cf. Pierre Mesnard, 'Le commerce épistolaire comme expression sociale de l'individualisme humaniste', in *Individu et société à la Renaissance* (Bruxelles 1967), p.15.

6. Elisabeth Labrousse, 'Obscurantisme et lumières chez Pierre Bayle', *Studies on Voltaire* 26 (1963) (reprinted in *Notes sur Bayle*), p.1037, who sees this international and trans-confessional ideal as 'une préfiguration du "philosophe" des générations ultérieures'.

7. On Remond, see Dubois, p.516-33.

j'observe que la vérité étant l'ame de l'Histoire, il est de l'essence d'une Composition Historique que le mensonge n'y entre pas; & ainsi, quand même toutes les autres perfections s'y trouveroient, elle n'est pas une Histoire, mais une Fable & un Roman, si la vérité lui manque. Il n'en va pas de même d'un Ouvrage de Poësie, ou de Rhétorique. [...] J'entens par mentir, non seulement l'invention entiere d'un fait faux; mais aussi la suppression ou l'addition de certaines circonstances qui peuvent servir ou à disculper les gens ou à les charger.[8]

While the statement echoes La Mothe Le Vayer[9] and, behind him, Bodin (*Methodus*, p.280), a greater severity is in evidence here. The 'histoire fabuleuse' of these writers, with its rhetorical flavour, suppression, and half-truths, becomes an 'histoire mensongère' ('Hercule', footnote R). The opposition, moreover, contains the antidote. That is to say, if history is not to be transformed into a 'Fable' or a 'Roman', then the practices of a Remond must be rigorously excluded from the historical *récit*. Together with the earlier sixteenth-century reactionaries against the corrupting influence of oratory[10] and, more recently, the Cartesians,[11] Bayle posits the notion of an intellectual ascesis, whereby a kind of mental hygiene is the basis for the search for truth.

It would be a mistake, however, to assume that Bayle is entirely derivative in his notion of the activity proper to the Republic of Letters. His ideals, owing much both to humanism and to classicism, testify to a dynamic unification of the two aesthetic theories, inasmuch as his 'goût classique'[12] is tempered with erudition. This 'rhétorique des citations' (Fumaroli, p.471) also displays the preoccupations of the moralist in its notion of the *probité* necessary to the man of letters: 'Ce que l'on a dit de l'Orateur est encore plus nécessaire à l'Historien: sa définition doit être, "vir bonus narrandi peritus", un honnête homme qui sçait narrer les événemens' ('Remond', footnote D). The adage, borrowed from Quintilian,[13] is significant not only in its application but also its translation. As in the sixteenth-century reaction to decadent eloquence, erudition, an alternative rhetorical mode, is conceived as inseparable from conscience[14] – a reversal of

8. 'Remond', footnote D; cf. 'Usson', footnote F. The opposition *fable/vérité* is to be found in Bodin, *Methodus*, p.280; the maxim 'la verité est l'âme de l'Histoire' is attributed to Polybius by La Mothe Le Vayer (*Du peu de certitude*, xiii.417) which is perhaps Bayle's source in this remark.

9. La Mothe Le Vayer, *Discours de l'histoire*, in *Œuvres*, ii.156ff.; note 8 above.

10. Fumaroli, p.392ff.; the preoccupation with the frontiers of truth and fiction is also typical of the *grand siècle*: cf. Bernard Magné, *Crise de la littérature française sous Louis XIV: humanisme et nationalisme* (Lille 1976), i.138.

11. Labrousse, *Pierre Bayle*, ii.39ff.; cf. Tocanne, p.371-448.

12. Cf. Claude Chantalat, 'Les Idées littéraires de Pierre Bayle dans le *Dictionnaire historique et critique*', Unpublished doctoral thesis, University of Paris IV (Sorbonne), 1983, p.140. I am most grateful to M. Chantalat, who allowed me to read the chapter on history before the defence of his thesis.

13. Identified by Bayle in 'Pericles', marginal note 203.

14. Fumaroli, p.685ff.; cf. 'Hall (Richard)', footnote B.

the imbalance consequent on the Fall and of Jesuit rhetoric, dominated by imagination[15] – and literary success is not to be separated from 'une grandeur d'âme extraordinaire'.[16] *Bonus*, however, becomes *honnête*, revealing a seventeenth-century transfiguration of the sixteenth-century ideal. Influenced both by the shift in the latter half of the grand siècle in the conception of the *honnête homme*, who increasingly becomes an *homme de bien*, and by the ideals of neo-Stoicism, Bayle presents the good historian as one whose literary output is founded on his espousal of a Christian-Stoic code of behaviour.[17] It is the purpose of this chapter to explore firstly the intellectual prophylaxis and secondly the moral asceticism fundamental, to Bayle's mind, to the aim of the *République des lettres*, namely *la recherche de la vérité*.[18]

A herculean diligence is the prerequisite of historical composition. Apart from the cases where the writer is an eyewitness of the events he describes, past happenings must be painstakingly reconstructed from a wide variety of original and derivative sources, often in a number of different languages. The *savant* is exhorted to follow the example of historians like William Camden, whose devotion to duty knew no bounds:

Par inclination naturelle il s'attacha principalement à rechercher les Antiquitez de son païs, & [...] des anciens peuples Britanniques: il vouloit traiter à fond de leur origine, de leurs mœurs, & de leurs loix. Il étoit nécessaire pour cela, non seulement qu'il entendît tout ce que les Grecs & les Latins nous ont laissé concernant la grande Bretagne, mais aussi l'ancienne Langue de cette Ile, l'ancien Breton & l'ancien Saxon. Il faloit qu'il examinât les anciens Itinéraires, qu'il fouillât dans les Archives, qu'il consultât une infinité de vieux papiers. Il ne négligea rien de tout cela: ses diligences & ses soins furent extrêmes.[19]

Camden's exemplary scholarship resides in his linguistic and philological skills, his geographical knowledge and his use of documents assiduously accumulated. The conception of ideal scholarship owes much to the juridical procedures of sixteenth-century Gallican humanists, '[qui] accordent plus de crédit au texte

15. Fumaroli, p.326ff.

16. *CG*, letter II, §i, *OD*, ii.12a. The phrase is used to describe de Thou and Mezerai, who come nearest – in their mastery of prejudice – to Bayle's ideal historian. Cf. also 'Hercule', footnote B.

17. The notion of *honnêteté* is multivocal in Bayle's work and the term is used to denote both *civilité mondaine* and moral integrity. Both senses are used with reference to the scholar. On the one hand, he is called to treat his fellows with civility and on the other, where sources and the act of writing are concerned, the term *honnête* and its variants are used, for the most part, in a moral sense. For the ambivalence of the term, see Tocanne, p.236-49, an ambivalence already present in the treatise by Nicolas Faret, *L'Honneste homme ou l'art de plaire à la Court* (1630), ed. Magendie (Paris 1925), p.xlv, xlvi. Bayle read this work: cf. *CPD*, §LXXVII, no.xxiii, *OD*, iii.301b; on Bayle's Stoicism, below, p.189ff.

18. Fumaroli p.475ff., for Bayle's forebears in these ideals.

19. 'Camden', *in corp.*; cf. 'Adriani', *in corp.*, 'Alegambe', *in corp.*

de la loi, à la pièce justificative, au témoignage écrit, qu'à la "bourre" orale que l'avocat est tenté d'ajouter à ces éléments de preuve' (Fumaroli, p.686-87, and *passim*). The exhortation to imitate the British historian might appear gratuitous in a century remarkable for its erudite enterprises, whether in secular or ecclesiastical history.[20] As the case of Maimbourg evinces, however, the seventeenth-century *érudit* has to contend with a historian turned *avocat*, whose learned activity is based not on documentation alone but also on imagination. The historian turned controversist spares himself the 'peine' of research by, in the first place, inventing without scruple 'contes', whose sole aim is to blacken the reputation of the opposing party or individual. Examples abound in the *Dictionnaire*. On the Protestant side, for example, the accusation of sodomy clouding the reputations of Calvin and Beza is placed in this category.[21] The 'Contes malins & bouffons' with which Protestant controversists peppered the life of St Francis of Assisi are a striking instance of the denigration of Catholicism ('François (d'Assise)', footnote G). In the case of the heterodox, Bayle repeatedly alludes to the horrible deaths that heretics – among them Nestorius[22] – reputedly die, an indication to the orthodox 'de l'empreinte de la punition divine'.[23] In the second place, as accounts of conversion from one religion to another illustrate, research is frequently done in a spirit of malignity. The researcher collects 'pele-mele, avec des bruits vagues, les faits qui pouvoient avoir quelque certitude, & ceux qui pouvoient recevoir un mauvais sens'.[24] Consequently, if the historian does emulate Camden, he will often assemble a set of documents not uniformly trustworthy. To assiduity must be added selectivity: the *savant* is to discriminate the facts which have been invented from those capable of substantiation.

The resurrection of Beza's supposed sodomy by François Eudes de Mézeray, one of Bayle's favourite and most trusted historians,[25] stimulates the enunciation

20. Cf. Bruno Neveu, *Un historien à l'Ecole de Port-Royal: Sébastien Le Nain de Tillemont 1637-1698* (The Hague 1966), *passim*, and, by the same author, 'Sébastien Le Nain de Tillemont (1637-1698) et l'érudition ecclésiastique de son temps', in *Religion, érudition et critique*, p.21-32. Bayle expresses reserves concerning the erudition of the Congregation of St Maur: cf. 'Gregoire I', footnotes P, Q, R and S, added in 1702. His respect for Camden may also contain an indirect reflection on the contemporary trend away from erudition, as evinced by the popularity of histories of the Maimbourg variety (cf. Martin, ii.840ff.).

21. 'Calvin', footnote Q; 'Beze', footnote U; 'Bolsec', footnote K.

22. 'Nestorius' *in corp.*; such deaths are read by the popular historian as *notae* or signs of heresy.

23. 'Alciat (Jean-Paul)', footnote D; Naudé, *Apologie*, p.18-19, notes and censures similar historical practices.

24. 'Sponde', footnote C; cf. 'Weidnerus', footnote A.

25. On Mézeray, see Wilfred Hugo Evans, *L'Historien Mézeray et la conception de l'histoire en France au XVIIe siècle* (Paris 1930), *passim*. Pintard, p.28off., traces an evolution from credulity to criticism in Mézeray's historical practice. The co-existence of these two attitudes in the *Histoire de France* explains the divergence between Bayle's and Leclerc's appreciations of the historian. The former

of certain techniques of discrimination. In the first place, again reminiscent of sixteenth-century Gallican humanism (Fumaroli, p.686, and *passim*), the 'Historien étourdi' is opposed to the 'Historien judicieux'. The former is guilty of wilful credulity: 'C'est un grand défaut, que d'être tout prêt à croire ce qui se publie au desavantage de ses ennemis, vrai ou faux, douteux ou certain' ('Loyola', footnote Q). The judicious historian is to cultivate a sceptical disposition and should be found among 'les gens qui ne s'arrêtent pas aux préjugez & ne se rendent qu'à la certitude': 'Défions-nous & des unes & des autres, & ne décidons rien qu'après une forte discussion des faits' ('Marillac', 2nd article, footnote A). Scepticism is universal, directed against sources both favourable and inimical to the subject matter and is only to be abandoned in exchange for a certainty based not on an inner persuasion – often no more than *prévention* – but on a careful examination of factual data. The procedure is the exact counterpart of that employed by Maimbourg. In the Jesuit's rhetoric, 'la mémoire-imagination' is the dominant faculty. In Bayle's ideal, like that of his Gallican forebears, 'jugement' is the 'faculté maîtresse, soutenue par la mémoire-réminiscence' (Fumaroli, p.687, and *passim*). Perhaps echoing Montaigne, historical composition is seen to depend not only on herculean scholarship but also on the finesse of an informed judgement.

Giving voice simultaneously to the objectives of Renaissance and Enlightenment thinkers, Bayle intimates that the fact to be judiciously examined is equipollent to the source. The separation of truth from error operates at the level of the available documents. The 'Historien judicieux' embarks on 'une recherche critique de la vérité à travers les textes oubliés, falsifiés, mal interprétés, qui en portent témoignage'.[26] Mézeray follows Bolsec, Sponde, Remond and Saintes in his biography of Beza ('Beze', footnote U):

Ce ne sont point des gens qu'il faille croire dans les faits personnels qu'ils reprochent à leurs Adversaires, à moins qu'ils ne les apuient sur des Actes authentiques; desorte que Monsr. de Mezerai, n'aiant fait que suivre un Claude de Saintes, & un Florimond de Remond, qui n'ont aporté aucune preuve de leurs médisances, s'est fait un grand tort auprès des personnes de jugement.

By 'Actes authentiques', the *philosophe* of Rotterdam means the judicial deposition of witnesses contemporaneous to the event. In the cases of Calvin and Beza, such evidence, easy to find at the time, is lacking. In its absence, the historian may conclude that 'le fait en question est chimérique'. The truth of

sees Mézeray, with some exceptions, as a critical writer, while the latter dismisses him as a credulous historian ([Jean Le Clerc], *Parrhasiana, ou Pensées diverses sur des matières de critique, d'histoire, de morale et de politique*, Amsterdam 1699-1701, i.195).
26. Fumaroli, p.686, and below, p.119ff.

the fact depends not, as in the case of Maimbourg, on a received tradition[27] but on its documentary pedigree. 'Sources involontaires' are more reliable than derivative ones.

'Témoignages involontaires',[28] however, may either not exist or be unavailable to a writer. Consequently, the author of the *Dictionnaire*, echoing Bodin (*Methodus*, p.295), recommends certain procedures whereby data based on derivative sources may be screened for reliability. Attention is again fixed on the source but now the historian is to exercise a more sophisticated judgement. Certitude is possible:

l'on peut être persuadé d'un fait, ou d'un dessein, ou d'un motif particulier, lors que tous les partis en conviennent; lors qu'étant infame à l'un des partis, il ne laisse pas d'être avoué par ceux à qui il est infame; ou bien lors qu'étant glorieux à l'un des partis, il n'est pas contesté par l'autre.[29]

Three principles of discrimination are here enunciated. First comes the criterion of universal consent: a fact may be considered certain when all witnesses are in agreement.[30] As is clear, however, from the Bayle-Maimbourg debate and sectarian history in general, uncontested facts are rare and a standard for testing the *prévention* of a *récit* must be devised. Secondly, the test of ingenuous confession may be used: data are acknowledged as reliable if, in attesting them, the witness diminishes the party to which he belongs. Thirdly, the scholar may apply the rule of uncontested advantage: a narrative is deemed certain if the credit it reflects on one party is not disputed by another. While the first of these principles appeals to the scholar's diligence, the last two invoke his discernment. Once he has assembled his materials, he is to decide the ideological bias of his source and, filtering one through another accept only as certain those facts which represent a vanquishing of prejudice on the part of his witnesses (cf. Bodin, *Methodus*, p.295-98).

The devotion to truth demanded of the historian is inseparable, then, from the perusal, broadly speaking, of written sources, and historical certitude is a function of adequate and reliable documentation.[31] A dynamic relationship exists, however, between the scholar and his sources. On the one hand he tracks down the origin of his facts, on the other he is frequently obliged to decide if

27. Below, p.119ff.; cf. 'Guebriant', footnote B.

28. Labrousse, 'La méthode', p.463.

29. *CG*, letter II, §i, *OD*, ii.11b. Bayle holds these methodological principles in common with many of his contemporaries; cf. Perry, p.60.

30. This is the only case where Bayle admits universal consent as a criterion of truth. It is criticised at length both as a theological and as a philosophical criterion in the *Pensées diverses* and the *Continuation*.

31. Labrousse, 'La méthode', p.450.

these origins are worthy of credence. Consequently, the standard of certitude becomes either the impartial document or a position deduced from a collection of sources. In all cases, a reversal of the Maimbourg-type relationship to the facts is in evidence. By diligence and judgement, the good historian submits his mind and imagination to documentary evidence, perceived as a check on invention and *prévention*, the fortes of the credulous and injudicious historian. The critically established source constitutes the basis for that intellectual ascesis required of the man of letters.

The primacy of the source as the foundation of historical verity is most amply illustrated by Bayle's understanding of the place of harangues and miracles in the historical *récit*. The two cases pick up and reverse the oppositions between oratory and erudition, credulity and *bon sens*, *rhéteur* and *philosophe* to be found in the critique of Maimbourg. The opinion of seventeenth-century aesthetic theorists is divided *vis-à-vis* the propriety of harangues (Tocanne, p.112). On the one hand, speeches are admitted by Bernard Lamy and are seen as an opportunity for the historian to exercise his rhetorical skills. While normally historical style is to be characterised by 'la clarté & la briéveté', this does not mean that 'un Historien qui est bon Orateur ne puisse faire usage de son éloquence':

L'occasion s'en presente assez souvent. Comme il est obligé de rapporter ce qui a été dit, aussi bien que ce qui a été fait, il y a des Harangues à faire dans l'histoire, où les figures sont necessaires pour peindre la passion de ceux qu'on fait parler.[32]

For Lamy, harangues are not necessarily reported speech. On the contrary, they are a fictitious and dramatic means of representation whereby historical persona are made to reveal their passions, plans or inner thoughts. Moreover, while the historian may have evidence to corroborate the details unveiled in these speeches, he is not limited by that evidence. He may attribute to the actors of history feelings and reflections he intuitively presumes them to have nourished.

On the other hand, ambivalence is the keynote of Rapin's opinion of the place of harangues in the historical narrative. While welcomed as an embellishment, they are also seen as inimical to *bon sens*:

Un petit discours fait à propos dans une Histoire, par un Acteur d'un caractere à en faire, qui soit convenable à la personne & au sujet dont il s'agit, peut avoir sa grace, étant en son lieu. Mais ces Harangues en forme, à la tête d'une Armée, quand on va au combat [...] ne sont presque plus d'usage dans les Histoires bien sensées: & les plus sages prennent le parti de faire parler indirectement leurs personnages, disant les choses en géneral.[33]

32. Bernard Lamy, *De l'art de parler* (Paris 1676), p.204.
33. René Rapin, *Réflexions sur l'histoire*, in *Œuvres* (Paris 1725), ii.281.

The propriety of speeches is determined by their *vraisemblance*: convoluted rhetoric is not a medium proper to a soldier in the heat of battle (Rapin, ii.280). To animate the *récit*, the author may include only those speeches which neither misrepresent the personality nor falsify the context of the supposed orator.

Bayle's sentiments on the matter reveal at one and the same time an awareness of contemporary theory[34] and a critical distance from it. In the first place, the position represented by Lamy is rejected by implication: 'Il regnoit beaucoup d'abus dans les Harangues que les Historiens raportoient: ils les composoient eux-mêmes selon leur caprice, & vouloient bien que l'on crût qu'elles avoient été prononcées actuellement' ('Guicciardin', footnote K). The weight of the criticism is carried by the expressions 'abus' and 'caprice': speeches are an abuse because they are fictional and therefore untruthful. Like Bodin before him, our author maintains that 'on ne peut rechercher tout ensemble l'agrément et la vérité' (*Methodus*, p.300), if rhetorical embellishment is allowed to usurp the place of historical truth. Moreover, given that harangues are the fruit of 'caprice' and not of the source, they represent a writer negligent of intellectual ascesis: he manipulates and does not serve the documentary evidence.

In the second place, the author of the *Dictionnaire* is sympathetic, while for not quite the same reasons, to the cautious position represented by Rapin:

Je tombe d'accord qu'un Historien peut représenter les gens selon ce qu'ils pensent, encore qu'ils ne le disent pas: mais cela demande deux conditions; l'une qu'il soit manifeste ou tout-à-fait vraisemblable qu'ils pensent une telle chose; l'autre, que l'on avertisse qu'ils ne disent pas cette chose, mais qu'ils font assez conoître qu'ils la pensent.[35]

More wary than his classical predecessor, Bayle, as in the critique of Maimbourg, attempts to reconcile Bodin's emphasis on verity and the contemporary preference for *vraisemblance*. The acceptance of harangues depends not on their literary propriety but on their representational veracity: they must express the actual thoughts of the historical character. Furthermore, to avoid all possible confusion, a distinction is to be drawn between the historian's oratory and the character's thoughts, a position faithful to Bayle's conception of history as an erudite activity. The historian is asked to be faithful and to be seen to be faithful to his sources. He is to distinguish for the sake of his readers between fact and fiction, between his own literary inventions and documentary evidence.

The place of the paranormal in the historical narrative also receives careful consideration from Bayle, stimulated undoubtedly by his reading of the provi-

34. Bayle read Rapin's *Réflexions* and cites it frequently in the *Dictionnaire*: see for example, 'Mariana', footnote D.
35. 'Musurus', footnote D; cf. Bodin, *Methodus*, p.309, where a similar position is implicit in the comparison of Guicciardini and Jove.

dential historians of the sixteenth century (Dubois, *passim*) and the contemporary resurgence of the supernatural as a supposed sign of the legitimacy of politico-religious parties.[36] Despite his critique of credulous historians, Bayle does not recommend a policy of total exclusion of miracles from the narrative. On the contrary, the scholar is advised to avoid the two extremes of excessive credulity and unmitigated hostility.[37] Surprising as it may seem, for the sake of what might anachronistically be termed the 'histoire des mentalités', the historian is advised to be a 'fidéle raporteur' of the stories of the paranormal found in his sources:

un Historien qui raconte la terreur qu'une Comete, qu'une éclipse, qu'une inondation exciterent dans un païs, à cause qu'on les prenoit pour des présages sinistres, & qui n'oublie pas les processions, & les autres cérémonies religieuses qui furent ordonnées pour détourner ces présages, ne sort nullement de la sphere d'Historien; car ce sont des faits aussi curieux, aussi instructifs que les batailles, que les sieges, que les traitez d'alliance.[38]

In harmony with his own age, Bayle takes his distance from spurious miracles but, while an *éclairé*, unlike his Enlightened heirs he is not bereft of a certain 'sens du sacré'. The remark, in its echo of a similar position in La Mothe Le Vayer,[39] is worthy of an author steeped in the letters of the Renaissance. The 'univers magique' of the earlier century may be restricted but it is not excluded; no longer an object of credence, it is still retained for its curiosity value. That is to say, leaving aside the question of the ultimate truth of certain attitudes to the supernatural, the attitudes are interesting *in themselves*, as a gauge of the intellectual climate of certain periods of history.

Having established the validity of the supernatural as a historical topic, our author continues by counselling discernment; some paranormal phenomena are more worthy of inclusion than others (*CPD*, §lxiii, *OD*, iii.280a):

En premier lieu, je souhaiterois qu'un Historien ne fît point l'honneur à des bruits vagues qui n'ont encore paru dans aucun Livre, de les faire changer d'état, je veux dire de les tirer de l'obscurité des conversations pour les transporter à l'imprimerie. Bien entendu qu'ils n'aïent été abandonnez des Ecrivains qu'à cause de leur peu de fondement & de leur peu de vraisemblance.

The observation explains the *historical* reasons for the hostility to Agreda. The Spanish mystic, in recording visions deemed spurious, caused them to 'changer d'état' and, having been printed, private extravagances bid fair to become public

---

36. Tocanne, p.116, 121ff.; Labrousse, 'The political ideas', p.248 and 275, n.60; Jean de Viguerie, 'Le miracle dans la France du XVIIe siècle', *XVIIe siècle* 140 (1983), esp. p.330.
37. Labrousse 'La méthode', p.452.
38. *CPD*, §LXIII, *OD*, iii.282a, and §III, *OD*, iii.192b-193a; cf. 'Junon', footnote DD.
39. La Mothe Le Vayer, *Discours de l'histoire*, in *Œuvres*, ii.169ff.

belief (above, p.28-30). Only those miraculous tales which possess *vraisemblance* and verity, inasmuch as they express a widely held belief, merit inclusion. Oral traditions, as distinguished from popular practices, are not to become written traditions. A further discernment operates at the level of the written source: some 'chroniqueurs' are as unworthy of credence as the oral tradition. The term 'chroniqueur' is not limited to the authors of annals but is extended by its context to all those writers who lend the 'poids de leur autorité' to the 'bruits populaires sur des batailles vûës en l'air [...] sur des voix nocturnes etc'.[40] Once more the *savant* is invited to sieve his documents in order to determine whether the miracles reported are substantiated only by 'bruits vagues' or, more properly, by 'les monumens les plus authentiques', and only the latter may be included in the narrative.

Furthermore, the critical attitude demanded of the author is to be limited to the source. In a remark sensitive to the use of the paranormal for the defence of sectarian or political causes, Bayle maintains that the historian's *métier* excludes all doctrinal consideration of the verity of miracles (*CPD*, §LXIII, *OD*, iii.281b):

Je ne voudrois pas [...] qu'on tombât dans un excès de négation ou de Pyrrhonisme. Je voudrois même qu'un Protestant qui composeroit une histoire des Croisades se gardât bien d'entrer en dispute sur les miracles de Saint George, ou de tel autre Saint de la Communion de Rome. Je ne parle pas d'une dispute où par des raisons de fait tirées des circonstances, & des témoignages historiques on combatroit quelque tradition. Cette espece de combat doit être permise aux Historiens: je parle d'une dispute par lieux communs, ou par des raisons générales; elle seroit mal placée dans une histoire. Rien n'est plus fastidieux qu'un Historien qui s'érige en Controversiste.

The Protestant, a little naively given Jurieu's recent excursus into supernatural tales (above, ch.2, n.57), is thought to be in most danger of turning history into controversy, where miracles are concerned. Such use of history for doctrinal ends is repudiated and instead, looking back at his own practice in the *Dictionnaire*, its author argues for a critical rather than an iconoclastic treatment of the miraculous.[41] The caution which it is the historian's duty to inspire in his readers[42] is not to be exploited as a convenient vehicle for the propagation of a religious creed.

The position on harangues and miracles testifies to the presence of an alternative rhetoric in Bayle's conception of history, the rhetoric of sources which holds in tension the humanist and classical criteria of *vraisemblance* and

---

40. *CPD*, §LXIII, *OD*, iii.281b.
41. Above, p.27-30. Bayle does practise a historical iconoclasm (below, p.233ff.) but it is subject to certain scholarly exigencies. Cf. 'Constance', footnote B; 'Jonas' (1st article), footnote B.
42. *CPD*, §LXIII, *OD*, iii.281a.

*vérité*. The devotion to truth and reason, the ethic of the Republic of Letters, becomes, in the case of the historian, 'la religion des sources', an oft-repeated phrase in the *magnum opus*. Consequently, the exhortation to the *savant* to 'se tenir dans les bornes de la vérité' ('Botero', footnote C) is the counterpart of the admonition to the historian not to 'se hasarder à sortir des bornes de ce qu'il copie'.[43] The historical enterprise is an erudite activity which, by filtering fact from opinion and oral or popular tradition, aims to exclude the human factor from historical composition. As with the sixteenth-century philologists and jurists, Bayle's hostility to error and ignorance proceeds not so much from 'le goût de détruire' as from 'la passion de retrouver' (Fumaroli, p.686). The 'application aux sciences', proposed as a prophylactic for the 'préjugez de l'enfance' – child epistemology being a type of fallen adult epistemology[44] – finds a historical parallel in the 'application aux sources', conceived as the corrective to imaginative and decadent historiography and a path to that elusive ideal, historical impartiality and objectivity.

Research is but the first step in the gargantuan effort required of the historian. The material, once collected, must be sorted and written up. Inevitably, given the extensive nature of the initial documentation, the historian will be constrained to condense his findings ('Alegambe', *in corp.*). All histories, and especially general ones ('Sabellicus', footnote B), are necessarily abridgements of their sources. While abridgement is both necessary and desirable, Bayle has three reasons for fearing its abuse. Firstly, through lack of ability, the narrative may be an incomplete account of events ('Guebriant', footnote F):

On voit là un exemple de ce qui arrive presque toujours à ceux qui donnent des Abrégez; ils omettent plusieurs circonstances, sans lesquelles un fait n'est qu'une petite masse brute & informe, comme l'éprouvent ceux, qui après l'avoir lu dans une Histoire étendue, comparent l'idée qu'ils en ont avec celle qu'un Abrégé leur en donnoit.

Incomplete versions constitute a mutilation beyond recognition of historical fact. The problem is not so acute while the *abrégés* can be compared with more extensive histories. Were the latter to be lost, as in the case of many Greek, Roman and medieval sources, the complex tapestry of events would also be lost to posterity. Secondly, certain genres, whether that of the *Vita* or the satirical *Vita renversée*,[45] positively encourage incomplete narratives. Consequently, the biographer or historian will be disappointed if he looks to the *Vita* for his facts ('Patin', *in corp.*):

43. 'Agrippa', footnote C; cf. 'Cassius Longinus', 3rd article, footnote A.
44. *CPD*, §XXIII, *OD*, iii.220b; above, p.83-84 and corresponding notes.
45. For the notion of certain satirical *Vitae* as a *renversement* of *éloges*, cf. Jean-Robert Armogathe, 'Les vies de Calvin aux XVIe et XVIIe siècles' in *Historiographie de la réforme*, p.45-59.

On seroit trop délicat si l'on trouvoit à redire, que l'Auteur de cet Eloge n'ait point donné l'Histoire de Guy Patin. C'est ainsi qu'en usent les faiseurs d'Eloge: ils ne s'amusent presque jamais à nous aprendre d'où est un homme, ni comment il s'est poussé; ils ne parlent de ses actions qu'au cas qu'elles se raportent d'une façon distinguée aux vertus dont ils le louent.

The *Vita* is a declamation on a theme and the oratorical exigencies of the genre dictate the omission or inclusion of certain facts ('Basta (George)', footnote B). Consequently, the quasi-biography which results may mislead its readers by its omissions: its subject will appear more virtuous or depraved than he was in reality. The third abuse, whether it occurs alone or with the other two, is the most dangerous; here the historian becomes a lettered Procrustes whose abridgements are determined by his prejudice. The reflection occurs with reference to Maimbourg (*CG*, letter v, §iii, *OD*, ii.28b):

Car enfin quand on est ainsi possédé d'une passion dominante de se venger, & de faire sa Cour aux Princes, on accomode les faits dont on a besoin à sa passion, à peu près comme ce Procrustes, dont Thesée delivra le monde, égaloit ses prisonniers à la mesure de son lit: S'ils étoient plus grands, il leur coupoit le superflu; s'ils étoient plus petits, il leur allongeoit les membres.

In this case, abridgement is a deliberate falsification of data where the historian's *prévention* is the selector. Misrepresentation, whether deliberate or not, is a recurrent feature of the historical narrative. To eliminate it is impossible. If history is to live up to the ideal of impartiality and objectivity, it must be controlled. To this end, certain techniques are advanced to enable the historian to avoid mutilating his data.

In the first place, the *philosophe* of Rotterdam insists that, while condensation reduces the facts, it must not omit any of the essential details ('Arsinöé', 2nd article, footnote C):

Un Abrégé doit ressembler aux pygmées, qui ont toutes les parties du corps humain, mais chacune à proportion plus petite que celles d'un homme de belle taille. Apetissez dans un Abrégé les parties d'une narration, tant qu'il vous plaira; mais ne les retranchez pas entiérement.

Completeness is the order of the day. As Bayle observes elsewhere, both 'la bonne foi historique' and 'la netteté du récit' demand, in the second place, that 'quand tous les autres Livres du monde seroient brûlez, la seule Histoire d'un homme aprît à tous les Lecteurs s'il a dit ou s'il a fait une telle chose'.[46] Behind this statement is the 'hantise de la décadence', that anxiety common to humanist and classical thinkers concerning the possibility of a new Dark Age, destructive

---

46. 'Baudoüin', footnote A; cf. 'Buchanan', footnote M. Superfluous details, however, are seen as a distraction which tires the reader: 'Andronicus' (1st article), footnote B.

of learning and human achievement.[47] The verity and reliability of a good history lie in its replacement value: its capacity to supply for all previous accounts in the event of their loss. This preoccupation lies at the heart of the *Dictionnaire* and its abundant citations: a historical monument, its very size might well protect it from impending doom. Its survival would compensate for the loss of the thousands of books cited and preserved within its pages.

A full picture is all the more necessary, given the notion, shared by Bayle with contemporary and humanist theorists, of history as a vehicle for moral instruction.[48] While a consensus existed concerning the moral purpose of history, opinion was divided as to how this was to be accomplished. On the one hand, some felt it legitimate to weight the *récit* with 'maximes' and 'sentences', which ineluctably lead the reader to the moral lessons the narrator wishes to draw.[49] On the other, thinkers like Rapin and Bayle and, behind them, Bodin (*Methodus*, p.298) advise that the reader be allowed to draw his own conclusions from a complete exposition of the facts (Rapin, ii.287-89). Bayle urges the writer neither to 'cacher les défauts des grands hommes' ('Luther', footnote R) nor to 'fomenter la haine du mal en le décrivant plus noir & plus haïssable qu'il n'étoit effectivement' ('Mahomet', *in corp.*). In fact, 'le premier but de l'Historien doit être de conserver la mémoire des bonnes actions & de faire craindre l'infamie aux mauvaises'. Moreover, echoing Bodin, he maintains that the reader is to be spared the maxims and moral reflections with which historians love to pepper their accounts:[50]

Ils devroient faire un Narré qui ne contînt que les principes ou que les premisses du raisonnement, le lecteur tireroit lui-même la conclusion soit qu'il s'agit de blâmer, soit qu'il s'agit de louer. Il sufit donc de bien exposer les faits.[51]

The concern is that of protecting the reader's liberty of judgement. While the historian may *suggest* a line of interpretation, he is to avoid, in Bodin's words, 'toute appréciation anticipée [... qui] semble bien porter préjudice aux faits rapportés, en imposant des préjugés divers aux esprits peu avertis' (*Methodus*, p.298). The ideal common to erudite classical and humanist thinkers is that of unmediated narration and it is this mirage which leads Bayle to speak of history as a mirror,[52] held up to the past, wherein, without authorial inter-

---

47. Zuber, 'Guez de Balzac', p.140. Below p.186.
48. Bodin, *Methodus*, p.280; La Mothe Le Vayer, *Du peu de certitude*, in *Œuvres*, xiii.416-17.
49. Jean Le Clerc, *Parrhasiana*, i.182ff.
50. 'Louïs XI', footnote N; cf. 'Sforce', footnote E.
51. 'Louïs XI', footnote N; cf. below, p.237-38.
52. 'Orose', footnote G; 'Manichéens', footnote D; history, to Bodin, is 'l'image de la vérité' and 'un tableau des actions passées' (*Methodus*, p.298).

ference, the reader may learn and judge the actions of his forebears.

In the third place, again opposing 'histoire savante' to 'histoire éloquente', Maimbourg's critic advises the observation of a strict chronological order in all historical writing.[53] The desire for brevity is no excuse for confusion:

On ne peut pas excuser ces fautes en disant qu'on a voulu être court, car la premiere chose que l'on se doit proposer dans un Ouvrage, c'est de donner dans le goût du monde, qui est sans doute de voir regner l'éxactitude chronologique, dans tout ce qui a du rapport à l'Histoire.[54]

Exactitude and sequential narration are part of that desire for completeness noted above. A deeper preoccupation, however, also informs the insistence on order ('Caussin', footnote G):

Je suis assûré que la plupart des Eloges des Hommes illustres sont tout pleins de semblables Anachronismes, & que l'on y commet plus souvent que dans les Livres de Scholastique le Sophisme *à non causa pro causa*. Pour éviter cela, il faudroit toujours donner la forme d'Annales à l'Histoire des grans Hommes.

Eulogy, an oratorical use of history on a given theme, is particularly open to the charge of confusion. The implication is clear: reshuffling the events of history allows the narrator to mould the facts to his own ideological ends. Responsibility may thereby be attributed to the wrong group or individual, as in the case, for example, of the sixteenth-century civil wars: confusion in the sequence of Catholic and Protestant persecutions allowed authors to clear their own politico-religious party of blame.[55] Chronological exactitude is necessary, therefore, to the ideal of unmediated history: it acts as a check on the mystification of historical data.

Finally, the necessity to protect the facts and the reader from the undue influence of the scholar's partiality inspires the third of Bayle's recommendations: the historian should cite his sources. Citation was not universally practised by *savants* in the *grand siècle*. Indeed, according to Jean Le Clerc, its validity is disputed, a dispute forming part of the 'querelle des Anciens et des Modernes'. Those following the Ancients deem citation unnecessary: 'Les uns croient qu'il n'est nullement nécessaire de citer, & que le Lecteur se doit fier au choix & à la sincerité de l'Historien; sans lui demander de qui il a appris les faits qu'il rapporte.[56] Blind faith is demanded of the reader by authors of this

---

53. Bodin, *Methodus*, p.283, makes a similar demand on the historian. Adrien Baillet, *Jugemens des sçavans sur les principaux ouvrages des auteurs* (Paris 1685-1686), ii.133, sees the demand for chronological sequence as typical of 'le goust de nostre siecle'.
54. *NRL*, juillet 1684, art.v, *OD*, i.92b; cf. 'Alegambe', footnote C.
55. See 'Macon' and 'Beaumont'; Jehasse, p.102.
56. Le Clerc, *Parrhasiana*, i.144. The author also argues that failure to cite facilitates the corruption of historical truth by 'l'esprit Romanesque' (p.147-49).

persuasion: the scholar's sincerity is a sufficient gauge of his good faith. To the Moderns, of whom Le Clerc is one, the historian's propensity to err makes sincerity an insufficient criterion of *bonne foi*. The historian is to 'citer par tout', for citation is the only means of testing the exactitude of an author.

In his praise of William Selden, Bayle enters the debate unequivocally on the side of the Moderns:

[Guillaume Selden] est fort exact à citer ceux dont il emprunte quelque chose, & il prie les Lecteurs de ne prendre pas cette exactitude pour une ostentation de science. C'est assurément le meilleur parti que celui de bien citer les Autheurs qui nous rendent du service.[57]

To both authors, citation represents a progress in historical science which the authority of the Ancients must not be allowed to crush. While their position announces later developments in historiography (Momigliano, p.10, 11, 25), their reasons are altogether those of the *grand siècle* and its Cartesian spirit.[58] Le Clerc articulates this mood:

On soûtient donc que l'on n'évite de citer, qu'afin que personne ne puisse examiner l'Histoire, que l'on raconte, en comparant la narration avec celles des Historiens qui ont écrit auparavant. Car le moien d'examiner ce que l'on avance, sans citer personne en particulier; à moins que d'avoir tous les Historiens dont on s'est servi, & de les avoir bien lûs, & bien mis dans sa mémoire? Peu de gens en sont capables [...][59]

Le Clerc is as sceptical as Bayle concerning the historian's ability to write with impartiality. Thus, he muses, following the method of the Ancients, it is possible to 'donner tel tour que l'on veut à l'Histoire'. The opposition is between a historical practice which is esoteric and authoritarian and one open to verification. The demand for citation both establishes the reader's right to check the veracity of the historical *récit* and controls the development of those oppressive historical traditions noted in the case of Maimbourg.[60]

While the *philosophe* of Rotterdam does not express his position in the same way, the 'servitude de la citation'[61] to which he submits throughout his published work, together with his reiterated laments concerning authors who do not cite,[62]

57. *NRL*, juin 1684, art.vi, *OD*, i.71. Some argued that citation was inspired by an arrogant and ostentatious spirit, to which Bayle retorts that arrogance is more evident in those who do not cite, for such writers want the work of others to be attributed to themselves. 'Cavalcante', footnote I; 'Aristote' (1st article), footnote C; 'Erasme', footnote CC. For Bayle's sympathy to the 'Moderns', see Labrousse, 'Le paradoxe de l'érudit cartésien, Pierre Bayle', in *Religion, érudition et critique*, p.59

58. Labrousse, *Pierre Bayle*, ii.39-68; on the association of Cartesianism and critical humanism, see below, p.130-32.

59. Le Clerc, *Parrhasiana*, i.146-47; cf. 'Hosius', footnote B.

60. See above, p.74-75; below, p.119ff.

61. 'Préface de la première édition', in *Dictionnaire*, i.IV.

62. 'Marillac, (Louis de)', footnote K, *in fine*.

bear witness to a similar spirit. He goes one step further, for space allows him to quote sources at length in the footnotes to the *Dictionnaire* (i.vi):

Et parce qu'il s'est commis beaucoup de supercheries dans les Citations des Auteurs, & que ceux qui abregent de bonne foi un Passage n'en savent pas conserver toûjours toute la force, on ne sauroit croire combien les personnes judicieuses sont devenues défiantes. Je puis dire avec raison que c'est une espece de témérité en mille rencontres, que de croire ce qu'on attribue aux Auteurs, lors qu'on ne raporte pas leurs propres paroles. C'est pourquoi j'ai voulu mettre en repos l'esprit du Lecteur; & pour empêcher qu'il ne soupçonnât ou *subreption* ou *obreption* dans mon raport, j'ai fait parler chaque témoin en sa Langue naturelle; & [...] j'ai allongé quelquefois [l'endroit nécessaire], afin que l'on comprît mieux de quoi il étoit question, ou que l'on aprît incidemment quelque autre chose.

The anatomy of error, to which the *Dictionnaire* is an eternal monument, uses citation as one of its most incisive instruments. The *magnum opus*, composed by an 'écrivain judicieux', aims to train the reader to be a 'personne judicieuse', to examine all positions put forward by its author. The remark establishes the *scholarly* perspective of thee articles 'Agreda' and 'Nestorius'. Polemical they may be, but the conscientious quotation of the sources from which they are drawn actually invites a reader/author dialogue and the penetration of the true objectives of the entries. In a word, both Bayle and Le Clerc are concerned for the *scrutability* of the historian. They both favour a kind of historical composition which promotes the principle of *examen* over the *principe d'autorité*.[63]

Prophylactic erudition is insufficient to contain the scholar's credulous and procrustean tendencies. To good scholarship the historian must add virtue. Maimbourg, as we have seen, was seduced into using history as propaganda by his ambition and avarice. To the desire to use learning to acquire wealth and powerful patrons, Bayle opposes both practical guidelines and an ideal of asceticism, enabling the *savant* to retain his liberty of judgement. In the first place, echoing La Mothe Le Vayer and, behind him, Lucian,[64] the historian is advised to avoid writing about contemporary affairs. The French historian Du Haillan is proposed, in this instance, as an example to be emulated ('Haillan', footnote E):

Les Raisons, qui portérent [Du Haillan] à terminer son Ouvrage à Charles VII, marquent qu'il entendoit les devoirs d'un Historien. J'entens principalement la Réfléxion qu'il a faite qu'on s'expose à une fâcheuse alternative quand on travaille à l'Histoire des

63. 'Ovide', footnote G: 'Voici ses paroles: il est nécessaire que je les produise, afin de faciliter la voie de l'examen à ceux qui voudront se convaincre si j'en tire ou non le sens véritable'. Cf. 'Mariana', footnote D; 'Bonfadius', footnote D.

64. La Mothe Le Vayer, *Discours de l'histoire*, in *Œuvres*, ii.146-47; Lucian, *How to write history* (London 1959), p.71. Many of Bayle's ideals for letters are strikingly similar to those proposed by Lucian.

Monarques qui sont morts depuis peu de tems. Il faut, ou dissimuler la vérité, ou irriter des personnes de qui l'on a tout à craindre. Le premier de ces inconvéniens choque l'honneur & la conscience de l'Historien; l'autre choque sa prudence: il vaut donc mieux ne rien dire.

A choice between expediency and conscience is forced on the historian of contemporary affairs. If he decides in favour of conscience, then opposition to his work will eventually trammel his scholarly output. If, on the other hand, he opts for expediency, historical truth will inevitably suffer. Surprising as it may at first seem in one who argues that truth is the soul of history ('Remond', footnote D), in the face of this dilemma Bayle recommends a prudent silence ('Capriata', footnote C). Prudence is not a betrayal of truth and conscience but a protection of them. It not only safeguards history from alteration – more difficult to correct at a later date – it also shields the *savant* from temptation and ensures his liberty to continue his work.

In the second place, Bayle frowns on patronage and dedicatory prefaces. To his mind, they compromise the scholar's integrity:

Car, autant que seroit loüable la sincérité d'un Historien qui auroit blamé justement la conduite d'un Monarque, & raporté fidélement les succès honteux qui l'auroient accompagnée, autant pourroit-on blâmer son imprudence s'il lui dédioit son Livre. C'est d'ailleurs la coutume de piper aux Souverains à qui l'on adresse un Ouvrage. On aspire à quelque pension, ou à quelque gratification; on sait donc ce qu'il faut dire & ce qu'il faut taire. On s'est réglé là-dessus dans tout le cours de l'Ouvrage, où l'on a parlé de leurs actions. Leur dédier un tel Ouvrage, qu'est-ce autre chose que notifier d'entrée de jeu qu'on a renoncé à la liberté, & qu'on cherche maître? N'est-ce pas pour le moins faire préjuger cela?[65]

The reflection pinpoints the irreconcilability of patronage and dedications with sincerity and objectivity. It is not inconceivable to Bayle that a historian who dedicates his work to a monarch has none the less avoided partiality. The dedication, however, prejudices the reader against the *bonne foi* of the author: it is frequently an indication that the scholar has cut his *récit* to please his patron. The historian is not only to reject sponsorship but also to eschew any appearance of patronage.

Such practical guidelines are common coinage in the 'Réflexions sur l'histoire' of Bayle's day.[66] The enunciation of a value system proper to the Republic of Letters announces the more personal voice of Bayle as a moralist. The spirit in evidence in the dedicatory preface is likened to the 'esprit mercenaire' which

---

65. 'Capriata', footnote D; cf. 'Haillan', footnote M. Bayle's position is shared by many of his contemporaries; see Perry, p.62. For the wider context of patronage in the *grand siècle*, a widespread practice, see Magne, i.314ff.; Raymond Picard, *La Carrière de Jean Racine* (Paris 1961), p.313-25, 359-75.

66. Rapin, *Réflexions sur l'histoire*, in *Œuvres*, ii.307-12; Le Clerc, *Parrhasiana*, i.152.

informs the world at large. The general run of humanity, he muses,

Ce sont des personnes qu'on ne contente presque jamais, toûjours prêtes à demander de nouveaux honneurs, & de plus grans appointemens, à se plaindre de la petitesse des récompenses, à étaler leurs services, à murmurer si on les oublie pendant que l'on songe à d'autres, à menacer de se retirer, à faire paroître leur mécontentement par des démarches brusques, audacieuses, etc.[67]

To this pessimistic picture of the *homo homini lupus*[68] is opposed an ideal of disinterestedness which is to characterise the man of letters: '[les] Muses [...] devroient jouïr [de la gloire] d'inspirer à leurs Sectateurs un véritable desintéressement, & un généreux mépris des richesses, & des récompenses publiques'.[69] There is a hint not only of Epicurean or Stoic simplicity but also of a new *élite* in this picture of scholarly simplicity. The *passions du cœur* of a Maimbourg are undermined by that *générosité* of spirit recommended by the neo-Stoics and Descartes[70] as a check on the baser instincts. The *savant* is to distinguish himself from the *peuple* – whether peasant, bourgeois or aristocrat – by being content with his books and the satisfaction of his basic needs.[71] His 'application continuelle à composer de bons Livres' is to be regarded not as a basis for the pursuit of wealth but as 'une civilité envers le public' ('Alciat, (André)', footnote G). In a word, the scholar is to be characterised by a single-minded consecration to 'l'instruction du public'.[72] Indeed, if fame is important to the man of letters then he is reminded that the 'grandeur' and 'beauté' 'du don gratuit' alone earn for the *savant* the only title worth possessing: 'un bon titre de noblesse dans la République des Sciences'.[73]

The Cartesian-Stoical overtones of the position are integrated, however, into a Christian-Stoic[74] conception of the ethics of the Republic of Letters. Echoing

67. 'Haillan', footnote M. It is interesting to note that Faret, in his *Honneste homme*, evokes in similar terms the *esprit mercenaire* of the Court. The behaviour of the *honnête homme/homme de bien* is therefore opposed, as is Bayle's historian/*honnête homme*, to the *homme mondain* (Faret, p.8, 33ff.).

68. On the Hobbesian context of this much cited adage in the *grand siècle*, see Pintard, i.552.

69. 'Haillan', footnote M. The ideal of disinterested scholarship is one which Bayle holds in common with the Renaissance: see Jehasse, p.61-62.

70. Descartes, *Les Passions*, §L-LIV, p.105-109.

71. This notion of the *respublica literaria* as 'une caste savante' was current among the *libertins érudits*: see Pintard, p.77-79.

72. 'Peiresc', *in corp.*; 'Hall (Joseph)', footnote B.

73. 'Haillan', footnote M; 'Launoi, (Jean de)', footnote B; 'Préface de la première édition', §VI, in *Dictionnaire*, i.x.

74. On the development of Christian Stoicism in the seventeenth century, see Julien-Eymard d'Angers, 'Le renouveau du stoïcisme au XVIe et au XVIIe siècles', in *Recherches sur le stoïcisme*, p.1-32, and by the same author, 'Le stoïcisme en France dans la première moitié du XVIIe siècle', in *idem*, p.33-105. The author distinguishes between the Stoicism of Descartes and that of Christian humanism: the latter is open to 'la foi révélée', the former 'se [renferme] dans les limites de la raison' ('Le renouveau', p.28-29). He argues, however, that Stoicism amongst Protestant humanists

the image the humanists had of themselves, Bayle presents Pierre Bunel as a type of the ideal scholar ('Bunel', *in corp.*):

[cet honnête homme] fut encore plus recommandable par ses bonnes mœurs, que par la délicatesse de son style. On ne le vit point courir après les richesses, & après les établissemens de la fortune: content du nécessaire, il ne s'appliquoit qu'à la culture de son ame.

The *honnêteté* of the scholar's erudition is to be accompanied by an ethical behaviour, liberating him for the 'culture de son ame'. In the commentary on this 'portrait du cœur', occurring in a related footnote, the *philosophe* of Rotterdam presents 'ce mépris des biens & des dignitez, qui faisoit le caractere de notre Bunel' as a practical expression of 'les préceptes de Jesus-Christ touchant le mépris du monde'. Moreover, the sixteenth-century scholar is seen somewhat naively as putting into practice the first proposition of the Reformed catechism: 'Ceux de la Religion ont un petit Catéchisme, où la prémière Demande est, "Pourquoi Dieu nous a-t-il mis au monde?": Le Catéchumene répond, "pour le connoître & servir".'[75] That is to say, to the image of the venal historian, represented by Maimbourg, is opposed the picture of the ascetic scholar who controls his passions – avarice and ambition – in order to devote himself entirely to the pursuit of learning. Not only that, such unworldliness is presented as a profoundly spiritual approach to the profession of letters.[76] The *honnête homme*, whose single-minded scholarship is disinterested, not only serves but also honours God with his pen.

The dialogue between classicism, ethics and scholarship continues in the consideration of the style proper to history. The ambivalence to oratory evinced in the reaction to Maimbourg reappears in a distinction of two styles, one for rhetorical, the other for historical purposes. With Rapin, Bayle argues that, given the rhetorician's task of stirring his audience to agreement, he may legitimately devote more attention to developing a 'style figuré', 'flatteur' and 'pompeux', which appeals to the passions and the imagination of the public.[77] Such a style cannot, however, be used in history, whose aim is to enlighten rather than to persuade. This rationalistic conception of 'le discours historique' is very clearly expressed by Rapin:

L'Histoire qui est simple & naïve, & qui ne veut point m'en faire accroire, doit me laisser

has no adherents in the *grand siècle* ('Le stoïcisme', p.79), an argument undermined by the case of Pierre Bayle; see below, p.189ff.

75. 'Bunel', footnote C; cf. 'Préface de la première édition', §VI, in *Dictionnaire*, i.x, where the 'désintéressement' of the scholar is seen as part of the charitable disposition recommended by the Gospels.

76. On the spirituality of the act of learning, see Fumaroli, p.685-87; Tocanne, p.410ff.

77. 'Baudoüin', footnote E; 'Theopompe', footnote C.

le cœur libre pour juger plus sainement de ce qu'elle me dit. L'Eloquence, qui par son caractere est un Art imposteur, peut entreprendre sur ma liberté, en s'efforçant de me persuader malgré moi. Mais l'Histoire qui se renferme dans les bornes d'une instruction toute pure, ne peut avec bien-seance se servir de figures, que pour ôter au discours sa froideur naturelle, & pour le rendre moins ennuieux.[78]

The remark is typical of that suspicion of eloquence as an 'Art imposteur' – parallel to a similar sixteenth-century attitude (Fumaroli, p.427ff.) – to be found among *érudits* in the latter half of the seventeenth century. Its appeal to the heart precipitates the uninformed consent of the mind, an epistemology of persuasion, in Bayle's terms, depraved in the *theological* sense (see above, p.81ff.). *Bienséance* becomes the criterion of the style appropriate to history, an opinion echoed in a variety of remarks on historical style, scattered in the *magnum opus*. 'La grandeur', muses Bayle, '& la majesté du sujet doit attirer toute l'attention de l'Ecrivain',[79] and style merely adds 'agréments' to the narrative.[80] This is not to argue that questions of style are extrinsic to historical composition, for to the 'style figuré', appealing to the imagination, is opposed the 'style simple', appealing to the mind alone, which is to typify history. The qualities of 'gravité', 'simplicité' and 'netteté' –[81] also noted by Bodin (*Methodus*, p.300) – are both recommended and praised when observed in historians: 'M. Spon s'est conduit [dans son Histoire] selon les veritables regles de l'art Historique, qui demande beaucoup d'ordre, un style net, court, simple, sans affectation, sans figures, ni autres ornemens oratoires'.[82] The 'style simple' is a fitting companion to the ideal of historical objectivity. It constitutes that unmediated discourse which, leaving the heart or the imagination untouched, allows the reader's judgement to function unfettered.

The question of the propriety, or *bienséance*, of unmediated discourse was to the fore in the debates concerning Christian eloquence that took place between Jansenists and Protestants following the publication in 1671 of Nicole's *Prejugez legitimes*. The dispute revitalises not only the reaction to Garasse's *Doctrine curieuse* (Fumaroli, p.323ff.) but also the critique of Jesuit eloquence and *la parole satirique* undertaken in Pascal's *Provinciales*.[83] In his evaluation of the arguments, Bayle uses the criteria of 'la raillerie chrétienne' present in the

78. Rapin, *Réflexions sur l'histoire*, in *Œuvres*, ii.273; cf. *La Logique*, III, 20, p.340-42; 'Spinoza', footnote A.
79. 'Theopompe', footnote C; cf. 'Ermite', footnote G.
80. 'Maimbourg', footnote D; cf. 'Emile', footnotes C and D.
81. 'Camden', *in corp.*; 'Remond', footnote D; 'Theopompe', footnote C.
82. *NRL*, janvier 1685, art.iv, *OD*, i.202. The ideal of unmediated discourse is one shared by Bayle with his contemporaries, see Peter France, *Rhetoric and truth in France* (Oxford 1972), *passim*; Michel Foucault, *Les Mots et les choses* (Paris 1966), p.59ff. and 92ff.
83. Pascal, *Les Provinciales*, letter XI, p.193ff.

*Provinciales*, their sources and their followers, drives a wedge between them and Jansenist satire and offers a more radical interpretation of the ethics of invective. Invoking the rule of *decorum*, later to be used by our author in his critique of Maimbourg,[84] Nicole argues from the 'esprit de calomnie' of the Reformers' discourse in the sixteenth century that 'une malignité si noire & une haine si implacable' necessarily prove that the Reformation was the fruit of the devil and not of the Holy Spirit.[85] That is to say, as summarised later by Bayle, 'la médisance est le caractere perpétuel de l'Heresie' ('Beze', footnote B). 'Médisance' is, however, an equivocal sign of heresy, since it is capable of being reversed against Port-Royal, whose 'éloquence', as our author later drily observes, 'outre toutes choses, & principalement l'invective'.[86] Consequently, in *Le Renversement de la morale de Jésus-Christ* of the following year, Arnauld picks up the definition of that 'éloquence [...] qui soit digne, je ne dis pas d'un Théologien & d'un Chrestien, mais mesme d'un honneste homme', earlier given in the *Perpétuité* (1669-1674) and the *Provinciales*, and applies it to the case in hand. To the authors of the *Perpétuité*, Christian eloquence is 'sage, modeste, judicieuse, sincere, veritable' and expounds the truth 'd'une maniere propre à la faire entrer dans l'esprit & dans le cœur'.[87] The preacher must, therefore, stir the heart to embrace the truth which the mind perceives. Arnauld very cleverly turns this definition into a defence of the 'expressions trop dures' used by the Jansenists in their many controversies. For, he argues, to use the word 'fausse' to describe an opinion which is 'veritablement impie' is to appeal only to the mind: 'quand la notion de fausseté seroit suffisante, pour en détourner l'esprit des lecteurs, je serois obligé d'y joindre celle d'impiété pour en détourner encore leur cœur avec plus de force & d'efficace'.[88] Here is an epistemology of persuasion – worthy of the inquisitorial eloquence of Garasse (Fumaroli, p.327) – which justifies a certain satirical turn of phrase. Truth turns 'médisance' into an expression of pastoral concern: thereby, the public is made to flee errors which would otherwise lead to damnation.

The two Protestant replies singled out for attention by Bayle are those by Jean Claude in his *Défense de la Réformation* (1673) and Jean Graverol, *L'Eglise protestante justifiée par l'Eglise romaine* (1682). Neither author is insensitive to the reversibility of the Jansenists' argument for, as Graverol remarks, 'ce célébre

84. Fumaroli, p.330. Above, p.76.
85. Nicole, *Prejugez*, ch.11, p.270, 272, 273, 291; cf. *La Perpetuité de la foy de l'Eglise catholique touchant l'eucharistie* (Paris 1669-1674), bk.XI, ch.8, p.131-32.
86. *NLC*, letter v, §iii, *OD*, ii.193b; cf. Claude, *La Défense*, part II, ch.6, p.149-50.
87. Above, fn. 83. *Perpétuité*, bk.XI, ch.8, p.130.
88. *Le Renversement de la morale de Jésus-Christ, par les erreurs des calvinistes, touchant la justification* (1672), in *Œuvres*, xiii.84.

M. Arnaud fait dans son *renversement* l'Apologie du style de nos Réformateurs, en voulant défendre le sien' (p.269). Jansenist pastoral concern becomes in Claude's defence 'une véritable compassion' (*La Défense*, p.151):

bien loin qu'on doive imputer ce qu'ils en ont dit à une haine ou à une aversion implacable contre l'Eglise Romaine, comme fait l'Auteur des Préjugez, il le faut au-contraire attribuer à une véritable compassion qu'ils ont euë pour le peuple de Dieu, de le voir si mal instruit, si mal conduit, si mal gouverné, & à un desir ardent de procurer une bonne réformation dans tout le corps de l'Eglise Latine. Et plus leur compassion étoit grande, plus leur étoit-il difficile de traiter cette matiére sans donner atteinte aux personnes en qui la source de tout le mal résidoit [...].

That is to say, a parallel epistemology of persuasion is implicit in the Protestant's argument. Catholic error had caused such an 'assoupissement' in its devotees (and such horror in the Reformers) that emotive and vehement expressions were necessary 'pour réveiller les hommes de ce profond sommeil où ils paroissoient étre depuis long-tems' (p.150). In a word, truth still whitewashes *médisance*; this time, however, the Janus-face of truth is Protestant.

None the less, the second stage of the argument from 'les circonstances du tems' constitutes, for Bayle, 'la meilleure Apologie qu'on puisse faire'.[89] To Claude's mind, the Reformers had been provoked: firstly, by the 'défense opiniâtrée qu'on faisoit des erreurs & des abus' and, secondly, by the 'persécutions qu'ils avoient à soûtenir'. Thus, Roman Catholic 'opiniâtreté' forced the *réformés* to employ strong expressions in order to unmask 'la grossiéreté des abus que la Cour de Rome défendoit' and 'pour fortifier leurs fréres qu'ils voyoient par tout dans les fers des Inquisitions'.[90] Nevertheless, such a defence has the disadvantage of inadvertently encouraging reciprocal violence in language. Consequently, it is Graverol's emphasis on the *décalage* between the literary styles of the sixteenth and seventeenth centuries which earns Bayle's approval. The Reformers, when not writing in Latin, used a 'vieux Gaulois', poles apart from the 'nouvelle civilité' of the *grand siècle*.[91] While the distinction mitigates the culpability of the *réformés*, it does not, for Bayle, excuse their violent discourse: *vieux Gaulois* and moderation are not mutually exclusive. Nor is he happy with the argument from epistemology; it fails to establish which party, if any, has a right to speak vehemently:

On dira sans doute que ces exemples n'autorisent que les injures qui partent d'un véritable zele pour la vérité, & qu'ainsi les Hérétiques ne peuvent pas s'en servir. 'Vous avez raison', répondra le Socinien, '& ainsi tout ce que vous êtes de Papistes & de Calvinistes dans le monde, devez vous [en] départir [...] & me le laisser à moi, qui parle

89. *NLC*, letter VI, §xi, *OD*, ii.201a.
90. Claude, *La Défense*, p.150-51.
91. *NLC*, letter VI, §xi, *OD*, ii.201a; Graverol, p.261.

pour la vérité contre les Hérésies que vous enseignez.'[92]

If truth justifies *médisance*, every heretic who sincerely believes he possesses the truth may legitimately vituperate his opponent. The argument simultaneously deprives the Jansenists and the Calvinists of their defences and prepares the ground for the more radical solution: a solution, moreover, with the side-effect of reversing against Jansenism the attacks against Protestantism. Arnauld's justification of satire by truth is shown to constitute a 'renversement de la Morale de Jesus-Christ'.

Returning to an earlier debate between the Jansenists and the Jesuits, Bayle indicates from Arnauld's *Réponse à la lettre d'une personne de condition* (1654), the source for the *Provinciale* letter on the subject,[93] that Port-Royal justifies its vehemence by appealing to Scripture and the Church Fathers. The Almighty, in his banishment of Adam and Eve from paradise, the prophets inspired by the Holy Spirit, Jesus Christ in his censure of the Jews and Pharisees, the apostles and Fathers from Tertullian to Chrysostom, are proven to have used and considered it legitimate to use *raillerie* and indignation in their discourses against their opponents.[94] To Bayle's mind, such arguments are an 'abus de la parole de Dieu', an attempt to 'canoniser [nos défauts]' and to make them 'vénérable sous la protection divine'.[95] While the special authority of God and those inspired by him – prophets and apostles – sanctions these examples of vehemence, it cannot be extended to the common run of humanity.[96] The Fathers – here Bayle speaks with a Protestant voice[97] – as fallible human beings, are an example to be followed with caution.[98] With divine exceptions, therefore, authors and preachers are bid to remain within 'le chemin battu de l'Evangile'[99] and to follow the spirit of the Gospel:

Il est certain que l'esprit général de la Religion Chretienne est la douceur, la modestie, l'humilité, la patience. Toute la vie de Jesus-Christ nous est un modele de ces admirables vertus. Ses discours ne respirent que cela; il nous recommande sans cesse de n'offenser personne, non pas même ceux qui nous offensent [...] La vie & les exhortations de ses

92. *NLC*, letter VI, §viii, *OD*, ii.199b; the question recurs in 'Luther', footnote T, and a similar conclusion is reached.

93. Pascal, *Les Provinciales*, letter XI, p.196, n.1.

94. [Antoine Arnauld], *Réponse à la lettre d'une personne de condition touchant les règles de la conduite des saints Pères dans la composition de leurs ouvrages, pour la défense des vérités combattues ou de l'innocence calomniée* (dated 20 mars 1654), p.11ff. The work is reprinted in the *Œuvres*, vol. xxvii.

95. *NLC*, letter VI, §§i & ii, *OD*, ii.196a; cf. below, p.168ff., for the place of this attitude in Bayle's hermeneutic.

96. *NLC*, letter VI, §vii, *OD*, ii.199b.

97. Cf. *PD*, §CIII, *OD*, iii.71a-b; Jean Daillé, *Traicté de l'employ des saincts peres* (Genève 1632), p.292-300, and 'Daillé', and footnote H, for Bayle's appreciation of the work.

98. *NLC*, letter VI, §ix, *OD*, ii.200a.

99. *NLC*, letter VI, §vii, *OD*, ii.198b.

Apôtres tendent principalement à nous former à la pratique de ces vertus.[100]

While for the defenders of *médisance* truth was the justification of *la parole satirique*, for the *philosophe* of Rotterdam truth necessitates the eschewing of violence. In practice, to follow the spirit of the Gospel means that writers and preachers are to 'soutenir les interêts de la vérité, sans sortir des bornes de la modestie'.[101] In a word, embracing the position of Christian and Erasmian humanists, Bayle maintains that *raillerie* is not only an improper proof, it is utterly at variance with Christian apologetics.[102]

The rhetoric of denunciation (Fumaroli, p.328) is to be replaced, where error must be censured, by an art of correction based not on insult but on charity. The critic is to distinguish between the sin and the sinner, the doctrine and the heretic, the error and the erring:

Savons-nous bien précisément, si un homme qui passe pour Hypocrite, est Hypocrite? Savons-nous bien précisément, si celui qui s'oppose au progrès de la vérité, le fait par malice, ou par ignorance? Ne faut-il pas que l'indignation qui nous est permise contre le vice en général, s'appaise en faveur de la personne vicieuse qui nous doit être toûjours chere? Ne faut-il pas que les déclamations véhémentes poussées contre le péché en général, se convertissent en douces exhortations, quand il s'agit de guérir le péché en particulier? Car si vous traitez la personne du pécheur comme vous traitez le péché, ce que vous faites a plûtôt l'air d'une querelle d'Allemand, que d'une œuvre charitable.[103]

Bayle's position, like that of his humanist forebears (Fumaroli, *passim*), could not be more clear: the justification of stylistic violence by confessional orthodoxy becomes impossible; he has shifted the criterion of *médisance* from doctrine to ethics. Consequently, the writer for whom vehement style is an expression of 'le doigt de Dieu' appears as a charlatan, eager to mask moral failing by a misguided appeal to Christian teaching. Christian charity demands that divisive and hostile feelings be rigorously excluded from all discourse directed against an opponent.

100. *NLC*, letter VI, §v, *OD*, ii.197-98; cf. letter XXI, §xx, *OD*, ii.320b-21a.

101. *NLC*, letter VI, §iv, *OD*, ii.197a. The opposition between satire and the spirit of the Gospel, already present in *PD* (§CLXX), returns in the *Avis important*, e.g. 'il n'y a pas de corruption plus opposée à l'esprit du Christianisme que cet acharnement satyrique' (*OD*, ii.,564b-65a and also 567b-68a). The coherence of the view of satire in this work with the earlier *NLC* and the later (or contemporaneous) *Dissertation sur les libelles diffamatories* leads me to adhere to Elisabeth Labrousse's argument, that Bayle contributed to the first draft of the *Avis* left to him by Larroque (*Pierre Bayle*, i.219-21). Not only do similar political and literary themes recur throughout our author's writings but the Scriptural and patristic sources are the same in all passages and works treating the satiric mode.

102. Cf. Fumaroli, p.330, and Corrado Vivanti, *Lotta politica e pace religiosa in Francia fra cinque e seicento* (Torino 1974), p.13-14, for Bayle's antecedents.

103. *NLC*, letter VI, §vi, *OD*, ii.198b; cf. 'Alciat, (Jean-Paul)', footnote D; 'Erasme', footnote I. The position is seen by Bayle as a rejection of Ciceronian eloquence: see *NLC*, letter VI, §§xiii, xiv, *OD*, ii.201b-202b.

The affinities of Bayle's position on style and his arguments on toleration, later developed at length in the *Commentaire philosophique*, are remarkable. In the first place, a similar epistemology pervades both positions: violence, whether physical or verbal, stirs the heart and the passions in such a way as to cloud the judgement.[104] As a persuasive technique violence necessarily produces hypocrisy and martyrdom or 'opiniâtreté' in opinion and is self-defeating.[105] Religious toleration and stylistic moderation are presented as a more effective means of persuasion: the mind, liberated from the disruptive influence of the passions, is free to consider the opinions presented to it.[106] In the second place, the connection between orthodoxy and stylistic or physical violence is shown to lead to generalised aggression: heretic and orthodox alike are convinced of the 'objective' truth of their respective positions. In consequence, verbal and physical brutality are *both* deprived of their legitimacy by an appeal to the *subjectivity* of religious certitude.[107] In the third place, the argument from Christian ethics in matters of style has its exact counterpart in the *Commentaire philosophique*, where persecution is portrayed as undermining both natural law and the spirit of the Gospel (see below, p.165ff.). Moderation in style and toleration in religion are, therefore, both seen as a practical expression of 'la Morale de Jesus-Christ'. Bayle's position is, at one and the same time, rationalist and moralistic. The 'style simple' becomes in the issue of 'la parole satirique' a literary mode concerned with things rather than words.[108] Emotive language, as an *acte de violence* against the conscience, must be abandoned for the naked communication of mind with mind ('Amphiaraüs', footnote I), wherein the word serves the truth and is compatible with evangelical *douceur*. Consequently, arguing by analogy, to the verbal manifestations of passion and vengeance in Maimbourg the *philosophe* of Rotterdam opposes a more radical interpretation of the 'style sévère' (Fumaroli, p.436ff.) as 'le discours de la tolérance': the pen must not be wielded like a sword. The position throws light on the tenor of the articles

---

104. *NLC*, letter IX, *OD*, ii.217ff.; *CP*, part II, ch.9, *OD*, ii.427ff.
105. Labrousse, 'The political ideas', p.242.
106. *CP*, part II, ch.1, *OD*, ii.393ff.
107. *CP*, part II, chs.7 and 8, *OD*, ii.419ff.
108. Arnauld saw this concern with things rather than words as typically Protestant (*Le Renversement*, in *Œuvres*, xli.86). Peter France indicates, however, that a rationalist approach was also to be found among the Jansenists (p.27-28; cf. Fumaroli, p.3). It is interesting to note, moreover, that the conception of the 'style simple' as unmediated discourse and its opposition to the 'style figuré', which is seen as a medium proper to the expression of *passion*, is present in *La Logique*, I, xiv, p.131 (*Œuvres*, xli.236). However, while the authors deem it necessary to employ a 'style simple' in philosophical discourse, the 'style figuré' is deemed necessary for preaching, where man's salvation is at stake. Bayle links his attitude to Maimbourg's satirical discourse with the definition of 'fausse éloquence' given in the *Logique* (*CG*, letter XI, §iii, *OD*, ii.47b; *Logique*, III, xx, p.340 in *Œuvres*, xli.342).

'Agreda' and 'Nestorius'. The urbanity of the one and the tolerant perspective of the other testify to a reconciliation of conviction and *douceur* which, by masterly irony and a *rhétorique des sources*, attempts to provoke 'le rire des *honnêtes gens*'.[109]

Good learning is complemented, then, by an *honnêteté*, not only moral but profoundly Christian, albeit with Stoical overtones. The spectre of Maimbourg, however, hangs over Bayle's reflections; the fallibility and moral weakness of human nature bore from within and threaten to render impossible any approximation to the ideal of the *République des lettres*. Consequently, to the ideals are added the means whereby they may be implemented to a greater or lesser degree. Firstly comes the tentative suggestion that godliness and good learning may in some cases result from the influence of divine grace and, secondly, that criticism can produce a utilitarian version of the same qualities (below, p.189ff.). A passing remark in the discussion of the 'style modéré', analysed above, hints at the necessity of divine intervention in the profession of letters. It occurs during the protestations against the justification, from Scripture and the Fathers, of *raillerie* and *injures*.[110] Addressing his fictitious correspondent, Bayle observes (*NLC*, letter VI, §ii, *OD*, ii.196a):

Vous ne haïssez point la raillerie, ni moi non-plus; mais au moins avons-nous la discrétion de ne pas prétendre que ce soit une vertu Chretienne. Nous avouons que c'est un défaut, & une suite du peché originel, dont nous serions déja guéris, si notre régeneration étoit un peu plus avancée.

Given that satire is a verbal expression of a *cœur dépravé*, abandonment of stylistic vehemence is fleetingly presented as the fruit of regeneration and sanctification.[111] It would be unwise to attribute too much importance to the remark. It is not inconceivable, however, that to the notion of the Republic of Letters as an intellectual élite characterised by a distinctive value system, Bayle adds that of a learned elect, divinely empowered to honour the godhead with the pen.[112]

The elect are few in number and still subject to failure. In the second place,

---

109. Fumaroli, p.327; below, p.233ff.

110. The justification of satire by Scripture and the Fathers is a commonplace with a long tradition. For example, Beza saw fit to defend Calvin in this way in his edition of the Reformer's *Opera*: cf. Olivier Millet, 'Calvin pamphlétaire', in *Le Pamphlet en France au XVIe siècle*, Colloque du Centre V. L. Saulnier, 1983.

111. Regeneration seems to be confused here with sanctification: see Rébelliau, p.24, for the background to this.

112. 'Launoi, (Jean de)', footnote B, where the theologian's disinterested pursuit of truth is presented as a sign that 'la Providence n'abandonne pas entiérement le genre humain à la corruption'. Beaujot draws a similar conclusion from the *Pensées diverses*; see Pintard, i.512 for the elitism of the *libertins*, by whom Bayle is influenced; Labrousse, *Bayle* (Past Masters), p.5, 52.

the author of the *Dictionnaire* stresses the importance of criticism as a means of alerting the scholar to his failings and stirring him to greater efforts. Some writers are resentful of criticism (*Projet*, vi.2980):

quand on censure [les Auteurs], on s'expose à leur propre ressentiment, s'ils vivent encore, ou à celui de leur famille, s'ils sont décédez. Or ce n'est pas un petit ressentiment que celui de Messieurs les Auteurs: ils passent pour extrémement sensibles, mal-endurans, & vindicatifs; & l'on diroit que leur parenté se croit obligée à perpétuer après leur mort, l'amour aveugle qu'ils ont eue pour les productions de leur Esprit.

Resistance to criticism is presented as the fruit of *amour-propre*. The author's reputation is wounded and his self-esteem suffers a blow. Bayle is impatient with such self-interest:

Enfin, il faut que l'on considere, que l'intérêt du public doit l'emporter sur celui des particuliers, & qu'un Auteur ne mérite point de complaisance, lorsqu'il est assez injuste pour aimer mieux que ses Fautes demeurent cachées, que de voir le public désabusé.

Private interest must give way before public good. The *savant* wedded to the truth above all things will readily accept any criticism which contributes to *la recherche de la vérité*.

The fraternal and gentle spirit, defended in the discussion of the *discours modéré*, is to prevail, palliating the injury to *amour-propre*. The scholar is to remember his own weakness and avoid insult, in the knowledge that one day the roles may be reversed.[113] Courtesy, moreover, is a prerequisite for the pursuance of the ideals of the lettered Republic; by avoiding personal animosity, it allows men of learning to strive together after truth:

plus on critique les choses avec raison, plus on montre combien il est difficile d'être parfaitement éxact. Or en portant si haut l'idée de la parfaite éxactitude, on engage les Auteurs à être plus sur leurs gardes, & à examiner tout avec un extreme soin. L'homme n'est que trop accoutumé à demeurer au deça des regles; il faut donc les reculer le plus qu'on peut, si l'on veut qu'il joigne de près le point de la perfection.[114]

113. 'Henichius', footnote A, cf. 'Suetone' (2nd article), footnote A and 'Catius', footnote D; *Projet*, §vi, in *Dictionnaire*, iv.2980-81; cf. 'Polonus', footnote B. The desire not to offend the *amour-propre* of an author indicates the influence of Nicole (*Essais de morale*, Paris 1671, i.254-301), cited by Bayle in the *NLC*. The Jansenist's notion of fraternal correction includes the means to 'conserver la paix avec les hommes' in the act of criticism. The critic is instructed to couch his critique in such a way as to make the *amour-propre* of the person being criticised serve the good intentions of the critic. This conception of the *manière honnête et civile* of correction is present in Saint-Réal's *De la critique*, in *Œuvres* (Amsterdam 1750), iv.189-202, on which Bayle draws, not without reserves, in 'Catius', footnote D. For the manifestations of this attitude in the Renaissance, see Mesnard, 'Le commerce épistolaire', p.29-31; Jehasse, p.242.

114. *Projet*, §vii, in *Dictionnaire*, iv.2981; cf. *Dissertation sur les libelles diffamatoires*, iv.2956; not only is an author to be open to criticism, he is also actively to solicit it: 'Abelly (Antoine)', *in corp.* and footnote A; *Projet* ..., §ii, in *Dictionnaire*, iv.2977.

This idea of perfect scholarship, shared by Bayle with humanist thinkers (Huppert, *passim*), is the final justification of fraternal correction. Criticism sets the scholar's aspirations soaring to attain the elusive ideal. The emphasis, like that of the *Dictionnaire*, is on the open-endedness of historical scholarship and, far from pessimistic, reveals a belief in the *perfectionnement* of history. Complete impartiality and objectivity may not be of this world but the man of letters, by interaction with his critically minded fellows, may be taught to approach ever nearer to perfection.

In conclusion, the manifesto of the Republic of Letters, Bayle's conception of ideal scholarship and scholars and his own unremitting practice testify to an implicit and occasionally explicit dialectic in his historiography. To decadent eloquence is opposed the rhetoric of sources, to malicious satire *la douceur évangélique*; the *historien étourdi* is challenged by the *historien judicieux*, his authoritarian historiography by exactitude and examination of sources. Moreover, the dialectic reposes on a conception of two *kinds* of history: the one informs and propagates a received tradition, the other embarks on the voyage of rediscovery known in humanist circles as *le retour aux sources* (below, p.119). In other words, Bayle stands simultaneously at the crossroads of the development of historical scholarship and the dawn of a new age. The dialectic of rhetoric and erudition continues in the next century, reaching a synthesis only in the nineteenth century in that modern scholarship of which our author is one of the founding fathers.[115] Nevertheless, while the *Dictionnaire* and the related works are publications ahead of their time, in their espousal of certain ideals and of a notion of the spirituality of the act of learning they belong to an earlier and perhaps, given the success of Maimbourg, even an anachronistic age. Not only that, the opposition between the critically established fact and its source and popular, imaginative culture and tradition may announce the Enlightenment, but its presence in the writings of the *philosophe* of Rotterdam, far from a *libertinage*[116] or an early positivism (Delvolvé, *passim*), is the fruit of a gaze turned both inwards and on the past. Scholarship, undertaken in an Erasmian spirit, is a pursuit executed *sub specie aeternitatis*: whether by grace or a Christian-Stoic mastery of the self, the writer is answerable not to politico-religious leaders but to God. The concern with truth at all costs is a religious commitment in the deepest sense. The elect or élite of the Republic of Letters may write very differently from the Maimbourgs of this world, but their espousal of truth over confessionalism is not a sign of latent unbelief but a response to a higher calling.

---

115. Momigliano, p.1-27; Kelley, *passim*.

116. Historians like Pasquier, who approached their sources critically, were accused by Garasse of libertinism (Huppert, p.172ff.).

They too are committed writers, committed to the ideals of the *République des lettres*. The ideals may be secularised, the spirituality diluted, but they none the less reside in a fundamentally theological vision of the world and its microcosm, the lettered fraternity. Theology and scholarship, moreover, continue hand in hand in the methodological considerations to be explored in our next chapter.

# III. History, criticism and faith

# 5. 'Les têtes de l'Hydre':[1]
## theological method and historical method

Lactance, le Ciceron des Theologiens, nous donne un precepte [...] ce
sçavant Theologien nous advertit que le premier degré de sagesse [...] est
de cognoistre

*Quid solidum crepet, & pictae tectoria linguae*

discerner & choisir le vray d'avec le faux, trier le diamant entre les
hapelourdes, & en un mot ne se laisser surprendre à aucune chose, pour
laquelle on puisse estre quelque jour soupçonné d'une trop grande legereté.
*Primus*, dit-il, *sapientiae gradus, est falsa intelligere.*

Gabriel Naudé, *Instruction à la France sur la verité de l'histoire des freres de la
Roze-Croix*[2]

Bien des gens sans doute s'inscriront en faux contre l'exemple de la Papesse
Jeanne. On peut dire qu'elle a donné occasion à un des plus grands
problêmes historiques, qui peut-être ayent jamais été proposez. Presque
tout le monde étoit déjà disposé à regarder comme une fable tout ce qu'on
a dit d'elle, lorsque feu M. Spanheim publia un Ouvrage pour soûtenir le
contraire. Cet Ouvrage, & la belle Traduction méthodique & abrégée que
M. L'Enfant en donna, fit revenir bien des gens de cette pensée. Les raisons
de M. Spanheim ne parurent néanmoins pas convaincantes à M. Bayle, il
promit de les refuter d'une maniére qui ne souffriroit pas de replique. On
assûre qu'il a tenu parole, & que cela se trouvera dans le Supplement de
son Dictionnaire, qu'on imprime actuellement à Rotterdam.

Sallengre, *Memoires de litterature* (i.45-46).

A DUALITY necessarily results from the interplay between pessimism and ideal-
ism in Bayle's conception of the Republic of Letters. That is to say, the division
of the scholarly community into ethical and unethical writers inevitably entails
a conception of the learned enterprise as a war, from within and without,
between truth and error. As the critique of Maimbourg illustrates, moreover, a
conception of history arises out of this duality, wherein the co-existence of *la
vérité* and *le mensonge* leads to a notion of two historical traditions:

On supose que le mensonge est toûjours postérieur à la vérité; mais cela n'est point

---

1. The phrase is Bayle's, in *Projet*, §i, *Dictionnaire*, iv.2976, but the image of the scholar as a
Hercules vanquishing the hydra is common to sixteenth-century scholars. Cf. E. F. Rice, Jr., 'The
humanist idea of Christian antiquity and the impact of Greek patristic work on sixteenth-century
thought', in *Classical influences on European culture (1500-1700)* (Cambridge 1975), p.202.

2. Gabriel Naudé, *Instruction à la France sur la vérité de l'histoire des frères de la Roze-Croix* (Paris
1623), p.17-18.

certain par raport aux relations: il n'arrive que trop souvent que les fausses précédent les vraies, ou qu'elles n'en soient jamais suivies; il arrive très souvent que les véritables, & les fausses se forment à la même heure, & ainsi elles courent dans les siecles à venir sous les auspices d'une Tradition également vieille.[3]

Quite apart from being characteristic of Bayle's approach to history, the statement reflects a division in historiography at the end of the seventeenth century. Increasingly scholars distinguish the *ars critica*, a method of interpreting and criticising sources, from the *ars historica*, essentially a rhetorical and derivative treatment of history (Momigliano, p.2, 7, 11). To the author of the *Dictionnaire*, however, the two are frequently confused, notably in histories soundly documented but which fail to cite their sources (above, p.102ff.). The composition of history, then, depends on the discernment and separation of the two traditions.

The pessimism inherent in his perception of historical error as frequently anterior, if not contemporary, to historical truth implies that the first concern of the *ars critica* is to pursue and defuse 'le mensonge',[4] associated in Bayle's mind with the *ars historica*. Such in fact is the stated intention of the *Dictionnaire*, presented in the *Projet* (1692)[5] as a 'Chasse aux Fautes' (*Dictionnaire*, iv.2978-79):

J'ai dessein de composer un *Dictionaire*, qui, outre les Omissions considérables des autres, contiendra un Recueil des Faussetez qui concernent chaque Article. Et vous voiez bien, Monsieur, que si, par exemple j'étois venu à bout de recueillir, sous le mot *Seneque*, tout ce qui s'est dit de faux de cet illustre Philosophe, on n'auroit qu'à consulter cet Article pour savoir ce que l'on devroit croire, de ce qu'on liroit concernant Seneque dans quelque Livre que ce fût: car si c'étoit une Fausseté, elle seroit marquée dans le Recueil, & dès qu'on ne verroit pas dans ce Recueil un fait sur le pied de Fausseté, on le pourrait tenir pour véritable.

The *Dictionnaire* espouses the critical as opposed to the rhetorical tradition. Three images are used by the author to describe this projected enterprise: the *Dictionnaire critique* is presented as 'la pierre de touche des autres Livres', 'la Chambre des Assurances de la République des Lettres' and 'la Clef des Sources'.[6] In other words, the historical pyrrhonism for which our author is famed is a mitigated one: the 'Chasse aux Fautes' enables the critic, a scholarly

---

3. 'Usson', footnote F; cf. *Dissertation sur les libelles diffamatoires*, §VIII, *Dictionnaire*, iv.2951-52. In 'Usson' historical pyrrhonism is presented as a 'desordre qui doit principalement sa propagation au partage qui se fait dès le tems même qu'une chose arrive'.

4. See Naudé, *Apologie*, p.3-4, and La Mothe Le Vayer, *Du peu de certitude*, in *Œuvres*, xiii.417-18, for a similar pessimism.

5. This early conception of the *Dictionnaire* was altered, however, in response to public demand. See 'Préface de la première édition', *Dictionnaire*, i.1.

6. *Dictionnaire*, iv.2978-79; Naudé, *Apologie*, p.3-4, also espouses a notion of the work of criticism as the touchstone of other works.

Hercules, to bring the hydra of error to bay and thereby restore the truth to its rightful precedence.[7]

The preface to the first edition of the *Dictionnaire* (1697) suggests the means whereby the hydra of error is to be tracked and destroyed. When first mooted, the work was to be essentially one of 'Critique', and the use of the term is both self-conscious and symbolic. In discussing the validity of composing a purely critical *Dictionary*, the author points out that the errors he has collected 'ressemblent à celles qui ont été observées par les grans Critiques' and, in a marginal note, refers his readers to a work by Scaliger.[8] To the mind of the *philosophe* of Rotterdam, the great humanist enterprises of the sixteenth century constitute the inspiration and model for his *magnum opus*. A commentary on the seventeenth-century critic Reinesius, some years later, leaves us in no doubt as to the import of the association:

Ceux qui sont capables de juger d'une matiére de Litérature n'ont pas plutôt lu quelques pages de ses Ecrits, qu'ils le mettent hors du rang de ces Humanistes qui n'ont que de la mémoire, & qu'ils le placent parmi ces Critiques qui vont au delà de leur lecture, & qui sçavent plus de choses que les Livres ne leur en ont enseignées. La pénétration de leur esprit leur fait tirer des conséquences, & leur suggere des conjectures qui les conduisent à la découverte des thrésors cachez. Ils éclaircissent par ce moien les lieux les plus sombres de l'Erudition, & ils étendent les bornes de la science de l'Antiquité.[9]

The notion of two traditions reappears, this time based on an opposition of the faculties proper to historical composition: rejecting *mémoire-imagination*, our author establishes the *ex fontibus* approach to history on *mémoire-réminiscence-jugement* (above, p.92). Consequently, while the *Dictionnaire* is frequently referred to as an 'Ouvrage de Compilation', it is not conceived as the work of a 'simple copiste'. On the contrary, inspired by his forebears, 'les grans Critiques', Bayle is intent on selecting from the documentary evidence available to him the true reading of historical events. Like them, he is 'à la recherche de la plus authentique tradition de la vérité' (Jehasse, p.11, 39, 41).

The pursuit of authentic tradition is as double-edged for Bayle as it was for

---

7. Cf. *Projet*, §IX, *Dictionnaire*, iv.2984, and 'Beaulieu', footnote F, for the famous statement concerning the ontological superiority of certain historical facts over mathematics.

8. 'Préface de la première édition', §I, *Dictionnaire*, i.I, and marginal note I. For Scaliger, see Jehasse, *passim*.

9. 'Reinesius', *in corp.*. The article is an addition to the second edition of the *Dictionnaire* (1702). It might be noted in passing that Bayle's ideal scholar goes beyond the Rabelaisian ideal of the *abysme de science* and joins with Montaigne's emphasis on the *jugement* (*Essais*, I, 26). It is undoubtedly this perception of the formative nature of erudition which inspires the notion of its superiority to mathematics – a branch of human knowledge which Bayle never appreciated. Erudition has, then, for Bayle, the same didactic function as mathematics had for Descartes: it teaches the ability to discern truth from error. This conception of erudition is already present in that 'fourth generation' humanist Gabriel Naudé (*Apologie*, p.3-4, 634ff.).

the humanists. They, like him, were 'à la recherche d'une vérité qui désabuse'.[10] Inevitably, given Bayle's preoccupation with error, the term 'désabuser' recurs frequently under his pen. It is the scholar's task to disabuse his reading public of their acceptance of erroneous traditions, that is to say, of the 'fables', 'contes' or 'erreurs populaires', which they might otherwise accept as true.[11] In the seventeenth century, this perception of the pedagogic function of scholarship or philosophy is common to *libertins*, Cartesians and Protestants. In Bayle's theory and practice, however, the textual criticism of the humanists is transformed via *libertinage*, Cartesianism and Calvinism into a historical methodology.[12] The method evolves gradually to maturity. In the *Pensées diverses* theology, philosophy, and history form a critical kaleidoscope which serves to debunk the 'erreur populaire' of credulous belief in comets as supernatural phenomena. Later, in the *Continuation des Pensées diverses*, the author points out the similarity between his approach to superstition and the scholarly endeavours of two of his intellectual heroes – the Protestant David Blondel and the Catholic Jean de Launoy. This self-identification brings the historical methodology implicit in the work on the comet out into the open. Moreover, the controversy surrounding the history of Pope Joan and the methodology therein employed by Blondel – at once theological *and* historical – is revamped by the author of the *Dictionnaire*. By fusing diverse tools and traditions – theological, philosophical and historical – he creates the lethal criticism of the *magnum opus*, designed to eradicate human error of all kinds. But first let us consider the genesis of the historical method as it appears in 1682-1683, in the *Pensées diverses sur la comète*.

The focal point of the attack on superstition in this early work is credulity, the credulity of the masses, whether they be learned or unlearned. In fact, the fictitious correspondent to whom the *Lettre sur la comète* is addressed is a Doctor of the Sorbonne and the author's aim is to demonstrate and thereby disabuse the Doctor of the factors which contributed 'à vous rendre peuple'[13] in the matter of cometary superstition. Comets are, however, but one of the subjects of the essay and the critique is broadened – in a fashion reminiscent of *libertin*,

10. Marc Fumaroli, 'Aux origines de la connaissance historique du Moyen Age: humanisme, réforme et gallicanisme au XVIe siècle', *XVIIe siècle* 114-115 (1977), p.5.

11. Cf. 'Antonio'; 'Alciat, (Jean-Paul)', footnote E; 'Bochart', 2nd article, footnote B; 'Hercule', footnote L; 'Pythagoras', footnote L. The term 'désabuser' is also frequently associated with the name of Jean de Launoy.

12. R. Pintard outlined the influence of *libertinage érudit* upon Bayle's methodology and suggested the link with Cartesianism and Protestantism (*Le Libertinage*, p.573ff.). Elisabeth Labrousse investigated the Cartesian avenue (*Pierre Bayle*, ii.39ff.), and the theological dimension to the methodology was suggested by Rex, *Essays*, p.98. It is this last emphasis which is explored in detail in this chapter, while the other two are taken into consideration.

13. *PD*, §VIII, *OD*, iii.12b.

Cartesian and Calvinist attacks on 'erreurs populaires' – to include a wide variety of popular beliefs. Astrology, the belief in lucky and unlucky days, superstition about names and fear of eclipses, all pass before Bayle's dissecting gaze.[14] Moreover, an opposition between 'science' (knowledge) and superstition informs the two phases of the dissection. The first phase demonstrates the ridiculous nature of these beliefs *per se*, by appeals both to philosophy and to psychology. The piercing light of science flushes out the credulity inherent in what appeared to be authoritative positions (*PD*, §§IV-VIII). The second phase is dependent on the first. If intellectual justification is lacking, then the authority of the age-old multitudes who welcomed these phenomena with superstitious awe – pagans, modern and ancient Christians and modern infidels all jostle for a place in Bayle's gallery of the credulous – is made null and void.[15]

Here we hit on the nerve of the demonstration, the desire to unmask and disarm the criteria of truth which support superstitious belief. Three criteria are singled out for attention: *antiquitas, multitudo, auctoritas* and, as Walter Rex has demonstrated, this critique is inseparable from the Protestant onslaught on Catholic claims to be the custodians of religious truth.[16] Not only is the question of historical truth implicit in the argument – the debate as to which confession is more faithful to apostolic doctrine is a historical one[17] – but also the terms used by Bayle as a means of disguising his polemical concerns reveal analogies between his approach to history and the Calvinist approach to religious truth.

In the first place, the critique of *antiquitas* is based on two related oppositions. Firstly, pagan superstition is contrasted with the purity and simplicity of the Early Church. The passage indicates the source of the superstitious beliefs present in Roman Catholicism (*PD*, §LXXXIX, *OD*, iii.59b-60a):

Quand nous n'aurions pas l'aveu de tant de grands personnages, il seroit bien facile de prouver qu'en effet c'est une maladie originairement venüe du Paganisme. Car outre que ceux qui ont prêché la Religion de Jesus-Christ, n'ont enseigné rien de semblable, il paroît par les monumens de l'antiquité qui nous restent, que toutes ces superstitions étoient en vogue parmi les Gentils.

The passage, in its echo of the myth of the purity of the Early Church – a myth

---

14. *PD*, §§XVII-XXII, XXV-XXVIII, XXX-XXXII, L-LVI, respectively.
15. *PD*, §§XXVIII-XXXI, L, LXXIX.
16. Rex, *Essays*, p.3-74, and below, p.122ff.
17. Pontien Polman, *L'Elément historique dans la controverse religieuse du XVIe siècle*, Universitas Catholica Lovaniensis, series II, vol.23 (Louvain 1932), *passim*; Rébelliau, p.4-92; Snoeks, *passim*; Gustave Thils, *Les Notes de l'église dans l'apologétique catholique depuis la Réforme*, Universitas Catholica Lovaniensis, series II, vol.30 (Louvain 1937), *passim*.

dominating Protestant ecclesiological thought at the time[18] – and of some of the dominant trends of the eucharistic controversy, establishes the existence of two ecclesiastical traditions. Protestant polemicists were keen to demonstrate that the Catholic doctrine of the eucharist was both superstitious and a corruption of the faith of the Early Church (Snoeks, p.9, 36.). Here the emphasis becomes an opposition between the continuity of paganism and Catholicism and their combined divergence from 'la Religion de Jesus-Christ'. In other words, primitive verity – the superior tradition – was steadily obfuscated by a second and erroneous tradition, that of pagano-Roman Christianity.

A second comment, which again draws on standard Calvinist theories,[19] reveals that the infiltration of Christianity by paganism was both deliberate and so gradual as to be imperceptible to eye-witnesses (*PD*, §LXXXV, *OD*, iii.56a):

quand on se fut apperçu dans l'ancienne Eglise, que la trop grande simplicité du culte que les Apôtres avoient enseigné, n'étoit pas propre pour le tems où la ferveur du zele s'étoit un peu ralentie, & qu'ainsi il étoit de la prudence Chrétienne d'introduire dans le service divin l'usage de diverses cérémonies, on s'arrêta surtout à celles qui avoient eu le plus de vogue parmi les Païens: soit parce qu'en général on les trouva propres à inspirer du respect aux peuples pour les choses saintes, soit parce qu'on crut que ce seroit le moïen d'apprivoiser les Infidels, & de les attirer à Jesus-Christ, par un changement en quelque façon imperceptible.

The statement is part of an ironic defence of the similarities between paganism and Catholicism – Bayle wears a Catholic mask[20] – which undermines the confession the author purports to be defending. 'La prudence Chrétienne', here a neutral term indicating evangelistic zeal, led clerics to change the tradition received from the Apostles. In other words, the syncretism of pagano-Catholicism represents a deliberate departure from the apostolic tradition it claims to uphold. *Antiquitas* it may have, but its antiquity diverges from verity and is but a perpetuation of error. Having departed from the truth of Scripture and the rule of primitive Christianity, the church of Rome is no longer the church of Christ.

The contrast between apostolic and Catholic Christianity stimulates the second opposition, that between Calvinism and Catholicism. Again, the context is an ironic defence of Catholicism, this time of its *criterium veritatis* (*PD*, §CXXVII, *OD*, iii.81b):

Que vous semble de cette pensée, Monsieur? Vous n'oseriez la traiter d'absurde, comme fait Lactance; car elle vous fera voir que l'esprit de la Religion Catholique étoit déja

18. Pierre Jurieu, *Prejugez legitimes contre le papisme* (Amsterdam 1685), i.4, and René Voeltzel, *Vraie et fausse Eglise selon les théologiens protestants français du XVIIe siècle* (Paris 1956), p.15.
19. See above, ch.1, n.81.
20. Rex, *Essays*, p.36ff.

dans la Ville de Rome avant la naissance de Jesus-Christ, puisque voilà des Romains qui déclarent, qu'à la verité ils ne refuseront pas les éclaircissemens des Philosophes, mais que néanmoins ils s'en tiendront aveuglément à la tradition & à la coûtume. Je suis bien aise que nous puissions nous prévaloir de cette antiquité contre les Calvinistes, qui ne s'en veulent raporter qu'à leur propre sens.

Significantly, Calvinism replaces the Early Church in the opposition to pagano-Catholicism. The conclusion is threefold. Firstly, far from being faithful to apostolic tradition, the Roman Catholic appeal to the criterion of *antiquitas* ranges it with the pagans against Christianity. Secondly, antiquity is portrayed as obscurantist in its refusal of verity. Just as the ancient Romans refused in practice the more enlightened teachings of the philosophers, so the Catholics, by implication, refuse the teachings of Christ in order to adhere blindly to their pagan traditions. Thirdly and also by implication, the Calvinists are aligned with the *testes veritatis*: the philosophers, early Christians and, finally, the Protestants form a cohort who, rejecting erroneous traditions and superstition, espouse the truth.[21] The Calvinists and the tradition they represent appear in stark contrast to the degeneration of Christianity embodied in Catholicism. They have rediscovered the ancient verity of the religion of Jesus Christ.

As a later remark in the *Critique générale* implies, this critique of *antiquitas* contains a methodology, which is as much historical as theological. Bayle is defending Calvin's uncompromising attitude to Catholicism (*CG*, letter XI, §iii, *OD*, ii.48a):

J'avouë qu'il y eût eu plus de prudence humaine à ne point pousser les choses si loin: mais il s'agissoit de remettre les choses dans l'état, où Jesus-Christ & ses Apôtres nous les ont laissées: il faloit remonter à l'idée de pureté & de spiritualité qui fait le caractere essentiel du Christianisme. Ainsi point de quartier, point de ménagement, point de restes de Judaïsme & du Paganisme, qui avoient peu-à-peu envahi tout le culte extérieur de la Religion.

Present in this assertion is one of the claims of Calvinist historiography: the imperceptible changes introduced by Catholicism had reduced the Church at the time of the Reformation to such a condition of spiritual darkness that its affiliations with primitive Christianity were no longer recognisable.[22] Consequently, as the phrases 'il s'agissoit de remettre' and 'il faloit remonter' indicate, Calvinism is a voyage of rediscovery through the centuries of erroneous traditions

21. The notion of an invisible Church or *testes veritatis* which resisted Roman superstition and hegemony stems from the treatise by Flaccius Illyricus (*Catalogus testium veritatis qui ante nostram aetatem reclamarunt* (1556)) and thereafter dominates much Protestant historiography: see Dubois, p.27ff.; Bernard Dompnier, 'L'histoire religieuse chez les controversistes réformés du début du XVIIe siècle: l'apport de Du Plessis Mornay et Rivet', in *Historiographie de la Réforme*, p.22ff.; Snoeks, p.53.
22. For example, Claude, *La Défense*, p.150.

and aims to recover the authentic tradition of truth. The statement also expresses the paradox of the Protestant approach to ecclesiology. The recognition of an evolution or a degeneration in Catholicism is accompanied by a negation of historicity in the case of Calvinist belief (Dompnier, p.22). Calvinists merely reinstate the primitive purity of the apostolic age. The reinstatement of the traditions of early Christianity, however, not only demands a 'retour aux origines', it also requires a 'retour aux sources', the Scripture and ecclesiastical histories of the first three centuries of the Christian church. Once rediscovered, the primitive sources become normative and discriminatory, the basis on which falsehood is separated from truth. In a word, theology and history fuse: the Calvinist is also a historian, consumed, like the humanist, by a desire to return to the original source, enabling him to restore 'la plus authentique tradition de la vérité'.[23]

Two explicit connections between theological and historical methodology occur, albeit somewhat hazily, in the manner chosen to disguise the polemical thrust of the work. Firstly, the reference to the imperceptible shifts of Christianity towards superstition is at one point phrased in terms of historical composition (*PD*, §XCIX, *OD*, iii.67a):

Je n'examine point s'il est vrai au pié de la lettre, qu'on étoit plus crédule en ce tems-là, que du tems du Paganisme. Il me suffit de savoir qu'on l'étoit beaucoup: & de-là vint que peu après on s'avisa d'écrire l'Histoire d'un air romanesque, & d'ajoûter mille fables aux faits des vaillans hommes, comme étoit Roland, neveu de l'Empereur Charlemagne.

The statement is obviously more symbolic than accurate. However, the choice of symbol is significant: just as the history of Christianity is seen as a conflict between two traditions, one superstitious, the other veridical, so historiography is divided between 'Histoire' – ideal or perfect history – and 'histoires' – the rhetorical or *romanesque* historical practice of a Maimbourg.

A second, earlier reference to history explicitly links 'histoires' and superstition. Cometary superstition is to be found, argues Bayle, among 'Auteurs de profession', a term including the historian. Their authority, however, is questionable. Where the paranormal is concerned, 'les Savans sont quelquefois une aussi méchante caution que le peuple':[24]

Tite-Live nous en fournit une forte preuve: car quoique ce fût un homme de grand sens, & d'un génie fort élevé, & qu'il nous ait laissé une Histoire fort aprochante de la perfection, il est tombé néanmoins dans le défaut de nous laisser une compilation insuportable de tous les prodiges ridicules, que la superstition Païenne croïoit qui devoient être expiez [...] Quel desordre ne voit-on pas dans ces grands & immenses

23. Dubois, p.32-33; below, p.233ff.
24. *PD*, §XLVII, *OD*, iii.35a.

volumes, qui contiennent les Annales de tous les différens Ordres de nos Moines, où il semble qu'on ait pris plaisir d'entasser sans jugement & par la seule envie de satisfaire l'émulation ou plûtôt la jalousie, que ces Sociétez ont les unes contre les autres, tout ce que l'on peut concevoir de miracles chimériques?[25]

A significant alteration has occurred in the now familiar passage from pagan to Catholic superstition: it is the historical *récit* which is now at issue. The implication is that, in Bayle's mind, 'histoires' bear the same relationship to 'Histoire' as superstition bears to true piety. Arguing by analogy, just as Calvinists strip superstition of its pretensions to antiquity and restore truth to its pristine simplicity, so the critic anatomises and defuses the mechanisms of historical superstition. In both cases, the rejection of certain traditions, be they religious or historical, is perceived as the only reliable means to the restoration of truth.

The critique of the second criterion, *multitudo*, is as rich in its implications for history as is that of *antiquitas*. In this instance, 'la multitude des suffrages' is opposed to the 'petit nombre'[26] of the elect or the élite and the opposition is weighted in favour of the latter. The argument has three phases. Firstly, the opposition between superstition and 'science' is used to prove that the *consensus omnium* is a sign of error rather than of truth. For, argues Bayle, if universal consent is allowed to be decisive, then pagan superstition must be accepted as true (*PD*, §XLV, *OD*, iii.33a):

on ne prescrit pas contre la verité par la tradition générale, & par le consentement unanime des hommes: autrement il faudroit dire que toutes les superstitions que les Romains avoient aprises des Toscans, sur le fait des augures & des prodiges, & toutes les impertinences des Payens sur le Chapitre de la Divination, étoient autant de véritez inconstestables, puisque tout le monde en étoit aussi prévenu que des présages des Cometes.

Given that superstition has already been derided in all its forms as preposterous and opposed to truth, the fact that the majority of pagans were superstitious is positive proof that *multitudo* is inseparable from error.

Secondly, this refusal of *multitudo* in general terms becomes, by a subtle shift of emphasis, a resistance to its use as a test of theological questions. Thus, observes Bayle to his fictitious correspondent:

Ainsi ce ne sont pas les Philosophes en tant que Philosophes, qui ont contribué à vous rendre peuple en cette occasion, puis qu'il est certain que tous leurs raisonnemens en faveur des malignes influences, font pitié. Voulez-vous donc que je vous dise en qualité d'ancien ami, d'où vient que vous donnez dans une opinion commune, sans consulter l'oracle de la Raison? C'est que vous croïez qu'il y a quelque chose de divin dans tout ceci […]; c'est que vous vous imaginez que le consentement général de tant de nations

25. *PD*, §v, *OD*, iii.11a.
26. *PD*, §vii, *OD*, iii.12a.

dans la suite de tous les siecles, ne peut venir d'une espece d'inspiration, *vox populi vox Dei*; c'est que vous êtes accoûtumé par votre caractere de Théologien à ne plus raisonner, dès que vous croïez qu'il y a du mystere [...].[27]

The reference to theology and the *vox populi* shifts the debate into the realm of confessional differences. As Bayle was later to point out, it is the Roman Catholic use of the *consensus omnium* as a divinely instituted criterion of truth which is here at issue (*APD*, *OD*, iii.172b). The observation is designed to reveal the inconsistency of the Catholic position: Jansenist or Cartesian Catholics refuse *multitudo* as a criterion in philosophy, while bowing before it in theological questions.[28] To Bayle, however, if universal consent is unreliable in philosophy it must not be invoked as a source of truth in theology. And it is here that the Cartesian tone of the *Pensées diverses* becomes unmistakably Calvinist.[29] The *docteur* of the Sorbonne is called upon to distinguish his position from those both of the superstitious *peuple* and of his inconsistent co-religionaries: the authority of *multitudo* is to be rejected in matters both theological and philosophical.

Epistemology is added to theology in the third phase of the argument. Echoing one of his favourite books, *La Logique de Port Royal*, Bayle distinguishes between external and internal signs of truth:

L'Auteur de l'*Art de Penser*, remarque fort judicieusement, que la plûpart des hommes se déterminent à croire un sentiment plûtôt qu'un autre, par certaines marques extérieures & étrangeres, qu'ils jugent plus convenables à la vérité qu'à la fausseté, & qu'ils discernent facilement; au lieu que les raisons solides & essentielles qui font connoître la vérité, sont difficiles à découvrir. De sorte que comme les hommes se portent aisément à ce qui leur est plus facile, ils se rangent presque toûjours du côté où ils voïent ces marques extérieures. Or comme vous savez, Monsieur, l'antiquité & la généralité d'une opinion passent volontiers dans notre esprit pour une de ces marques extérieures.[30]

Not only is the *consensus omnium* by definition an equivocal sign of truth but also, in the light of the previous links with pagan and Catholic superstition, it is shown to be as often associated with error as with truth. Consequently, its ability to convince is a factor not of its truth content but of human psychology. Man's 'paresse naturelle' seduces him into accepting the opinion of 'le plus grand nombre', for by so doing he avoids the arduous demands of 'la recherche de la vérité'. In other words, the multitude of fallen humanity, enticed by error,

27. *PD*, §VIII, *OD*, iii.12b; Rex, *Essays*, p.36ff.
28. Henri Busson, *La Religion des classiques* (Paris 1948), p.375, n.2; Rex, *Essays*, p.40-43.
29. Rex, *Essays*, p.40-43; Cantelli (p.18-22) argues that Bayle uses Malbranchian Jansenism to disguise his own atheistic critique of the *consensus omnium* as a criterion of truth. The interpretation fails to do justice to the intellectual and psychological coherence of the methodology developing from theology to humanism.
30. *PD*, §C, *OD*, iii.68b; *CPD*, §IV, *OD*, iii.193b; *Logique*, III, xx, §vi.

is opposed to the select few who, motivated by the *libido sciendi* or divine grace, will accept nothing but the truth.[31]

The stage is now set for Bayle to state his unequivocal support for the minority. Dismissing his correspondent's *vox populi, vox dei* as an 'aphorisme qui autoriseroit les pensées les plus ridicules si on le suivoit', he concludes: 'il nous est fort permis de compter pour rien les suffrages d'une infinité de gens crédules & superstitieux, & d'acquiescer plûtôt aux raisons d'un petit nombre de Philosophes' (*PD*, §XLVIII, *OD*, iii.36a). Majority opinion is unreliable given the facility of belief typifying the *peuple*. Critical reason and investigation are the property of a few and it is their opinions which carry weight, despite their paucity of numbers. The dismissal of the authority of the *multitudo* is not, however, limited to philosophy and theology, for a statement, later linked by the author of the *Dictionnaire* to the critical enterprises of Jean de Launoy, broadens the field of vision to include history:

Souvenez-vous, Monsieur, de certaines opinions fabuleuses à qui l'on a donné la chasse dans ces derniers tems, de quelque grand nombre de témoins qu'elles fussent apuïées; parce qu'on a fait voir que ces témoins s'étant copiez les uns les autres sans autrement examiner ce qu'ils citoient, ne devoient être comptez que pour un: & sur ce pied-là concluez, qu'encore que plusieurs nations & plusieurs siecles s'accordent à accuser les Cometes de tous les désastres qui arrivent dans le monde après leur aparition, ce n'est pourtant pas un sentiment d'une plus grande probabilité, que s'il n'y avoit que sept ou huit personnes qui en fussent, parce qu'il n'y a gueres davantage de gens qui croïent ou qui aïent cru cela, après l'avoir bien examiné sur des principes de Philosophie.[32]

History is one of the disciplines where truth-claims are based on 'la pluralité des voix': many historians reach their conclusions in much the same way as the *peuple* arrive at their theological or scientific positions. That is to say, the acceptance of received tradition is equated with the uncritical transcription of facts from one historian to the next. The position on history is, however, more radical. While in the other disciplines, probability is on the side of the minority, in history the multitude of witnesses is boldly rejected in favour of one source. In other words, given that in historical questions the multitude of witnesses derive their facts from one source, that original source is alone accepted as authoritative. Just as in religious thought the *éclairés* are distinguished from the *superstitieux*, so in history the *historien judicieux*, informed by his source, is opposed to the multitude of *historiens crédules* who propagate fables and error from source to source. This reductionist approach will achieve full significance in the *Dictionnaire*; at this early stage, it forms the basis of the critique of the third criterion: *auctoritas*.

31. See *CPD*, §XXIII, *OD*, iii.220a.
32. *PD*, §VII, *OD*, iii.12a-b; cf. *CPD*, §IV, *OD*, iii.193a-b.

The conflict at this stage of the argument is between the *principe d'autorité* and the *principe d'examen*, an opposition which informed the respective positions of Catholic and Protestant polemicists in the eucharistic controversy. On the one hand, to the Catholic, the *magisterium* of the Church possesses an authority similar to that of Scripture which allows doctrines not explicitly stated in Holy Writ, such as transubstantiation, to be received as true. On the other, to the Protestant, patristic and later writings merely testify as historical documents to the past beliefs of the Church.[33] Far from being normative, such documents are to be submitted to the control of Scripture, which alone decides those doctrines capable of being held as true. The believer and theologian are to examine all truth-claims, patristic or otherwise, in the light of the first source of Christian belief. As the following statement indicates, Bayle's sympathy is entirely on the side of *examen*:

Je vous l'ai déja dit & je le répete encore; un sentiment ne peut devenir probable par la multitude de ceux qui le suivent, qu'autant qu'il a paru vrai à plusieurs, indépendamment de toute prévention, & par la seule force d'un examen judicieux, accompagné d'exactitude, & d'une grande intelligence des choses: & comme on a fort bien dit, qu'un témoin qui a vû est plus croïable que dix qui parlent par ouï-dire; on peut aussi assûrer qu'un habile homme qui ne débite que ce qu'il a extrêmement médité, & qu'il trouve à l'épreuve de tous ses doutes, donne plus de poids à son sentiment, que cent mille esprits vulgaires qui se suivent comme des moutons, & se reposent de tout sur la bonne foi d'autrui.[34]

If the two criteria already analysed can be signs either of error or of truth, then it necessarily follows that their authority is at best equivocal. Examination is necessary to the discernment of truth: 'il ne faut pas compter les voix, il faut les peser', muses Bayle in echo of Montaigne.[35] The *savant* is called upon to determine whether certain traditions depend for their authority on popular credulity ('cent mille esprits vulgaires') or on the careful examination of a few 'habiles hommes'. Now, while the intention is polemical, the terms of the disguise broaden the statement to include all disciplines. The application to history is particularly obvious since the eye-witness or original source is considered normative and superior to subsequent and derivative sources. Consequently, the 'autorité du fait' is substituted for the 'autorité des personnes'. Only those *savants* whose authority is based on a private examination of factual data may be accepted as witnesses to the truth, be it religious or historical.

Theology, history and philosophy fuse, then, at this early date and lay the

33. Snoeks, p.235ff., 333ff.; cf. Daillé, *Traicté de l'employ*, *passim*.
34. *PD*, §XLVII, *OD*, iii.35b. In later years, however, Bayle came to appreciate the difficulties inherent in the *principe d'examen*. See 'Nicolle' and 'Pellisson' in the *Dictionnaire*.
35. *PD*, §XLVIII, *OD*, iii.35b. Montaigne, *Essais*, II, 10, 11, 12, and III, 8; cf. Labrousse, *Pierre Bayle*, ii.63, n.96.

basis for the historical methodology of the *Dictionnaire*. To some critics, however, Bayle's method is inspired more by the *libertins érudits* and Cartesianism[36] than it is by Calvinism. It cannot be disputed that the *philosophe* of Rotterdam holds certain methodological principles and conceptions of learning in common with these two systems of thought. Firstly, a duality is shared by all, insofar as claims to certitude depend on the rejection of *multitudo* in favour of the positions of a critical minority.[37] Secondly and contingent upon this, the rigorous critique of unsubstantiated traditions and *erreurs populaires* forms a leitmotiv in all three attitudes.[38] Moreover, the similarity between his own historical method and Cartesian philosophical attitudes is pointed out by Bayle himself ('Goulu, (Jean)', footnote F):

Il faudroit en quelque façon dans les matieres de fait suivre le conseil que Mr. Descartes donne à l'égard des Spéculations Philosophiques, éxaminer chaque chose tout de nouveau sans avoir autre égard à ce que d'autres en ont écrit. Mais il est infiniment plus commode de s'arrêter au témoignage d'autrui, & c'est ce qui multiplie prodigieusement les témoins des faussetez.

The pursuit of the original source is seen as the erudite equivalent of the Cartesian 'recherche de la vérité' by a return to first principles: truth, whether historical or philosophical, is not received by tradition, it is rediscovered or reconstructed.

The statement also contains, however, a major betrayal of Cartesianism. Nothing could be more inimical to the spirit of Descartes than the association of his mathematically inspired methodology with erudition, a domain of human endeavour which he despised for its lack of certitude.[39] Consequently, such a betrayal argues for another influence on Bayle's methodology. The principles associated by Elisabeth Labrousse with a transposition of Cartesian method into history[40] are to be found, almost ten years before the publication of the *Discours de la méthode*, in a work by Gabriel Naudé. In the *Apologie pour tous les grands personnages qui ont esté faussement soupçonnez de Magie*, the rejection of certain

36. Pintard, i.573ff.; Labrousse, *Pierre Bayle*, ii.39-68; 'Le paradoxe', p.53-70; and *Bayle* (Past Masters), p.50.

37. Naudé, *Instruction à la France* and *Apologie, passim*; Rex, *Essays*, p.36-38.

38. Naudé, *idem.*; Malebranche, *De la recherche de la vérité*, bk.i, ed. Geneviève Rodis-Lewis (Paris 1965), i.1ff.

39. This fact is noted by Elisabeth Labrousse ('Le paradoxe', p.53), whose answer to the problem differs somewhat from my own.

40. Firstly, Bayle substitutes for *la vérité de la raison, la vérité de fait* (Labrousse, *Pierre Bayle*, ii.51-52); secondly, for clear and distinct ideas he proposes a scrupulous respect for the document (ii.55-56); thirdly, the plurality of witnesses is replaced by the preference for the original source (ii.57); finally, both reject the argument from authority in favour of the examination of the data by the individual (ii.58).

'erreurs populaires'[41] concerning the reputation of some famous men is informed essentially by two methodological principles.

In the first place, the dismissal of *multitudo* as a criterion of truth is executed in the same radical fashion as in the later *Pensées diverses* (Naudé, *Apologie*, p.17):

Or pour nous delivrer de toutes ces absurditez, il ne faut que considerer l'ordre de ceux qui descrivent ces belles fantaisies, & monter des uns aux autres jusques à ce que l'on ait recogneu le premier, & peut estre l'unique de ceux qui nous les ont données.

That is to say, given that the suspicion concerning certain leading figures depends on the testimony of 'Historiens, Démonographes & Auteurs de crédit' who have for the most part copied each other without verification, the multitude of sources may be reduced to one: the original source from which they all derive.[42] In the second place, this tradition of credulous scholarship is opposed to that of critical humanism in an observation revealing by implication Naudé's own methodology (*Apologie*, p.638-39):

[les esclaves du Pedantisme] ont coustume de ne travailler que le plus legerement & au moins de frais qu'ils peuvent sans qu'ils veulent s'amuser à la recherche longue & difficile des premiers Autheurs, & du sujet qu'ils ont eu de semer toutes ces fables & calomnies, ny gehenner aussi leur jugement sous la diverse consideration des circonstances qui les accompagnent pour les luy faire ruminer, recuire & repasser par l'estamine de la raison, & en tirer une resolution solide & veritable.

The opposition, to be found later in Bayle, between 'fables', or the credulous historian, and sources, or the judicious historian, is already in place (see above, p.59ff.). The authority of well-known writers counts as nothing for Naudé, who praises instead the pursuit and critical examination of the original source. The method is also linked with the names of Erasmus, Montaigne and Scaliger, among others (*Apologie*, p.7ff.), writers who figure in Bayle's pantheon of literary heroes. Given, firstly, his discovery of the *Apologie* in 1675[43] and the many references to it in the *Pensées diverses* and the later works, secondly, his espousal of similar apologetic aims in the article 'Nestorius' (above, p.55), and thirdly,

41. Naudé, *Apologie*, p.*4r. It was this aspect of Naudé's thought which most impressed Bayle; see his letter to Jacob, 21 July 1675, in Paul Denis, 'Lettres inédites de Pierre Bayle', in *RHLF* 19 (1912), p.436.

42. Naudé, p.*7v. The *consentement universel* as a criterion of truth is also refused (p.634, 636-37). This radical reduction of a multitude of historical sources to the one from which they all derive is seen by Elisabeth Labrousse (*Pierre Bayle*, ii.62) as the most original aspect of Bayle's transposition of the Cartesian method into history. While the principle is undoubtedly associated with Descartes by Bayle's contemporaries (cf. *Logique*, III, xx, §vi), its presence in Naudé and Blondel (below, p.135ff.), both before Descartes and in a context of the critique of sources, argues against its being either original to the *philosophe* of Rotterdam or exclusive to Cartesianism.

43. Letter to Jacob, 21 July 1675, Denis, in *RHLF* 19 (1912), p.427-37; Labrousse, *Inventaire*, no 99, p.89.

his self-identification with critical humanism in the *Dictionnaire*, we may argue that, despite certain affinities with Cartesianism, his historical method owes more to the *ex fontibus* approach to learning than it does to the philosophical method of Descartes.

A further betrayal remains to be discussed: to integrate Cartesianism and libertine principles into a theologically based discourse is to extend critical reason beyond the limits prescribed by both systems (see n.28 above). In this, however, Bayle is not alone. In a letter home from Geneva in 1671, he indicates that his much admired professor of theology Louis Tronchin was among the first Protestant theologians to harness Cartesianism to Calvinism in the war against Catholicism:

Il [Louis Tronchin] est dégagé de toutes les opinions populaires & de ces sentimens généraux qui n'ont point d'autre fondement que parce qu'ils ont été crûs par ceux qui nous ont précédés sans être soutenus de l'autorité de l'Ecriture. Ce n'est rien pour lui que d'apporter qu'un tel & un tel, que les Universitez, que les Académies ont condamné une chose; il examine les raisons pourquoi ils l'ont fait, & s'il les trouve justes, il les embrasse & non autrement [...] vous ne sauriez croire quels avantages il tire de la philosophie de Mr. Descartes, dont il fait assez ouvertement profession, pour combattre ceux de l'Eglise Romaine.[44]

The observations which follow this enthusiastic appraisal of the Saumur-trained theologian are concerned with his application of Cartesian principles to the eucharistic controversy. Firstly, Calvino-Cartesianism functions as a critique of tradition, both the traditions of Roman Catholicism and the academic philosophical tradition by which it is inspired. Secondly, like Naudé for Bayle, Descartes in Tronchin's thought forms the basis of a sceptical critique of commonly received notions, 'erreurs populaires'. Thirdly, Cartesian metaphysics, as later in the articles 'Agreda' and 'Nestorius', become part of the critique of the physical doctrine of transubstantiation: the Aristotelian distinction of essence and attributes informing Catholic eucharistic dogma is impossible from the viewpoint of Cartesian substance and modes.[45] This more famous use of Descartes[46] should not blind us, however, to the association of Cartesianism in Bayle's account with a theological method where the *source*, Scripture, is normative and forms the basis for independence of thought and the rejection of weighty traditions. If, as Walter Rex has observed, it is to Tronchin that Bayle

44. Letter to his father, 21 September 1671, *OD*, ib, p.10b; cf. Labrousse, *Inventaire*, no 6, p.72; *Pierre Bayle*, i.103; Walter Rex, 'Pierre Bayle, Louis Tronchin et la querelle des donatistes', *BSHPF* 105 (1959), p.102. On Tronchin, see Jacques Solé, 'Rationalisme chrétien et foi réformée à Genève autour de 1700: les derniers sermons de Louis Tronchin', *BSHPF* 128 (1982), p.29-43.
45. Cf. above, ch.2, n.19.
46. Rex, *Essays*, p.121ff.

owes his 'redécouverte intellectuelle du protestantisme',[47] then it is also to this much admired mentor that the author of the *Pensées diverses* owes the affinities with Cartesianism in his historical methodology. That is to say, by a kind of intellectual alchemy whose elements are partly visible in the above remark, Bayle's studies in Geneva, reinforced by his perusal of *La Logique de Port-Royal*, lay the basis for the link between the methods of Cartesianism, Calvinism and critical humanism. The Cartesian method enters history via theology and Bayle's perception of the implications of Cartesian-Calvinism for history operates via the annexation of arguments from *libertinage érudit*. Such a diversity of trends hints at what will become obvious in the *Dictionnaire*: theology may have inspired history but in the *magnum opus*, it is the latent humanism – common to both[48] – which provides the exit from the duality of error and truth.

The link between the methodology of the *Pensées diverses* and that of Bayle's later activity as a critic is established by the author himself in 1704. The observation, in the *Continuation*, is addressed to his fictitious correspondent:

Vous souhaitez de savoir si quand j'ai dit que 'l'on a donné la chasse dans ces derniers tems à certaines opinions fabuleuses, de quelque grand nombre de témoins qu'elles fussent apüiées', j'ai eu en vue Mr. de Launoi qui a détruit plusieurs traditions générales, & nommément l'histoire de la Papesse. Je vous répons qu'oüi, & qu'à l'égard de ce dernier point, je considérois principalement ce que le docte David Blondel a communiqué au Public. Je ne fais point difficulté de mettre parmi les fables l'histoire de la Papesse, & de dire même qu'il y a peu de faux contes que l'on puisse réfuter par des raisons plus convaincantes. Si vous lisez un jour dans le suplément de mon *Dictionnaire* le long article que j'ai dressé là-dessus, & qui est déja tout prêt, vous avouërez, je m'assûre, que je ne parle pas en l'air.[49]

The opposition in Bayle's thought between *conte, fable* and *peuple* and *vérité, docte* and *éclairé* is reproduced here in a passage whose association of theology and history in the works of Launoy and Blondel is rich in implications (see above, p.29-30). Firstly, the quotation from the *Pensées diverses* relegates the legend of the occupation of the Holy See by a female pope between the deaths of Leo IV (d. 7 July 855) and Benedict III (d. 17 April 858) to the realm of 'superstitious history' evoked in that work. Secondly, Bayle's association of Launoy both with his essay on the comet and with his contribution to the Pope Joan controversy implies that a continuity exists between Launoy's critical activity and his own, both in its earlier and in its later manifestations. Finally, by linking his own work to that of Launoy and Blondel, the author of the *Dictionnaire* situates his

47. Rex, 'Pierre Bayle, Louis Tronchin', p.104; *Essays*, p.127ff.; Elisabeth Labrousse, 'Pierre Bayle et ses correspondants genevois', *Bulletin de la Société de l'histoire et de l'archéologie de Genève* 19, no 2 (1969), p.142.

48. Y. M.-J. Congars, *La Tradition et les traditions: essai historique* (Paris 1960), p.183ff.

49. *CPD*, §IV, *OD*, iii.195a; the reference is to *PD*, §VII, quoted above, p.129.

historical criticism within a tradition of textual and historical criticism both with humanist and Gallican foundations. Let us first examine the principles informing Bayle's rejection of Pope Joan as a creation of over-heated imaginations.[50]

As the generous quotations from Blondel's *Familier esclaircissement de la question si une femme a esté assise au Siege papal de Rome entre Leon IV, & Benoist III*[51] imply, the *philosophe* of Rotterdam's self-identification with his co-religionary operates on the methodological level. In the first place, the relegation of Pope Joan to the land of fables depends on a transfer of the historico-theological opposition between tradition and verity into the realm of historical criticism. The transfer functions on three levels, the first of which, reminiscent of Naudé, is a distinction between the source and the later additions to it. According to Bayle, the earliest source, Anasthasius the librarian's chronicle, which dates from the ninth century, never mentions the female pope. However, given that no autograph of the chronicle has survived, the argument is based on a hypothesis from chronology and common sense. The accession of Joan to the Holy See becomes a nonsense if the sequence of papal successions is taken into account. If, as all the chronicles maintain, Benedict III was the immediate successor of Leo IV, then to argue that Joan became pope at the latter's demise is to portray the Holy See as occupied simultaneously by *two* popes:

nous dirions qu'un même Ecrivain n'a pas pu dire toutes ces choses, & qu'il faut de toute nécessité que les Copistes aient joint ensemble sans jugement ce qui avoit été dit par différentes personnes. Ne faudroit-il pas qu'un homme fût fou, ou ivre, ou qu'il revât, s'il narroit qu'Innocent X étant mort on lui donna promptement pour Successeur Alexandre VII, qu'Innocent XI fut Pape immédiatement apres Innocent X, & siégea plus de deux ans, & qu'Alexandre VII lui succéda? Anastase le Bibliothécaire seroit tombé dans une pareille extravagance, s'il étoit l'Auteur de tout ce qu'on trouve dans les Manuscrits de son Ouvrage qui font mention de la Papesse. Disons donc que ce qui concerne cette femme-là est une piece postiche, & qui vient d'une autre main.[52]

In other words, the absence of the original source leads the author of the *Dictionnaire* to reconstruct it from other data. The reconstructed source is then used to establish that the story of the *papesse* comes from another and later hand. The principle, none the less, remains the same: verity, equated with the original source, is opposed to tradition, perceived as accretions to that source.

In the second stage, Bayle questions the reliability of these additions by opposing primitive to later traditions. The story of Pope Joan is present in three

50. The Pope Joan fable has recently inspired a twentieth-century romantic reconstruction: Claude Pasteur, *La Papesse* (Paris 1983).

51. David Blondel, *Familier esclaircissement* (Amsterdam 1647), is quoted extensively by Bayle in 'Papesse', an addition to the posthumous edition of the *Dictionnaire*, but composed before 1704 at the latest. For Blondel, see Rex, *Essays*, p.109ff.

52. 'Papesse', footnote A; cf. Blondel, *Familier esclaircissement*, p.6.

later chronicles, those of Marianus Scotus, Sigebert and Martin Polonus, which date from the eleventh, twelfth and thirteenth centuries, respectively.[53] In the absence of the autograph, however, other means must be found to establish the primitive tradition, prior to opposing its witness to the later chronicles. The technique chosen, in this instance, is one much favoured by Bayle,[54] that of 'l'argument négatif' ('Papesse', footnote G):

Un homme, qui seroit vuide de tout préjugé, n'auroit besoin que de l'Argument négatif pour rejetter le Roman de la Papesse. Ce n'est pas que je prétende qu'à l'égard de toutes sortes de faits le silence des Auteurs contemporains soit une bonne raison de les nier. On ne doit prétendre cela qu'à l'égard des événemens insignes [...].

Given that the occupation of the Holy See by a woman would indeed be extraordinary, the silence of contemporary witnesses is conclusive for the author of the *Dictionnaire*. For 'il est moralement & même physiquement impossible, que tous les Historiens du tems se taisent sur les Aventures de [la Papesse]'. If the validity of the *argument négatif* is accepted, then the story of the female pope has its origin, not in primitive tradition but in the minds and imagination of later chroniclers. The argument is only conclusive, however, if the primitive tradition is perceived as normative. As in the theologico-historical methodology, Bayle perceives later developments or additions as a corruption or degeneration to be carefully discriminated from the 'tradition authentique'.

The third stage depends on the earlier ones: the contemporaneity of the witness becomes the criterion of historical truth. Consequently, even the earliest mention of Pope Joan is rejected as legendary, given that it occurs two centuries after the events are purported to have taken place. This principle, which informs the historical criticism of the *Dictionnaire* as a whole, is most clearly stated apropos of the biography of Aesop:

Un homme qui se tient bien sur ses gardes ne croit guere touchant la vie d'un particulier les traditions de deux siecles: il demande si les faits qu'on conte ont été mis par écrit au tems de leur nouveauté; & si on lui dit que non, mais que la mémoire s'en est conservée de pere en fils & de vive voix, il sait bien que le Pyrrhonisme est le parti de la sagesse.[55]

The contemporary witness is opposed both to ancient and to oral traditions. That is not to argue that contemporaneity is a guarantee of truth. Rather it implies that *less* variation will occur if the episode is written down while still

53. 'Papesse', footnotes B & C; cf. Jacques Basnage, *Histoire de l'Eglise*, vol.i, bk.VII, ch.12, p.409-10.

54. See 'Brachmanes', footnote A; 'Cattho', footnote B; 'Hyperius', marginal note 15, where the *argument négatif* is associated with the name of Launoy; 'Zuerius', footnote P, *in fine*; *CPD*, §LXIII, *OD*, iii.280a-b. The argument played an important role in Protestant controversy against Roman Catholic tradition; cf. Snoeks, p.334ff.

55. 'Esope' (1st article), footnote B; cf. Blondel, *Familier esclaircissement*, p.16-17.

fresh in the minds of the eye-witnesses:[56] given the defects of human memory, if left to tradition the episode will be altered beyond all recognition. By its silence or its information, a contemporary source allows the historian to close in and seize the truth.

To the rejection of tradition in favour of the verity of the original source is added the opposition between *multitudo* and 'celui qui seroit seul de son sentiment'. The argument is provoked by the great number of witnesses, from both confessions, who could be produced to support the legend of the female pope. On the one hand, many Catholics had accepted the fable until Protestants began to use it as a polemical tool. On the other, not only did Bayle's co-religionaries refuse to believe later Catholic repudiations but many also persisted in their credulity after David Blondel's refutation ('Papesse' *in corp.* and footnotes G, H). Bayle adds his voice to that of his hero by a two-fold refutation of the *consensus omnium* as a criterion of historical truth.

Firstly, he refuses what might be called the 'harmonisation principle'[57] in favour of the witness of the original source and those who have recourse to it. Considerable variation exists not only in the later but also in the earliest accounts of the *papesse*. Instead of according equal weight to each of the witnesses and thence attempting to reconcile or harmonise their variations, Bayle attributes the variants to the inexactitude which reigns among copyists ('Polonus', footnote B):

On pouvoit copier [la Chronique] pour son usage particulier. Tel homme qui n'étoit pas riche aimoit mieux prendre cette peine que de dépenser de l'argent pour le prix du Livre. Rien n'empêche que cet homme ne s'attachât plus aux choses qu'aux expressions, & qu'afin d'avoir plutôt fait, il ne sautât ce qui lui sembloit inutile, & qu'il n'abregeât certaines phrases, & qu'il ne substituât ses paroles à celles de l'Original. On écrit beaucoup plus vite quand on fournit soi-même les expressions, que quand on copie celles d'un autre; car la peine de se détourner pour jetter les yeux sur un Manuscrit fait perdre beaucoup de tems, & l'on en gagne beaucoup si l'on ne fait que copier ce que l'on pense. Un Copiste qui prend le sens de toute une période, & qui l'exprime selon son goût particulier, achevera dans un jour ce qui en demanderoit deux si l'on suivoit mot à mot le Manuscrit.

The variants are deprived of their authority by being presented as corruptions of the source. Consequently, if the truth concerning the *papesse* is to be established, 'il faut qu'un Auteur éxact s'arrête à la source'.[58] The principle is

---

56. Cf. *RQP*, §IV, *OD*, iii.509a: 'Ce n'est que par l'écriture que les faits parviennent à un état de consistence.'

57. The term is often used to describe certain kinds of biblical exegesis, where contradictory passages in Scripture are harmonised into agreement (James Barr, *Fundamentalism*, London 1977, p.55ff.).

58. 'Brasavolus', footnote B; cf. Blondel, *Familier esclaircissement*, p.23.

consistent with the historical practice throughout the *Dictionnaire*, where the earliest available source is the criterion used to distinguish 'le texte d'avec la brodure de celui qui cite',[59] even and indeed especially if the 'brodures' are present in a multitude of writers.

Secondly, echoing Blondel,[60] the author of the *Dictionnaire* categorically refuses to accept the multitude of witnesses as a criterion of historical truth:

> Ceux qui réfutent le Conte de la Papesse établissent clairement que l'on ne la peut placer entre Leon IV, & Benoit III. Ils en donnent des Démonstrations Chronologiques, qu'ils apuient sur des Passages évidens des Auteurs du IX Siecle. D'où il résulte que le prémier qui a parlé de la Papesse deux Siecles après, est indigne de toute créance, & que ceux qui dans la suite ont débité la même chose se sont copiez les uns les autres sans remonter à la vraie source, & sans faire aucun examen, & par conséquent que l'on ne doit faire aucun fond sur leur multitude.[61]

The opposition is by now a familiar one. The credulous masses are here represented by a class of authors whose lack of critical judgement leads them to propagate and lend authority to error. Consequently, not only is the witness of the multitude conceived as void of authority, its numerical superiority is also refused. As Bayle observes elsewhere ('Jodelle', footnote C):

> Il faut prendre garde que les Copistes d'Hondorf, ou ceux qu'il a copiez, en quelque nombre qu'ils puissent être, ne valent pas tout ensemble l'autorité d'un témoin, pendant qu'ils ne citent personne ou qu'ils se citent l'un l'autre.

The notion of two traditions, one popular and superstitious, the other learned and critical, has reached full autonomy at this point. The opposition is no longer between two theologies but between two approaches to learning. The popular current finds its parallel in a written tradition which develops independently of original sources, while the other, the critical trend, is represented by those scholars for whom the verity of the source is normative. And historical truth is established by the sifting of the former by the latter: the *ars historica*, which retained its dominance, according to Momigliano (p.2), until the nineteenth century, is already discredited in Bayle's eyes, in favour of the *ars critica* (cf. Devolvé, p.228-29). The presence in Blondel of principles not only parallel with but which directly inspire Bayle's own practice implies that a methodology,

---

59. 'Anacreon', footnote D; above, p.94ff.

60. 'Ainsi (selon que je puis appercevoir) Marianus est la premiere & seule source d'où tous les ruisseaux des Escrivains posterieurs sont derivez, & je ne croy pas (apres en avoir descouvert à nud le vice inexcusable) qu'il soit aucun besoin de passer plus avant en l'examen de ceux qui n'ont fait que copier les uns des autres, sans sçavoir si le premier avoit esté bien fondé: Quand les tesmoins se leveroyent à centaines, voire à milliers pour donner des depositions digerées de la sorte, il n'y auroit ame bien faitte qui daignast avoir esgard, soit à leur nombre, qui ne devroit jamais faire de contrepoids contre la verité & la raison; soit à leur discours' (*Familier esclaircissement*, p.70-71).

61. 'Papesse', footnote I; cf. *CPD*, §XII, *OD*, iii.205b-206b.

originally inspired by theology, becomes in maturity a late seventeenth-century version of critical humanism. While in the controversy concerning Pope Joan confessional overtones have receded, Bayle's method remains distinct from the humanist methodologies of his contemporaries. The opposition by analogy between verity, source, *ars critica* and superstition, fable, *ars historica* continues to dominate his notion of historical duality. In fact, it is this opposition which both informs the article on Jean de Launoy and stimulates Bayle's self-identification with this theologian.

Jean de Launoy's infamous reputation as a 'dénicheur des saints'[62] is the focal point of the article devoted to him in the *Dictionnaire*. The reason is clear: Launoy's critical onslaught on legendary or apocryphal saints leads Bayle simultaneously to admire the theologian's critical temper and to welcome him as a fellow *résistant* to superstition. While Launoy is praised for his ability to 'discerner le vrai & le faux dans les Matieres Historiques', he is also portrayed as a saboteur of 'plusieurs fausses traditions [...] et superstitions': 'il étendit sa critique jusques sur les dévotions; & il auroit coûté quelques Saints au Kalendrier si l'on eût suivi ses raisonnemens' ('Launoi (Jean de)', *in corp.*). The observation goes beyond admiration, for it contains a tacit recognition of a methodology consistently associated by Bayle with Launoy. In his *De auctoritate negantis argumenti dissertatio* (a work much cited in the *Dictionnaire*), Launoy maintains that a tradition which possesses no proof or title deeds, as it were, of its origin must be abandoned.[63] And, as Bayle intimates, it is the *argument négatif* which led Launoy, like Blondel before and our author afterwards, to reject certain mariological traditions and legends of the saints.

The *philosophe* of Rotterdam is not unaware that Launoy's endeavours form part of a tradition which precedes and follows him. The Catholic theologian's Gallican sympathies are not neglected.[64] Thus, while Launoy and 'ses imitateurs' repudiate schism, they strive to preserve the precedence of 'la tradition objective ou documentaire' over the 'tradition active ou magistère vivant' (Congars, p.24off.). This conflict within Catholicism – echoing to 'Agreda' – becomes, in Bayle's view, a resistance by the Gallicans to the 'zèle indiscret' of the more superstitious *ultramontains* (above, p.27-28). Moreover, as the case of Launoy illustrates, this resistance finds expression in a certain kind of scholarship and historical research; the community of St Maur is presented as continuing the work of Launoy in the *Acta sanctorum*: 'Il faut même dire en leur honneur qu'ils

62. Cf. Louis Ellies Du Pin, *Bibliothèque des auteurs ecclésiastiques du dix-septième siècle* (Paris 1708), iii.98-184, *passim*.

63. *De auctoritate* (Paris 1662), *passim*; Niceron, *Mémoires pour servir à l'histoire des hommes illustres dans la république des lettres* (Paris 1727-1745), xxxii.113; Busson, *La Religion*, p.309ff.

64. Martimort, *Le Gallicanisme de Bossuet*, p.566-67, 607-608.

rejettent beaucoup de fables, & que leur sincérité les expose tous les jours aux mêmes plaintes qui ont été faites contre Mr. de Launoi' ('Launoi (Jean de)', footnote G). The early confessional opposition between Catholic superstition and Protestant verity is replaced, in a manner reminiscent of the generalisation within the article 'Agreda', by a more sophisticated perception of ecclesiastical conflict. Gallican Catholics, motivated by a respect for written tradition, conceived of as normative, also reject fables from history and superstition from religion (footnote P).

This inclusion of Jean de Launoy and his imitators in the critical tradition of scholarship leads to a trans-confessional notion of the critical elect or élite, similar to parallel developments in Bayle's ecclesiology (below, p.226-30). Some, he muses, have equated Launoy's rejection of certain ill-founded traditions with the position espoused by the Protestant Flaccius Illyricus in his *Catalogus testium veritatis* (n.21 above). The reference to the sixteenth-century historian is completed by a contemporary reference, to Jacques Basnage, the Huguenot ecclesiastical historian ('Launoi (Jean de)', footnote H):

Voiez l'excellente Histoire de l'Eglise que Mr. Basnage publia l'an 1699, en 2 volumes in folio. C'est là qu'on trouve la destitution de tant de faux Saints, & de tant de faux Martyrs, qu'en comparaison de cet Océan, l'entreprise de Mr. de Launoi n'est qu'un ruisseau.

The Gallicans are annexed, with a glorious disregard for confessional niceties, to the *testes veritatis* who, throughout the centuries, rejected both the imperium of the Roman See and its sanction of additions to the primitive verity of the Early Church.[65] That is to say, the oppositions at the heart of the article 'Agreda' and the deployment of Du Pin's image of the Nestorian heresy against the orthodox reading of the episode not only repose on a notion of an alternative history (below, p.233-40) but also constitute a self-identification with a cohort of historians conceived of as subversives of authoritarian historiography, its superstitions and oppression of underprivileged minorities. Launoy, the community of St Maur, Jacques Basnage, and Bayle represent a group of scholars all motivated by a similar aim: the deployment of the original source or the primitive tradition against all later legends, fables or accretions to that source, conceived of as ideological expressions of authoritarianism.

The conception of the superstitious majority undergoes a similar transformation, and here Bayle simultaneously joins hands with Blondel and Launoy. His perception of the opposition to his two predecessors' critical endeavours forms the point of contact. Firstly, the Catholic theologian's application of the *argument*

---

65. n.21, above; it is interesting to note that the theological notion of the *testes veritatis* is now applied to history.

*négatif* was decried by many of his co-religionaries as destructive of the divinely instituted apostolic tradition.[66] The outcry does not escape the author of the *Dictionnaire* ('Launoi (Jean de)'):

Il étoit difficile que ce docte Théologien écrivit tant de Volumes contre les Maximes des flateurs du Pape, & contre les Superstitions, & les prétendues éxémptions des Moines, sans se faire beaucoup d'ennemis. Il éprouva sur ses vieux jours, qu'il avoit choqué un parti fort redoutable.

The analysis of the opposition to Launoy, in its echo of the articles 'Agreda' and 'Nestorius', expresses a typically Protestant perception of Roman Catholicism. The theologian's enemies, like those of the fifth-century heresiarch, are portrayed as an assertive *political* party, backed by the Holy See, whose *refusal* to reform 'les abus', as in the case of the Spanish mystic, is motivated by self-interest; financial or controversial advantages were at stake:

Les protecteurs de la fausse dévotion ne voudront jamais reculer, ils trouvent trop bien leur compte à ne démordre de rien, & ils sont assez puissans pour se garantir de toute contrainte. La Cour de Rome les secondera, & les soutiendra. [...] On fait périr en herbe les fruits du zêle discret.[67]

Despite the fact that Launoy bases his arguments 'sur des preuves incomparablement plus solides que les Objections', his influence on the superstitious belief of his co-religionaries is negligible. Not only that, his critical historiography, on which his subversion of abuses is based, meets with a similar fate. Hagiography and the *ars historica* hold their own against judicious scholarship and the *ars critica*. For credulity pulls the strings of power.[68]

A similar analysis of opposition to Blondel indicates not only that Bayle extends the notion of power-based rejection of criticism explicitly to history,[69] but also that he conceives of Protestantism as controlled by a parallel authoritarian approach to enlightened scholarship. The outcry which followed his co-religionary's exposure of the fabulous nature of the female pope is interpreted as a refusal of truth in favour of party interests ('Papesse', footnote G):

Ne peut-on pas dire que ceux qui soutiennent avec tant de chaleur que l'Histoire de la Papesse est véritable, consultent plutôt les intérêts de leur cause que l'état & la condition des Preuves? Car s'ils étoient vuides de toute passion ne se souviendroient-il pas que le silence des Auteurs contemporains leur a paru plusieurs fois une raison invincible contre mille Traditions que la Cour de Rome allégue?

66. *JS*, lundi 16 mars 1665, p.75-76; lundi 13 juin 1701, p.265-66; Busson, *La Religion*, p.311ff.
67. 'Launoi (Jean de)', footnote Q; for the notion of the superstition of the *peuple* as a source of revenue to Rome, see also 'Nestorius', footnote N, and Pierre Du Moulin, *Des Traditions et de la perfection et suffisance de l'Escriture saincte* (Sedan 1631), p.111.
68. 'Launoi', footnote Q; cf. Naudé, *Apologie*, p.22.
69. The notion of a political base behind the *ars historica* is in evidence in 'Bezanites', footnote B.

Protestant reaction to Blondel is but another example of that 'esprit de girouette' which according to Bayle all too frequently characterises his co-religionaries.[70] That is to say, the use of the primitive tradition and the *argument négatif* to prove the discrepancy between Roman Catholicism and the apostolic tradition is now exposed as a base opportunism. If truth had been their cause, Protestant polemicists would not have scrupled to accept Blondel's parallel use of the same methodology. Instead, some of his co-religionaries refused to read the *Familier esclaircissement*, condemning it as the work of an author in the pay of Rome:

> Voilà quel étoit le langage des plus modérez; & c'est ainsi que l'on parlera toûjours, lors que l'intérêt de Parti aura plus de part à ce qu'on dira, que les idées de l'ordre, que les idées de l'honnête, que l'amour de la vérité en général. Je dis en général; & ce sont deux choses bien différentes, qu'aimer la vérité en elle-même, & qu'aimer le Parti que l'on a une fois pris pour la véritable, & que l'on est bien résolu de ne prendre jamais pour faux.[71]

The statement highlights the existence within Calvinism of the *prévention* and *esprit de parti* heretofore linked with the name of Maimbourg and such historians. The tone of surprise reveals the naivety upon which Bayle's realism reposes: Calvinist – and in the case of Launoy, Gallican – convictions, as a result of their rejection of tradition and superstition, are presented as synonymous with the pursuit of truth. The presence of resistance to verity within Protestantism represents a departure from its original vocation, even if the latter is conceived of somewhat idealistically by Bayle.

This departure from the original mandate of the Reformation as Bayle perceives it provokes a link between Protestant authoritarianism and Catholic oppression of its critics ('Blondel (David)', footnote I):

> L'Eglise Romaine est toute remplie de gens qui jugent la même chose de ceux qui réfutent les Légendes: on les traite d'Hérétiques, ou de fauteurs d'Hérétiques; de sorte que de part & d'autre, un Homme, qui n'a point pour but de se confirmer par ses recherches & par ses études dans tous les préjugés de sa Communion, s'expose à de grans inconvéniens.

Authoritarian refusal and repression of the truth are not the property of one confession.[72] On the contrary, they are the tools of all those who see love of truth as inferior to party allegiance or self-interest. To this oppressive religion

---

70. The term is usually applied to the Reformed swing from absolutism to republicanism, which Bayle sees as a rationalised self-interest.

71. 'Blondel', footnote I. It is interesting to note that, in his early years, Bayle himself was hostile to Blondel (letter to Jacob, 21 July 1675, *RHLF* 19 (1912), p.427-28); this more mature attitude is indicative of the submission of confessional interests to the pursuit of truth which characterises his later years.

72. For the shift towards authoritarianism within Protestantism, see Rébelliau, p.41ff.; Bayle, *CPD*, §xxii, *OD*, iii.218a.

and, by extension, historiography is opposed the open-ended scholarship and religious convictions of the *testes veritatis*, whose devotion to verity on occasion precipitates the questioning of long-standing, even cherished beliefs or historical traditions. The critique of Agreda, the defence of Nestorius are part of a methodological and historiographical vision wherein the historian and the critic are committed, not unlike Du Pin, to redressing the historical record, a redressal likely to provoke opposition and oppression from the majority, now also trans-confessional and concerned to maintain its dominance and spurious traditions (below, p.214ff.). Bayle's frequent allusions, moreover, to 'l'Inquisition des Livres'[73] implies that the credulous majority's oppression of the critical minority is frequently authoritarian. Against such opposition the critic in the final analysis is powerless. Bayle's pessimism dominates as he sighs over the fate of Launoy and Blondel: 'Le mal est sans remède' ('Launoi (Jean de)', footnote Q). The optimistic notion – which seemed to inform the *Projet* – of the *ars critica* as the tool of a literary Hercules, whose pursuit of the hydra of the *ars historica* would end in the triumphant restoration of the truth, recedes into darkness.[74]

The final *impuissance* of the critic raises, however, one final question: what purpose has scholarship if, as Bayle observes in the *Commentaire philosophique*, 'les Livres [...] ne [produisent] aucun changement' (*OD*, ii.357a)? Two justifications of the literary profession occur in his work. The first is revealed, by implication, in the article on Launoy (footnote Q):

Quelques Docteurs, plus éclairez & plus courageux que leurs Confreres, desabuseront une infinité de particuliers, & n'aporteront aucun changement aux cérémonies publiques. [...] leur Critique, fût-elle beaucoup plus sévére qu'elle ne l'est, ne serviroit tout au plus qu'à l'instruction des particuliers.

The pessimism is mitigated. While the scholar cannot hope to sway public opinion as a whole, he may expect to convince some more open-minded individuals, motivated like himself by the love of truth. This may seem to amount to an élitism; it is rather, in our opinion, a secularisation of the notion of the elect. The scholar cannot know in advance those who will respond to the truth. He must cast his pearls indiscriminately before the reading public, in the confidence that those who have ears to hear will respond.

Secondly, Bayle's own espousal of truth rather than expediency in the debate with Jurieu over the *honnêteté* of atheists provokes the following observation. That guardian of orthodoxy may prefer to deny the existence of virtuous atheists, he muses, but as for myself (*APD, OD*, iii.178a):

73. *CG*, letter v, §vi, *OD*, ii.29b; 'François, (d'Assise)', footnote F; Preface to the 2nd ed. of the *Recueil de quelques pièces curieuses concernant la philosophie de M. Descartes* (1684), in *OD*, iv.186a-b.
74. 'Luther', footnotes O and Z *in fine*; *CPD*, §xxxix, *OD*, iii.242b.

pour moi je ne me prêterai jamais à ce ministere politique. La destinée de David Blondel ne me fera jamais peur. La médisance se déchaîna contre lui d'une maniere très-scandaleuse, lorsqu'il eut écrit contre la tradition de la Papesse. Notre délateur, s'il avoit été de ce tems-là, n'auroit point manqué de crier que ce Livre étoit scandaleux, & qu'il tendoit à diminuer l'aversion pour l'Antechrist, & à ôter aux bonnes ames la consolation qu'elles tiroient de cette aventure burlesque & honteuse au Siege Romain. De tels vacarmes font mille fois plus de tort au bon parti que notre méthode Philosophique, qui veut que l'on rende justice à tout le monde sans exception, & que l'on préfere la verité à toutes choses.

The statement is both moving and revealing in its psychological self-identification with Blondel. The submission of scholarship to party ideologies becomes a political, even Machiavellian[75] abuse of truth. At this point the link with Naudé, a counsellor of such abuses,[76] is broken and the anticipation of the Enlightenment comes to the fore: the refugee of Rotterdam becomes a *philosophe avant la lettre*. In the final analysis, the scholar researches and publishes because that is his vocation. The influence of his critical endeavours is not only both unpredictable and inscrutable, it is also profoundly subversive. His task is to have the courage of his conviction that the truth must be preferred to all personal advancement, self-interest or party allegiance.[77] The hydra of error may vanquish the scholarly Hercules but the latter is to fall 'la plume à la main'. None the less, as in the critique of Maimbourg and the ethics of the learned Republic, theology may yield to unaligned truth, but the service of verity is still perceived as more useful to 'le bon parti' than the propagation of error. Reformation theology and humanist scholarship continue, albeit ideally, to be the mutual handmaids of primitive and authentic tradition.

Bayle *libertin*, humanist, Cartesian, or Protestant? It is the pessimism of his vision of scholarship which gives a personal note to his methodology. Despite its Augustinianism, the later humanism, to which the author of the *Dictionnaire* appeals, retains a confidence in the power of the *humaniores litterae* to transform men and society (Jehasse, *passim*). Similarly, Calvinist polemicists and *libertins érudits* share a triumphalism and a confidence in the power of truth, where their respective battles against superstition are concerned.[78] Finally, Descartes's persuasion of the novelty and merit of his *méthode* lends a tone of self-assured didacticism to his writings (France, p.40ff.) absent from those of the *philosophe* of Rotterdam. It is not to other ideologies but to Bayle's experience that we must turn to give coherence to his methodology. From his earliest years, the author of the *Dictionnaire* experienced at first hand the uneven battle between

75. Naudé, *Science des princes*, ii.27-31.
76. Above, p.54-55; Pintard, i.561-63.
77. A position held by Blondel, *Familier esclaircissement*, p.100ff.
78. Blondel, *Familier esclaircissement*, p.105-106; Naudé, *Instruction*, p.17-20, 39.

144

truth and error, as he was later to express it. Born into a persecuted minority, he was forced into exile by lack of religious liberty, and his later years were dogged by the disputes with Jurieu, where political machinations achieved more than truth. The final word must be given not to a Calvinist theology but to one Calvinist's psychology:[79] Bayle's siege mentality remains as an index of his life-long devotion to the discernment of truth from the many-headed monster of error and superstition.

79. Labrousse, 'Le paradoxe', p.69.

# 6. The Ariadne's thread: Bayle and Scripture

> Les estrangers n'ont autre chose à nous reprocher, sinon, que comme un
> autre Thesee, estans engagez sous d'autres imperfections, dans ce labyrinthe
> de la nature, ils s'en desgagent plus facilement par le moyen du filet
> d'Ariadne, j'entends l'usage & la pratique de la raison.
>
> Gabriel Naudé, *Instruction à la France sur la vérité de l'histoire des frères de
> la Roze-Croix*[1]

> Vous vous imaginerez peut-être qu'en raisonnant sur les perfections de
> l'homme ils auroient pû s'élever plus facilement jusqu'à l'existence d'un
> esprit créateur de toutes choses. Mais soyez sûr que sans la lumiere révélée
> les réflexions sur les qualitez de l'homme ne leur auroient pas fourni le fil
> d'Ariadne pour sortir du labyrinthe, elles auroient pû au-contraire les faire
> errer de plus en plus.
>
> Pierre Bayle, *Continuation des Pensées diverses*[2]

BIBLICAL exegesis, a discipline as old as the sacred writings themselves, reaches
a crossroads in the closing years of the *grand siècle*.[3] The wealth of information
concerning pagan antiquity,[4] the claims of other civilisations to be more ancient
than Judeo-Christianity[5] and the ever-increasing popularity of voyage literature
inject Christian apologetics with a note of strident insecurity (Hazard, p.186
and *passim*). The main crisis is provoked, however, less by external than by the
internal problems attaching to Holy Writ. The test case is that of the Mosaic
authorship of the *Pentateuch*. Four authors bear the responsibility, in the minds

---

1. Naudé, *Instruction*, p.3-4. The author is reproaching the French for their credulity in the
Rosicrucian affair.

2. *CPD*, §CXII, *OD*, iii.343a.

3. Auvray, p.140-41; Albert Monod, *De Pascal à Chateaubriand: les défenseurs français du christianisme de 1670 à 1802* (Paris 1916; reprint, Genève 1970), p.50.

4. Both Isaac de La Peyrère in his *Prae-Adamitae* (1655) and Pierre-Daniel Huet in his *Demonstra-
tio evangelica* (1697) attempted to harmonise profane and sacred history; cf Richard Popkin, *The
History of scepticism from Erasmus to Spinoza* (Berkeley, Los Angeles, London 1979), p.218-20, and
by the same author, 'The development of religious scepticism and the influence of Isaac de La
Peyrère's pre-Adamism and Bible criticism', in *Classical influences*, ed. Bolgar, p.271-80; Auvray,
p.86-89. Bayle read both works but greeted their hypotheses with caution: see, for example, 'Caïn',
footnote A; 'Peyrere'; 'Zoroastre', footnote H.

5. Paul Pezron wrote *L'Antiquité des tems rétablie & défenduë contre les juifs & les nouveaux
chronologistes* (Paris 1687) and the *Défense de l'antiquité des tems, où l'on soûtient la tradition des Pères
& des Eglises, contre celle du Talmud; et où l'on fait voir la corruption de l'hébreu des juifs* (Paris 1691),
proposing the chronology of the Septuagint as a means of reconciling profane and sacred chronology.
Bayle read both works with interest (see 'Akiba') but sticks to the chronology of the Hebrew Bible.
On this, see D. E. Curtis, 'Pierre Bayle and the expansion of time', *Australian journal of French
studies* 13 (1976) p.197-212; Hazard, p.58ff.

both of their contemporaries and of later historians, for the consternation seizing theologians, apologists and intellectuals of both confessions.[6] While the four – Thomas Hobbes in the *Leviathan* (1651), Isaac de La Peyrère in the *Systema theologicum* (1655), Spinoza in the *Tractatus theologico-politicus* (1670), and Richard Simon in the *Histoire critique du Vieux Testament* (1678) – frequently differ in the details of their arguments, all are agreed on one issue.[7] In the words of Simon: 'Moïse ne peut être l'Auteur de tout ce qui est dans les Livres qui lui sont attribués'.[8] To question Mosaic authorship in a century dominated by the 'dictation theory' of biblical inspiration[9] is to undermine the crucial link between God and the text of Scripture. Predictably, the four authors' temerity met with swift condemnation. Hobbes was denounced as an atheist.[10] The works of La Peyrère and Spinoza were loudly condemned by Catholics and Protestants alike.[11] Simon's *Histoire critique* was no sooner printed than it was suppressed (Auvray, p.46ff.). Hence the notion, common to both many later historians and biographers of Richard Simon, that 'liberal' biblical scholarship was trampled into oblivion by outraged 'orthodox' intellectuals and theologians.[12] The truth, however, is not so simple.

Pierre Bayle, in the December issue of the *Nouvelles de la République des lettres* (1684), appeals to intellectual history to elucidate the reaction to Simon. Echoing the latter's 'Préface', the journalist sees Simon's plight as another example of traditional opposition to scholarly endeavour:[13]

6. A. Bernus, *Richard Simon et son Histoire critique du Vieux Testament* (Lausanne 1869), p.64ff.; Auvray, p.62-64.

7. Hobbes, *Leviathan* (London 1651), part III, ch.33, p.199-207, esp. p.200. For La Peyrère, cf. Auvray, p.63; Popkin, p.218-20; Jean Steinmann, *Richard Simon et les origines de l'exégèse biblique* (Paris 1960), p.54-57; Spinoza, *Tractatus*, ch.8 (New York 1951), p.120-32; Bayle was shocked by this work when he read it in 1679: see letter to Minutoli, 26 May 1679, *OD*, iv.574b; no 158 in Labrousse, *Inventaire*; the early horror is still visible, moreover, in 'Spinoza'.

8. Richard Simon, *Histoire critique du Vieux Testament* (Rotterdam 1685), 31b and p.***2r. This edition was read by Bayle. The quotation is the title of chapter 5 of the work and, according to Auvray (p.46), it was this chapter in particular which sent Bossuet post-haste to Le Tellier to have the work suppressed.

9. Auvray, p.89, and E. Mangenot, 'Inspiration des saintes écritures', in *DTC*, vol.vii, part 2, p.2068-266, esp. p.2202; cf. François Laplanche, 'L'Ecriture, le sacré et l'histoire: le protestantisme français devant la Bible dans la première moitié du XVIIe siècle', doctoral thesis, Université de Paris-Sorbonne, 1983, i.84ff.

10. Laplanche, *L'Evidence*, p.7.

11. For La Peyrère, see Popkin, *The History*, p.219-20; for Spinoza, see Paul Vernière, *Spinoza et la pensée française avant la Révolution* (Paris 1954), i.121-63.

12. Auvray, p.176; Steinmann, p.7.

13. Firstly, the use of the word 'persecution' to describe the reaction to Simon indicates that Bayle felt a great deal of sympathy for the exegete: Bayle frequently espouses the cause of persecuted individuals or minorities (above, p.31ff.). Secondly, many methodological affinities exist between the two writers. Simon not only opposes the sentiments of 'un seul docteur' to those of 'la Tradition' (cf. Auvray, p.139), but he is also a 'démolisseur' of popular ideas (p.57). It is not inconceivable,

Quelles persécutions n'excita-t-on pas dans le dernier siecle contre plusieurs sçavans Théologiens qui avoient osé soûtenir, que la Vulgate n'étoit pas tout-à-fait correcte? Cependant c'est une chose dont presque tout le monde convient aujourd'hui. Nôtre siecle nous a fait voir quelque chose de semblable depuis-peu, & en général on peut dire que ceux qui ont travaillé sur cette sorte de choses, n'ont été goûtez qu'après de longues traverses. C'est pourquoi les amis de M. Simon doivent se promettre, que le tems & la patience procureront à son Livre le privilége qui lui a été refusé jusques ici.[14]

The observation rings true to the confidence in scholarship which characterises Bayle at this early date (above, p.120-21). Simon's critical approach to Scripture will eventually conquer a public opinion whose reluctance is merely a part of the growing pains experienced by all new ideas. Twentieth-century analyses confirm the insight. As Paul Vernière has demonstrated in the case of Spinoza, even the latter's enemies were constrained to make concessions to his main theses. Public outcry is accompanied by subterranean *glissements* towards Spinozist and Simonian exegetical positions.[15] Bayle's prediction, perhaps unknown to himself, is being realised as he writes. The generation of scholars to which he belongs is typified by an ambivalence to the biblical criticism they publicly profess to abhor.[16]

Intellectual disagreement is an insufficient explanation for the violent reaction to 'liberal' exegesis. Ideology is reinforced by psychology. From his detached position in Rotterdam, the future author of the *Dictionnaire* detects a note of panic in the precipitate condemnation of the *Histoire critique du Vieux Testament* (*NRL, OD*, i.191a):

Je ne sçai si l'on ne pourroit pas dire qu'il y a certaines matieres si delicates, que pour

then, in this period when the methodology of the *Pensées diverses* was maturing into the historical method, that Simon's work functioned as a catalyst to that development and, as such, was welcomed less cautiously than in Bayle's later years.

14. *NRL*, décembre 1684, art.xi, *OD*, i.191a-b.

15. Vernière, i.121-63. While Auvray maintains ('Richard Simon et Spinoza', in *Religion, érudition*, p.201-14) that Simon was not influenced by his forebear, it is legitimate to apply the above argument to both authors, since their contemporaries always spoke of them in the same breath.

16. Justel's remark to Leibniz in 1677, a year before the *Histoire critique*, is significant in this respect: 'Nous aurons bientôt une critique historique sur les livres de la Bible où il y aura des choses hardies. L'auteur soutient que le canon de l'Ecriture n'a été fait qu'après la captivité (c'est aussi le sentiment de Spinoza), que le sanhédrin pouvait ajouter et ôter ce qui lui plaisait de l'Ecriture qu'il croit avoir été maltraitée comme les autres livres. Il y a plusieurs autres choses de cette force-là qui me paraissent terribles. Cependant cet ouvrage sera bon et utile' (*Corresp. Leibniz*, no 262, 30 July 1677, quoted by Vernière, i.110). An unwitting testimony to a *divided* public opinion is given by Richard Simon's (a homonym of the exegete) *Le Dictionnaire de la Bible* (Lyon 1693). The twenty-one articles I have examined all testify to an uncritical and conservative approach to Scripture. However, the 'Introduction à l'écriture sainte', written by the R. P. Lamy of the Oratoire, which opens the work, is inspired by Richard Simon the exegete and Louis Cappel (cf. *Le Dictionnaire de la Bible*, p.4) and is, therefore, radically different in tone from the *Dictionnaire* as a whole.

peu que l'on y touche, l'on jette l'allarme dans les esprits. Or quand une fois ces émotions de zele sont excitées, il est assez mal aisé qu'on examine les choses profondement. On n'écoute gueres que les premieres apparences: on craint, je ne sçai combien de suites fâcheuses, je ne sçai combien d'abus, & on n'écoute que cela, soit qu'en effet on n'ait pas la capacité nécessaire pour pénétrer plus avant, soit que le zele de Religion nous grossisse les objets, & nous persuade qu'il faut user de diligence, & ne point perdre de tems en Réponse & en Répliques.

The statement echoes the analysis of the party-psychology of Maimbourg (above, p.59ff.). To Bayle's mind, the initial shock felt by theologians whose biblical criticism differs from that of Simon forestalls judicious examination of the execrated work. In other words, agreement or at least tolerance might have been reached had the *passions* not obscured the real issues. For as Simon, echoed by our author, had been at pains to point out, the application of the *ars critica* to the text of Scripture is neither novel nor revolutionary.[17] The all-important difference between Simon and his humanist forebears is one of degree rather than of kind. His more rigorous and rationalist criticism causes a series of shock waves because his contemporaries fear the imminent disappearance of cherished positions in a morass of transposed passages and textual variants.[18] Paradoxically, the series of replies to Simon's work is permeated by a conspiracy of silence: the execrated exegete remains anonymous when refuted.[19] Unable to accept the logical conclusion of a hitherto acceptable *ars critica*, Simon's contemporaries choose instead *la politique de l'autruche*.

Given the climate of tension, Bayle's open-minded and sympathetic analysis is on the one hand exemplary and on the other misleading. Leaping ahead to the *Dictionnaire*, it is curious to note that, while the *Histoire critique* is used as a *texte d'appui* in for example the articles on Rabbis,[20] its presence in the biblical articles is reduced to one – albeit highly significant – allusion (below, p.162-64). Moreover, despite his acute enjoyment of voyage literature and his acquaintance with the controversies over biblical chronology, Bayle continues to propose on the whole a traditional and linear chronology of Scripture (above, n.5). Not

17. Simon, 'Preface, *Histoire critique* (1685), p.*2rff. The preface occurs only in the 1685 edition and, while purporting to be written by the editors, is actually by Simon himself (cf. Auvray, p.79). The contention that the *H.C.* merely continues an *ars critica* popularised in the Renaissance is confirmed by modern scholars: cf. Bernus, p.55ff.; Robert Mandrou, *Des humanistes aux hommes de science* (Paris 1973), p.36ff., and Vernière, p.121ff.

18. Cf. H. Margival, *Essai sur Richard Simon et la critique biblique au XVIIe siècle* (Paris 1900). This edition was unavailable to me; references are to his earlier series of articles in the *Revue d'histoire et de littérature religieuse* 1-5 (1896-1900), which are reproduced in the book. Cf. art.iv, 'La publication de l'*Histoire critique du Vieux Testament*', *Revue*, ii.233-38, for an interpretation similar to my own.

19. Bossuet, *Discours sur l'histoire universelle*, ii.23, *Œuvres*, xxxv.190ff.; Bayle to Minutoli, 1 January 1680, *OD*, iv.579a, no 165 in Labrousse, *Inventaire*.

20. For example, 'Abrabanel', marginal note 34.

only that: although the *Pentateuch* certainly causes him problems, the reiterated references to Moses as its author,[21] together with the acceptance of the Bible as a unique and divinely inspired source, imply a personal adhesion on his part to traditional conceptions of Scripture.[22] We are constrained to admit, then, that, despite his proclamations of sympathy, the author of the *Dictionnaire* both shares the ambivalence and participates, to a certain extent, in the conspiracy of silence.[23] His reasons, however, differ from those of his contemporaries. While for the latter the 'liberal' exegesis constitutes both an internal and external threat, for the former the conflict is internalised and subsumed under the dialectic of reason and faith.

The biblical articles are informed – broadly speaking – by two sets of problems: humanism versus Scripture on the one hand and ethical rationalism versus biblical ethics on the other.[24] In the first of these, Bayle's indication of the symbiotic nature of his historical method and biblical interpretation ('Abraham', *in corp.*) implies that he will scrupulously apply his own *ars critica* to the sacred text. An examination of his evolving notion of source in this instance reveals, however, that biblical criticism, feared for its rationalism, is subject to certain ideological positions derived from a Protestant theology of Scripture. The

21. 'Abel', article and footnotes A and C; 'Abimelech', footnotes B and C; 'Arimanius', footnote A; 'Cham', footnote F; 'Eve', footnote D; 'Lamech', footnote D; and 'Marie', footnote C, which maintains that Moses was 'inspiré de Dieu'. Moreover, Bayle's refusal at one stage in the *Commentaire philosophique* (II, 4, *OD*, ii.407a) to question Mosaic authorship, even when to do so would facilitate his own argument, is very significant. Elisabeth Labrousse argues that Bayle's apparent acceptance of Mosaic authorship is but 'une concession aux idées du lecteur moyen' (*Pierre Bayle*, ch.11, n.53, ii.331). I disagree with this interpretation for three reasons. Firstly, had Bayle wished to question Mosaic authorship, he would not have hesitated to do so: another *erreur populaire* would simply have been chalked up to the list of his *bêtes noires*. Secondly, his preferred biblical commentaries date from the first quarter of the seventeenth century: Rivet, *Theologicae et scholasticae exercitationes CXC in Genesin* (1633), and Cornelius à Lapide, *Commentaria in Pentateuchum Mosis* (1616). Thirdly, at the risk of overplaying my argument, I would suggest that preference for one source over another always indicates both a psychological and an ideological foundation on which the choice is based. In this case, the choice implies a predilection for conservative scholarship and a self-identification with its exegetical presuppositions.

22. Labrousse, *Pierre Bayle*, ch.11, ii.317-18; for Bayle's acceptance of the divine inspiration of Scripture, see also E. D. James, 'Scepticism and fideism in Bayle's *Dictionnaire*', *French studies* 16 (1962), esp. p.312-14.

23. This interpretation differs from that of Elisabeth Labrousse (*Pierre Bayle*, ch.11, ii.317-45), who sees Simon as a catalyst in Bayle's development from his earlier rigidly Reformed position to a more liberal biblical scholarship. The position is reiterated by Laplanche, 'L'Ecriture', iv.853-54. For our reasons, see below, p.153-54 and 162-64.

24. For a list of these articles, see Appendix II. It is somewhat artificial to separate the two sets of problems, since they are both permeated with a similar methodology, notably, the opposition of a literal or Reformed interpretation to that of the Church Fathers or Catholic tradition in general. None the less, two separate crises are provoked in Bayle's thought by the inter-related questions and it is our purpose to seize the dynamics of these crises.

theological note continues in the pursuit of valid hermeneutics. Rabbinical and Catholic exegesis comes under attack and is replaced by hermeneutic procedures characteristic of the Calvinist tradition. Embarrassed, none the less, by some of the more difficult passages, Bayle perceives the shortcomings of his own interpretative modes. An uneasy co-existence of Calvinist and Simonian techniques results: the inconsistency is noted but not resolved *per se*. The presence of a fideistic approach to the difficulties of biblical interpretation indicates, however, a possible escape route. The exegete may flee from the maze of his own inquisitive reason by trusting unquestioningly to the Ariadne's thread of divine revelation.

This precarious balance of reason and faith is reversed in the second of our considerations. Distrust of reason is replaced by rationalist hermeneutics, first mooted in the *Commentaire philosophique*. The debates on toleration had shown Scripture to be a *nez de cire* whose dicta could be turned against the spirit of peace and charity essential, in Bayle's view, to the Christian religion. Reason and its counterpart, natural law,[25] become the guarantors of biblical meaning. As Walter Rex has demonstrated, despite its extremism this position is the fruit of developments within Calvinism in the seventeenth century (*Essays*, p.121-93). Less noted, perhaps, are its links with Calvinist exegesis.[26] The connection becomes obvious in the *Dictionnaire*, where the lives of the patriarchs are scrutinised and found wanting in the light of natural law. The critique, far from being a threat to Scripture, is conceived by Bayle as entirely consistent with the will of its divine author and hermeneutic procedures traced through André Rivet[27] to Jean Calvin. Nevertheless, the consideration of Manichean arguments brings the fatal flaw to light: rationalist ethics sunder the Divinity, who cannot be *both* omnipotent and beneficent. At this point a parallel fideism comes into operation. Fearing the labyrinthine recesses of his own reasoning, Bayle grasps

25. Labrousse, *Pierre Bayle*, ch.9, ii.257-89.

26. Howard Robinson (*Bayle the sceptic*, p.164) noted the influence of Calvin: 'The citation of Calvin's judgement well illustrates the way in which Bayle constantly supported his boldness.' None the less, his conclusion that our author quotes Calvin the better to undermine traditional belief is impossible in the light of Bayle's spontaneous use of Calvinist hermeneutic procedures. For this, see below, p.158-62.

27. André Rivet, minister of the Reformed Church in Thouars and chaplain to the La Trémouille family, was later called to the Theological Faculty at Leiden (1620), where he upheld the orthodox position developed at the Synod of Dordrecht. Theologically he is held to be a direct descendant of Calvin. For this, see Huibert Jacob Honders, *Andreas Rivetus als invloedrijk gereformeerd theoloog in Holland's bloeitijd* ('s-Gravenhage 1930); also *La France protestante*, viii.444-49. Bayle appreciates Rivet's theological position and his 'grande lecture' ('Calvin', footnote S and marginal notes 84-85). This critique of the patriarchs against the standards of natural law was also a prominent feature of the exegesis of the Saumur school; Bayle may have become acquainted with it in Geneva or through his reading (Laplanche, 'L'Ecriture', iii.720ff.). The common source is, however, Calvin and Bayle may have taken his inspiration directly from the sixteenth-century Reformer.

the lifeline of faith. His attitude to Scripture, then, is nothing if not inconsistent. A beleaguered Bible, a Calvinist theology and an unquiet mind all contribute to make Holy Writ problematical to him. While his solutions are often self-destructive, his motives in advancing them stem from a desire to maintain the religious authority of divine revelation. His inconsistencies point beyond themselves to the religious compulsion by which they are inspired. Let us not, however, anticipate our conclusion: it is time to explore, in detail, the first of our considerations.

In an age when the relationship borne to the Hebrew Bible by its various copies and manuscripts is a subject of acrid dispute,[28] Bayle is neither contentious nor rigid in his choice of the biblical sources for his articles. He possessed and used copies of the Septuagint, the Greek New Testament, the Vulgate, the Genevan Bible and other more modern translations, such as that of Mons, which he particularly liked.[29] As a general rule, he refers his readers to French translations – occasionally to the Vulgate – and has recourse to the earlier texts only when discussing problems of interpretation, suggested by exegetes or by his own reading.[30] None the less, while references to the Hebrew Bible and Greek New Testament are few in number, their tenor indicates that they are both perceived as *the* source, from which all other texts and copies derive.[31] This is not to argue, however, that Bayle believes the Scripture, as known in his day, to be inerrant. In fact, as early as 1671, he not only evinces sympathy, albeit second-hand, towards the critical enterprises of Louis Cappel,[32] he himself also asks questions concerning New Testament variants.[33] But a certain tension is obvious at this stage. The young

28. On this question, see Jean-Paul Pittion, 'Intellectual life in the Académie de Saumur (1633-1685): a study of the Bouhéreau collection', Ph.D. thesis, University of Dublin (Trinity College), 1970, p.115ff. I am grateful to J.-P. Pittion for providing xeroxes of the relevant chapters. Laplanche, 'L'Ecriture', ii.255ff.

29. See, for example, and respectively, 'Abel', marginal note 44; 'St. Jean (l'Evangéliste)', marginal note 5; 'Abraham', marginal note 24; 'Ovide', footnote H. Bayle also frequently quotes Marot's translation of the Psalms: see 'Abel', marginal note 39.

30. 'Agar', footnotes C and G, respectively.

31. Bayle's Hebrew was, at best, mediocre. Consequently, in the *Dictionnaire* he uses the works of biblical scholars who themselves work from the Hebrew. The works he consulted and cites are, almost without exception, from the pens of Protestant *érudits*: for example, Johannes Henricus Hottingerus, *Historia orientalis* (1660) ('Abel', marginal note 25), and Johannes Henricus Heideggerus, *De historia patriarchum* (1689) ('Abimelech', marginal note 43). He appreciates, however, G. A. Saldenus, *Otia theologica* (1684), undoubtedly for its rich erudition (see *NRL*, juin 1684, art.vi, *OD*, i.71-74), which he puts to good use in the *Dictionnaire*. For the way Bayle handles the early copies, see 'Agar', footnote G, and 'St Jean'. For the notion of the ideal text, see *NRL*, octobre 1684, art.xiii, *OD*, i.153b-55a.

32. For Cappel, see n.28 above; Bayle, letter to Jacob, 21 September 1671, *OD*, iB.14b; Labrousse, *Inventaire*, no 8.

33. Letter to his father, 21 September 1671, *OD*, iB.11b; Labrousse, *Inventaire*, no 6; letter to Jacob, cited in n.32. The first raises questions concerning variants on Judas's death (Matthew

## 6. The Ariadne's thread: Bayle and Scripture

Bayle's acceptance of the dictation theory of inspiration means that to accept variants is to question the doctrine of inspiration: 'ne se pouvant faire que deux choses éloignées l'une de l'autre, aïent été dictées aux Ecrivains Sacrez'.[34] Not only that, once variant readings are accepted, critical reason and not Scripture becomes the criterion of religious truth:

Je trouve que c'est fort affoiblir l'autorité des Ecritures, & qu'il faudroit bien se garder de la soumettre à la raison des hommes [...]; mais d'autre côté on ne peut nier qu'il n'y ait des endroits de l'Ecriture où on ne lit pas comme il y avoit au commencement, puisqu'à peine deux exemplaires, même des plus anciens, se trouvent conformes en ces endroits-là, l'un portant un mot, l'autre en portant un autre, & moins encore peut-on nier qu'un habile homme ne pût changer quelques mots qui feroient un sens plus juste que ceux qui sont aujourd'hui dans le texte.

Ambivalence is the keynote, an ambivalence which comes from Bayle's knowledge of the disputes between editors of the classics. He fears that Scripture will suffer the same fate as Horace, Virgil or Cicero: different critical judgements will create rival texts, each claiming to be the most authentic. Nevertheless, the opposition between the text 'd'aujourd'hui' and that which existed 'au commencement' reveals a certain acceptance of biblical criticism. The recognition of variants is an *interim* stage in the restitution of an *ideal* text – the Scripture as originally given. In other words, reason and its counterpart, biblical criticism, are allowed to function only under the authority, not of Scripture itself but of a certain theology of Scripture. The critic's task is to restore a text whose full divine origin and correspondence with divine actuality are presupposed.

By 1685, the period when the *philosophe* of Rotterdam is reading the works of Richard Simon,[35] the position has evolved into a more mature appreciation of biblical criticism. The comment occurs in a review of Simon's projected Polyglot,[36] where the journalist is explaining to his readers why the presence of variant readings poses no threat to a Protestant doctrine of biblical authority:

ce n'est point la Doctrine des Protestans, que chaque Livre, chaque Chapitre, & chaque Verset de l'Ecriture, soit la base & la regle de la Religion. En effet quand on leur objecte qu'il y a des citations dans la Bible qu'on ne trouve plus, & qu'on en infere qu'il s'est perdu quelque Livre Canonique, ils ne font point difficulté d'avouër que quand cela

---

xxvii.5 and Acts i.18) and the second concerning the interpretation of John viii.22. Neither is conceived of as a challenge to the authority of Scripture, since the first was suggested to Bayle by a minister whose classes he was attending and the second was offered for discussion to Jacob's friends in the ministry.

34. To Jacob, 21 September 1671, *OD*, iB.14b.

35. For a list of Bayle's reviews of works by Simon, see Labrousse, *Pierre Bayle*, ii.324, n.29.

36. The two works, *Novorum Bibliorum polyglottorum synopsis* (Ultrajecti 1684) and *Ambrosii ad Origenem epistola, de novis Bibliis polyglottis* (Ultrajecti 1685), appeared anonymously, though Bayle seems to have suspected the identity of their author (*NRL*, octobre 1684, art.xiii, and janvier, art.ix, *OD*, i.153b-55a, 209a-11a).

seroit vrai, leur foi n'en recevroit point de préjudice, parce que les véritez nécessaires au salut, se trouvent assez clairement contenuës dans ce qui nous reste. Il faut dire la même chose touchant les petites altérations, qu'on pretend qui se sont glissées dans le texte de l'Ecriture. Que les Copistes ayent pris une lettre pour une autre en quelques endroits, cela n'y fait rien; le corps des véritez révélées n'est pas attaché à cinq ou six voyelles, ou consonantes; il est répandu dans tout le Canon; & on ne laisse pas de l'y rencontrer, quoi que toutes les paroles ne soient pas précisément les mêmes qu'elles étoient au commencement.[37]

Here, the relaxed acceptance of the biblical *ars critica* depends on a dual notion of Scriptural truth: truth essential and truth inessential to salvation. No criterion (apart from that of self-evidence) is given to distinguish one kind of revelation from the other. Nevertheless, variants occur, according to our author, only in those passages unimportant to salvation. The statement represents a somewhat ambiguous development from the earlier position. On the one hand, undoubtedly impressed by Simon's work, Bayle now freely acknowledges the necessity of critical scholarship to biblical studies. It is the means whereby copyists' errors may be rectified. On the other, not only does the reconstitution of the ideal text remain the end of the *ars critica* but the truths essential to salvation are also presented as being, for the most part, in their pristine condition. Curiously, this notion of an *Urtext*, either still partially available to man or capable of restoration, is a misunderstanding of Simon's enterprise. To the latter, the biblical text is not *'un*, véritable, seul inspiré, [mais] le lieu de convergence de différentes leçons'.[38] In other words, despite his apparent acceptance of the new-style exegesis, Bayle's conception of its function is radically different. His continuing espousal of the ideal text effectively muzzles criticism, as Simon understands it. In a word, Bayle's attitude to the source is dogmatic rather than positivist.

The pursuit of valid hermeneutics in the columns of the *Dictionnaire* continues

37. *NRL*, janvier, art. ix, *OD*, i.211a. The statement echoes the well-worn Reformed argument that biblical truth necessary to salvation is both clear and perspicacious. On this, see Laplanche, 'L'Ecriture', *passim*, for the place of the argument in the exegesis of leading Protestant thinkers; also François Wendel, *Calvin*, trans. Philip Mairet (London 1963), p.153-60.

38. Jacques Le Brun, 'Sens et portée du retour aux origines dans l'œuvre de Richard Simon', *XVIIe siècle* 131 (1981), p.196. Le Brun indicates that the notion of the ideal text, a Renaissance concept, was entirely abandoned by Simon (p.187, 197). Bayle's conception of biblical criticism is parallel to his historical methodology, wherein the object of criticism is the reconstitution of ideal history. This is the basis of my disagreement with Elisabeth Labrousse, cf. above, n.23, for Bayle's sympathy towards Simon is based on a *misunderstanding* of the latter's biblical criticism: a misunderstanding altogether understandable given, firstly, the conceptual framework within which Bayle approached Simon, and secondly, the volume of reading imposed on him by the composition of the *NRL*. (On this, Elisabeth Labrousse, 'Les coulisses du journal de Bayle', in *Pierre Bayle le philosophe de Rotterdam*, p.97-141, reprinted in *Notes sur Bayle*.) I am inclined to believe, given the evolution in his attitude to Simon (see below p.162-64), that, at this early date, Bayle had read only the Prefaces and Introduction to the *Histoire critique*, from which his entire review of the book is drawn.

this dogmatic note. On first appearances, however, the critique of patristic and rabbinical exegesis, which occupies approximately 60 per cent of the space given to the Bible, seems to be but the application to Scripture of the dualistic method devised for history.[39] The reappearance of the lexis 'fables', 'romans', 'légendes', etc.[40] confirms this perception. Like the historical practice of Maimbourg, the figurative exegesis of 'Messieurs les Ebraisans' ('Cham', footnote D) is conceived of as a flight into esotericism: 'Distillateurs des Saintes Lettres, vous seriez moins blâmables, si vous abusiez de votre loisir dans des distillations chymiques, pour la recherche du fantôme de la Pierre Philosophale' ('Eve', footnote A). In other words, just as those in search of the philosopher's stone lacked scientific data, so patristic and rabbinical exegesis is devoid of textual justification. The criticism, like that of Maimbourg, is not without a note of moral censure, a fact which explains the re-emergence of the terms 'aveuglement', 'extravagance', 'fausseté', and 'vision'[41]. The figurative and allegorical modes used by these exegetes constitute an exegetical tradition,[42] whose mysticism is the fruit of imagination rather than meditation on the text.

This hositility to 'mystiquerie',[43] characteristic of Bayle's generation, is insepa-

---

39. In the course of this critique, Bayle gaily lists one scurrilous story after another, drawn from rabbinical and patristic sources. This apparent disrespect for Scripture has caused a lot of critical ink to be spilt and led to interpretations of Bayle as a free-thinker. I am entirely convinced by Elisabeth Labrousse's sensitive treatment of the subject (*Pierre Bayle*, ii.331ff.), to which one remark might be added. Craig B. Brush has pointed out (*Montaigne and Bayle, variations on the theme of scepticism*, The Hague 1966, p.293) that the biblical articles were, for the most part (see Appendix II), 'composed when Bayle still intended to confine his *Dictionnaire* largely to a list of errors committed in other works, hence the number of fantastic, even scurrilous, rabbinical traditions recounted in the notes'. We can be sure of this chronology, since our author states in the Preface to the first edition that the publication of Simon's *Dictionnaire de la Bible* (1693) caused him to abandon his plans to include many more articles on biblical heroes (*Dictionnaire*, i.II). Thus, given that the scurrilous stories are part of the *chasse aux fautes*, they must be read as part of the dialectic of the pursuit of truth, in this case the true interpretation of Holy Writ. The remark raises an interesting methodological point: in our opinion, if more attention were paid to the chronological development of Bayle's thought and the overall context of the individual asides, many misinterpretations might be avoided.

40. The lexis, applied to patristic and rabbinical modes of exegesis, particularly the allegorical, tropological and occasionally typological modes, is present already in the reviews of the *NRL* devoted to biblical topics. It recurs in the *Dictionnaire* in the first and all later editions: for example, 'Abraham', footnote M; 'Agar', article and footnotes E and I; 'Sara'; 'David', footnote A (1702); 'Eve' article and footnote E. Laplanche, 'L'Ecriture', i.61ff., demonstrates that this hostility to allegory is typical of the humanist exegetes and, later, the Reformers.

41. *NRL*, juillet 1686, art.ii, *OD*, i.592a-94b; 'Abel', footnote G; 'Abimelech', footnotes C and E; 'Abraham' (1702), article and footnote B; 'Caïn', article and footnote B.

42. 'Fausses traditions' ('Agar', footnote A), which are most frequently associated by Bayle with the names of Origen, St Augustine and St Chrysostom: an association also made by Richard Simon (*Histoire critique*, p.371bff., 386aff., 391bff.), and Jean Calvin (cf. Wilhelm Vischer, 'Calvin, exégète de l'Ancien Testament', *Etudes théologiques et religieuses* 40, Montpellier 1965, p.224).

43. The word was a favourite one of Richard Simon's: see Steinmann, p.414. Bayle also considers

rable, in his mind, from the dynamic relationship of history and theology. Commenting on modern exegetes, he observes:

C'est au P. Salian que j'en veux [...] En vérité, cela n'est gueres pardonnable qu'à des Auteurs frais émoulus d'une Régence de Rhétorique; & je suis fort persuadé, que les Sirmonds, les Pétaus, les Hardouïns, & les autres grands Auteurs de la Société des Jésuites, jugeroient de cela comme j'en juge.[44]

Salian's invention of a death-bed 'Harangue', which he attributes to Adam, is attacked as evincing 'trop de liberté' towards Holy Writ. The form of the criticism is most significant. As the reference to three 'Grands Critiques' implies, rhetorical extravagance is opposed to careful textual analysis. In other words, exegesis for Bayle is yet another domain where the tradition of the *ars rhetorica* is in conflict with that of the *ars critica*, and the *Dictionnaire* enters the fray on the side of the latter.[45] Scripture alone is the source of the biblical articles – 'Quand je parle ainsi je m'arrête à la Narration de l'Ecriture'[46] – and is opposed

allegory as a flight from, rather than an attempt to cope with, the problems of Scripture: see 'Judith', footnote A.

44. 'Adam', footnote N.

Jacques Salian, S.J. (1557-1640): rector of the Collège of Besançon and, later, in Paris, of the Collège of Clermont, was an ecclesiastical historian of respectable erudition but who occasionally lacked judgement.

Jacques Sirmond, S.J. (1559-1651): a classical scholar, he taught rhetoric in Paris and after 1590 worked in Rome as secretary to the Father General Aquaviva. There he developed his taste for history and numismatics and returned to Paris in 1608, preceded by his reputation as a scholar. He became confessor to Louis XIII in 1637 and at his death left behind a vast *opus* of editions of the early Fathers and dissertations on the same.

Denis Pétau, S.J. (1583-1652): classical scholar and editor, in contact with Isaac Casaubon, taught rhetoric in Rheims and La Flèche and was later called to Paris (1618), where he taught for 20 years at the Collège de Clermont. He contributed numerous editions, chronological tables and literary criticism to the scholarly world.

Jean Hardouin, S.J. (1646-1729): a contemporary of Bayle, he became librarian at Louis-Le-Grand in 1683 and later edited Pliny's *Historia naturalis* as part of the series dedicated to the Dauphin's instruction. He was also an antiquary and devotee of numismatics. His contentious spirit earned him many enemies.

It is significant that Sirmond and Pétau are mentioned in this context, for they were both among the 'jésuites érudits' (Fumaroli, p.392ff.) who reacted against the 'corruption' of eloquence. That is to say, Bayle's attitude to Scripture and Scriptural commentaries is parallel to his humanist historical method. Cf. Laplanche, 'L'Ecriture', i.61ff., for the influence of humanist on Reformed exegesis.

45. See also 'Caïn', footnote C, and 'St. Jean', footnote A. The parallel with the critique of Maimbourg is also suggested by the following remark on a rabbinical commentator: 'Ce qu'il y a de plus étrange, c'est qu'ils apuient toutes ces chimeres sur des paroles de l'Ecriture, qu'ils tordent & qu'ils sophistiquent misérablement' ('Eve', footnote G (1702)). That is to say, by their infidelity to the text of Scripture, rabbinical and patristic commentators indulge in what Bayle sees as procrustean alterations to the text: see above, n.41, p.155. Moreover, rabbinical modes are also linked, in our author's mind, with superstition: cf. 'Esechiel', footnote C and marginal note 8.

46. 'Marie', footnote B; cf. 'Aaron'; 'Eve', *in corp.* and esp. footnote D.

to all other positions not characterised by submission to the sacred text.

The ambiguity inherent in Bayle's conception of Scripture as source deprives this methodological opposition, however, of its apparent positivism. The critique of rabbinical modes continues in the article 'Eve', where the author is considering interpretations of the Fall and, more particularly, of the serpent's reported powers of speech – a source of embarrassment to generations of commentators.[47] According to the Rabbi Abarbanel, the serpent's speech is a poetic image for the bad example he gave to the woman. The beast which, by definition, could not speak, simply climbed the tree and ate the forbidden fruit. Eve, seeing it had come to no harm, was tempted to follow its example. Bayle's comment is short but indignant: 'N'est-ce pas mépriser l'Ecriture encore plus qu'Eve n'auroit méprisé la défense, que d'expliquer ainsi un Récit où il est parlé si précisément d'un Dialogue entre le serpent & la femme?' ('Eve', footnote A). The argument works by analogy, while the antecedents differ in each case. The Rabbi's alteration of the exact formulations of *Scripture* is presented as an offence parallel to Eve's disobedience to the *divine commands*, and an even more serious one. That is to say, the earlier distinction between truth essential and inessential to salvation has disappeared. In its place is an attitude implying that every detail of the story of the Fall, as we know it, corresponds to the original divinely inspired text. Hence the severity of the rebuke: the slightest alteration of the text is conceived of as a derogation of divine authority.

Reasons for this apparent discrepancy between theory and practice are given in the same footnote. The explanation takes the form of an admonition:

Gardons-nous bien de croire, ou que Moïse a trop abrégé cette Narration, ou que suivant le génie des Orientaux, il cache sous le voile de quelques Fables ce funeste événement. Ce seroit trop commettre les intérêts de nos véritez fondamentales [...]

The remark reveals the *a priori* nature of Bayle's exegesis. His penchant for the Augustinian doctrine of the Fall transforms the story of the serpent into a passage of Scripture essential to salvation. By definition, the narrative is held to be in its pristine condition and is to be interpreted without alteration. In effect, something of a hermeneutic circle is created: the Bible supposedly gives rise to a theological tradition while, in practice, that tradition is the criterion and guarantor of biblical meaning. In other words, the rejection of rabbinical exegesis is an attempt to prevent Bayle's theological tradition from being damaged by modes of interpretation that might make the Bible mean something

47. Cf. L. Tillemanus Andreas Rivinus, *Serpens iste antiquus seductor, ad mentem doctorum Judaeorum & Christianorum exhibitus* (Lipsae 1685), reviewed by Bayle, *NRL*, juillet 1686, art.ii, *OD*, i.592a-94b. On this article, cf. Walter Rex, 'Bayle, Jurieu and the politics of philosophy: a reply to Professor Popkin', in *Problems of Cartesianism* (Kingston, Montreal 1982), p.83-94.

else. While the target is different, the attitude is parallel to contemporary reaction to Simon: psychology and ideology unite to resist an alternative exegesis.

This hostility to Judeo-patristic exegesis is commonplace in Bayle's generation.[48] None the less, a comparison with the attitude of the *Histoire critique du Vieux Testament* reveals its particularly Protestant tone. Simon's rejection of figurative and allegorical modes is informed by a distinction, in the case of the Church Fathers, between their critical and their spiritual insights (p.386a). On the one hand, ranging himself with the 'Moderns', Simon argues that progress in the critical sciences makes the enterprises of the patristic age obsolete.[49] On the other, his appreciation as a Roman Catholic of the status of tradition as a correlative revelation (p.***4v) enables him to preserve the spiritual instruction present in patristic commentaries. To his mind, the exegesis of the Early Church Fathers may have certain 'scientific' deficiencies but its contribution to the understanding of 'la verité de la Religion Chrêtienne' is not to be underestimated (p.386a). No such distinction exists in the *Dictionnaire* where, as we have seen, the lexis 'romans', 'chimères' and 'fables' is applied to Rabbis and Fathers alike. Not only that, the spiritual insights of the Fathers are often described as 'impertinences', 'effronteries' and even 'impiété'.[50] And on one celebrated occasion Bayle goes so far as to oppose the ethical insights in the exegesis of his co-religionary, André Rivet, to those of St Augustine: 'C'est une chose étrange, que ces grandes Lumieres de l'Eglise, avec toute leur vertu & tout leur zèle, aient ignoré qu'il n'est pas permis de sauver sa vie, ni celle d'un autre, par un crime.'[51] Superior spiritual instruction is to be sought and found in modern and (let there be no doubt) Calvinist exegesis. In this Bayle is merely applying to hermeneutics a methodological principle fundamental to Reformed epistemology. Before him Daillé and Rivet, in works cited and commended in the *Dictionnaire*, both reject the insights of Rabbis and Fathers ('Cabbala Pontificiorum').[52] The Fathers' mystical spirituality constitutes, to their minds, a deformation of the meaning of Holy Writ, terminating in the substitution of 'orales suas traditiones in locum scripturae'. Their insights were to be given no

---

48. Cf. Bertram Eugene Schwarzbach, *Voltaire's Old Testament criticism* (Genève 1971), p.42ff.

49. Simon, *Histoire critique*, p.****1v. The passage is worth quoting for its obvious affinities with Bayle's historical methodology: 'nous voyons aujourd'hui des personnes sçavantes qui se contentent de recueillir tout ce qu'ils trouvent dans les Livres des Peres sur l'Ecriture, comme si les Peres avoient mieux réüssi que les autres Interprétes de la Bible. Ceux qui recherchent la verité en elle-même, & sans préoccupation, ne s'arrêtent point aux noms des personnes, ni à leur antiquité, principalement lors qu'il ne s'agit point de la foi.'

50. *NRL*, juillet 1686, art.ii, *OD*, i.593b; 'Marie', footnote D; 'Elisée', footnote B; 'Eve', footnotes A and C.

51. 'Abimelech', footnote A; see 'Augustin', footnote G, for a commentary on the saint's exegesis.

52. André Rivet, *Isagoge, seu Introductio generalis ad Scripturam sacram Veteris et Novi Testamenti* (1617), in *Operum theologicorum quae Latinè edidit* (Roterodami 1651-1660), ii.986b.

quarter since 'l'Escriture saincte est la seule reigle [de la foi]'.[53] Paradoxically, the echo of this position by Bayle means that Judeo-Catholic traditions are rejected in the name of another (albeit Calvinist) tradition. That is to say, Scripture is incorporated into a theological discourse which in turn determines the epistemological status of Scripture.

The confessional note continues in the two hermeneutic procedures proposed as alternatives to rabbinico-patristic modes. The most illuminating example of the first rule occurs in the article 'Caïn', where Bayle is commenting on the multitude of ingenious explanations given to explicate why God refused Cain's sacrifice (footnote C; cf. Hebrews xi.4):

C'est deviner, c'est tirer des coups en l'air, que de s'amuser à la recherche des défauts extérieurs qui pouvoient être dans les offrandes de Caïn. Peut-être n'y manquoit-il rien de ce côté-là; peut-être n'oublia-t-il que les bonnes dispositions du cœur, à quoi Dieu regarde principalement. Nous voions que St. Paul n'attribue qu'à la foi d'Abel la superiorité qu'il eut sur son frere.

The criticised exegetes err because their explanations are extra-scriptural imaginative inventions. Recommended instead is a hermeneutic procedure which explains the obscure by the clearer passages. The procedure depends on the unity of sense which the *philosophe* of Rotterdam – faithful to, among others, the Calvinist tradition[54] – assumes to exist between Old and New Testament. Given that God is the author of both Testaments, the New may be used to explicate the Old and vice versa. The exegete's task is to track down this inner unity of sense: his conclusions are to be but the mirror of a self-interpreting Scripture.

As the second rule indicates, however, this is not to argue that the biblical commentator is a passive instrument of the divine voice. God's communication with mankind is both verbal and textual and, as such, demands that the exegete should determine the true, that is to say, the original sense of the given words. For Bayle, 'le sens naturel des paroles de l'Ecriture' ('Sara', footnote A) is found by taking the words 'au pied de la lettre':[55] the literal meaning is the natural and divinely inspired sense. In cases of a multivocal lexis, the commentator is to choose the meaning which is most 'vraisemblable', 'probable', or

53. Daillé, *Traité de l'employ*, p.442; see p.333ff. for the view of patristic exegesis as 'jeux d'imagination' and p.113ff., 157ff., for the opposition of rhetorical exaggerations of the Fathers to the text of Scripture. A similar attitude permeates Calvin's and Rivet's exegesis.

54. The unity of the two Testaments is an Augustinian principle of exegesis used both by humanists and by Reformed exegetes. Cf. Pittion, p.112, and corresponding notes, and Laplanche, 'L'Ecriture', *passim*.

55. Cf. 'Eve', footnote B, no IV. In this, Bayle is faithful to the sixteenth-century humanist and Reformed tradition (Laplanche, 'L'Ecriture', i.75ff., and *passim*) and also to the spirit of his time (Schwarzbach, p.31ff.).

'raisonnable'.[56] The criteria for determining the probable sense are never stated but may be inferred from the instances where scriptural ambiguities are discussed. The article 'Samson' is a typical example. There the author discusses the curious contention that 'par les paroles de l'Ecriture, qui nous aprenent que les Philistins le firent moudre, il faut entendre qu'ils le firent coucher avec leurs femmes, afin d'avoir la race d'un si brave homme'. Four procedures are used, proving in this case inconclusive, but which echo the methods employed in the other articles. Firstly, the word *moudre* is shown to be ambiguous by an examination of different translations (the Genevan Bible and the Vulgate). Secondly, the literary context of the word is discussed. Thirdly, appeal is made to occurrences in the profane writers of Antiquity. Finally, the testimony of scholars who have consulted the Hebrew is alleged.[57] In other words, when the literal sense is not obvious, the exegete has recourse to the critical disciplines. Biblical and ancient grammar and morphology are indispensable to the discovery of the inspired sense of Scripture. This is not perceived, however, as a submission of the sacred text to critical reason. On the contrary, given the verbal nature of revelation, the critical disciplines are accepted as the handmaids of Scripture. As in the earlier reviews of Simon's work, reason is joined without tension to Holy Writ, insofar as it facilitates the discovery of the theological sense of the Bible.

The limitation of biblical meaning to the literal and grammatical sense proves, however, to be an insufficient basis for hermeneutics, as Bayle is himself aware. On two quite separate occasions he alters his exegetical procedures to accommodate some thorny biblical passages. In the first place, as early as 1686, he rejects *both* literal and allegorical explanations of the serpent's powers of speech in the story of the Fall. To the description of rabbinical allegories as a 'puérilité', he adds:

En comparaison de cette pensée, l'absurdité de plusieurs Rabins qui ont crû que le Serpent dont parle Moïse n'étoit qu'une simple bête, est fort supportable, quoi qu'au fonds ce soit un étrange aveuglement que de croire que des bêtes brutes soient capables de tout ce que Moïse rapporte du Serpent qui séduisit Eve.[58]

The *philosophe* of Rotterdam is caught in a dilemma, given his refusal to alter the biblical narrative, his hostility to allegory and the impossibility of literalism in this instance. The solution, given ten years later in the *Dictionnaire*, as these parallel quotations indicate, is the result of an evolution.

---

56. Respectively, 'Abimelech', footnote C; 'Abel', footnote F, and 'Cham', footnote B.
57. 'Samson', footnote A; cf. 'Abel', footnotes B and F; 'Abimelech', footnote C; 'Abraham', footnote C; 'Job', footnote D. Laplanche, see 'L'Ecriture', ii.277f., for the heritage behind this interpretation of the literal sense as the grammatical sense.
58. *NRL*, juillet 1686, art.ii, *OD*, i.592b; cf. *RQP*, IV, §xxv, *OD*, iii.1075b.

## 6. The Ariadne's thread: Bayle and Scripture

| 1686 | 1697 |
|------|------|
| Quoi qu'il en soit, il faut confesser que Moïse ne dit pas un seul mot qui signifie clairement qu'il veut qu'on croye qu'il y avoit là un Démon caché [...] | Le sentiment le plus véritable, savoir qu'Eve fut séduite par le Demon caché sous le corps d'un serpent, a été joint à mille suppositions par la licence que l'esprit humain s'est donnée.[59] |

While in 1686 Bayle is aware of the traditional theological explanation, it is only in 1697 that he accepts it as the most 'natural' sense of the passage. Basing our argument on his favourite sources for the biblical articles, the evolution reveals a preference for Calvinist hermeneutics. The Jesuit Cornelius à Lapide maintains that the devil merely took the *form* of a serpent, that is to say, no *actual* serpent was involved in the incident.[60] To Rivet, however, whom our author follows, such an interpretation is inconceivable, given that it is 'sensum historicum excludens'. His own interpretation respects common sense, the historical and literal meaning, and theology: 'Dicendum est igitur, verum fuisse serpentem qui Evam adortus est, sed permissione divina à daemone possessum, qui in serpente loquebatur & ratiocinabatur.'[61] The hermeneutic principle informing this explanation – also that of the Calvinist interpretation of the *Hoc est corpus meum*[62] – is as follows. When the literal meaning is impossible (the standard of judgement is the *lumen naturale*) the words become signifiers of a spiritual sense. The excesses of allegory are to be avoided, however, by the harmonisation, as in the case of the serpent, of the literal and the spiritual sense.[63] Thus, both for Rivet and for Bayle the serpent remains a beast but the beast is a victim of demon possession. This choice of a specifically Calvinist interpretation indicates

---

59. *NRL*, juillet 1686, art.ii, *OD*, i.592b and 'Eve', footnote A, no V, *in fine*.

60. Cornelius à Lapide (1567-1637), whose real name was Cornelis Cornelissen Van den Steen, a Belgian Jesuit, studied the humanities, philosophy and theology with the Jesuits of Maëstricht, Cologne, Douai and Louvain. It was in this last city that he entered the Society of Jesus (1592). He later taught Hebrew and Holy Scripture in Louvain, whence he was called to Rome in 1616, where he taught until his death. His intention was to explicate the literal sense clearly and methodically but, in fact, he frequently has recourse to allegory (*DTC*, xvi.818, and Vigoureux, vol.ii, part 1, p.1014-15). His *Commentaria in Pentateuchum Mosis* appeared in 1616 and went into many editions. It attracted by its erudition, although Simon's opinion is somewhat disparaging (*Histoire critique*, p.423a). I have used the edition of Antwerp 1671 for the interpretation of the serpent: see p.78ff.

61. Rivet, *Theologicae et scholasticae exercitationes CXCI in Genesin* (1633), in *Operum*, i.113a. For the link between the literal and the historical sense in the seventeenth century, cf. Laplanche, 'L'Ecriture', ii.403ff.

62. Rex, *Essays*, p.75-193, *passim*. This principle also informs Bayle's interpretation of the anthropomorphisms in the Bible (see *CG*, letter xxviii, §xvii, *OD*, ii.134a-b; 'Rimini', footnote B, and many other passages in *CPD* and *RQP* Cf. also Jean-Robert Armogathe, 'De l'art de penser comme art de persuader', *La Conversion au XVIIe siècle*, Actes du Colloque du Centre méridional de rencontres sur le XVIIe siècle 12 (1983), p.29-41.

63. *Isagoge*, in *Operum*, ii.931a.

that, as in the critique of allegory, the author of the *Dictionnaire*'s hermeneutics depend, in the final analysis, on theological or religious considerations.[64]

The second set of problems arises in the article 'David', whose fidelity to the biblical text is scrupulous. In the course of the article Bayle realises that his respect for the apparently sequential order of the narrative necessitates the attribution to Saul of two incomprehensible lapses of memory. In the first place, while still a young shepherd, David was summoned to the royal court to soothe with music Saul's mental derangement. Yet some few years later, just after David's victory over Goliath, the monarch failed to recognise the youth to whom he owed a debt of gratitude.[65] In the second place, according to Scripture, David had two opportunities to slay Saul and seize the throne but his generous nature prevented his availing himself of either. Strange as it may seem, Saul fails to refer to the first occasion when he finds himself spared for the second time.[66] These parallel accounts provoke similar commentaries from Bayle, which none the less contain significant differences:

Si une Narration comme celle-ci se trouvoit dans Thucydide ou dans Tite-Live, tous les Critiques concluroient unanimement que les Copistes auroient transposé les pages, publié quelque chose en un lieu, répété quelque chose dans un autre, ou inséré des morceaux postiches dans l'Ouvrage de l'Auteur. Mais il faut bien se garder de pareils soupçons lors qu'il s'agit de la Bible.

Si je voiois deux Récits de cette nature, ou dans Elien, ou dans Valere Maxime, je ne ferois pas difficulté de croire qu'il n'y auroit là qu'un fait, qui aïant été raporté en deux manieres auroit servi de sujet à deux articles ou à deux chapitres [...] Je laisse au Pere Simon, & à des Critiques de sa volée, à examiner s'il seroit possible que les Livres Historiques du Vieux Testament raportassent deux fois la même chose.[67]

The two earlier attitudes to biblical criticism reappear simultaneously in an uneasy relationship between a radical re-organisation of the sacred text and an anxiety concerning the resultant challenge to its authority. The second remark intimates Bayle's sympathy towards Simon's techniques.[68] The activity of the

---

64. Simon argued that this preference for the theological sense was the antithesis of criticism.

65. 'David', *in corp.* and footnotes C (1697), D (1702); cf. 1 Samuel xvi.20 and xvii.55.

66. 'David', footnote K (1697), H (1702); cf. 1 Samuel xxiv and xxvi.

67. Respectively, 'David', footnotes C (1697), D (1702), and K (1697), H (1702).

68. To my knowledge Simon does not suggest, at least in the *Histoire critique*, that the book of Samuel is not in its 'original' order. The principle of parallel accounts is cautiously stated in the preface and illustrated by the example of the two-fold abduction of Sarah (cf. Genesis xii.12ff. and xx.1ff.). In the second case, Scripture reports that Abimelech brought Sarah to his harem, despite the fact that she was, given a linear chronology, 90 years old. Simon prefers to argue that the order of the narrative was confused by the copyists (*H.C.*, p.***3r-v). The fact that Bayle applies the *principle* to the book of Samuel argues for a familiarity with and acceptance of Simonian techniques. Before concluding that he thereby attempts to rid himself of his Calvinist heritage, two further points must be taken into consideration. Firstly, according to Vischer (p.228) and Laplanche, ('L'Ecriture', i.77ff.), Calvin, influenced by the humanists, believed that the narratives of Old

sacred authors is no different from that of the profane historian: both work from an antecedent document, whose parallel accounts were read as two separate incidents. Gone is the equation of the text as it stands and the original words of the divine author. Absent, too, is the notion of the inspiration or dictation of the original text. The Bible is now equated with any or all of the profane texts of Antiquity.[69] The historical books of the Old Testament are submitted to the critic, whose specialist knowledge alone is capable of creating a coherent text. This calm association of 'la raison des hommes' and 'la parole de Dieu' seems to depend on the earlier distinction between fundamental and inessential truths of Scripture. A minor discrepancy in the life of the psalmist is unlikely to raze the whole edifice of revelation. The critic achieves parity with Scripture although the scope of his activity is still limited by the antecedent doctrine of Scripture.[70]

The anxiety of the first remark is, therefore, all the more difficult to explain. Not only does it follow a less radical approach – the copyists and not the authors are the source of the discrepancies – but it too is concerned with the historical narratives of the Bible. We may only assume that, having internalised 'liberal' hermeneutics, Bayle perceives their logical conclusion: the authority of the source they claim to explicate is imperilled. An intellectually acceptable procedure becomes a psychological impossibility, as religious certitude threatens to disappear in the wake of rationalist criticism. The resultant *impasse* is not resolved at this juncture. In the article 'Lamech' (1st article), however, the obscurity of that patriarch's speech to his wives leads not to critical questions concerning variant readings but to a novel view of Holy Writ as an expression of the divine character.[71] The remark takes the form of a cross-reference to an

Testament prophets had suffered a similar fate at the hands of the copyists. Secondly, the ambivalence of Bayle's position may be judged from his handling of the abduction of Sarah. For a moment he seems inclined to follow Simon, for the two stories, by his own admission, 'se ressemblent comme deux gouttes d'eau' ('Sara', footnote B). However, the commentary turns into a censure of the patriarchs, all the more culpable for having twice committed the same sin ('Sara', footnote B). In this Bayle faithfully adheres to the Calvin/Rivet interpretation (cf. Rivet, *Exercitationes*, in *Operum*, i.277aff.). It might be added that Bayle's long discussion of Sarah's age ('Sara', footnote E), which is supposed to have inspired Voltaire's mockery (see 'Abraham', *Dictionnaire philosophique*, Paris 1961, p.2-6), draws directly on Rivet, even to the extent of appealing to certain contemporary women as examples of beauty persisting in middle years (given the longevity of the patriarchs, 90 is considered to represent middle-age). Cf. Rivet, *Exercitationes*, in *Operum*, i.277aff.

69. This attitude to the historical books of the Old Testament is very near to the position expressed by Jean Le Clerc in the *Sentimens de quelques théologiens de Hollande* (1685). There Le Clerc on the one hand places the historical books of the Old Testament on the same level as the profane works of Antiquity, while on the other arguing for a special providential guidance in the case of Scripture. The criteria for establishing the veracity of Scripture are, however, no different from those used to establish the reliability of an ancient historian. Cf. Labrousse, *Pierre Bayle*, ii.328ff., for Bayle's hostility to the work on its appearance.

70. Cf. Labrousse, *Pierre Bayle*, ii.327.

71. 'Lamech', article and footnote D. Referring in the third person to his own earlier remark,

earlier statement made in 1686, when Bayle was discussing the peculiarities of the story of the Fall:

de la maniere que Moïse raconte ce funeste événement, il paroît bien que son intention n'a pas été que nous sçussions comment l'affaire s'étoit passée, & cela seul doit persuader à toute personne raisonnable, que la plume de Moïse a été sous la direction particuliere du S. Esprit. En effet si Moïse eût été le maître de ses expressions & de ses pensées, il n'auroit jamais enveloppé d'une façon si étonnante le récit d'une telle action; il en auroit parlé d'un stile un peu plus humain, & plus propre à instruire la postérité; mais une force majeure, une sagesse infinie le dirigeoit de telle sorte qu'il écrivoit non pas selon ses vûës, mais selon les desseins cachez de la Providence. [72]

In this somewhat back-handed use of the proof of the divinity of Scripture from the majesty of its style, [73] the holy text achieves the status of a Christian mystery. Unlike the work of a human author, where clarity is to be expected, the Bible, as a divinely dictated text, necessarily contains obscurity. The difficulties met by the exegete are transformed into a proof of the divinity of Scripture: they point beyond themselves to the 'Sagesse infinie', whose thoughts are not man's thoughts and whose expressions at times defy man's understanding.

At this point we are perilously far from the Calvinist insistence on the clarity of the self-interpreting Scripture and dangerously near to the mock fideism of Voltaire. [74] None the less, while the statement subverts one trend in Bayle's thought, it is consistent with his frequent recourse to a theology of Scripture in order to cope with methodological problems. The theology is slightly altered but the intention is the same: the sacred text must be spared the destructive tendencies of human reason. The comments are not, however, to be read as an attempt to pre-empt biblical criticism. The Bible may at times share the obscurity inseparable from Christian mysteries but at others its dicta are clear and capable of intellectual apprehension. The approach of the critic is two-fold. He applies his skills to the explication of Scripture. If the text is resistant, he may choose to conclude that its expressions, unclear to him, are clear to its divine author. Then he places his hand over his mouth and bows before the inscrutable wisdom

---

Bayle observes: 'Au reste, je ne prétens pas combattre généralement parlant, la Pensée de ceux qui prennent pour des marques d'inspiration dans les Récits de Moïse, certaines singularitez qui sont de telle nature, qu'il ne semble pas qu'un Auteur les eut jamais emploiées, s'il avoit été le Directeur de son Ouvrage.' At marginal note (12), Bayle refers the reader to *NRL*, juillet 1686, art.ii.

72. *NRL*, juillet 1686, art.ii, *OD*, i.592a; cf. Labrousse, *Pierre Bayle*, ii.331-33. We should not be surprised by this sudden *volte-face* on Bayle's part, since, according to René Voeltzel ('Jean Le Clerc (1657-1736) et la critique biblique', in *Religion, érudition*, p.49-50), both Le Clerc and Simon bowed before the mysteries of Scripture, which their critical hypotheses could not unravel. Cf. Laplanche, 'L'Ecriture', iv.1023, who argues that the conflict between theology and criticism ends in the *Deus absconditus*.

73. This proof was a common-place of Reformed apologetics: cf. Laplanche, 'L'Ecriture', *passim*.

74. See, for example, Voltaire's article 'Abraham' in the *Dictionnaire philosophique* (p.2-6).

of God, who is hidden even in the act of self-revelation. Fideism is the final safeguard of a beleaguered Bible.

In 1686, the *philosophe* of Rotterdam put pen to paper in order to counteract the (this time) Catholic insistence on a literalist interpretation of the words 'Compelle intrare', to be found in the parable of the banquet.[75] The parable portrays a host – equated by commentators with Christ – whose guests cry off at the last minute. The blind and the lame of the town, invited to come instead, do not fill the tables. The host then instructs his servant: 'Et le Maître dit au Serviteur, va par les chemins & par les hayes, & contrains-les d'entrer, afin que ma Maison soit remplie.'[76] The Catholics, consistent with the doctrine of transubstantiation, which is based on a literalist interpretation of the *hoc est corpus meum*, read the statement literally, thereby justifying constraint in religious matters. In the *Commentaire philosophique* the Calvinist rejection of transubstantiation is extended to the defence of toleration. The extension is effected by a shift in the understanding of *lumière naturelle*, the criterion by which the notion of a transformation of the bread and wine into the body and blood of Christ is found to be repugnant.[77] The following quotation illustrates that shift (*CP*, I, i, *OD*, ii.367a):

je me contente de réfuter le sens littéral [des] Persécuteurs.

Je m'appuie, pour le réfuter invinciblement, sur ce principe de la lumiere naturelle, 'que tout sens littéral qui contient l'obligation de faire des crimes, est faux'. S Augustin donne cette regle & pour ainsi dire, ce *Criterium*, pour discerner le sens figuré, du sens à la lettre.

The guarantor of the sense of Scripture is reason seconded by ethics: a literalist interpretation which suggests unethical behaviour is false. The proof that constraint in religious affairs is unethical will preoccupy Bayle for the greater part of the *Commentaire*. At this early stage, however, he is concerned to justify the use of a rationalist ethics as a criterion to which the Bible itself is subject.

The justification takes the form of a theory of divine revelation which concentrates on the chronological sequence of human relations with the god-

---

75. Catholic insistence on the literal sense of Scripture was, by this stage, a well-worn apologetic tool. Cf. Rébelliau, *Bossuet*, p.12; Armogathe, 'De l'art de penser comme art de persuader', p.29-41; Laplanche, 'L'Ecriture', i.107ff.

76. *CP*, I, i, *OD*, ii.367; cf. Luke xiv.15ff.

77. Rex, *Essays*, p.155ff. Rex provides the intellectual background to this shift in the understanding of the *lumen naturale*. Since our purpose is to study Bayle's exegesis, the more complex question of the influences on the *Commentaire philosophique* must be left to one side. Suffice it to say that the rationalist and ethical approach to Scripture was in germ in Calvinist hermeneutic procedures, in contexts other than the eucharistic controversy – although Bayle's position was undoubtedly fortified by this controversy and the instruction of his teachers in Geneva (Laplanche, 'L'Ecriture', iii.543ff. and iv.856ff.).

head. In the beginning, that is in the Garden of Eden, according to Bayle, Adam had a two-fold knowledge of God: immediate and mediate. The first is a direct and perfect communion with the Almighty, the second a kind of primitive ethical theology, used to evaluate the justice of God's commands: '[il] est fort aparent à l'égard d'Adam [...] qu'il a connu la justice de la défense verbale de Dieu, en la comparant avec l'idée qu'il avoit déja de l'Etre suprême'.[78] A certain critical distance is conceived to operate right at the start of man's existence. The divine command was not accepted *per se* but because its justice was verified in the light of an antecedent knowledge of God's character. This simultaneously trims the godhead of much of its majesty and authority and grants mankind a certain amount of autonomy. Obedience to divine decrees hangs less on their inherent authority than on a human appraisal of their justice. Man's immediate knowledge functions as a criterion of truth to which the Divinity itself is subject.

After the Fall, this critical distance is transformed into a testing of supernatural phenomena by the light of reason. While man's immediate knowledge of God was impaired by original sin, communication from the Divinity continued under a different form: the patriarchs were visited by visions and voices relaying the will of God. However, given the malevolent intentions of the 'mauvais Anges', man needed a criterion to distinguish true from false supernatural utterances (*CP*, I, i, *OD*, ii.369a):

Et cette regle n'a pû être autre chose que la lumiere naturelle, que les sentimens d'honnêteté imprimez dans l'ame de tous les hommes; en un mot que cette Raison universelle qui éclaire tous les esprits, & qui ne manque jamais à ceux qui la consultent attentivement, & surtout dans ces intervales lucides, où les objets corporels ne remplissent pas la capacité de l'ame, soit par leurs images, soit par les passions qu'ils excitent dans notre cœur.

There is a continuity between man before and after the Fall, inasmuch as immediate is replaced by an innate knowledge, capable of distinguishing right from wrong. In other words, natural law, a kind of primitive post-lapsarian revelation of the will of God, now functions as a criterion. The capacities of natural reason have certainly been impaired by the Fall but, given favourable epistemological circumstances – the silence of the imagination and the passions – the truth may be apprehended.[79] The autonomy of man continues, even in his

---

78. *CP*, I, i, *OD*, ii.369b. This and the ensuing stages of the argument seem to be a somewhat original application of Amyraut's covenant theology to exegesis. On Amyraut, see Laplanche, 'L'Ecriture', iii.539ff.

79. Rex, *Essays*, p.155ff., indicates the influence of Malebranche (*Recherche*, vol.i, bk.III, ch.6). A word might be added on the problem of Bayle's Augustinianism. It was argued (above, ch.3, n.124) that Bayle's approach to Maimbourg reveals his application to history of the theological notion of total depravity. Ensuing discussions with Elisabeth Labrousse have led me to believe that the conflict between our respective interpretations arises out of the ambivalence in Bayle's own attitude to

fallen state: he accepts and submits to revelation when it conforms to the dictates of natural law. There is, however, no real opposition between reason, natural law and Revelation: God is the author of them all. If a vision or personal revelation, accorded to the patriarchs, commanded an act contrary to natural law, it is deemed contrary to the will of God.

A notion of precedence emerges, none the less, with the advent of *la loi positive*. The patriarchal age yielded to the age where divinely inspired and recorded Revelation – whether in the Old or the New Testaments – was the rule of faith and conduct. Surprisingly, however, far from taking precedence over natural reason and natural law, the divinity of Scripture is established by *la lumière naturelle* (*CP* I, i, *OD*, ii.369b):

Il a falu que Dieu ait marqué ce qui venoit de lui d'une certaine empreinte, qui fût conforme à la lumiere interieure qui se communique immédiatement à tous les esprits, ou qui du moins n'y parût pas contraire; & cela fait, on recevait agréablement, & comme venant de Dieu, toutes les loix particulieres d'un Moïse & d'un autre Prophete, encore qu'elles ordonnassent des choses indifférentes de leur nature.

Two interdependent criteria of truth are given here. The divinity of Scripture is accepted either as a result of the absolute continuity between the light of reason and that of Revelation or because biblical dictates are not contradictory to those of natural law. This effectively means, in Walter Rex's words, that the authority of Scripture is subjected to 'the absolute negative authority of reason' (p.111).

In practice this chronology of Revelation is transformed into a 'hermeneutic chain' whose three crucial links, natural reason, natural law, and Holy Writ must remain unbroken if the true sense of Scripture is to be discovered. One example will suffice. Using one of his favourite didactic methods, Bayle posits a hypothetical discussion between a *Casuïste* and the author of the *Commentaire*. The former is said to argue 'qu'il trouve dans l'Ecriture qu'il est bon & saint de maudire ses ennemis' (*CP*, I, i, *OD*, ii.369a). In his reply, Bayle appeals to the argument from epistemology: the Scripture to which his opponent appeals 'n'est qu'une vapeur bilieuse de tempérament'. That is to say, the *apparently* Scriptural argument of the Casuist is in fact the fruit of a post-lapsarian psychology of the soul. He has falsified the hermeneutic procedure by allowing

Augustinian theology. The ambivalence can be eliminated by arguing that, although Bayle maintains that human beings can perceive the true and the good, their fallen nature prevents their acting on either (this is frequently the position of the *PD* and the *CPD*). This harmonisation is, however, in our opinion, a betrayal of Bayle's thought, where both the Augustinian position and the rationalist appeal to man's ability to act on his ethical insights (*CP*) co-exist. The question, complex as it is, merits a study which would explore the ways in which the demands of controversy cause Bayle to alter his position. For a brief account, see below, p.189ff., and Ruth Whelan, 'La religion à l'envers: Bayle et l'histoire du paganisme antique', in *Les Religions du paganisme antique dans l'Europe chrétienne XVI-XVIIIe s.* (Paris 1987), p.115-28.

the *lumière naturelle* to be dominated by the passions. In a very real sense the Catholic insistence on a literalist interpretation of the *compelle intrare* is seen to constitute the *imposition* of a 'depraved meaning' on the sacred text: a meaning, moreover, which will be sabotaged throughout the *Commentaire philosophique* by an insistence on toleration as the only doctrine which respects the absolute continuity – established by God himself – between natural and revealed law. While the dangers inherent in this essentially rationalist exegetical mode are half-perceived at this stage, it is in the *Dictionnaire* that the real crisis occurs.[80]

The problem of Old Testament moral standards arises in one of the two groups of articles devoted to the patriarchal age: 'Abimelech', 'Abraham', 'Agar', 'Sara' and, linked by cross-references, 'Acindynus (Septimus)' and 'Sophronie'.[81] Two cases of dubious morality are discussed, namely Abraham and Sarah's reiterated dissimulation of their marital status, and the legitimacy of the patriarch's sexual relations with Hagar.[82] In the first case, two famines, separated by an interval of twenty-five years, drove the couple from their home

80. It is clear from Bayle's discussion of the violent sentiments expressed by the Psalmist, Elijah's slaying of the prophets of Baal and the command, recorded in Deuteronomy xii.12ff., whereby idolators were to be exterminated (see *CP*, *OD*, ii.368a, 409a and 407a-409a, respectively) that these passages embarrassed him. They were, in fact, used by his opponents to justify intolerance. At this stage, however, he contents himself with arguing, firstly, that the severity of the Mosaic law is abrogated by the New Testament ethic of peace and charity (Erasmus also refused any interpretation of Scripture which would authorise violence: Laplanche, 'L'Ecriture', i.61). Secondly, both David and Elijah were presided over by 'une providence spéciale' (p.368a), which means that their conduct cannot be transformed into a general principle. By the time the *Dictionnaire* appeared, however, everything had changed, for Jurieu, against whom the articles 'Elie' and 'David' are directed, had claimed in the interval the support of a special Providence in defence of his political ideas (cf. Rex, *Essays*, p.197-255). Thus, as Bayle himself indicates ('Elie', footnote B and marginal note 12), the article 'Elie' contains a shift in his own position. Both Elijah and David are deprived of the support of divine Providence for their acts of violence (cf. 'David', footnote D (1697), withdrawn at the request of the Consistory: see the judgements of 17 November 1697 and 17 December 1697, *Actes du Consistoire de l'Eglise wallonne de Rotterdam*, in *Dictionnaire*, ed. Beuchot, xvi.287-300 and n.100). What this in effect means is that Scripture is itself threeatened by the criterion of natural law, now the standard by which parts of the Bible may be considered both canonical and inspired (cf. 'Judith', and footnotes A and B). It is this, together with the Manichean arguments, which precipitates the 'second' fideistic answer to the dilemmas posed by rationalism (see below, p.175-79) and corresponding notes.

81. We touch here on the question of the genesis of the articles of the *Dictionnaire*, for not only are 'Abraham', 'Sara', 'Agar', and 'Abimelech' linked together in Rivet's commentary, the discussion also spills over into a consideration of a case concerning Acyndinus, noted by St Augustine, and the reaction of the early Christian lady Sophronia to attacks against her virtue (*Exercitationes*, in *Operum*, i.281ff.). It is apparent to anyone reading Rivet and the *Dictionnaire* in parallel, that our author used Rivet as a 'reading guide', following up the references given by that author. The often bizarre selection of biographies which Bayle offers in his *magnum opus* may, then, result from the leads given by his many sources.

82. See Genesis xii.12ff., xx.1ff., xvi.1-15, xxi.8-21; 'Abimelech', footnotes B and C; 'Sara', footnotes A, C, and E; 'Agar', footnote C.

to the protection of Pharaoh of Egypt and Abimelech of Gerar respectively. Sarah, despite her advanced age, was a woman of striking beauty and Abraham feared he would be murdered in order to facilitate her abduction. Since they were also half-brother and half-sister, the patriarch advised his wife to pass herself off as his sister. Unfortunately, while the ploy saved Abraham's life, it precipitated his spouse into the harems of the respective monarchs. But for divine intervention, Sarah's virtue would have been compromised.[83] According to Jesuit exegetes, given the patriarch's consanguinity the introduction of Sarah as Abraham's sister does not constitute a lie.[84] Bayle rejects this contention, revealing as he does so not only his moral rigorism but also his confessional allegiance.

The argument is directed against the 'doctrine des équivoques', popularised and ridiculed in the *Provinciales*, whereby, in the words of Sanchez, 'il est permis d'user de termes ambigus, en les faisant entendre en un autre sens qu'on ne les entend soi-même'.[85] To the *philosophe* of Rotterdam, however, any reply which does not respect the intention of the person asking the question must be seen as a lie ('Sara', footnote D):

Ceux qui combatent la mauvaise morale d'un Lessius, & de quelques autres Jésuites, mettent en fait que c'est mentir, que de faire des réponses qui ne se raportent pas à l'intention de celui qui vous interroge. Ces réponses ont beau ne contenir que la vérité, elles ne laissent pas d'être menteuses [...] En un mot, la suppression d'une vérité est un mensonge effectif, toutes les fois qu'elle est destinée à faire faire de faux jugemens à l'auditeur [...] Abraham & Sara sont dans le cas.

The Casuist argument to the effect that 'c'est l'intention qui règle l'action' is reversed to read that the intention is to be *deduced from* the action. Consequently, the effect of the dissimulation practised by Abraham and Sarah on the two monarchs implies that it was certainly their intention to deceive, and, as such, they are to be censured for what must necessarily be called a lie. This unapologetic approach to the moral failings of biblical heroes has long been interpreted as a 'profanation – on Bayle's part – of the sacredness of sacred

83. Cf. the discussion of the problem by the R. P. Gabriel Daniel, *Réponse aux Lettres provinciales de L. Montalte ou Entretiens de Cleandre et d'Eudoxe* (Cologne 1696). (This edition used by Bayle, p.342-67.) Daniel uses the case of the patriarch's lie to defend the 'doctrine des équivoques' and fortifies his position by appealing to St Augustine's interpretation. It must be concluded, then, that Bayle's position is iconoclastic but, like Rivet and Calvin before him, it is an iconoclasm directed against a certain theological tradition and not against Scripture itself.

84. 'Non mentitur Abram', writes Cornelius à Lapide, 'erat enim Sara eius soror eo sensu, quo dicam, c.20, v.12' (*Commentaria*, p.149a; cf. p.187a). Lapide belonged to the Molinist/Baist school of thought; his exegesis cannot therefore be separated from his theological position. I am grateful to Jacques Le Brun for this and other information on Lapide.

85. Respectively, 'Sara', footnote B, *in fine*, and Pascal, *Les Provinciales*, letter IX, p.164. The quotation is translated by the author from Sanchez, *Opus morale*.

history'.[86] The fact is, however, as Bayle is aware, that Jean Calvin and André Rivet both speak in similar terms of the patriarchs' lapse. The affinity becomes strikingly obvious in the second stage of the discussion.

The debate centres – as does Rivet's commentary, which Bayle follows step by step – on St Augustine's interpretation of the incident and the question as to whether the end can justify the means. Augustine and, to a certain extent, Calvin present Abraham's special destiny as a justification of his fear. In other words, given that the Christ was to come from the patriarch's descendants, he was obliged to save his own life in order to father Isaac. While Calvin condemns the means chosen, inasmuch as Sarah was placed in a potentially adulterous situation, Augustine dares not censure the patriarch.[87] Bayle's intervention takes the form of a long commentary on the problem, followed by a quotation from Rivet:

Un grand Théologien comme lui [St Augustine] ne devoit-il pas savoir, que notre vie, qui n'est qu'un bien temporel & périssable, ne doit pas être assez précieuse pour nous sembler digne d'être rachetée par la désobéissance à la loi de Dieu? [...] je ne dis rien des abimes de la corruption, que l'on ouvre de toutes parts sous nos pieds, en nous disant qu'une chose, qui seroit un crime, si on la faisoit sans avoir dessein de sauver sa vie, devient innocente, lors qu'on la fait pour sauver sa vie. [...] Qui ne voit, que si une telle Morale avoit lieu, il n'y auroit point de précepte dans le Décalogue, dont la crainte de la mort ne nous dispensât? [...] Ecoutons un Théologien [Rivet], qui, pour avoir vêcu plusieurs siecles après ce Pere, ne laisse pas d'être meilleur Moraliste sur ce point. 'Qua in re mirum est talem ac tantum virum potuisse dubitare, cum ex sacra Scriptura constet apertissimè, malum aliquod poenae, nunquam esse redimendum malo culpae, & vitam potius esse deponendam, quam ut eam nobis aut aliis servemus, id facientes ex quo Deus offenderetur.'[88]

The argument has four stages. Firstly, the interpretation of the episode is similar, in its double movement, to the hermeneutics of the *Commentaire*

---

86. Howard Robinson, 'Bayle's profanation of sacred history', *Essays in intellectual history* (New York 1929), p.147-62. (I am grateful to the Cambridge University Library for providing me with a xerox of this article.) It is interesting to note that Cornelius à Lapide records and espouses Bellarmin's condemnation of Calvin for a similar 'profanation' (*Commentaria*, p.164b-65a).

87. Rivet, *Exercitationes*, in *Operum*, i.281a; Calvin, *Commentaires de M. Jean Calvin sur les cinq Livres de Moyse* (Genève 1564), p.99-100, and Augustine, *De Sermone Domine in Monte*, I, 16, in *Opera* (Antwerpiae 1576-1577), iv.337b-39a. It is in the course of his commentary on the definition of that fornication which is considered a legitimate reason for divorce (Matthew v.31-32) that Augustine tells the story of Acyndinus's lust. The wife, who saved her husband's life by granting one night to the tyrant, is presented as both chaste (for it was not she who desired the monarch) and charitable (p.339a). Her act of 'fornication' is not a legitimate cause for divorce, since it was an act of obedience to her husband, who took advantage of the apostle's recommendation in 1 Corinthians vii.4. (The discussion and application of this verse to Sarah and Abraham occurs in *Adversus Faustum Manichaeum*, xxii, 33, *Opera*, vi.170a.) For Bayle's attitude to the application of this verse to 'un tiers & un quart', see 'Anabaptistes', footnote M at marginal citation 53.

88. 'Acindynus (Septimus)', footnote C, and Rivet, *Exercitationes*, in *Operum*, i.281a.

*philosophique*. The rejection of a Catholic interpretation – shared, curious to note, by St Augustine and the Jesuits – depends on a maxim drawn from natural law: namely, 'Il n'est pas permis de sauver sa Vie ni celle d'un autre par un Crime.'[89] Secondly, the behaviour of the patriarchs is opposed to the law of God. Natural and divine law concur in their condemnation of the act. Implicit at this stage is the earlier notion of a post-lapsarian psychology of the soul, giving rise to a faulty exegesis. St Augustine certainly knows that the law of God should not be sacrificed to expediency but, in this instance, his judgement is clouded. Thirdly, Bayle alludes to the pernicious consequences of the Augustinian interpretation. Failure to censure the patriarchs' sin creates a precedent capable of subverting all the precepts of the *Decalogue*. To the three elements of his hermeneutic chain he adds, in the fourth place, a citation from Rivet. The quotation forms an integral part of the argument, inasmuch as it too is opposed to St Augustine and for similar reasons. The appeal to Rivet constitutes, however, more than an appreciation of his moral rigorism. Bayle, more perceptive than his critics, identifies his own exegesis with that of his forebear.

The identification proceeds on the methodological level. Firstly, referring to the earlier commentary, it is clear that Rivet is keen to establish a critical attitude towards Scripture:

Non est enim quod omnia Patrum facta excusemus, vel omnia quae à scriptura commemorantur, probari posse putemus; sed id tantum eorum acta utriusque generis maximè insignia afferri, ut sciamus eos homines fuisse, & quantumvis essent sanctissimi, lapsos aliquando, saepè per errorem, ut de hoc facto credendum: Quod non solum Doctissimi Ebraeorum culpant: sed etiam inter veteres Christianos fuerunt.[90]

The fear, present in Bayle's analysis, is obvious here, albeit differently expressed. The exegete is worried lest the development of a biblical hagiography – which fails to censure glaring moral faults – leads to the undermining of the ethical standards of Scripture. Consequently he maintains that the biographies of biblical heroes are to be tested (*probare*) and claims the authority of an exegetical tradition to justify this apparently inconoclastic approach.[91] Secondly, while the criteria by which the morals of the patriarchs are to be judged are not mentioned, they may be deduced from Rivet's practice, as also from his theoretical work on exegesis, the *Isagoge*. His analysis of the patriarchs' lie indicates that he is working from a principle of natural law and that the infringement of that law is read as an offence against God. Not only that but, in the *Isagoge*, Rivet argues

89. 'Abimelech', footnote A, *in fine*.
90. Rivet, *Exercitationes*, in *Operum*, i.282a.
91. Rivet also deliberately associates his exegesis of the passage with that of Calvin and defends the latter against Cornelius à Lapide, p.270ff. Cf. Laplanche, 'L'Ecriture' (iii.543ff.) for a similar exegesis in the Saumur school.

for the absolute continuity between the *lumen naturale* and the *propositiones revelatae in verbo Dei*.[92] The two positions are not welded together, as in Bayle's hermeneutic. It is easy, none the less, to imagine how, in the heat of composition, the earlier exegete's position was interpreted as the exact counterpart of that of the author of the *Dictionnaire*.

The two additions to the article 'Sara' in the 1702 edition of the *Dictionnaire*, which reinforce the author's severe judgement of Abraham's sexual relations with Hagar, testify to the consistency of his hermeneutic procedures. Footnotes I and K, forming a commentary on the additional note C of the article 'Agar', seek to undermine St Augustine's *apologia* for the patriarch. To Augustine Abraham's uncomplaining dismissal of Hagar, at his wife's instigation, implies that he had eschewed lust and taken a concubine only for the worthy purpose of procreation. Properly understood, Abraham and Hagar's relations are worthy of praise as an act of obedience to Sarah.[93] Bayle could have seen this as an attempt at a historical reconstruction of the mentality and customs of antiquity. Instead, he maintains his earlier position ('Sara', footnote K):

> si le commerce du Patriarche avec sa servante est mauvais en soi, il ne devient pas légitime par l'aquiescement d'Abraham aux desirs de Sara; les conseils, ni les suggestions d'une femme ne disculpent point le mari à l'égard des choses illégitimes [...] N'abîmeroit-on pas aujourd'hui les Baunis, & les Escobars, s'ils enseignoient que pourvu qu'on se proposât uniquement de laisser des successeurs, une femme pourroit animer son époux à jouïr de leur servante, & un mari pourroit suivre ce beau conseil?

The worthy end of procreation is incapable of justifying the immoral means to that end, and again the spectre of *la morale relâchée* hangs over the analysis. The standard by which the concubinage is judged to be immoral is, as the article 'Lamech' (1st article) reveals, that of natural law. 'La Loi monogamique' was established 'dans le Paradis terrestre' and ought, therefore, to have ruled the patriarchs' behaviour. Curiously, Rivet is not produced here as a *texte d'appui*. The reason is simple: the much-admired exegete holds a more relativistic, historical understanding of polygamy. It existed for a time, by divine permission, so that the world as yet in its infancy might be populated.[94] Bayle turns elsewhere for his authority.

It seems probable, given that the references to Calvin's commentary on *Genesis* occur only in the second edition of the *Dictionnaire*, that Bayle read (or

---

92. Rivet, *Isagoge*, in *Operum*, ii.942b, and Honders, p.130-45. I am most grateful to Jean-Michel Dufays, who read and summarised this chapter for me.

93. Augustine, *De civitate Dei*, XVI, 25, in *Opera*, v.197a. Augustine again argues from 1 Corinthians vii.4.

94. Rivet devotes many pages to the question (*Exercitationes*, in *Operum*, i.176a-85b).

re-read?) it in the interval between the two editions (1696-1701).[95] We can only conjecture as to why he has recourse at that precise moment to the writings of the sixteenth-century Reformer. If the scandals which broke out after the publication of the first edition of his *magnum opus* are borne in mind, however, the tenor of the quotations from Calvin suggests a disguised *apologia* for the 'maniere si peu respectueuse' which Bayle was said to use toward '[les] Saints Patriarches'.[96] The *apologia* has three stages. Firstly, the Reformer is singled out for his *franchise* ('Sara', footnote I):

La maniere ronde & franche, dont Calvin juge de cette conduite du mari & de la femme, fait voir clairement qu'il ne cherchoit point de détours. Il en dit son sentiment avec la derniere liberté, & il se sert de tout le droit que la Raison & l'Ecriture nous donnent de prononcer sur la qualité d'une action. [...] C'est là le langage d'un Casuiste qui ne bïaise point [...].

Picking up a phrase which recurs obsessively in the Reformer's commentaries ('la Raison & l'Ecriture') Bayle pinpoints the methodological principle behind Calvin's frank censure. Given that no judgement of the act is provided by the Scripture, the exegete may appeal to reason to supply the silence. Far from being in conflict, reason complements the Scripture in the Reformer's exegesis. Again ignoring the niceties of historical context, Bayle indicates that his rationalist exegesis is practised by no less a representative of orthodoxy than Jean Calvin.

The second stage deepens the impression of a self-identification on Bayle's behalf. For he stresses the fact that the Reformer's severe judgements stem from his espousal of natural law as an exegetical tool:

Ma seconde Remarque est que les lumieres de Calvin sont beaucoup plus pures sur ce point-là que celles des anciens Peres. Il condamne nettement & sans détour la conduite d'Abraham & Sara. Il ne leur cherche point d'excuses dans l'usage de la polygamie établi déjà parmi les Nations, il prétend que ce n'étoit pas à eux à choquer la Loi qui lie les mariez un avec une.[97]

The opposition of a 'Calvinist' exegete to the early Fathers, present in the analysis of Rivet, occurs again here. The purity of the Reformer's exegesis results from his respect for the totality of Revelation, whether in its natural or

95. Bayle may even have used Rivet as a guide, remembering his defence of Calvin against the charge of profanation of sacred Scripture (cf above nn. 86, 91). The charges against Calvin are discussed in detail in 'Sara', footnote I.

96. The sentence is from the abbé Renaudot's *Jugement* on the *Dictionnaire*, which was circulated by Jurieu (cf. Labrousse, i.246-48, and Bayle, *Réflexions sur un imprimé*, in *Dictionnaire*, iv.3025) and was repeated by the minister in his *Philosophe de Rotterdam accusé*, p.60-61, from which the quotation is taken.

97. 'Sara', footnote K. Laplanche, 'L'Ecriture', iii.720ff., demonstrates that Amyraut also defends his ethical, rationalist exegesis by appealing to Calvin.

written form. In his hermeneutics, according to the author of the *Dictionnaire*, an absolute continuity exists between the law of nature and the law of Scripture, and the absence of value judgements in the biblical narrative means that the deeds of the patriarchs are to be judged in the light of the former.[98] In other words, the Bible is subject to an antecedent Revelation, held to come from God himself – a position, for all that, rationalist in its implications. While Bayle's position is more extreme, the appeal to Calvin is intended to lend a certain authority to his exegesis: the *Dictionary* articles are but a part of a Reformed tradition of biblical interpretation.

Finally, to this Calvinist pedigree Bayle adds an indication of the utility of his exegesis. The comment points to a salutary iconoclasm present in the Reformer's commentaries ('Sara', footnote K):

En troisieme lieu j'observe, que la liberté que Calvin a prise de censurer fortement cette action de Sara, & de son époux, est incomparablement plus utile à la Morale Chrétienne, que le soin qu'ont pris les Peres de justifier Abraham & son épouse. Ils ont sacrifié les intérêts généraux de la Morale à la réputation d'un particulier; & peu s'en faut que je n'aplique à tou ceux qui sont animez de cet esprit ce bon mot de Ciceron: 'Urbem philosophiae proditis dum castella defenditis.'

Here the two sets of problems present in the biblical articles coalesce, insofar as both are directed against a patristic exegesis, considered noxious in its effect. A confessional opposition is set up, echoing the contentions of seventeenth-century Huguenot polemicists, wherein Calvinist hermeneutics is presented as a defence and Catholic exegesis as a betrayal of Christianity.[99] That is to say, Bayle fears that patristic hagiography, in its protection of the reputation of the patriarchs, will expose the Bible to the *irrisio infidelium*: the glorified immorality of biblical heroes will be read as a reason to reject the religion which venerates them. Consequently, as Labrousse has so judiciously observed, Bayle's biblical iconoclasm is directed less against the Scripture itself than against an exegetical tradition, one whose superstitious interpretations are to be sabotaged.[100]

98. Laplanche, 'L'Ecriture', iii.720ff. for Calvin's exegesis and attitude to the patriarchs; Wendel, p.30-31, 206-208, for the importance of natural law in Calvin's thought.

99. Laplanche, *L'Evidence*, i.105 and *passim*.

100. *Pierre Bayle*, ii.332, n.55, and 333ff. Here Bayle's Protestantism touches the chord common to the thinkers of Augustinian persuasion in the seventeenth century, be they Oratorian, Jansenist or Calvinist. This 'courant sévère' unites in a common desire to defend the Scripture against rationally or morally lax interpretations. For reasons of space, the article 'David' has been deliberately excluded from this analysis. Furthermore, as Walter Rex has demonstrated (*Essays*, p.197-225), the target of the article is different from that of the others. Certain methodological principles common to all the articles may, however, be traced. Firstly, the article devoted to the Psalmist is also iconoclastic in its thrust, while the hagiography to be sabotaged is now a Protestant one. That is to say, just as Bayle attempts to deprive *la morale relâchée* of its scriptural basis, so he tries to strip Jurieu's political position of its biblical justification. Secondly, the same hermeneutic procedures

## 6. The Ariadne's thread: Bayle and Scripture

These preoccupations place Bayle nearer in spirit to the exegesis and concerns of his own confession than it does to the mock-seriousness of Voltaire. The potential reversibility of his arguments – which the *Encyclopédie* will not be slow to note[101] – cannot be laid to his account. During his lifetime he was known to sigh over the gradual disappearance of an erudite reading public. It is this, in our opinion, which contributed to the eighteenth-century image of the *philosophe* of Rotterdam as an author who thumbs his nose at everything sacred. The rising generation of writers and *honnêtes gens* could hardly be expected to read his exegesis in the context of the long-forgotten confessional disputes and apologetic traditions which inspire it. Stripped of this context, however, it is hardly surprising that a thought as highly allusive and a literary style as apparently irreverent[102] as Bayle's should transform him into a figurehead of the Age of Reason. It must, moreover, be admitted that the tensions created in his work by his preoccupation with Manicheism did little to facilitate comprehension on the part of the next wave of writers.

The question raised by the series of articles in the *Dictionnaire* devoted to Pyrrhonism and the problem of evil is too vast to be adequately treated in a conclusion.[103] We shall content ourselves with a consideration of the arguments in footnote B to the article 'Pyrrhon', concerning the 'ethics' of the Fall. There

are used to censure David's behaviour. The passage is worth quoting, since it provides a summary, by our author himself, of the conceptual framework of the biblical articles. 'Mais le profond respect que l'on doit avoir pour ce grand Roi, pour ce grand Prophête, ne nous doit pas empêcher de desaprouver les taches qui se rencontrent dans sa vie; autrement nous donnerions lieu aux profanes de nous reprocher, qu'il suffit afin qu'une action soit juste qu'elle ait été faite par certains gens que nous vénérons. Il n'y auroit rien de plus funeste que cela à la Morale Chrétienne. Il est important pour la vraie Religion, que la vie des Orthodoxes soit jugée par les idées générales de la droiture & de l'ordre' ('David', footnote D (1697, withdrawn in 1702)). Natural law must, then, be added to Scripture if the pernicious effects of glorified sin are to be avoided. Finally, as Haydn Mason (p.33) and Walter Rex (*Essays*, p.252-55) have argued, our author's unremitting emphasis on the immorality of Old Testament heroes, and notably David, drives a wedge between the two Testaments. It is not, in our opinion, Bayle's desire to imply that the Christian religion is founded on a ridiculous and immoral Old Testament. None the less, caught in the vice-grip of his own problems and polemical intentions, he triggers off a problem which the eighteenth-century *philosophes* will delightedly turn against the Revelation that Bayle apparently wants to defend.

101. This has been documented by Mason, p.25-34, and Rétat, *Le Dictionnaire, passim*.

102. Cf. Ruth Whelan, 'The wages of sin is orthodoxy: the *Confessions* of Saint Augustine in Bayle's *Dictionnaire*, *Journal of the history of philosophy* 26 (1988), p.195-207.

103. The problem of Bayle's Manichean, Pyrrhonist and fideistic leanings has been more than adequately treated by others: cf. for example, Brush, p.160-331; James (above, p.150, n.22), and the reply by H. T. Mason, 'Pierre Bayle's religious views', *French studies* 17 (1963), p.205-17; Labrousse, *Pierre Bayle*, ii.153ff., and 346ff.; and Sandberg, *passim*. While I adhere to the spirit of Sandberg's work, namely its attempt to seize a paradox and a tension in Bayle's thought, I disagree with his assessment of the chronology of our author's move away from rationalism (p.26ff.): for, as we have seen, rationalism and distrust of reason co-exist in the later years. Richard Popkin's article 'Pierre Bayle's place in 17th-century scepticism', in *Pierre Bayle le philosophe de Rotterdam*, ed. Dibon, p.1-19, provides a helpful analysis of the paradoxical nature of our author's position.

Bayle's rationalism not only plays devil's advocate but also, in his critique of traditional theological explanations of that 'funeste evenement', he comes dangerously near to blasphemy. The argument is presented in the form of a dialogue – a fact which should immediately alert the critic to its *didactic* intentions[104] – between an *abbé pyrrhonien* and an *abbé catholique* and contains a three-fold opposition between natural law and the behaviour of the Divinity at the time of the Fall. In the first place, divine passivity is confronted with the self-evident maxim that evil must always be prevented, where possible ('Pyrrhon', footnote B):

Il est évident qu'on doit empêcher le mal si on le peut, & qu'on peche si on le permet lorsqu'on le peut empêcher. Cependant, notre Théologie nous montre que cela est faux: elle nous enseigne que Dieu ne fait rien qui ne soit digne de ses perfections, lorsqu'il soufre tous les desordres qui sont au monde, & qu'il lui étoit facile de prévenir.

The statement highlights in summary form a conflict between divine omnipotence and beneficence which is treated at length elsewhere in the *Dictionnaire*. In theory, God had the power to stifle evil at birth, either by choosing to create a different world or by granting a special grace to man in order to empower him to resist evil. The fact that he did not, if reason and/or natural law is our guide, implies either that he is not all-powerful or that he is not all-good ('Manichéens', footnote D). Hence, by default, God may be said to be the author of sin. This rationalist, blasphemous conclusion is tempered, however, by the presence of the theological interpretation of the Fall, wherein God's perfections are in no way diminished by the birth of evil. None the less, Bayle's use of natural law as a criterion in exegesis has led his critics to believe that his sympathies are other than theological in this matter.[105]

Original sin is the subject of the second opposition, which is permeated by a similar ambivalence. Here, the doctrine of the transmission of Adam's sin to the rest of mankind is considered ('Pyrrhon', footnote B):

Il est évident qu'une créature, qui n'existe point, ne sauroit être complice d'une action mauvaise. Et qu'il est injuste de la punir comme complice de cette action. Néanmoins notre doctrine du péché originel nous montrre la fausseté de ces évidences.

The comment undermines the Augustino-Calvinist explanation of the mode of transmission of original sin. Following Augustine, Calvin argues that the corruption and consequent judgement of all mankind stems from an ordinance

---

104. It would be impossible to document Bayle's use of dialogue as a pedagogic form. Apart from the fact that most of the miscellaneous works are written in epistolary form – a kind of dialogue – the *CP* and the *Dictionnaire* bear witness to the multitude of dialogues invented as an art of persuasion and demonstration.

105. For example, Mason, *passim*.

of God. That is to say, designating, as it were, Adam as a representative of the whole human race, the Almighty condemned all mankind in him (Wendel, p.195). It is precisely the legitimacy of this judgement which is opposed to self-evident principles: an inexistent being cannot be accused of criminal complicity. Thus, in the light of natural law the judgement of the whole human race in Adam cannot escape the charge of injustice. The final 'néanmoins' appears, in consequence, as more of an after-thought than an alternative. It appears to be proposed as an ineffective palliative to an incurably corrupt Providence.

The final opposition, informed by Bayle's pessimism, undermines Augustinian and Cartesian cosmogony:

Il est évident qu'il faut préférer l'honnête à l'utile, & que plus une cause est sainte, moins elle a la liberté de postposer l'honnêteté à l'utilité. Cependant, nos Théologiens nous disent que Dieu aiant à choisir entre un monde parfaitement bien réglé & orné de toute vertu, & un monde tel que celui-ci, où le péché & le desordre dominent, a préféré celui-ci à celui-là, parce qu'il y trouvoit mieux les intérêts de sa gloire.[106]

With something of a sleight of hand, the purpose of divine Providence in creating the world finds itself ranged with *l'utile* against *l'honnête*. Consequently, the notion of the glorification of God as the final cause of Creation, espoused by Calvin and Malebranche (to name but two of Bayle's sometime models), is turned on its head. The strength of the argument lies in its *a posteriori* reasoning. The sin and misery which dominate the world point to a God whose purpose of glorification is incompatible with virtue ('Manichéens', footnote D). That is to say, on three accounts, the self-same ethical principles which Bayle elsewhere sees as compatible with Reformed hermeneutics are turned against both a Reformed theology and the Scripture which informs it.

In the face of the outraged protestations of his contemporaries, the *philosophe* of Rotterdam staunchly maintains the propedeutic function of his arguments:

Il est plus utile qu'on ne pense, d'humilier la Raison de l'homme, en lui montrant avec quelle force les Hérésies les plus folles, comme sont celles des Manichéens, se jouent de ses lumieres, pour embrouiller les véritez les plus capitales. Cela doit aprendre aux Sociniens, qui veulent que la Raison soit la regle de la Foi, qu'ils se jettent dans une voie d'égarement, qui n'est propre qu'à les conduire de degré en degré jusques à nier tout, ou jusques à douter de tout, & qu'ils s'engagent à être batus par les gens les plus exécrables. Que faut-il donc faire? Il faut captiver son entendement sous l'obéissance de la foi, & ne disputer jamais sur certaines choses. En particulier, il ne faut combatre les Manichéens que par l'Ecriture, & par le principe de la soumission, comme fit saint Augustin.[107]

---

106. 'Pyrrhon', footnote B; cf. Wendel, p.141ff. and 171ff.; Henri Gouhier, *La Philosophie de Malebranche et son expérience religieuse* (Paris 1926), p.15-40.

107. 'Pauliciens', footnote F. This position is maintained consistently throughout the *Dictionnaire*: see, for example, 'Arminius', footnote E; 'Charron', footnote I; 'Manichéens', footnote D; 'Pyrrhon',

The force of Bayle's seemingly blasphemous arguments is here explained. A strategy rather than a conclusion, it is intended – to use one of his own expressions – to 'battre son ennemi sur son propre fumier'. Aware of the rationalism which informs both his own theology and hermeneutics and that of his contemporaries, the author of the *Dictionnaire* does an about-turn and demonstrates the final bankruptcy of reason when confronted with the mysteries of faith.[108] Like the final attitude in the face of Simonian exegesis, however, the position is more of a paradox than a solution: it attempts to hold in tension two mutually exclusive approaches to Scripture. The sacred text is, at one and the same time, subject and lord of reason. In matters of ethics, reason and natural law become the final court of appeal while in the doctrine of divine Providence, also concerned with ethics, Scripture alone must be the guide through a labyrinth of possible but execrable conclusions. It is little wonder that contemporary and later critics were unwilling to credit the sincerity of Bayle's fideism. A philosophical sorcerer's apprentice, he unleashes a dialectical process which, carried one step further, will end in total pyrrhonism.

In conclusion, a word must be hazarded on the tortured subject of Bayle's beliefs. Far be it from us to presume to gaze upon the heart, let us be content instead with certain indications pointing if not to faith, at least to a refusal of doubt. It is significant, in the first place, that the author of the *Dictionnaire* is not alone in his ambivalent attitude to faith and reason. The contemporary attitude to Simon is but one example of a tension under which a whole generation labours. The joint authors of the *Logique de Port-Royal* – to cite a work appealed to on many occasions by Bayle, in support of his fideism – simultaneously teach the right use and the limitations of reason.[109] Thinkers influenced both by Cartesianism and Augustinianism, *érudits* labouring both to combat error and preserve the truth, and writers like Pascal[110] – another point of reference for Bayle – attempting to compose a rational apologetic for an essentially irrational

footnote C; 'Simonides', footnote F; *CPD*, §xx, *OD*, iii, p.214b. It is not insignificant that in his final recommendation of the submission of reason to faith, Bayle frequently either quotes the Mons translation or the *Logique de Port-Royal* and often refers to Pascal as a model of this attitude. The implication is that he identifies his own position with that of Port-Royal, whose attachment to Christianity has never been doubted.

108. The strategy is consistent with Bayle's rejection of the, to his mind, 'Erreur pernicieuse' which consists in maintaining that 'ce qui est vrai en Philosophie est faux en Théologie'. In situations of conflict, philosophy must be revised to harmonise with theology (cf. 'Hoffman, Daniel', footnote C, and 'Luther', footnotes II, KK). That is to say, our author is attempting to force rationalist theologians into an *impasse* and constrain them to admit the bankruptcy of their rationalism.

109. *La Logique*, iv, 1. A preliminary *sondage* of the way Bayle uses the *Logique* indicates that, apart from his use of it as a *texte d'appui* for certain factual information, he appeals to the work as a support both for his scepticism and his fideism.

110. 'Zenon (l'Epicure)', footnote D.

act of faith, are all caught in a dialectic parallel to that of the *philosophe* of Rotterdam.[111] None forces the problems to such extreme conclusions but all, at some point, abandon reason in favour of a faith which, according to the temperament in question, is more or less rational.[112] In the second place, the sincerity – if a historian of ideas may risk the word – of Bayle's hostility to reason is corroborated by a thematic study of the *magnum opus*, together with the miscellaneous works. Repeatedly, through all the editions of the *Dictionnaire*, theologians and philosophers attempting to establish either the reasonableness of Christianity or the rationality of the act of faith are criticised and censured. Their efforts are dismissed not only as ill judged but as a 'licence de l'esprit humain' – one more unfortunate consequence of the Fall from innocence.[113] Moreover, as is well known, Bayle's final years were embittered by a series of disputes with the rationalist theologians Jacquelot and Le Clerc. Rationalist theology could not be allowed to replace the simplicity of that 'Vertu théologale', the act of faith, granted by the grace of God.[114] Finally, while we cannot know if Bayle himself experienced that grace, the self-contradiction involved in the simultaneous *oui et non* given to reason points beyond logical incoherence to psychological coherence.[115] It testifies, in the words of Paul Hazard, to 'un effort conscient de sa volonté, [qui] lui [permit] de ne pas accomplir le dernier pas'.[116] In a word, Bayle's refusal to accept the logical consequences of his own rationalism belongs less to the enlightened century of Voltaire than to the tragic vision present in the *siècle de Louis XIV*.

111. Cf. Anthony Levi, 'La psychologie de la conversion au XVIIe siècle: de François de Sales à Nicole', in *La Conversion au XVIIe siècle*, p.19-28.

112. Cf. Popkin, 'Bayle's place', *passim*.

113. Cf. n.108 above; 'Arminius' *passim*.

114. 'Eclaircissement sur les Pyrrhoniens', §v, in *Dictionnaire*, iv.3004; cf. 'Spinoza', footnote M. It is interesting to note the terminology used by Bayle to describe this final abandon of reason in favour of faith. Words such as 'holocauste', 'sacrifice', 'recourir à la grace', etc. imply that the final fideism is perceived as a salvific act accomplished only by supernatural intervention: cf. 'Acosta', footnote G, a historical character with whom Bayle has long been held to identify. It may be that the paradoxical mixture of rationality and irrationality in Bayle's conception of faith is another facet of the conflict common to his contemporaries, a conflict which results from the psychology of the soul inherited from medieval thought: cf. Levi, 'La psychologie de la conversion au XVIIe siècle'.

115. This conclusion is influenced by Lucien Goldmann's understanding of Racine and Pascal. It seems to me, *mutatis mutandis*, that the dialectic of reason and faith is an attempt on Bayle's part to seize and articulate a reality – call it supernatural – which both impinges on and defies reason. Thus, the dialectic in Pascal and Racine between the world and the supernatural order finds a parallel in Bayle's conflict, albeit on the epistemological level, concerning a God who is both bound and 'unbound' by reason (*Le Dieu caché*, Paris 1959, *passim*, esp. p.68-69, 157ff.). Cf. also Labrousse, *Pierre Bayle*, ii.294-304.

116. Hazard, i.150-51.

# IV. Theology and history

# 7. 'Le doigt de Dieu' and 'le théâtre du monde':[1] the philosophy of history

> Sçavoir, c'est connoître les choses par leurs causes; ainsi sçavoir l'Histoire, c'est connoître les hommes qui en fournissent la matiere, c'est juger de ces hommes sainement; étudier l'Histoire, c'est étudier les motifs, les opinions, & les passions des hommes, pour en connoître tous les ressorts, les tours, & les détours, enfin toutes les illusions qu'elles sçavent faire aux esprits, & les surprises qu'elles font aux cœurs.
>
> Saint-Réal, *De l'usage de l'histoire*[2]

> Je pourrois vous alléguer encore d'autres conjectures, sur la cause qui a retardé l'impression de l'Histoire du Calvinisme: mais outre que ce n'est pas une chose dont vous vous souciez beaucoup, je ne voudrois pas répondre que tout ce que j'en dirois, & tout ce que j'en ai dit, ne soient de pures imaginations. Il n'est rien de si difficile que d'attraper, sur des apparences spécieuses, la vraye cause, & le principal ressort des actions de l'Homme. Les plus fins sont bien souvent ceux qui s'y trompent le plus, & qui donnent le plus grand sujet de rire aux personnes qui savent tout le mystere.
>
> Pierre Bayle, *Critique générale de l'Histoire du calvinisme*[3]

THE notion of ideal history, embraced, as we have seen, by Bayle and many of his humanist forebears and contemporaries,[4] is synonymous with a conception of the historical narrative as a faithful reflection of historical events. That is to say, in a Utopia of Letters, the historian is merely the amanuensis of a past resurrected in its integrity or critically restored to its pristine condition. In 1702, however, in the additional article 'Remond', the author of the *Dictionnaire* tempers naivety with realism, indicating that, even in ideal conditions, history is never a resurrection but a conceptual reconstruction of the past:[5]

---

1. The first phrase is used as a metaphor of divine Providence and causation in history by writers in the *grand siècle* (for example Bossuet, *Discours sur l'histoire universelle*, II, 1, in *Œuvres*, xxxv.163). The second is an image which places its user in the role of the spectator/actor (cf. 'Laurentio', footnote A; Jean Rousset, *La Littérature de l'âge baroque en France*, Paris 1953, p.66-72; Jehasse, p.570ff.).

2. Saint-Réal, *De l'usage de l'histoire* (1671), ed. René Demoris and Christian Meurillon (Lille 1980), p.2.

3. Bayle, *CG*, letter I, §i, *OD*, ii.7b.

4. Above, p.87ff. E. H. Carr (*What is history?*, Harmondsworth 1980, p.8ff.) maintains that this notion of 'unmediated history' was also common in the nineteenth century, a fact which explains Delvolvé's reading of Bayle as a positivist *avant la lettre*, a reading untrue, as we shall see, to the dialectic between fact and conviction in Bayle's historical practice.

5. Cf. Raymond Aron, *Introduction à la philosophie de l'histoire: essai sur les limites de l'objectivité historique* (Paris 1981), p.49, 101, 104, 114, 123.

183

Un Historien ne sçauroit être trop sur ses gardes [...] Il y a des formes de Gouvernement, il y a des Maximes de Morale & de Politique qui lui plaisent ou qui lui déplaisent. Ce préjugé le porte à favoriser un Parti plutôt qu'un autre, lors même qu'il fait l'Histoire d'un ancien Peuple, ou d'un Païs éloigné.[6]

In other words, the historicity of the historian,[7] at once actor and spectator of the historical pageant, transforms the historical quest into a dialectic between past and present, between fact and interpretation (Carr, p.22ff.). Consciously or unconsciously, the writer's present experience and ideological preferences focus his retrospective gaze, and the resulting reconstruction owes as much to the interpretative grid employed as to the texture of past events.[8] The remark is particularly aimed at historians like Remond, who actively seek to correlate past with present and thereby forge a diatribe against their own or the public's *bêtes noires* (above, p.59ff.), but it also has a more universal application. As Bayle observes elsewhere, a history free of authorial interference would have to be written by a 'Stoïcien qui n'est agité d'aucune passion'[9] and, unfortunately, 'le sage des Stoïques [est] chimérique'.[10] Selectivity is inseparable from history: while avoiding the Procrustean tyranny of the propagandist (above, p.72). The good historian none the less interacts in dialogue with his facts. Out of this dialogue is born the philosophy of history.[11]

To some historiographers, however, the scrupulous and apparently impersonal erudition of the *Dictionnaire*, its often bizarre selection of entries negate, in Bayle's case, the relativity of historical scholarship which he so ardently exposes in others. An antiquarian rather than a historian,[12] a collector of facts

6. 'Remond', footnote D; cf. above, p.59ff.

7. Carr, p.36; Aron, p.61. The term 'historicity' is, in the sense used here, a transliteration from the French and is taken to mean the historical context or roots of the historian, in a word, the historian as a historical subject.

8. Kelley, p.1-14 and *passim*; William Dray, *Perspectives on history* (London 1980), p.37, 42.

9. 'Usson', footnote F, and above, p.87ff.

10. *CP*, III, ch.20, *OD*, ii.463a.

11. Some historiographers (Kelley and Perry are the most striking examples among those I have consulted) assume that modern scholarship is 'value-free' and judge the writings of early historians and controversists as contributing unwittingly, despite their ideological bias, to the 'relentless progression toward truth, objectivity and a critical attitude' (Kelley, p.9) to be found, it is alleged, in twentieth-century scholarship. In our opinion, however, while modern scholarship may have become more 'scientific', it is still 'value-laden' inasmuch as the scholar is not merely a spectator, he is also an actor and the activities, experiences and convictions of past and present set his gaze and tune his interpretations. Indeed, it is the presence of perspective and interpretation in history which distinguishes the good historian from the mere *raconteur*, for the former alone has the ability to give coherence to his facts (cf. Carr, p.21ff, and *passim*). Thus, to detect interpretative grids in Bayle is not to diminish his scholarship. On the contrary, it accords him a niche in the pantheon of philosophers of history, heretofore denied him by those who perceive his work as that of an uncommitted *érudit*.

12. Momigliano, p.1-27, *passim*.

rather than a historical theorist, interested in 'les princes, l'Eglise, les savants [...] pour lui les trois éléments qui composent l'histoire',[13] Bayle is the prototype of the modern *érudit*, whose sole concern is the increase of knowledge (Cassirer, p.202-204). As with all caricatures, the portrait contains elements of truth. Never aspiring to the title or functions of a historian,[14] the author of the *Dictionnaire*, who consistently sees himself as a member of the 'tiers état de la République des Lettres', emphasises the deliberately random nature of his *magnum opus*.[15] Given, on the one hand, his conception of the *Dictionnaire* as a substitute library for scholars chagrined, like himself, by 'une disette prodigieuse [de] Livres' and, on the other, by the burgeoning industry of 'instruments de travail' in his day,[16] he determined not to repeat 'les Histoires des Hommes Illustres' to be found elsewhere: 'afin de n'exposer pas les Lecteurs à la fâcheuse nécessité d'acheter deux fois les mêmes choses'.[17] Consequently, as he himself observes, while many 'grans sujets' are noticeable by their absence, his *magnum opus* abounds in 'sujets inconus' and 'noms obscurs' (i.iv). His commentaries are no less unpredictable; 'tant de sécheresse à certains égards, tant de profusion à certains autres' are similarly attributed to public demand. To the constraints of circumstances is added a naturally unsystematic intellectual temperament: the self-portrait drawn as early as the *Pensées diverses* holds true for all his subsequent literary endeavours (*PD*, §1, *OD*, iii.9a):

je ne sai ce que c'est que de méditer régulierement sur une chose: je prens le change fort aisément; je m'écarte très-souvent de mon sujet: je saute dans des lieux dont on auroit bien de la peine à deviner les chemins, & je suis fort propre à faire perdre patience à un Docteur qui veut de la méthode & de la régularité partout.

Unashamedly 'primesautier', Bayle transforms his own taste into a style and presentation capable of providing 'assez de variété pour pouvoir croire que par un endroit ou par un autre chaque espece de Lecteur trouvera ce qui l'accomode'.[18] Finally, the historical scepticism for which he is renowned, together with his unremitting hostility to ideological history, lend credence to

---

13. Edouard Fueter, *Histoire de l'historiographie moderne*, trans. Emile Jeanmaire (Paris 1914), p.404.

14. On one occasion, at the instigation of his friends, Bayle wrote a life of Gustavus Adolphus of Sweden in order to obtain a post as official historiographer to William of Orange. The *vita* and the application were both, however, abandoned (cf. Labrousse, *Pierre Bayle*, i.194-95, n.94).

15. 'Préface de la première édition', in *Dictionnaire*, i.iv.

16. J. Michel, 'Bibliographies et instruments de travail au XVIIe siècle: aperçus sur l'éveil d'un monde moderne offrant à tous des commodités pour la recherche et l'étude', *Mélanges de sciences religieuses* 17 (1960), p.131-42; Neveu, *Un historien à l'école de Port-Royal*, p.213-37.

17. 'Preface de la première édition', in *Dictionnaire*, i.iii.

18. 'Préface de la première édition', in *Dictionnaire*, i.ii; 'Avertissement à la seconde édition', i.xvi; 'Poquelin', footnote F.

the opinion of Edouard Fueter that Bayle's historical research lacks 'la main vigoureuse qui unifie la matière historique et réduit la multitude des détails à quelques grandes lignes' (p.405). In other words, his work contributes little to the philosophy of history.

None the less, in the light of recent research, the *Dictionnaire* and the miscellaneous works, interrelated by a network of cross-references,[19] are seen to depend on a conception of history whose main trends may be quantified. Statistics reveal a significant imbalance of interest in the *magnum opus*: the meagre 12 per cent devoted to the Middle Ages is overshadowed by the 28 per cent allotted to pagan and Judeo-Christian antiquity; while modern times, and particularly sixteenth-century Europe, steal the show, with an impressive 60 per cent.[20] Attributable in part to the random factors outlined above, the selection is no less relative to the value system espoused by Bayle, for whom 'les Sciences' are subject to an alternation of degeneration and renewal:

[les Sciences] ne vont pas en augmentant. Parvenuës à un haut degré, elles font place peu à peu à l'ignorance; et, à leur tour, les Siecles barbares, parvenus au comble, font place à une nouvelle naissance de l'érudition. C'est ce que l'Histoire nous apprend.[21]

The dominance of modern times and Antiquity is to be attributed to a cyclical philosophy of history in which barbarity yields to periods of cultural endeavour and achievement, in turn succeeded by a new age of darkness.[22] Clearly, from this point of view, in the words of Elisabeth Labrousse, 'Bayle ne s'intéresse qu'aux plages lumineuses: aux époques de haute culture littéraire'.[23] The repeated oscillations from darkness to light are not, however, limited to the Republic of Letters. To Bayle's mind, the moral standards of individuals and groups subject to an alternation of 'réforme' and 'relâchement', international and internal politics in the successive 'élévations' and 'chûtes' of individuals

19. In our opinion, the cross-references in the *Dictionnaire* have been either wrongly or too little exploited. As the articles 'Agreda' and 'Nestorius' together with their network of cross-references illustrate, far from being mystifying data, the links are designed to clarify the individual articles by situating them in the thematic and ideological context of the work as a whole. Many interesting studies might be undertaken, using the cross-references as a basis for tracing the 'intellectual map' of the *Dictionnaire*.

20. Solé, 'Religion et vision historiographique', in *Religion, érudition*, p.120-30.

21. Quoted by Labrousse, *Pierre Bayle*, ii.459-60, n.43.

22. 'Gregoire VII', footnote T; 'Zuerius', footnote P, reflection XVII. A cyclical philosophy of history is quite reconcilable with an Augustinian world-view, given the *chiaroscuro* element in the thought of St Augustine and his followers. Cf. Gérard Ferreyrolles, 'Augustinisme et conception de l'histoire', *XVIIe siècle* 135 (1982), p.217, 237; Philippe Sellier, *Pascal et saint Augustin* (Paris 1970), p.19ff.

23. I have taken this quotation from the manuscript of 'Pierre Bayle et les deux antiquités', a paper given by Elisabeth Labrousse at the Warburg Institute, 2 February 1979, which she had the kindness to lend me.

and dynasties,[24] and the history of religion in its teetering from truth to superstition, from *douceur évangélique* to domination,[25] all testify to the fact that 'la vie humaine n'est qu'un théâtre de changement [et d'] inconstance' ('Nestorius', footnote N). This discernment of a pattern leads the *philosophe* of Rotterdam to inquire unceasingly – and here, despite its antiquarian tendencies, his work becomes that of a historian[26] – into the causes of decline and renewal. While two orders of causation are noted, one anthropocentric, the other theocentric, the interplay of the two orders in the areas of ethics, politics and religion, far from clear, is complicated even further by the shifts in vision resulting from a maturing judgement. It is the purpose of this chapter to analyse this shifting historical vision, thereby weaving together the threads of our study.

In the first place, the *Pensées diverses* and its *Continuation*, together with the *Dictionnaire*, all bear traces of an ongoing inquiry into the causes of moral *grandeur*. The 'augustinisme ambiant'[27] of the early work, reinforced by a more serious perusal of St Augustine obvious in the later writings,[28] excludes *sub specie aeternitatis* any notion of moral superiority apart from divine grace.[29] In the wake of the *Commentaire philosophique*, however, where the 'Morale de l'Evangile' is associated with a rationalist ethics,[30] Bayle, now under the influence of Stoicism,[31] is torn between admiration for the moral greatness of pagans and unbelievers and censure of their self-interested motives. Unresolved, the conflict (given both the mystery of grace and the efficacy of 'la Religion naturelle') nudges the interpretation of ethics towards secularisation. The investigation of the causes of political success and failure continues, in the second place, to widen the gap between sacred and profane. Two trends are already in evidence

24. 'Esope' (1st article), footnote I; 'Pericles', footnote K; 'Lucrece, (Titus)', footnote H; see below, p.230-31.

25. 'Nestorius', footnote N, and below, p.214ff.

26. Miriam Yardeni, 'New concepts of post-Commonwealth Jewish history in the early Enlightenment: Bayle and Basnage', *European studies review* 7 (1977), p.253, argues that this preoccupation with historical cause places Bayle in the ranks of first-rate historians.

27. Ferreyrolles, p.216. It is necessary to distinguish in the *siècle de St Augustin* between those who simply absorb an 'Augustinian atmosphere' (the early Bayle, for the most part) and those whose Augustinianism is based on careful study of Augustine.

28. Below, p.196ff. The apparent hostility of the article 'St Augustin' (see Whelan, 'The wages of sin is orthodoxy') is belied by the many occasions where Bayle cites Augustine with favour or in support of his own positions, whether historical or theological.

29. This is not to argue that unbelievers are necessarily immoral. On the contrary, as Bayle himself strove to prove in the *PD*, atheists quite often put Christians to shame in matters of moral integrity. To the Augustinian, however, virtue not inspired by grace is but civil virtue, that is to say, it is not salvific (below, p.189ff.); cf. *De civitate Dei*, XIV, 2, in *Opera*, v.158a-b, where St Augustine argues that the Stoics, for all their moral rigorism, live according to the flesh.

30. Above, p.165ff., and Rex, *Essays*, p.77.

31. Above, p.105-106, and n.74. The question of Bayle's Stoicism merits a full-scale study.

in the early work on the comet. On the one hand, its Augustinianism leads to censure of the ambition and guile noted in the conquests and reigns of key historical figures, notably Alexander and Louis XI. On the other, the attack on astrology and its concomitant determinism provokes a stress, not irreconcilable with Providence (Ferreyrolles, p.224), on the chance element in all human affairs.[32] The first edition of the *Dictionnaire* testifies to a reconciliation of Augustinianism and Machiavellianism (perhaps under the influence of Hobbes)[33] inasmuch as the passions and more corrupt side of human nature are accepted as an effective political force: an essentially anthropocentric concept of causation. The position, like that of so many thinkers influenced by the Italian writer,[34] is, however, one of reluctant realism, as the second edition of the *magnum opus* illustrates. For a series of additions, loosely connected to the article 'Timoleon', reveal a tension between 'prudence' and 'Providence' as causes of political *grandeur* and *décadence*. Unable to decide definitively between the two, Bayle takes refuge in fideism. Finally, Augustinianism and Machiavellianism coalesce in the vision of ecclesiastical history as a war between two traditions in which might triumphs over right. The typology of 'Nestorius' depends on the confessional opposition between truth and superstition of the *Pensées diverses*, a confessionalism continued in the *Critique générale*. There the superstition of which Agreda later becomes a type is seen to depend on a dichotomy of *devotional* practices, the one characteristic of Rome, the other of Geneva. The crisis of the Revocation leads not only to the detection of Machiavellianism in Church politics but to its application as a reading-grid to the ecclesiastical past. The universality and antiquity of Roman Catholicism depend on her superior guile and intrigues (an anthropocentric causation), while the *testes veritatis* are the elect of God, a sign of Providence in history. The elaboration of alternative signs of the true Church in the *Commentaire philosophique*, together with political and ideological changes in the *Refuge*, leads to a crisis in the *Dictionnaire*. The oppression of verity (no longer the property of one confession) through the ages leads to a quest after the Divinity, whose trace, like that of the true Church, seems to disappear from the sands of time. Augustinian, libertine and Reformed notions shift and fuse, then, to form a kaleidoscopic historical vision, giving

32. This emphasis on 'le nez de Cléopâtre' is typical of thinkers like Saint-Réal (see *De l'usage*, *passim*) influenced by the Machiavellian historiographical school (cf. Fueter, p.68ff., and Robert Flint, *History of the philosophy of history*, Edinburgh, London 1898, p.207-208). It is, however, also reconcilable with Providence (cf. Ferreyrolles, p.224, and Christian Meurillon, 'Saint-Réal et Pascal' in Saint-Réal, *De l'usage*, p.57-71).

33. Cf. Labrousse, *Pierre Bayle*, ii.103ff., and Tocanne, p.182ff., for the reconciliation of St Augustine and Hobbes in the *grand siècle*.

34. Etienne Thuau, *Raison d'état et pensée politique à l'époque de Richelieu* (Athènes 1966), *passim*, and Philip Butler, *Classicisme et baroque dans l'œuvre de Racine* (Paris 1959), p.176.

voice not only to Bayle's conflicts and inconsistencies but to those of a whole generation: mystery and rationalism, theology and *libertinage*, faith and scepticism, leitmotifs of writers' whose double-mindedness foreshadows – without deliberately preparing – the great divorce: the withdrawal of the Divinity from the stage of history.[35]

An incipient conflict between two mutually exclusive ideological traditions is already discernible in the paradox for which the *Pensées diverses* was later to become both execrated and celebrated: the inferiority of idolatrous religion to atheism.[36] Maintaining the link, in the lengthiest section of this early work, between paganism and Roman Catholicism, Bayle none the less shifts the attention to the relationship between faith and behaviour. The discussion, as Walter Rex has demonstrated (*Essays*, p.51ff.), subverts the contentious misreading by Catholic thinkers of the Reformed doctrine of justification – a dogma, according to Antoine Arnauld, in its stress on salvation by faith and not by works, inimical to moral uprightness in believers and non-believers alike.[37] In a somewhat gauche imitation of the polemical style of the *libertins*,[38] a series of examples is marshalled by Bayle to prove that crime and immorality are historically the most frequent bedfellows of superstitious paganism, in its ancient, modern and, notably, Catholic manifestations. Nero's crimes and Nero's respect for astrology and worship of images are indissociable.[39] Soldiers given to 'crimes' and 'ravages' are frequently motivated, as in the case of the Crusaders, by a superstitious religious zeal.[40] The prostitutes and abandoned women of Venice, Paris and Rome marry vice and litanies, contribute liberally to the Church from ill-gotten gains and fulfil ecclesiastical obligations in lieu of repentance.[41] Inevitable is the conclusion that virtue and belief, behaviour and conscience are frequently (though not necessarily)[42] at odds.[43] Considered in isolation, these observations are common-places of pulpit oratory throughout the ages.[44] Taken in conjunction with and indeed opposed to the historical examples of atheists

---

35. Ferreyrolles, p.241, who describes the seventeenth century as a *temps de partage* where a divorce between Providence and 'une histoire humaine' is in the making.

36. See above, ch.1, n.3.

37. Arnauld, *Le Renversement de la morale de Jesus-Christ, par les erreurs des Calvinistes touchant la justification* (1672), in *Œuvres*, xiii.93ff.

38. Rex, *Essays*, p.61-65.

39. *PD*, §CXXX, *OD*, iii.83a-84a.

40. *PD*, §§CXXXIX, CXL, *OD*, iii.89b-90a.

41. *PD*, §CXLII, *OD*, iii.91a-92b; Rex, *Essays*, p.55-56.

42. An exception is always made of those motivated by divine grace, e.g. *PD*, §§CXLVI, CLX, CLXXXVIII, *OD*, iii.94a-b, 103a-b, 121b.

43. *PD*, §CXXXVI, *OD*, iii.87a.

44. For example Jean Claude, *L'Examen de soy-mesme pour bien se preparer à la communion* (1682) (La Haye 1693), p.27ff., 39ff., etc.

and pagans famous for moral integrity adduced by Bayle, they seem to place the work within a libertine tradition deliberately subversive of the *Weltanschauung* of the 'Golden Age of Augustinianism'.[45]

Like La Mothe Le Vayer before him Bayle, no matter how religious his intentions, uses atheism as a foil in his investigation of the motivations of human behaviour. The earlier thinker also starts from a similar, if more timidly expressed, paradox: 'comme les Fideles ne laissent pas d'estre assez souvent vicieux, il n'est pas impossible non plus qu'un Infidele ne puisse exercer quelques vertus'.[46] The hypothesis, based on a popularised form of semi-pelagianism and liberally demonstrated with examples throughout his *De la vertu des payens* (1642), clings to the ethical rationalism of Erasmus in the face of the new-wave Augustinianism.[47] The position – perhaps inspired by Charron, the Saumur school and, more recently, Malebranche[48] – is not entirely absent from the later work on the comet, as the following parallel quotations illustrate:

| | |
|---|---|
| il n'est pas vray, que tout desir de gloire & d'honneur soit un vice, comme le pretendent ceux qui sont de l'avis que nous refutons; n'y ayant que l'ambition demesurée qui soit condamnable, & non pas le desir reglé d'une honneste gloire. Observons y encore la fausseté de cette autre maxime qu'ils deffendent, que c'est un crime de suivre la vertu, à cause d'elle-mesme [...] ils n'ont pas consideré que dans Saint Augustin la vertu n'est rien autre chose que l'amour de Dieu. D'où l'on peut conclure que suivre la vertu pour l'amour d'elle- | on a vû faire aux Epicuriens plusieurs actions loüables & honnêtes, dont ils se pouvoient dispenser sans craindre aucune punition, & dans lesquelles ils sacrifioient l'utilité & la volupté à la vertu. La raison a dicté aux anciens Sages, qu'il faloit faire le bien pour l'amour du bien même, & que la vertu se devoit tenir à elle-même lieu de récompense, & qu'il n'apartenoit qu'à un méchant homme, de s'abstenir du mal par la crainte du châtiment.[49]<br>[Bayle] |

45. The phrase is Sellier's: *Pascal et saint Augustin*, p.12, 15.

46. La Mothe Le Vayer, *De la vertu des payens*, in *Œuvres* (Paris 1656), i.542. For geographical reasons, I have been constrained to use two different editions of Le Vayer's works.

47. Jansenius's *Augustinus* was published in 1640 and is the spearhead of a new-wave Augustinianism which seems to outlaw, to Le Vayer's mind, the heroes of Antiquity from the historical pantheon of moral greatness. His work purposes to refute Augustinian 'Sophistes' (p.544) who exaggerate the theologian's position, arguing 'que hors le Christianisme il n'y a point de veritables Vertus' (p.542). It is conceivable, then, that Le Vayer, rather than being a far-sighted subversive (Pintard, *Le Libertinage*, i.139ff.), is, in fact, a nostalgic reactionary whose gaze, fixed on sixteenth-century values, is hostile to new developments in ethical theology. In this he is similar to Bayle, whose 'subversion', or anticipation of future trends, is often the result of his antiquarian interests: cf. above, p.115-16.

48. A. Prat, in his edition of the *PD* (Paris 1912), ii.123, n.1, indicates the similarities with Charron's *Livre de la sagesse*; cf. Rex, *Essays*, p.77ff., for the influence of the Saumur school and Malebranche on Bayle's ethical rationalism.

49. Le Vayer, *De la vertu*, in *Œuvres*, i.543; Bayle, *PD*, §CLXXVIII, *OD*, iii.114a; cf. *PD*, §CLXXXVIII, *OD*, iii.121b, where 'la Religion Chretienne' is said to teach 'la pratique des vertus les plus pures & les plus conformes aux lumieres de la droite Raison'.

mesme, c'est la suivre pour l'amour de
Dieu. [La Mothe Le Vayer]

Both authors recognise and admire not only the ideals but also the practice of
*honnêteté* in the ancient sages. While by a sleight of hand Le Vayer attributes a
religious motivation to the pursuit of virtue for its own sake, the future author
of the *Dictionnaire* goes one step further, separating ethics from any religious
inspiration: his ancient sages are virtuous 'sans croire qu'il y ait un Dieu'.[50] The
similarities, however, at this stage in Bayle's development, are more apparent
than real. Unmistakable as the *libertin* echoes may be,[51] the paradox of the
atheist bereft of the fear of God, whose behaviour is none the less God-fearing,
in Bayle's case forms part of a dialectic designed to establish morality *more firmly*
on an Augustinian foundation (Rex, *Essays*, p.51ff.). The fissures inevitable in
this use and abuse of a tradition inimical to the purpose of his work will appear
only later. Here, the virtuous atheist is subsumed under the contention that
'l'homme n'agit pas selon ses principes'.[52]

Sympathy becomes cynicism in the examination of historical examples of
virtuous infidels. The cases of Vanini, a martyr to atheism, and Lucretia, a
pagan celebrated for chastity, are alleged to prove the fundamental inconsistency
at the heart of ethical behaviour not inspired by divine grace. 'Le détestable
Vanini' is simultaneously an object of admiration and contempt for the *honnêteté*
visible in his refusal to escape death by disguising his sentiments.[53] His inconsistency is proven by two suggested alternative courses of action. He could have
committed perjury ('puisqu'il ne croïoit pas que l'hypocrisie eût été défenduë
de Dieu') or remained silent ('son système [...] ne l'engage à rien en faveur
d'autrui').[54] This surprising hostility finds its explanation in the analysis of
Lucretia's heroism, preceding the reference to the atheist martyrs. The inconsistency between the Roman woman's behaviour (she who resisted 'les sales
propositions' of Sextus, the King's son, and scorned life once she had been
abused) and the example of the pagan gods ('excessivement impudiques')
indicates that the pagans too cherished 'des idées d'honnêteté & de gloire
indépendamment de la Religion'.[55] With all the dogmatism of a young mind,

50. *PD*, §CLXXVIII, *OD*, iii.114a.
51. The dispute between Bayle and Jurieu concerning this work – which seems to have been
something of a pretext to mask their political disagreement (Labrousse, *Pierre Bayle*, i.299, n.84) –
was certainly based on certain misreadings by the minister. None the less, as the foregoing paragraph
indicates, the work does contain seeds of ethical rationalism, and Jurieu is perhaps less culpable
than Bayle's gifted polemics have made him in the eyes of posterity.
52. *PD*, §CXXXVI, *OD*, iii.87a; cf. Le Vayer, *De la vertu*, in *Œuvres*, i.542, who maintains a similar
position.
53. *PD*, §CLXXIV, *OD*, iii.111b.
54. *PD*, §CLXXXII, *OD*, iii.117a-18a.
55. *PD*, §CLXXX, *OD*, iii.115b-16a; see Whelan, 'La Religion à l'envers', *passim*.

the future author of the *Dictionnaire* subverts this apparent recognition of the force of natural law in pagan society and in a critique, perhaps innocently iconoclastic of the admiration of generations of humanists,[56] observes (*PD*, §CLXX, *OD*, iii.116a):

Si Lucrece avoit aimé la chasteté par un principe de Religion, ou ce qui est la même chose, si elle l'eût aimée afin d'obéir à Dieu, elle n'eût jamais consenti aux désirs de Sextus, & eût mieux aimé abandonner sa réputation à la calomnie, que de se soüiller dans un adultere. C'est pourtant ce qu'elle ne fit pas. Elle résista courageusement aux poursuites de ce Prince, quoiqu'il la menaçat de la tuer. Mais quand il l'eut menacée d'exposer sa réputation à une infamie éternelle, elle fit ce qu'il souhaitoit, & puis se tua. C'est une preuve évidente, qu'elle n'aimoit dans la vertu que la seule gloire qui l'accompagnoit, qu'elle n'avoit nullement en vûë de plaire à ses Dieux; car ceux qui veulent plaire à Dieu, choisissent plûtôt de passer pour infames devant les hommes, que de comettre le crime.

The passage not only testifies to an Augustinian reading of Antiquity[57] and, by extension, the events of history and individual biography, it also echoes almost verbatim the treatment of the case in the *Civitas Dei*.[58] The terminology is absent but not the concept of *concupiscence* and *charité* as alternative sources of behaviour.[59] That is to say, to Bayle, quite unlike La Mothe Le Vayer, both the apprehension, and the obedience to natural law, visible in the biographies of Vanini and Lucretia, stem from a 'desir de gloire', in turn the result not of a love of virtue but, in the latter's case, 'une passion incroïable pour la réputation d'honnête femme'.[60] The cynicism, similar to that of Jansenist *moralistes*,[61] is theological in origin. As Bayle was later to observe when summarising this section of the *Pensées diverses*, 'vertus extérieures' alone are attributed to pagans and atheists, whose highest perceptions and acts are 'ce que Saint Augustin appelle *splendida peccata*, des péchez brillans'.[62] Total depravity challenges semi-pelagianism in this reading of pagan Antiquity.

56. Guez de Balzac (for reference, cf. below, note 85) alludes to the story of Lucretia in such a way as to imply not only his own but a widely accepted admiration for her sacrificial chastity.

57. Cf. Zuber, 'Guez de Balzac et les deux antiquités', *passim*, for the notion of Augustinianism as a reading-grid for pagan Antiquity.

58. *De civitate Dei*, I, 19, in *Opera*, v.11b-12a. St Augustine notes the excessive desire for honour in Roman women; he opposes shame as a motive of behaviour to the virtue of genuine chastity, and his notion of the more commendable behaviour of Christian women in the same circumstances is repeated by Bayle as a judgement of Lucretia.

59. The terminology is absent but the concepts are present in the *De civitate Dei*, v, 13, 14, where the author notes love of praise and honour as motives of behaviour in the earthly city (in *Opera*, v.59b-60a). The terminology, common to seventeenth-century Augustinianism, occurs elsewhere in the *PD*: see §CXLVI and references given above, n.42.

60. *PD*, §CLXXX, *OD*, iii.115b.

61. Tocanne, p.169ff.; Paul Bénichou, *Morales du grand siècle* (Paris 1983), p.120-54.

62. *RQP*, II, §CXXXIV, *OD*, iii.772b, and Labrousse, *Pierre Bayle*, ii.109, note 26.

The notion of history as a vehicle for instruction, so dear to Bayle (above, p.100-101), is weighted, despite his obsession with impartiality, in favour of Augustinian theology and anthropology. While the presence of a 'discours augustinien' (above, p.59ff.) may be traced in the above instances, other examples both in the *Pensées diverses* and the *Dictionnaire* are informed, less obviously perhaps, by what might be termed a subterranean Augustinianism. Such is the case of Spinoza, whom critics have mistakenly assumed to express, as early as 1682, a desire to 'donner dignité et noblesse au libertinage nouveau'.[63] In fact, the passage opposes – as in the case of Vanini – the *honnêteté* of the philosopher's ascetic life to a significant detail, here his death, revealing the true motivation of his 'vertu extérieure' (see n.62). Spinoza bade all ministers of religion be excluded from his deathbed, a request which provokes the following cynical and unmistakably hostile comment from Bayle:

> Sa raison étoit [...] qu'il vouloit mourir sans dispute, & qu'il craignoit de tomber dans quelque foiblesse de sens, qui lui fît dire quelque chose dont on tirât avantage contre ses principes. C'est-à-dire, qu'il craignoit que l'on ne debitât dans le monde, qu'à la vuë de la mort, sa conscience s'étant réveillée, l'avoit fait démentir de sa bravoure, & renoncer à ses sentimens. Peut-on voir une vanité plus ridicule & plus outrée que celle-là, & une plus folle passion pour la fausse idée qu'on s'est faite de la constance?[64]

That is to say, with the pessimistic psychological acuity common to the day (above, n.61), Bayle presents his contemporary not as a conqueror but as a slave to vanity, one of the *passions de l'âme* (above, p.82-83). What from a more rationalist or Stoical point of view might appear as 'grandeur d'âme' and 'héroïsme' (Vernière, i.30), from the theological perspective adopted here is exemplary of reason as the blind instrument of egoism (Bénichou, p.171). In a word, the attitude of this early work belongs not to a pre-Enlightenment optimism but to the *démolition du héros* practised by Jansenists and their sympathisers in the latter half of the *grand siècle* (Bénichou, p.155-80).

In unison with Pascal,[65] the future author of the *Dictionnaire* uses the *contrariété* of human nature, unaided by divine grace, to carry the polemical point of the necessity of faith both to justification and more particularly sanctification. The psychoanalysis of Vanini and the like, in its identification of 'la passion dominante du cœur', 'la pente du tempérament' and 'la force des habitudes contractées' as the motives of their behaviour, is proof positive that they are not inspired by

---

63. Vernière, i.28; reiterated in Pierre Bayle, *Ecrits sur Spinoza*, ed. Françoise Charles-Daubert and Pierre-Françoise Moreau (Paris 1983), p.9-10.
64. *PD*, §CLXXXI, *OD*, iii.117a (cf. §CLXXIX); Vernière (i.31) maintains 'derrière la prudence des mots, décelons au contraire l'admiration', a position, to our mind, only possible if the *overall* context is neglected and the passage read in isolation from the other *exempla* adduced as proof of the legitimacy of Augustinian moral theology.
65. For Bayle and Pascal, see above, ch.3, p.83, n.118.

'l'amour de Dieu'.[66] With an assertiveness later eroded by age and experience, Bayle decrees complete moral integrity to be the sign of divine grace, obvious only in those who sacrifice their 'passion favorite' to obedience to God's commands:[67] a sign, he muses, as absent from inconsistent Christians as it is from atheists and pagans:

parce que tout ce qui a fait agir les Païens, soit pour le bien, soit pour le mal, se trouveroit dans une societé d'Athées, savoir les peines & les récompenses, la gloire & l'ignominie, le tempérament & l'éducation. Car pour cette grace sanctifiante, qui nous remplit de l'amour de Dieu, & qui nous fait triompher de nos mauvaises habitudes, les Païens en sont aussi dépourvus que les Athées.[68]

In other words, while, on the one hand, virtue and principles are dissociated in the case of unbelief and superstition, on the other, true faith is held to produce genuinely ethical behaviour. Curiously, however, while historical examples of the former abound, the latter remains without illustration.[69] A discreet allusion, it is true, links the elect and the *réformés*,[70] but such is its discretion that even the perspicacious reader cannot help but feel that the *Dieu caché* in history and biography is perilously near to the *Dieu absent*.[71] Herein lies the origin of the eighteenth-century reading of the work. Writers out of touch with Augustinian-ism will confuse its ambivalence towards atheism with subversion and its cynicism with prudence.[72] Nevertheless, Bayle is not wholly unresponsible for the misinterpretation: the exigencies of controversy provoke a shift in theology.

In the *Commentaire philosophique* (1686), the most rationalist of Bayle's works, he determines to subvert recent official propaganda justifying on principle the oppression of the Huguenot minority in France. Building on St Augustine's writings against the Donatists, Catholic authors, as we have seen (above, p.165ff.), presented the Scriptural *Compelle intrare* as a prototype of relations with heretics and schismatics. Bayle's dismissal of the Catholic interpretation of the scriptural passage is based in the first place on a reversal of the relationship between theology and philosophy. Theologians, he muses, despite a conception of their discipline as the Queen of sciences, recognise in practice 'que le tribunal suprême & qui juge en dernier ressort & sans apel de tout ce qui nous est

66. *PD*, §cxxxv, *OD*, iii.87b.
67. *PD*, §clxvi, *OD*, iii.106a-b.
68. *PD*, §clxxii, *OD*, iii.110a. Cf. *PD*, §§cxlvi and clxxxviii.
69. This is in part attributable to the fact that Bayle believes God alone can look upon the heart, such is the whole tenor of the *Commentaire philosophique*. None the less, historical figures such as Calvin, Erasmus and Melanchthon later seem to form part of an elect and conceivably might have been included.
70. *PD*, §clxiv, *OD*, iii.104b; cf. Rex, *Essays*, p.71.
71. Jehasse, p.499 and 588, makes a similar point for Justus Lipsius.
72. Rétat, p.15-60, 153-214, 353-441.

proposé, est la Raison parlant par les axiomes de la lumiere naturelle, ou de la Métaphysique'.[73] Careful to distinguish his position from that of the Socinians,[74] however, he hastens to discriminate between speculative and moral truths. While the former, doctrines such as the Trinity and hypostatic union, are subject to the Scripture, the latter are not only on a par but form the criteria of biblical meaning (above, p.165ff.). The *lumière naturelle*, whose sense is somewhat fluid in the *Commentaire* (Rex, *Essays*, p.153ff.), on the whole designates man's innate perception of ethical norms. A remark bearing traces of both Augustino-Calvinist and Cartesian influences (Rex, p.159-63) presents this innate principle in action (*CP*, I, i, *OD*, ii.368b-69a):

il faut soûmettre toutes les loix morales à cette idée naturelle d'équité, qui, aussi-bien que la lumiere Métaphysique, 'illumine tout homme venant au monde'. Mais comme les passions & les préjugez n'obscurcissent que trop souvent les idées de l'équité naturelle, je voudrois qu'un homme qui a dessein de les bien connoître les considérât en général, & en faisant abstraction de son intérêt particulier, & des coûtumes de sa patrie. [...] Je crois que cette abstraction dissiperoit plusieurs nuages, qui se mettent quelquefois entre notre esprit & cette lumiere primitive & universelle, qui émane de Dieu [...]

That is to say, while the pernicious effect of the passions, to the fore in the *Pensées diverses*, is acknowledged, under the influence of Tronchin (a favourite teacher) and, more recently, Malebranche, the comment reveals a new optimism (Rex, *Essays*, p.161-63). The tenets of natural law, a primitive revelation, may now be grasped by a silencing of the influence of custom and that *amor sui* previously seen to gnaw man's highest insights from within. Two conclusions follow. Firstly, implied rather than stated by the whole tenor of the work is the conviction that these divine truths, once perceived, can and should be implemented by mankind, no longer slave but master of the *passions de l'âme*. Secondly, and upon this rests the defence of toleration, natural law becomes a 'Religion naturelle' which exposes coercion as so many crimes committed against innate ethical perceptions (*CP*, I, i, *OD*, ii.371b.). In a word, the *Commentaire philosophique* and not the earlier work on the comet comes closer to that separation of religion and ethics said to prepare Enlightened deism (Rex, *Essays*, p.163, 186-87).

The notion of Catholic apologists, soon to be adopted also by Protestant thinkers,[75] that the true Church alone possesses the right to coerce belief in its doctrines, is met in the second part of the *Commentaire* by an insistence on the rights not only of conscience but also of the erring conscience. Here, the

73. *CP*, I, i, *OD*, ii.368a.
74. *CP*, I, i, *OD*, ii.367b; Rex, *Essays*, p.158.
75. References given above, ch.3, n.72.

imperious and self-evident dictates of natural law recede, replaced by the equally imperative directives of conscience, even if the latter is misguided in its understanding of ethical norms (Rex, *Essays*, p.173ff.). The argument has two stages; the first establishes the irrefragable nature of 'les lumieres de la conscience':

la premiere & la plus indispensable de toutes nos obligations, est celle de ne point agir contre l'inspiration de la conscience, & [...] toute action qui est faite contre les lumieres de la conscience est essentiellement mauvaise; de sorte que comme la loi d'aimer Dieu ne souffre jamais de dispense, à cause que la haine de Dieu est un acte mauvais essentiellement; ainsi la loi de ne pas choquer les lumieres de sa conscience est telle, que Dieu ne peut jamais nous en dispenser, vû que ce seroit réellement nous permettre de le mépriser, ou de le haïr, acte criminel *intrinsecè* & par sa nature.[76]

An individualistic note is sounded. *Amor Dei* is construed as an obedience not to ecclesiastical obligations but to inner convictions.[77] Hence, coercion in religious matters can never be right: its constraint on the conscience is equated with contempt for the godhead. In the second stage, individualism is joined by subjectivity. On the one hand, observes Bayle, an individual is to remain open-minded, ready to renounce 'ce qu'on a cru de plus vrai, si on nous le montre faux'.[78] On the other, given that scepticism in religion is reprehensible, the individual must decide on a course of action, 'soit que l'on se fixe au vrai, soit au faux'. That is to say, as the wealth of examples adduced proves, the standard of morality is no longer natural light but inner (and not necessarily well informed) persuasion. Consequently and paradoxically, a good action committed in bad faith is more culpable than a bad action committed in good faith.[79] Coercion of belief is again found wanting: its encouragement of hypocrisy is more pernicious than the misapprehensions of heresy (in the terms of the argument) innocently embraced. This new appreciation of natural law and conscience as motives of behaviour, despite their mutual contradiction (Rex, *Essays*, p.180), could lead to a radically altered reading of biography and history. In the first, Bayle joins hands with Le Vayer: in certain instances, obedience to natural light is also obedience to the Divinity. The second, bearing in mind the proviso of good faith, challenges the cynicism of his early years: the misguided integrity of a Vanini may now be construed as an act of heroism. The stage is set for the *Dictionnaire*, where dormant but hostile trends re-emerge to create a dual tribunal of human endeavour.

Taken in general terms, the *magnum opus* is informed, in all its editions, by

76. *CP*, ii, viii, *OD*, ii.425a; cf. Rex, p.178.
77. Cf. *CP*, ii, viii, *OD*, ii.424a-425b, etc.
78. *CP*, ii, viii, *OD*, ii.427b.
79. *CP*, ii, ix, *OD*, ii.428a.

an abivalence towards moral *grandeur*, an ambivalence generated by Bayle's earlier reflections. On the one hand, themes present in the *Pensées diverses* are re-asserted in two forms. The first, in, for example, the biographies of Epicurus and Spinoza, continues to use the virtue of reputed atheists as an example of the fundamental inconsistencies of human nature ('Epicure', footnote N). The integrity of Spinoza, ponders Bayle, may be 'étrange' but 'au fond il ne s'en faut pas plus étonner, que de voir des gens qui vivent très mal, quoi qu'ils aient une pleine persuasion de l'Evangile' ('Spinoza', *in corp.*). The second illustrates his notion of complete moral integrity as a sign of divine grace by historical examples, slight as they are. With his habitual sideways thrusts at institutionalised religion, the customary venality of clerics[80] is used to highlight the generosity to the poor and the simplicity of lifestyle of John Calvin: tokens of the presence of God in human nature.[81] On the other hand, while the Augustinian discourse is maintained in many of the entries, so attenuated is it in others that Bayle was obliged to append to the second edition (1702) a justification of his attitude to 'les bonnes mœurs de quelques personnes qui n'avoient point de Religion'.[82] Here the Augustinian stance is reaffirmed. 'L'amour-propre' and not 'l'amour de Dieu' forms the basis of the civil virtues of pagans and atheists, and the Augustinian dictum recurs: 'Ce n'étoient que des péchez éclatans, *splendida peccata*, comme saint Augustin l'a dit de toutes les belles actions des Païens'.[83] None the less, the additional article 'Lucrece', written during the same period,[84] testifies to what can only be called a schizophrenia in Bayle's analysis of the Roman woman's heroism. The fruit of his mature years, it embodies a head-on collision in his thought between Stoicism and divine grace, humanism and theology.

Sweeping away the cynicism of his early years, Bayle joins Guez de Balzac[85] in an accolade to the illustrious 'vertu' of the Roman woman. Caution and, at first sight, theology abandoned, he declares in frank contradiction to the *Pensées diverses* that 'j'ai toûjours été l'admirateur de cette illustre Romaine' ('Lucrece', footnote E). The new admiration involves, however, dissension from St Augustine, a challenge the author of the *Dictionnaire* is not loath to accept. The case study of Lucretia in the *Civitas Dei* forms part of an *ad hominem* reply to pagan derision of Christian women, violated during the Fall of Rome. Within a profane

---

80. See above, p.29, and below, p.220-21.
81. 'Calvin', footnote Z; cf. 'Nestorius', footnote N. There can be no doubt that the sixteenth-century *réformés* represent for Bayle a cyclical return to the purity of the Early Church.
82. 'Eclaircissement sur les athées', in *Dictionnaire*, iv.2986.
83. 'Eclaircissement sur les athées', §VI, in *Dictionnaire*, iv.2987.
84. The article was added to the second edition, as were the *Eclaircissemens*.
85. Guez de Balzac, *Dissertation de critique: Le Barbon*, in *Œuvres* (Paris 1665), ii.707.

and Stoical code of ethics, suicide seemed the only legitimate response to the physical and mental pollution consequent on the violation.[86] Hence, the Stoical defiance of misfortune visible in Lucretia's sacrifice of life to honour was adduced as proof of the inferiority of Christian ethics to those of pagan Antiquity. St Augustine maintains that no guilt attaches to a woman forcibly ravished, the apparent consent of the body is undermined by the refusal of the will,[87] a statement leading to a rhetorical question, iconoclastic in its intention. If Lucretia were non-consenting, she is guilty of homicide: she slew an innocent victim. On the contrary, if lust led to consent, then the heroine is an adulteress.[88] Bayle is impatient of an argument which 'prouve trop: car par un semblable raisonnement il faudroit blâmer une personne qui mériteroit de grans éloges' ('Lucrece', footnote D). Praise is due, in Balzac's phrase, to 'la plus belle fleur de l'Antiquité' for two reasons, one which echoes, a second which extends, the position taken by Bayle in 1682-1683. Firstly, considerations of self-interest were not absent from her action ('Lucrece', footnote D):

L'action de Lucrece ne doit exciter que des sentimens de compassion & d'admiration. Sa conduite fut éxempte de toute teinture d'impureté: ce fut un pur sacrifice à l'amour de la belle gloire; & l'on seroit aussi ridicule de dire qu'il entre de la prodigalité dans l'action d'un homme qui jette ses hardes afin de sauver sa vie à la nage, que de dire qu'il entra de l'impudicité dans la patience de Lucrece; car cette illustre Dame n'eut cette patience qu'afin de sauver sa réputation.

The identification of *amour-propre* as the motivation of Lucretia's suicide continues but is noticeably softened by a compassionate understanding of the act. That is to say, while the *philosophe* of Rotterdam's Christian background forbids him to condone this sacrifice to 'la belle gloire',[89] his more recent appreciation of the integrity of those who err in good faith brings him closer to the admiration for the Roman heroine expressed by generations of humanists.[90] A second and more striking *glissement* is also in evidence. The *Pensées diverses*

86. *De civitate Dei*, I, 16, 17, 18, in *Opera*, v.10b-11b.
87. *De civitate Dei*, I, 16, in *Opera*, v.10b-11a.
88. *De civitate Dei*, I, 19, in *Opera*, v.11b-12a.
89. It is clear that Bayle is hostile to the Stoic attitude towards and practice of suicide. While recognising that the Ancients committed suicide following 'des notions de grandeur d'âme', he none the less remarks drily: 'Il ne me souvient pas d'avoir remarqué qu'on demandât [aux Dieux] le pardon de ses péchez' ('Zia', footnote C). The article 'Sophronie', which tells the tale of a Christian woman who committed suicide for similar reasons, refrains from judgement. Her moral courage is noted, but Bayle is careful to emphasise that in this he merely quotes Eusebius.
90. André Rivet is perhaps a very good example of the erosion of theology under the influence of humanism. The critique of Abraham, whose cowardice motivated him to expose his wife to adultery in order to save his own life, leads Rivet to cite the case of Sophronia as exemplary of a more commendable conduct. While suicide of this kind should only be undertaken with specific divine guidance, Rivet cannot forbear observing: 'Quicquid sit, et talibus exemplis apparet pudicitiam & honestem, esse vitae huic temporali praeferendum' (*Exercitationes*, in *Operum*, i.181b).

undermine the seeming recognition of natural law as a moral force in pagan society, revealing it as subject to 'les passions humaines'. In the *Dictionnaire*, the Roman woman's courage is said to result from 'des idées d'honnêteté, & d'amour de la chasteté', fruits in turn of 'la Religion naturelle ('Lucrece', footnote E). The position is immediately reinforced by a eulogy of Lucretia drawn from the Jesuit Pierre Lemoyne, a writer distinguished for his defence of casuistry at the time of Pascal's controversial *Provinciales*.[91] In other words, Bayle appears not only to have altered his anthropology but also to have switched his theological allegiances. While stopping short of Le Vayer's position – *l'amour de la belle gloire* is not equated with *l'amour de Dieu* – he nevertheless accepts the possibility of integrity of action purely motivated by natural law. The *Weltanschauung* of the Golden Age of Augustinianism has begun to crumble.

Bayle, however, is clearly embarrassed by this ideological about-turn, an embarrassment augmented by the challenge to his earlier position brought by Du Rondel, a scholar with whom he differs on more than one occasion, over his reading of pagan Antiquity.[92] Du Rondel's justification of Lucretia is based on that idealistic syncretism typifying his work. The Roman woman's honour was satisifed by the convocation of the male members of the household, the recounting of the scandal and the suicide committed before their eyes. Her blood sacrifice appeased the gods, carefully distinguished from the lascivious deities of paganism as a whole, and consequently she entered the Elysian fields in an aureola of glory.[93] This two-tiered conception whereby the 'homicide de soi-même' is attributed, in the final analysis, 'aux motifs de Religion' draws Bayle into a reiteration of the Augustinian severity present in the *Pensées diverses*. Referring explicitly to the latter work and praising St Augustine's understanding of the case, he opposes the higher religious insights of Christian women subjected to similar assaults, 'qui se consolent en Dieu', to the baser reaction of the Roman heroine, who acted from an 'intérêt unique de sa réputation' ('Lucrece', footnote E). His learned friend's syncretism is also refuted by a renewed emphasis on the inconsistency between the ethical laxity of the pagan gods and the moral, if misguided, courage of Lucretia.[94] None the less, a note of dissatisfaction occurs.

So strong is the recent appreciation of misguided integrity and the force of

91. Pierre Lemoyne, *La Galerie des femmes fortes* (1647) (Leiden, Paris 1660), p.188-89.

92. Du Rondel and Bayle were good friends, as the dedication of our author's *Projet d'un Dictionnaire critique* to the former indicates. Labrousse, *Inventaire*, p.356-57, gives a list of their epistolary exchange. The two scholars also disagreed over Epicurus's atheism: 'Epicure', footnotes G and L.

93. Jacques Du Rondel, *Reflexions sur un chapitre de Théophraste* (Amsterdam 1686), p.80-103.

94. Cf. *NRL*, décembre 1685, art.v, *OD*, i.433a-434b, and 'Lucrece' footnote E; this is a return to the earlier emphasis on the discrepancy between belief and behaviour.

natural law that Bayle cannot rest within a purely Augustinian framework. The certainty that Lucretia acted from 'amour-propre' is also attended by the hypothesis that 'si elle eût été Chrétienne, je dis bien Chrétienne, elle eût agi autrement, & par un principe d'amour divin' ('Lucrece', footnote E). The observation hints at a more relativistic reading of history and biography, a hint buttressed by a further critique of Saint Augustine. Ostensibly claiming to give no personal support to the criticism, Bayle seems nevertheless secretly to welcome it ('Lucrece', footnote D):

saint Augustin a condamné [Lucrece] par des principes qu'elle ne conoissoit pas; car elle ignoroit les axiomes de la Religion Chrétienne qui défendent d'attenter à sa propre vie: elle eût donc pu se plaindre de ce qu'on la traduisoit devant un tel Tribunal: elle en eût pu décliner la jurisdiction, & demander d'être renvoiée à ses Juges naturels, à ces idées de la grandeur & de la gloire héroïque qui ont persuadé à tant de personnes qu'il vaut mieux mourir, que de vivre dans le deshonneur.

Stoicism, explicitly named later in the remark, is here opposed to Augustinian Christianity, as the *philosophe* of Rotterdam points to the injustice of judging Lucretia in the light of the latter when her absolute loyalty to the former is indisputable. That is to say, the earlier 'démolition du héros' has yielded to a recognition of the probity, from another point of view, of those trained in the pre-Christian 'école de l'Héroïsme.' This re-evaluation of the validity of Augustinianism leads in turn to the positing, as a compromise solution, of two tribunals of human endeavour. The Roman heroine, muses the author, cannot be justified 'au Tribunal de la Religion' but, once judged 'au Tribunal de la Gloire humaine', she wins 'la couronne la plus brillante'. Natural law has reached a parity with divine grace.

Despite the apparent attenuation of the divine presence in history implied in this position, Bayle's reading of human ethics is not yet deistic in its implications. Rationalist it most certainly is but, as the study of his sources implies, the rationalism is antiquarian rather than Enlightened.[95] Avid reader of sixteenth- and seventeenth-century humanists and avowed disciple of Grotius,[96] the author of the *Dictionnaire* responds to political tensions by introducing certain nuances into his previous and tenaciously held Augustinianism. The ethical rationalism of the *Commentaire* is strengthened by his reading of authors – Plutarch, Montaigne, Charron, Balzac – all influenced by Stoicism and transformed into a peculiarly hybrid reading of pagan Antiquity and, by extension, the whole course of human history. Walter Rex's demonstration of the influence of Saumurian rationalism on Bayle is borne out by the dual understanding of Providence in history

95. See above, p.115-16.
96. Labrousse, *Pierre Bayle*, ii.268-71.

advanced in the *Continuation des Pensées diverses*. Taking François Turrettini, the most conservative of his teachers at Geneva (*Essays*, p.139-40), as his authority, Bayle distinguishes between general and particular Providence (*CPD*, §CXXI, *OD*, iii.356a):

[Mr. Turretin] dit que de leur nature tous les hommes sont également corrompus, & que si les uns deviennent meilleurs que les autres, cela dépend de la grace par raport aux prédestinez, & de la Providence générale par raport aux réprouvez.

The universality of total depravity, momentarily hidden, returns to drive a wedge between Bayle and the next wave of writers (Rex, *Essays*, p.186). Optimism is replaced by theological hope: divine grace in the elect, and providential oversight in the reprobate, stay generalised corruption. Natural law has again receded[97] but, were Bayle systematic, might take its place as one of the instruments of a Divinity whose back-stage activity determines human endeavour in the 'théâtre du monde'. Nuance must not be equated with negation. Nevertheless, eighteenth-century writers determined to subvert Augustinianism are hardly at fault in their annexation of Bayle to their cause. Once the ideological climate has changed, the criticism of a loyalist all too easily becomes the guerilla tactics of an anarchist, at odds with the traditions of his day.

History and historical *exempla* in the *Pensées diverses* are in a sense both incidental and subject to its ideological thrust: the critique of superstition and its resultant determinism and moral inconsistency. Such are the cases of Alexander the Great and Louis XI of France, the one adduced as proof of the unforeseeable, the other of corruption in political affairs. In the first place, drawing on Plutarch for his information, Bayle reverses the Greeks' admiration for Alexander[98] in a remark simultaneously testifying to an antipathy to political ambition[99] and to methods reminiscent of those analysed in Naudé's *Coups d'état*.[100] The success of the 'grand perturbateur du genre humain' Alexander is attributed to the *cœur hardi* and *génie* evident in his repugnant

97. The secondary causes listed as divine curbs on corruption do not include natural law: 1. temperament; 2. education and instruction; 3. habit and nurture; 4. the laws of the country; 5. fear of infamy and concern for a good reputation (*CPD*, §CXXI, *OD*, iii.356a).

98. Bayle read and annotated Plutarch in 1672: cf. Leif Nedergaard, 'Manuscrits de Pierre Bayle', *Modern language notes* 73 (1958), p.36-39. Plutarch's treatment of Alexander is not free of a naive nationalism which turns the *vita* into a kind of political hagiography (Plutarque, *Les Vies des hommes illustres*, trans. Amyot, ed. Gérard Walter, Paris 1977, ii.322-413).

99. Alexander and Caesar are anti-types of the humanist ideal monarch; they represent expansionism for ambition as opposed to a 'religiously responsible use of armed might' (M. A. Screech, *Rabelais*, London 1979, p.165). Bayle's evolving attitude to Alexander is indicative, therefore, of a tension between the ideals of humanism and the political absolutism he never ceases to uphold.

100. Reference above, ch.1, n.114; on this, cf. Thuau, p.322ff., and Pintard, i.539ff.

Machiavellianism.[101] His conquests repose on the impiety and injustice whereby he drove 'de vive force de leur païs ceux qui le possedoient de bonne foi'.[102] This apparent recognition of man as master of his own destiny is undermined later in the work, however, by an appreciation of the *bonheur* and *Fortune* evidenced in the hero's victories.[103] Not only does war depend on 'mille rencontres fortuites' but also on 'la volonté de l'homme sujette à des passions qui changent du soir au matin'.[104] This latter emphasis, Augustinian in its view of the victor as subject to his baser instincts,[105] is neglected in favour of the first, glossed with hypothetical fortuitous events, destructive of the hero's triumphs. Had Alexander fallen ill or encountered opposition from Cyrus rather than Darius, muses the *philosophe* of Rotterdam, then 'les maux que l'ambition de ce Prince causa dans le monde' might have been avoided.[106] The reflection terminates with the following comment:

> Tout cela me fait dire, que les grands évenemens qui bouleversent le genre humain sont attachez à des circonstances si casuelles, qu'il n'est pas possible que le cours de la Nature nous en fournisse quelque présage assûré. [...] Un coup de pied de cheval qui en d'autres circonstances n'eût de rien servi, eût pû sauver la vie à des millions d'hommes, qui sont péris à cause d'Alexandre, & eût épargné au monde une infinité de miseres dont il a été désolé à l'occasion de ce Prince.[107]

The emphasis here, like that of Saint-Réal,[108] is on the contingency of historical events. The ·issue of war or any other human action is indeterminate. The celebrated 'nez de Cléopâtre' (Meurillon, p.63), the essentially unpredictable and minor event – albeit hypothetical in this case – decides the course of human history. While 'hazard', Fortune and Providence are implicitly linked in the *Pensées diverses* (Serrurier, p.66), it will be the task of the *Dictionnaire* to tease out the implications of that association.

Louis XI, the hero of that Machiavellian school of political thought in France

---

101. *PD*, §§CLII, CLIV, *OD*, iii.98a-99b; qualities inseparable from Machiavelli's ideal prince (cf. Niccolò Machiavelli, *The Prince*, ch.6, in *The Prince and other political writings*, trans. Bruce Penman, London, Melbourne, Toronto 1981, p.58).

102. *PD*, §CLIV, *OD*, iii.99b; Machiavelli counsels the taking of a state by force and the elimination of those opposed to the conqueror (*Prince*, chs.3, 5 and 8; Naudé, *Science des princes*, i.136-37).

103. *PD*, §CLIV, *OD*, iii.99b; Machiavelli also recognises the sway of Fortune in human affairs (*Prince*, ch.25, p.131-34), but his ideal Prince turns Fortune to his own ends.

104. *PD*, §CCXIII, *OD*, iii.133a.

105. Bénichou, p.145ff.; above, p.59ff.

106. *PD*, §CCXIII, *OD*, iii.133a.

107. *PD*, §CCXIV, *OD*, iii.133b. While Machiavelli also stresses the capricious nature of Fortune, the destiny of his ideal Prince is not decided by these caprices (cf. n.103 above): Naudé, *Science des princes*, ii.14ff., and Quentin Skinner, *Machiavelli* (Oxford, Melbourne, Toronto 1981), p.53.

108. Saint-Réal, *De l'usage*, p.8, 10.

known as the *raison d'état*,[109] appears in the work on the comet as exemplary of the discrepancy between belief and behaviour. His religious affiliations are evident in his exactitude 'à rendre à la Ste Vierge mille petites marques de dévotion extérieure'.[110] Not only did he have churches dedicated to the Virgin decorated at enormous expense, he also ordered that chapel bells be rung at mid-day as a reminder to recite the Angelus. This superstitious credence is opposed to Louis's immoral acts, but the immorality in this case is political. Moreover, Bayle seems to have forgotten his earlier and similar condemnation of Alexander because he contrasts Louis's immorality with Alexander's less reprehensible aspirations to conquest (*PD*, §CLII, *OD*, iii.98a):

Louis XI a fait profession toute sa vie d'une duplicité de cœur [...] oposée à l'esprit de la Religion Chretienne [...] Un fourbe, un Prince qui se moque de la parole donnée, qui tend des piéges à son prochain, qui s'agrandit par des voies obliques & par la fraude, me paroît plus criminel qu'un Conquérant qui, à l'imitation d'Alexandre, déclareroit sans aucune sorte de déguisement qu'il veut conquérir les Etats de ses voisins.

It is significant that Bayle draws his information from Pierre Matthieu's *Histoire de Louis XI*,[111] for the latter espouses a mitigated Machiavellianism obvious in his treatment and criticisms of the monarch's statecraft.[112] Adopting the perspective of the moralist, Matthieu condemns the hypocrisy of the Italian thinker and Louis XI, while none the less admitting a limited use of dissimulation in politics. Bayle's condemnation, however, is categorical and perhaps not unrelated to his attitude towards Louis XIV's statecraft *vis-à-vis* the Huguenots.[113] That is to say, while at this stage in his development the *philosophe* of Rotterdam is familiar with the theory and historical reconstructions of the Machiavellian school,[114] he repudiates both in favour of a notion of the monarch as subject to 'l'esprit de la Religion Chretienne'.[115] The opposition will be accentuated in the *magnum opus*, consequent on a more mature appreciation of the realism inherent in the Italian theorist's analyses.

The turn is evident in 1686, in a review of the former ambassador Amelot

109. Thuau, p.40; cf. Friedrich Meinecke, *L'Idée de la raison d'état dans l'histoire des temps modernes*, trans. Maurice Chevallier (Genève 1973), *passim*.

110. *PD*, §CLIV, *OD*, iii.100a.

111. [Pierre Matthieu], *Histoire de Louys XI, roy de France* (Paris 1610).

112. Thuau, p.65-66; Albert Cherel, *La Pensée de Machiavel en France* (Paris 1935), p.107-108, who demonstrates that Louis XI is, according to Matthieu, 'machiavélique avant Machiavel'.

113. The Huguenots condemned the measure taken against them as so much 'Politique et Raison d'Etat' (*HOS*, septembre, octobre, novembre, 1687, p.181) and above, p.31ff.

114. Prior to the composition of the *PD*, Bayle had read both Naudé's *Science des princes* and Machiavelli's *Prince* (*PD*, §CCXLIII, *OD*, iii.146b).

115. This is an attitude typical of the Christian humanist reaction to the increasing popularity of Machiavellian theory (cf. Thuau, p.46ff.).

de La Houssaye's translation of Machiavelli's *Prince*.[116] The preface to the text reveals the translator's whole-hearted acceptance of the principles of the work. Advancing 'le principe des deux morales', one proper to religion, the other to politics, Amelot stresses not merely 'l'utilité, mais la nécessité absolüe de ces maximes'.[117] Bayle's commentary on the preface is surprisingly favourable to its arguments:

On y lit, entre autres choses, cette pensée de M. de Wicquefort, 'Machiavel dit presque par tout ce que les Princes font, & non ce qu'ils devroient faire'. Il est surprenant qu'il y ait si peu de personnes qui ne croyent que Machiavel aprend aux Princes une dangereuse Politique; car au contraire ce sont les Princes qui ont apris à Machiavel ce qu'il a écrit. C'est l'étude du monde; & l'observation de ce qui s'y passe, & non pas une creuse méditation du Cabinet, qui ont été les Maitres de Machiavel. [...] Il faut par une malheureuse & funeste nécessité, que la Politique s'éleve au dessus de la Morale.[118]

The tone of world-weariness comes undoubtedly from the recent experience of Machiavellian techniques in the oppressive measures taken against the *réformés* in France.[119] This and a deepening acquaintance with the theoretical writings convince Bayle that the dogma is but a systematic expression of widespread political practice. None the less, while the rest of the article testifies to a continuing hostility to the politics of *raison d'état*, the above statement is at one with Amelot in its cynical acceptance of the two moralities. Ambivalence is the result. Machiavellian doctrine may be repugned but its methods are not merely efficacious, they are *de rigueur*: 'à l'égard des Souverains le péché est desormais une chose nécessaire'.[120] The recognition of Machiavellianism in practice is but a step away from a more vigorous perception of its presence in history. The threshold is crossed in the *Dictionnaire*.

In the article 'Machiavel' the earlier position is quoted and reinforced by reference to the verity of the maxim 'qui nescit dissimulare nescit regnare',[121] where affairs of state are concerned. Even greater familiarity with political theorists[122] now fosters an extension of the maxim into history both as *res gestae* and as narrative. Dismissing the prohibitions brought against the Italian theorist, Bayle observes ('Machiavel', footnote E):

puis qu'on permet, & qu'on recommande la lecture de l'Histoire, on a tort de condamner la lecture de Machiavel. C'est dire que l'on aprend dans l'Histoire les mêmes Maximes

116. Nicolas Machiavel, *Le Prince*, trans. Amelot de La Houssaye, 3rd edition (Amsterdam 1686): cf. *NRL*, cat.ii, janvier 1687, *OD*, i.740b-41a.

117. *Le Prince*, p.*5v; cf. Thuau, p.158-60.

118. *NRL*, cat.ii, janvier 1687, *OD*, i.740b-41a. Cf. Butler, p.176ff.

119. Cf. *NRL*, art.IV, novembre 1685, *OD*, i.412-414a.

120. *NRL*, cat.ii, janvier 1687, *OD*, i.741a.

121. 'Machiavel', footnote E; cf. Naudé, *Science des princes*, i.94.

122. Many more Machiavellian theorists and thinkers are quoted in 'Machiavel', footnote E.

que dans le Prince de cet Auteur. On les voit là mises en pratique: elles ne sont ici que conseillées. [...] Cela ne disculpe point Machiavel: il avance des Maximes qu'il ne blâme pas; mais un bon Historien qui raporte la pratique de ces Maximes la condamne.

The earlier appreciation of Machiavellianism as the theory of a pre-existent practice is here transformed into an analytical perspective adopted *vis-à-vis* the historical tapestry. Not only do the deeds of mankind embody the politics of dissimulation and manipulation but the historian must also, of necessity, become a practising Machiavellian analyst if his accounts are to be true to human actions.[123] None the less, the previous ambivalence returns. Faithful to his conception of the historian as a moralist (above p.59ff.), the *érudit* turned analyst, continues Bayle, must also encourage a critical distance from the corruption he portrays. Machiavellian history may otherwise and 'par accident' encourage the practice of these 'maximes très-mauvaises' ('Machiavel', footnote E), whose theory he never ceases to repudiate. This acquiescence to Machiavelli's relevance to history involves a shift in the image of conqueror and king: a shift also dependent on Bayle's preference for certain historians and their narrative modes.

Bayle's natural temperament inclines him towards the Machiavellian historiographical school, characterised by its pessimistic view of human nature (Fueter, p.84ff.). The momentary vision of Alexander as the toy of passion in the *Pensées diverses* becomes in the *Dictionnaire* the measure whereby sources are selected. Enrico Caterino Davila, Francesco Guicciardini and Fra Paolo Sarpi, to name but a few, are consistently chosen for the finesse of their psychological analyses of the course of human history.[124] This harmony of vision is also seen in Bayle's preference for memoirs and anecdotal narratives (Suetonius and Brantôme among a wealth of others),[125] precious sources for their revelation, according to Gabriel Naudé, of 'les plus grands secrets des Monarchies, les intrigues des Cours, les cabales des factieux, les prétextes & motifs particuliers'.[126] For if the passions of mankind are the mainspring of history, then the bizarre, the hidden, the depraved motivation becomes the concern of the historical analyst. The preference, however, is not unqualified, as the related articles 'Guicciardin' and 'Hobbes' indicate. In a footnote to the first, Bayle agrees with Montaigne's criticism of Guicciardini's unmitigated pessimism. Despite the essayist's own appreciation of the *bassesse* of mankind, he censures a historical analysis which invariably rejects virtue and reason in favour of 'quelque occasion vitieuse' or

123. If history is a mirror of the past (above, p.100) then Machiavellian analysis is necessary if the historical *récit* is to reproduce the Machiavellian practice of monarchs.
124. Fueter, p.84ff. Above, p.43.
125. 'Suetone', footnote D.
126. Naudé, *Science des princes*, i.45; cf. Saint-Réal, *De l'usage*, p.8, 10.

'quelque profit' as historical causes.[127] The comment is glossed in a footnote to the second article, apropos of Descartes's parallel criticism of Hobbes:

Mr. Des Cartes a raison de desaprouver qu'on 'supose tous les hommes méchans'; & cela me fait souvenir que Montagne, tout éclairé qu'il étoit sur les défauts du genre humain, ne trouve pas bon que Guicciardin attribue à de méchans motifs toutes les actions qu'il raporte dans son Histoire. Il est sûr qu'il y a des gens qui se conduisent par les idées de l'honnêteté, & par le desir de la belle gloire, & que la plupart des hommes ne sont que médiocrement méchans. Cette médiocrité suffit, je l'avoue, à faire que le train des choses humaines soit rempli d'iniquitez, & imprimé presque partout des traces de la corruption du cœur; mais ce seroit bien pis, si le plus grand nombre des hommes n'étoit capable de réprimer en plusieurs rencontres ses mauvaises inclinations, par la crainte du deshonneur, ou par l'espérance des louanges.[128]

Ostensibly a rejection of Machiavellian historiography, the statement in fact radicalises its analyses. The shift is made via Augustinianism (Tocanne, p.183ff.); the agreement with Montaigne is more apparent than real. The sixteenth-century author's defence of virtue and reason as historical causes is transformed by the gloss into the *splendida peccata* (*honnêteté* and *belle gloire*), so many *passions du cœur*, now conceived of as useful to the preservation of society. In other words, while in private morality the *philosophe* of Rotterdam, following St Augustine, holds man's enslavement to his passions as a sign of reprobation, in politics, faithful to Machiavelli, Naudé and Hobbes, he accepts private vices as public virtues.[129] The stage is set for the reversal in the *Dictionnaire* of the vision of Alexander and Louis XI present in the *Pensées diverses*.

The article devoted to Alexander not only continues to invert Plutarch's biography, in its filtering of the conqueror's life through a Machiavellian reading-grid, it also undermines the attitude of the earlier work on the comet. Plutarch, like the early Bayle, stresses the good fortune of a monarch born to reign, whose heroic deeds were inspired by a perusal of the *Odyssey* in his youth.[130] While not denying the role of *bonheur*, the author of the *Dictionnaire*, referring to his earlier position, now stresses the *prudence* (the word is important for its

---

127. Montaigne, *Essais*, II, 10, in *Œuvres complètes* (Paris 1962), p.399; cited by Bayle 'Guicciardin', footnote E.

128. 'Hobbes', footnote E; cf. 'Tacite', *in corp.* and footnote E. On the connection between Tacitus and Machiavelli, cf. Butler, p.161ff., and A. La Penna, 'Vivere sotto i tiranni: un tema tacitiano da Guicciardini', in *Classical influences*, ed. Bolgar, p.295, 301. The attitude expressed here by Bayle is common at the end of the seventeenth century: cf. J. H. Whitfield, 'Livy〉 Tacitus', in *Classical influences*, p.292-93.

129. Cf. *CPD*, §cxxv, *OD*, iii.361a; Labrousse, *Pierre Bayle*, ii.103ff. Cherel, p.174ff., misinterprets this position as reading that Bayle wished to 'justifier l'immoralité politique' (p.176); the argument fails to do justice to the nuances in Bayle's political and historical thought.

130. Plutarque, 'Vie d'Alexandre-le-Grand', in *Les Vies des hommes illustres*, ii.323-27.

Machiavellian connotations)[131] evinced in the hero's accomplishments. Admiration for this example of 'une Intelligence incarnée' is the keynote of the entry:

Qu'on ne dise pas que les occasions lui ont été favorables; & que tel Prince, qui dans une longue guerre ne gagne que peu de païs, auroit subjugué un grand Empire s'il avoit eu à combattre contre les Perses. Ce sont des excuses, ce sont des consolations peu solides. La rapidité avec laquelle Alexandre se servoit de l'occasion, & profitoit de ses avantages, lui eût fait trouver une moisson de triomphes, où bien d'autres Rois ne peuvent rien conquerir.[132]

Alexander embodies that *virtù* – moral and physical energy – unceasingly praised by the Italian theorist.[133] He may have been fortunate but he also created his own opportunities by his 'promptitude' and 'vigilance', superior courage, 'diligence' and 'une application constante'.[134] He also, like Machiavelli's Prince, joined the ferocity of the lion to the wiliness of the fox.[135] His 'promptes marches' ('Cesar', footnote C) were accompanied not only by 'intrigues' but also by surprise attacks: 'l'habileté à profiter de la déroute de ses ennemis' ('Cesar', footnote A). Finally, 'une fine politique l'obligea à faire croire qu'il étoit fils de Jupiter' ('Macedoine', footnote F); that is to say, he evidenced that supreme guile recommended by Machiavelli and his disciple Gabriel Naudé, the employment of religion to political ends.[136] As in the theatre of Racine,[137] sympathy to absolutism leads to a revision of the image of the hero, now set in the Machiavellian mould. This admiration for the conqueror, master and creator of his own destiny, is not, however, blind. Anxious to fulfil the role of the good historian, Bayle expresses reserves about Alexander's policies and personal morality.

The censure of the hero's cruelty – a characteristic, to the Machiavellian school, of competent government[138] – gathers momentum in the *magnum opus*. Now better informed, Bayle considers the aftermath of the taking of Tyre, a city which resisted Alexander's siege for many months, as an inexcusable episode in the conqueror's otherwise dazzling career. Having renewed his efforts,

il força la place, mais il deshonora sa victoire par sa cruauté. Il commanda qu'on mît le

131. 'Macedoine', footnote A; marginal note 2 gives a cross-reference to *PD*, §CCXIII; cf. Naudé, *Science des princes*, i.14-15.
132. 'Macedoine', *in corp.*; cf. 'Cesar', footnote B. The two articles are implicitly and explicitly linked by Bayle, perhaps under the influence of Plutarch's parallel Lives.
133. Machiavelli, *Prince*, chs., 6 and 7, p.58-70; cf. Skinner, p.39ff.
134. 'Cesar', footnotes A and C; these qualities are seen to be typical of Machiavelli's Prince in *PD*, §CCXLIII, *OD*, iii.146b.
135. Machiavelli, *Prince*, ch.19, p.107-17; cf. Naudé, *Science des princes*, i.94ff.
136. Machiavelli, *Prince*, ch.6, p.58-61; Naudé, *Science des princes*, i.111ff.; ii.32ff.
137. Butler, p.192 and *passim*.
138. Machiavelli, *Prince*, ch.17, p.100-103; Naudé, *Science des princes*, i.140ff.

feu aux maisons, & qu'on passât au fil de l'épée tout ce qui ne se seroit pas retiré dans les Temples, & il fit attacher en croix deux mille habitans qui étoient moins échappez à la fureur du soldat, qu'à la lassitude de tuer. [...] Il n'y a point aujourd'hui de Prince que mille volumes ne dégradassent de toute sa gloire, s'il faisoit la vingtieme partie de ce que fit alors Alexandre.[139]

The comment reveals that ambivalence towards the politics of 'raison d'état', inseparable from the absolutism of a Protestant under the reign of Louis XIV.[140] Machiavelli's insistence on the necessity of cruelty judiciously exercised led Naudé to cite the St Bartholomew massacre as an example of necessary cruelty, injudicious only inasmuch as some Huguenots escaped to tell the tale.[141] Protestant writers not only condemn the massacre but later denounce the Revocation and its related violence as one more example of the cruelty inseparable from 'Politique' and 'Raison d'état'.[142] For all his new admiration of the efficacy of Machiavellian techniques Bayle remains faithful to his earlier position. Reluctant in his realism, he continues to repudiate a political theory and practice wherein 'la Morale de l'Evangile', natural and international law are cast aside so that might can create right.

The entry also exhibits a tension between the Machiavellian and Augustinian reading-grids. A series of footnotes focus on the hero's private life and, using narrative techniques similar to those of Saint-Réal,[143] Bayle draws on the 'secrets' of biography not only to explain but also to undermine the public triumphs. The much admired conqueror excels both in 'les grandes vertus' and 'les grands vices' ('Macedoine', *in corp.*). Inordinately lascivious, his harem rivalled that of Solomon and his reception of prostitutes adequately testifies to his 'incontinence' and 'débordement' ('Macedoine', footnote I). Superstitious, 'jusqu'à la foiblesse feminine', he owed his conquests and defeats as much to the divinations of Aristandre as to his own superior judgement.[144] Excessive in

---

139. 'Macedoine', footnote L.

140. Louis XIV was compared by Racine and Boileau to Alexander the Great (cf. *PD*, §xcvii, and Racine's dedicatory Preface to the king in his *Alexandre le Grand*, in *Œuvres complètes*, ed. Raymond Picard, Paris 1980, i.175-76). It is not inconceivable, then, that these references in the *PD* to Alexander and to Louis XI are, in fact, veiled criticisms of Louis XIV and his treatment of the Protestants, criticisms which would have been recognised by contemporaries. This perception of the *PD* as a work of political as well as religious controversy is in keeping with the tone of the work (many of the additions to the second edition concern recent political events) and with our author's later literary activity, e.g., the article 'Nestorius' (above, p.31ff.). See Labrousse, *Pierre Bayle*, ii.474ff. and 497ff., for our author's attitude to the politics of *raison d'état*; also references, above, ch.3, n.74.

141. Naudé, *Science des princes*, i.392-93.

142. References above, note 113.

143. Cf. René Demoris, 'Saint-Réal et l'histoire ou l'envers de la médaille', in Saint-Réal, *De l'usage*, p.43-55.

144. 'Macedoine', footnote G, and 'Aristandre', *in corp.*

his love for wine, the supreme irony of his meteoric career lies in his ignominious death, the result of undue vinous indulgence ('Macedoine', footnote K). The most telling detail, however, is the insignificant cause of his ardent ambition. Alexander 'ne se proposoit que d'être loüé des Athéniens' ('Macedoine', footnote D); his conquest of the world reposes on the vain passion to be praised by posterity. Bayle's commentary is incisive:

N'est-ce point, me dira-t-on, être tout ensemble insatiable, & se contenter de peu de chose? N'est-ce pas une folie de s'exposer à tant de peines, & à tant de douleurs, pour l'amour d'une Harangue? [...] Je consens qu'on dise tout ce qu'on voudra sur les contradictions du cœur de l'homme, sur ses folies, sur ses extravagances [...]

For all his acceptance of the public utility of private vice, the *philosophe* of Rotterdam in this statement is nearer to Pascal than he is to Mandeville (Meurillon, *passim*). The irrationality of historical causation combines with pessimism to demystify the heroic individual. The procedure parallels that of Saint-Réal, inasmuch as 'le récit est l'occasion d'une chute, où le lecteur reconnaît, en un *semblable*, son propre néant' (Demoris, p.48). The perspective of the article is that of a realist and critic, profoundly influenced by the tragic vision of the *siècle de Louis XIV*.

The entry devoted to Louis XI in the *Dictionnaire* functions by apposition with that of Louis VII (1120-1180), nicknamed 'le Pieux', an apposition revealing further ambivalence to the politics of *raison d'état*. Throughout the seventeenth century theorists of this school set the former as a type of the Machiavellian prince in opposition to Saint-Louis (another monarch celebrated for his piety), espoused as an ideal by Christian humanists.[145] The image of Louis VII created in the *magnum opus* is exemplary of the Italian theorist's maxim 'que les princes ne peuvent pas toûjours gouverner leurs Etats avec le Chapelet en main' ('Machiavel', footnote E). The monarch's errors in statecraft result from an over-scrupulous 'délicatesse de conscience' ('Louis VII', footnote A). One error takes precedence over all others, namely, Louis's determination to divorce his wife Eléonor for her infidelity, a decision necessitating the restitution of her dowry. The kingdom of Aquitaine formed part of the said dowry and, six weeks after its restoration, Eléonor bestowed it in marriage on Henry II of England, thereby consolidating the position of one of France's most dangerous enemies. According to Bayle, two alternative courses of action were available to the monarch: he might either have accepted cuckoldry or refused to restore the

---

145. Manfred Tietz, 'Saint Louis roi chrétien: un mythe de la mission intérieure du XVIIe siècle', in *La Conversion au XVIIe siècle*, p.65, n.36, and Michel Tyvaert, 'L'image du roi: légitimité et moralité royales dans les histoires de France au XVIIe siècle', in *Revue d'histoire moderne et contemporaine* 21 (1974), p.538 and *passim*.

dowry. The one shocked his honour, the other his religious convictions, and his choice of the third course reveals his lack of *prudence*.[146] Arming himself with two quotations from Machiavelli, Bayle glosses the episode as follows ('Louïs VII', footnote H):

La dévotion & la piété sont incontestablement les plus grandes de toutes les vertus. Un Prince n'est pas moins obligé qu'un particulier à les posséder: & s'il aime mieux en observer les devoirs, que de conserver son Etat, il est devant Dieu l'un des plus grans hommes du monde; mais il est sûr, que selon le train des choses humaines, il n'y a rien de plus capable de ruiner une Nation que la conscience scrupuleuse de celui qui la gouverne. Si les voisins faisoient comme lui, on auroit à espérer de sa piété le plus grand bonheur dont les peuples puissent jouïr; mais si pendant qu'ils pratiquent toutes les ruses de la Politique, il se roidit à ne s'écarter jamais des regles sévéres de la Morale de l'Evangile, lui & ses sujets seront infailliblement la proie des autres Nations, & tout le monde dira qu'il est plus propre à la vie monastique, qu'à porter une couronne, & qu'il feroit bien de céder sa place à un Prince moins scrupuleux.

The acceptance of the Machiavellian reading-grid is here at its most radical. Despite a certain nostalgia for a world-wide Utopia governed by monarchs devoted to Christian ethics, Louis VII is tried and found wanting in accordance with the Italian theorist's conception of politics. For all its proximity to eighteenth-century attitudes, however, two features of the comment testify to its unquestionable affiliations with its own time. Firstly, the earlier recognition of the two moralities is transformed into a dual tribunal, divine and human, by which political action is judged. Bayle does not sneer at a piety which finds favour in the sight of God, he merely notes its subversion of the public good. Secondly, given the realistic acceptance of the subservience of morality to politics, by implication the hero of eighteenth-century historiography, Saint-Louis, becomes the type of the incompetent monarch, a typology possible only in the heyday of political absolutism (Tyvaert, p.543).

In contrast to *Louis le Pieux* comes Louis XI, 'un Prince très habile dans l'Art de régner: il étoit consommé dans les ruses de la Politique' ('Louïs XI', *in corp.*). While the ambivalence present in the article 'Macedoine' is not absent – our monarch '[d'une] humeur dénaturée, ne fut ni bon fils, ni bon pere, ni bon frere, ni bon mari'[147] – the emphasis is on the monarch's superior political judgement and the contribution made by his vices to the common weal. In the first place, his relations with King Edward of England embody that *prudence* so wanting in his pious forebear. Ridiculed as a coward for the unfavourable peace

146. That is to say, as his use of the term indicates, Bayle is judging Louis VII according to Machiavellian criteria (see above, n.131).

147. 'Louïs XI', *in corp.* Tyvaert, p.545, notes that these characteristics are consistently condemned by historians in the seventeenth century and argues for the ambiguity of attitudes to Louis XI, whose political activity, for all its efficacy, 'ne sortira complètement des enfers'.

terms made with his enemy in 1475, Louis's decision, muses the *philosophe* of Rotterdam, indeed constituted 'une rude mortification pour la France' but, properly understood, it was a 'coup de prudence', intended to sow disunity in the enemy camp ('Louïs XI', *in corp.* and footnote G). In the second place, the high taxation levied to finance his profligacy (footnote K) was compensated for by the interdiction on pillage imposed on his army (footnote L):

Voilà comment les mauvaises qualitez d'un Monarque sont quelquefois compensées par d'autres qualitez, qui font qu'à tout prendre les peuples ne sont pas plus malheureux, que sous un chef qui est bon & débonnaire. [...] Mais on peut aller plus avant, & dire que dans une même personne le mal & le bien se contrebalancent quelquefois de telle sorte, qu'il en résulte plus d'utilitez publiques, que d'une certaine bonté uniforme.

Realism becomes cynicism as the antagonism between morality and utility is illustrated by the opposition of Louis's balance of self-interest and ethics to the uniformly ethical government of a 'chef [...] bon & débonnaire'. Our monarch may have imposed high taxation but his interdiction constrained his soldiers to pay for the goods they appropriated, and the monies levied thereby returned to the coffers of the peasant. The frugality of the pious king[148] might have spared the people from the burden of taxation, but his *désintéressement* would also have pre-empted the greater circulation of wealth within the kingdom, evident under the reign of Louis XI.[149] Paradoxically, 'selon le train des choses humaines', the Machiavellian prince, with all his vices, is actually a better ruler than a monarch obedient to la 'Morale de l'Evangile', a conclusion utterly at variance with the more Augustinian *Pensées diverses*. This essentially rationalist and rationalising conception of the autonomy of political causation is undermined, however, by a series of observations on the failings of Louis XI's reign.

Significantly the entry 'Louïs XI' was added to the second edition of the *Dictionnaire*, at a time when Bayle had begun to swing away from the rationalism of his middle years. While in the article 'Macedoine', the demystification of heroic *grandeur* depends on the identification of fatal flaws, here the recognition of Louis's secret passions adds a certain mystery to the rise and fall of his political career. For all his superior guile, Louis failed to seize the opportunity of annexing Bourgogne to the French crown by the marriage of the *dauphin* to Marie, 'héritière de tous ces Etats' ('Louis XI', footnote R). The ostensible cause of this political error was his hatred of the inheritress's father, a 'passion personnelle' he was incapable of sacrificing to the public good. Bayle's commentary is not unlike that given to Alexander (footnote R):

148. 'Porcius', footnote B, seems to indicate that, ideally speaking, the good monarch, to Bayle's mind, is temperate and frugal.

149. 'Louïs XI', footnotes H and K, indicate, however, that Bayle's interpretation of Louis's vices as beneficial to the public good is not shared by all his sources.

Le Roi fut si aveugle qu'il laissa échapper cette occasion, la plus glorieuse & la plus avantageuse que le Ciel lui pût offrir. [...] Cela montre que les Monarques ne tournent pas toûjours leurs passions selon le vent de leur intérêt. On les accuse de ce défaut, on supose qu'ils se défont & de l'amitié, & de la haine, avec la derniere facilité, dès que leur grandeur demande qu'ils haïssent ou qu'ils aiment: cela peut être vrai ordinairement parlant; ils ont tout comme les particuliers certaines passions secretes, ou certaines antipathies, qui en quelques rencontres ne leur permettent pas de se gouverner autrement que selon l'instinct de cette disposition: ils lui sacrifient leur gloire, leur prudence, leurs intérêts les plus capitaux.

That is to say, even Louis XI, the type of the Machiavellian prince *par excellence*, is the slave rather than the ruler of his passions. Superior political judgement and skill do not suffice to make man master of his own destiny. The remark, however, goes beyond the realism of Saint-Réal. Following Philippe de Commynes,[150] Bayle attributes the King's *aveuglement* on this occasion to the intervention of divine Providence. At this point he again plays the dual role of the Machiavellian historical analyst and the historian turned moralist: God permitted the error as a punishment for 'la folle politique de Louis XI' ('Louïs XI', footnote R). This sudden appeal to a providential reading of political history is not, however, totally at odds with Machiavelli, who frequently attributes the bizarre and unexpected to the interventions of Fortune.[151] Nor is it at variance with Bayle's earlier analyses. The Divinity controls history by a 'sur-détermination' of rational and irrational causation:[152] the First Cause does not obliterate secondary causes, he merely directs them to his own ends. It is clear, none the less, from the article 'Timoleon', that Bayle is not entirely easy with this dual and chronologically separated appeal to human and divine activity as mutual causes of political success and decline.

The entry 'Timoleon' purposes to refute 'ceux qui soutiennent qu'il n'y a point d'autre source du bonheur que la prudence, ni d'autre source du malheur que l'imprudence',[153] a purpose subversive of the Machiavellian analysis of the lives of Alexander and Louis, as the appearance of the former in the footnotes indicates. While a series of remarks acknowledges the role of human endeavour

150. Comines is quoted as the *texte d'appui* for the providential interpretation of footnote R.

151. Machiavelli, *Prince*, chs. 7 and 25, p.62-70, 131-34; Skinner, p.39.

152. Labrousse, *Pierre Bayle*, ii.465-66.

153. 'Timoleon', *in corp.* I suspect, given the reference to Richelieu's political assumptions (footnote L) and the cross-reference to 'Mahomet II', an article also concerned with the interplay of *bonheur* and *Fortune*, that Bayle is here rejecting what is termed 'l'augustinisme politique', a rejection which is not unconnected with the plight of the *réformés*. For, as footnotes D and E to 'Mahomet II' indicate, if prudence is allowed as the cause of success, then, by extension, prosperity becomes the mark of 'la bonne cause' and the true religion, an argument subversive of the Reformed religion, a persecuted minority in France at the time. On political Augustinianism, cf. H. X. Arquillière, *L'Augustinisme politique: essai sur la formation des théories politiques du moyen âge* (Paris 1955), *passim*, and Ferreyrolles, p.224ff.

in political success, Alexander's conquests, as in the *Pensées diverses*, are again presented as 'moins l'ouvrage de la valeur que l'ouvrage de la fortune' ('Timoleon', footnote K). The contingency of historical events is such, muses Bayle anew, that a 'je ne sçai quoi', a 'caprice', a 'jalousie' can ruin the best-laid plans.[154] The observation echoes the identification of the passions as irrational historical causes present throughout his work; the erstwhile complementary intervention of Fortune/Providence now comes under scrutiny.[155] Her presence in history is unquestionable; the difficulty lies in providing a philosophical understanding of her operations: 'ce n'est point ôter la difficulté que de recourir à Dieu'.[156] Two possible explanations exist, the Augustinian hypothesis of a particular Providence '[qui] ménage immédiatement, & par des actes particuliers de sa volonté, ces occurences imprévues' and the Cartesian notion of an 'Agent infini' who creates 'un petit nombre de loix générales', thereby producing 'une variété infinie d'événemens'. Surprisingly, however, Bayle's earlier allegiance to the second of these[157] is swept aside by the contention that it renders Providence blind, subjecting her to predetermined general laws. This leaves only the first hypothesis, that 'il n'y a point de fortune sans la direction de quelque cause intelligente',[158] a conclusion causing no little embarrassment to the *philosophe* of Rotterdam (reflection VII):

il faut toûjours se souvenir que notre Théologie, & le langage commun de tous les Chrétiens fondé sur plusieurs Passages de l'Ecriture, établissent comme un dogme très certain que l'aveuglement de l'homme, sa témérité, sa folie, sa poltronnerie, sont assez souvent l'effet d'une Providence particuliere qui le punit; & que sa prudence, ses réponses à propos dans un interrogatoire, sa fermeté, son esprit, sont des faveurs inspirées par la Providence qui le veut sauver ou le faire prospérer.

The remark highlights the flight from rationalism of Bayle's last years. Like so many thinkers of his day, his earlier espousal of Cartesian causality denotes his rejection of the 'magical universe' typical of Renaissance thought.[159] The apparently 'closed universe' of the first edition of the *Dictionnaire*, wherein anthropocentric causation, rational and irrational, accounted for *grandeur* and *décadence* in history, becomes an 'open universe', in the second, subject to the interventions of a God who disposes all things according to his good pleasure. The ambivalence of Bayle's position, taken as a whole, reveals a shift in values.

---

154. 'Timoleon', footnote K, reflection IV; cf. Meurillon, p.63.
155. 'Timoleon', footnote K, reflection IV. There is a similar, if relaxed, interplay between *prudence* and *Providence* in Bossuet's *Discours*, III, 2 and 6, in *Œuvres*, xxxv.447-49, 528-29.
156. 'Timoleon', footnote K, reflection VI.
157. Labrousse, *Pierre Bayle*, ii.187ff.
158. 'Timoleon', footnote K, reflection VI.
159. Cf. Robert Lenoble, *Mersenne ou la naissance du mécanisme* (Paris 1971), p.6 and *passim*.

Sharing his Augustinianism with Bossuet,[160] he possesses none of the latter's confidence. The bishop of Meaux rarely hesitates to identify the hand of God in history, to affirm the divine support or repudiation of certain individuals or nations;[161] Bayle affirms the presence but rarely identifies the occurrences of 'le doigt de Dieu' in the affairs of men. His fideistic trust in a God '[qui] a dit lui-même que ses voies ne sont pas nos voies, & que ses pensées ne sont pas nos pensées'[162] is but a step away from the eighteenth-century neglect of divinity in favour of secondary and wholly anthropocentric causation.

The challenge to Catholic conceptual theology in the article 'Nestorius' and the hint that the truth of history lies in a *reversal* of the historical record[163] are a mature expression of trends already present in Bayle's earlier works. The *Pensées diverses*, a disguised work of religious controversy, not only revamps long-standing debates over the signs of the true Church,[164] it deliberately picks up and reverses the more recent image of ecclesiastical history present in Bossuet's *Discours sur l'histoire universelle* (1681).[165] Despite an Augustinian recognition of the vice and propensity to superstition typical of human nature, the bishop of Meaux holds to a triumphalist notion of his communion, a veritable 'miracle toujours subsistant, qui confirme la vérité de tous les autres: c'est la suite de la religion toujours victorieuse des erreurs qui ont tâché de la détruire'.[166] That is to say, while church history testifies to a conflict between truth and error, the former, as a result of Providential intervention,[167] always conquers the destructive forces of the latter. The triumph of verity is seen firstly in its antiquity. Anticipating the *Histoire des variations*,[168] Bossuet sees *nouveauté* as the sign of heresy in its severance from 'l'Eglise catholique, qui réunit en elle-même toute l'autorité des siècles passés, et les anciennes traditions du genre humain jusqu'à sa première origine'.[169] Secondly comes its unity and

---

160. Thérèse Goyet, *L'Humanisme de Bossuet* (Paris 1965), ii.252ff.

161. Ferreyrolles, p.237-41; Bossuet does allude, however, to the mystery in the historical tapestry (*Discours*, III, 8, in *Œuvres*, xxxv.556ff.).

162. According to Ferreyrolles (p.238), this respect for the mystery at the heart of human history is more faithful to St Augustine than the desire to identify the hand of God in specific historical events. The argument is borne out by an examination of the *City of God*, where Augustine frequently refers to the inscrutable purposes of the Divinity (e.g., IV, 17, XX, 2, in *Opera*, v.46b-47a, 257b).

163. Above, p.54-55.

164. Rex, *Essays*, p.3-74.

165. For the *PD* as a reaction to Bossuet, see above, p.25 and corresponding notes.

166. *Discours*, II, 31, in *Œuvres*, xxxv, p.434; cf. II, 19, (*Œuvres*, p.282). This conception of ecclesiastical historiography as a struggle is profoundly Augustinian: see *De civitate Dei*, I, 1; VI, 4, in *Opera*, v.5a-b, 68a-b.

167. *Discours*, II, 27, in *Œuvres*, xxxv.392ff.

168. Cf. Rébelliau, *passim*; Snoeks, p.21.

169. *Discours*, II, 31, in *Œuvres*, xxxv.431-32.

universality: sectarianism – 'des divisions scandaleuses'[170] – is the perennial characteristic of heresy, while the true Church is 'catholique et universelle [...] la suite, la succession, la chaire de l'unité' all belong to this communion, apostolic in its succession.[171] Finally and necessarily, if division and novelty typify heresy, authority is the leitmotif of a Church 'toujours attaquée, et jamais vaincue'.[172] For 'dans cette confusion de sectes qui se vantoient d'être chrétiennes [... Dieu] sut conserver [à son Eglise] un caractère d'autorité que les hérésies ne pouvoient prendre'.[173] Antiquity, universality, authority, the three criteria of the verity of Roman Catholicism, become, as we have earlier seen (above, p.122ff.), criteria of error in Bayle's work on the comet. Let us recapitulate the stages of the demonstration.

In the first place, the notion of two traditions, one erroneous, the other truthful, present in Bayle's historiography, reposes on a parallel conception of two ecclesiastical traditions, the one consistent with paganism, the other with 'la Religion de Jesus-Christ'.[174] *Antiquitas*, therefore, is an equivocal sign of truth: it may either be an antiquity as old as paganism, in Bayle's terms an antiquity of error, or an antiquity based on the sources of the Christian religion, the Scripture and the first three centuries of Church history – again in the terms of the work an antiquity inspired and founded on verity (above, p.122-25). By a series of *va et vient* between paganism and Catholicism, their mutual superstitious dread of natural phenomena,[175] their common cult of gods (saints) or virgins (the Virgin Mary) (*PD*, §cvff.), their constant inconsistency between spurious belief and immoral behaviour (above, p.189ff.), the *philosophe* of Rotterdam suggests that the antiquity causing Bossuet to wax lyrical[176] is, in fact, antiquity of the former kind. In other words, picking up the standard Protestant criticism of the Church of Rome,[177] Bayle argues that the converted pagans of the early Church 'ont conservé diverses erreurs en entrant dans le Christianisme, lesquelles ensuite se sont perpétuées par tradition'.[178] The perpetuity of Catholicism through the ages represents both a continuation of a 'maladie originairement venuë du Paganisme' and, by implication, a corruption of the purity of the primitive Church. The continuity, moreover, between pagan and Catholic Rome, together with their opposition to the early Church, reverses *nouveauté* as

170. *Discours*, II, 26, in *Œuvres*, xxxv.388.
171. *Discours*, II, 26, in *Œuvres*, xxxv.389.
172. *Discours*, II, 27, in *Œuvres*, xxxv.392.
173. *Discours*, II, 26, in *Œuvres*, xxxv.389.
174. *PD*, §LXXXIX, *OD*, iii.59b-60a.
175. *PD*, §§L-LI, *OD*, iii.37a-38a.
176. *Discours*, II, 31, in *Œuvres*, xxxv.431, for a passage of exceptional lyrical beauty.
177. Claude, *Défense*, ch.3, §2, p.17.
178. *PD*, §LXXXIX, *OD*, iii.59b.

a sign of error. If Rome corrupts primitive purity, then the novelties are hers, inasmuch as her doctrines and practices constitute a *departure* from verity as originally given (above, p.124-25). In a word, the criteria of truth and heresy, the marks of true and false confessions, become not the uncritical acceptance of traditions transmitted through generations but a dynamic interaction between tradition and primitive truth, discovered by a 'retour aux origines' (above, p.121).

In the second place, the reversal of the denotation of heresy by its divisions builds on the notion of Rome's departure from primitive verity. Maintaining that the continuity between pagan and Christian Rome demanded the implementation of certain changes in the doctrine and practices of the early Church, changes deliberately made for the purposes of evangelism, Bayle intimates that, far from apostolic in its succession, the Catholic church steadily undermined the tradition received from the Apostles (above, p.124-25). In other words, if divisiveness is a sign of heresy, then Rome not Geneva is heretical: it is she who emerges as a splinter-group from the true Church. Universality, moreover, is nothing if not an equivocal sign of ecclesiastical orthodoxy and truth. The errors of paganism, he muses, were accepted by the multitudes, and the history of human thought indicates that error as often as truth is embraced by universal consent (above, p.125, 127-29). Universality, synonymous with credulity and error, is opposed to the judicious pursuit of truth by a minority (above, p.127). At this point, the vision of history as a war between traditions of error and truth yields to a reading of ecclesiastical history as a conflict between the leaders of a majority (of whom St Cyril later becomes the type), by definition propagators of falsehood, and certain key figures in a minority (of which Nestorius later becomes the type), by definition *testes veritatis*. The Calvinists are not omitted from the analysis. Again, drawing on the history of human thought, Bayle argues that the majority consistently resists the enlightened insights or criticisms of the minority, a minority now including the philosophers of Antiquity, the early Christians and the Protestants (above, p.125). This historiographical vision is profoundly theological: Bayle links the denial of 'le véritable Roi de l'Univers' implicit in the superstition of the majority (above, p.21) to the machinations of 'le Démon [… qui] a fait tous les efforts imaginables pour entretenir l'idolatrie dans leur esprit'.[179] The position is not uncommon in the Calvinist polemical historiography of the age;[180] Bayle's maturing pessimism will, however, transform a theological common-place into the heterodoxy of Manicheism.

Finally, the authority of the Church of Rome comes under attack in the first

179. *PD*, §cxxii, *OD*, iii.86a; St Augustine also detects the Devil behind pagan superstition (*De civitate Dei*, vi, 4, in *Opera*, v.68a-b). Bayle's reversal of it against Catholicism is typical of the Calvinist historiographical tradition within which he works (Polman, p.225ff.).

180. See above, ch.1, n.81.

and, more vigorously, in the second edition of the *Pensées diverses*: the triumph of orthodoxy over sectarianism and heresy is seen to reside not in the exertion of a divine but in an all too human *political* authority. The argument depends on a *topos* of Protestant historiography. The advent of Constantine to the throne and the consequent institutionalisation of Christianity seduced many pagans in search of self-advancement to convert.[181] The converted pagans, 'sans aucune véritable vocation' and without any renunciation of former errors, brought, as a result, 'tous leurs préjugez [dans l'Eglise]'. The position underscores the two earlier criticisms. The authority of the Roman See, aided by 'le bras séculier', becomes responsible for the degeneration of Catholicism, and its unity and universality are the fruits of political 'clout' (above, p.38-39). Moreover, antici-pating the typology of the article 'Nestorius', the second edition of the work on the comet generalises the statement to include the predicament of contemporary Huguenots (above, p.50-52). The case represents a shift in the use of authority, for it is no longer a power which dazzles but one which constrains those outside the Church to convert. The triumph of Catholicism is now shown to depend on two kinds of corruption. The first is a corruption not a conversion of the persecuted heretic. On the one hand, the Huguenots, observes Bayle, are promised poverty, loss of privilege and employment, and a superfluity of 'peines' if they persist in their convictions.[182] On the other, they are offered 'mille douceurs' if heresy is abjured. Now, he continues, 'il faut être bien ignorant de ce qui se passe dans l'homme, pour ne pas savoir qu'il y a une infinité de gens dans ce siècle-ci, qui à ce prix-là feroient profession de croire tout ce qu'on voudroit'. In converting, however, the Huguenots are denying their convictions and thereby offending God.[183] The second is a corruption not an enhancement of the Church. Not only are the Huguenots, as false Catholic believers, likely to debase the docrine and practices of Rome,[184] but the 'extortion' of conversions 'à force d'argent, & à force de rendre malheureuse la destinée de ceux qui ne se convertissent point' is a denial of 'le véritable esprit du Christianisme'.[185] In a word, anticipating the article 'Mahomet' in the *Dictionnaire* (see above, p.51-53), the authority of Rome, to which the bishop of Meaux attributes its unity and universality, is not only spurious, by its opposition to the true spirit of

181. *PD*, §LXXXVI, *OD*, iii.57a.
182. *PD*, §LXXXVIII, *OD*, iii.58a.
183. *PD*, §LXXXVIII, *OD*, iii.58b.
184. *PD*, §LXXXVIII, *OD*, iii.59a-b. The argument is commonplace in the polemical literature of the time: cf. [Marc Antoine de La Bastide], *Considerations sur les Lettres circulaires de l'Assemblée du Clergé de France de 1682* (n.p. [1683?]), p.15, 102, 105, 128-37, and by the same author, *Réponse apologetique à messieurs du Clergé de France, sur les actes de leur Assemblée de 1682 touchant la religion* (n.p. 1683), p.63.
185. *PD*, §LXXXVIII, *OD*, iii.58a.

Christianity, it is proven to be a sign not of orthodoxy or divinity but of heresy and demonic inspiration.[186] The threads of the *Commentaire philosophique* are already in place.

The *Critique générale*, written in the interval between the first and second editions of the *Pensées diverses*, reinforces and extends its vision of ecclesiastical history to the devotional theology and praxis of Rome, of which Agreda later becomes a type. The Jesuit's *Histoire du calvinisme* is reversed. In the first place, adopting the *topoi* of Catholic church history, Maimbourg shifts the interpretation of *antiquitas* as a sign of orthodoxy from the continuity of doctrine to the perpetuity of devotional practices.[187] The truth of Catholicism and the heresy of Calvinism are seen, on the one hand, in the 'onction', 'ornement', and 'dévotion' of the former, which, 'entrant par les sens dans le fond de l'ame, l'attire & l'éleve par les choses visibles au Dieu invisible', and, on the other, in the 'sécheresse' and 'maigreur' of the latter's bare ceremonial, characteristic of 'tous les Héresiarques qui ont jamais été'.[188] Bayle's reply is twofold. The first, an argument from epistemology – parallel to the rejection of decadent eloquence (above, p.87ff.) – yields further insight into the hostility to Agreda in the *Dictionnaire*. Rome's luxurious devotions, 'la pompe des Cérémonies' and 'brillant[s] Panégyrique[s]'[189] are conceived of as a seduction of 'l'esprit des peuples'.[190] Their appeal to 'les sens & le cœur' enslaves the soul or mind and 'dans le fond il ne faut pas attendre qu'une ame, qui est attaquée par tant d'objets sensibles, se puisse réserver beaucoup de forces, pour s'élever aux objets intelligibles'.[191] That is to say, given that the heart is a depraved organ of perception Catholic ceremonial, far from a sign of orthodoxy, is the token of a depraved tradition, the devotional equivalent of the moral depravity of pagan worship. The second argument reintroduces the opposition pagano-Catholicism and primitive Christianity-Calvinism, as Maimbourg's reproach of 'sécheresse' becomes a source of holy joy (*CG*, letter xi, §3, *OD*, ii.48a):

Nous avons la gloire de voir que l'on nous reproche la sécheresse & la maigreur de notre Réforme, & qu'on l'oppose à la Majesté pompeuse des Cérémonies Romaines, de la même maniere que les Payens opposoient l'éclat auguste de leurs Cérémonies, à la simplicité des premiers Chretiens. Car il est faux que les premiers siecles de l'Eglise ayent eu cet attirail de Cérémonies, que l'on nous vante tant comme un moyen sûr de remplir l'ame d'une dévotion respectueuse; elles n'ont commencé proprement à

186. Cf. *CP*, i, 3, *OD*, iii.374a.
187. Maimbourg, *Histoire du calvinisme*, p.70-71; cf. Le Brun, 'Critique des abus', p.255.
188. Maimbourg, p.71, *CG*, letter xi, §3, *OD*, ii.47.
189. *CG*, letter xi, §5, *OD*, ii.48a.
190. *CG*, letter xi, §3, *OD*, ii.47b. This reverses the terms of Maimbourg's argument (cf. *Histoire du calvinisme*, p.71).
191. *CG*, letter xi, §5, *OD*, ii.48b.

s'introduire dans le service divin que sous les Empereurs Chretiens. Et c'est aussi ce temps-là que l'on donne pour l'Epoque de la diminution des graces spirituelles de Dieu, & de l'augmentation des prospéritez temporelles.

The historical process is again denied as Calvinism is seen to reinstate the purity of the early Church, corrupted by the compromise with paganism perceived in Roman Catholicism. Not only that, the degeneration results from a further compromise, this time with the world. Here the two later typologies 'Agreda' and 'Nestorius' find a unity. The link between Church and State – St Cyril and the emperor Theodosius – led, on the one hand, to the adoption by the former of the pomp and ceremony typical of the latter and, on the other, to the weakening of the spiritual graces typical of Nestorius and the spirit of primitive Christianity he embodies.[192] In a word, Rome's 'Majesté des Cérémonies' is transformed from a sign of orthodoxy into a denotation of heresy and schism.

The second argument depends upon the first. Anticipating Bossuet's *Histoire des variations*, Maimbourg uses the technique of the 'portrait à clé' to draw iconoclastic parallels between the Calvinists, the Vaudois and the Hussites. The Reformation is proven thereby to be a mere 'ramas des erreurs de quantité d'Héretiques, que l'Eglise avoit exterminez en divers tems depuis le dixieme siecle',[193] a resurgence and perpetuation of the hydra of heresy. Bayle, in his reply, accepts the parallel but deflects its disparaging intentions (*CG*, letter XI, §7, *OD*, ii.49b-50a):

J'ai considéré de plus que les doctrines que Calvin a débitées, ayant été plusieurs fois mises en avant par des personnes de mérite, c'est un signe que l'Eglise Romaine enseigne des choses qui ont paru chocantes & absurdes en divers tems à de grands hommes, ce qui jette de plus légitimes soupçons dans l'esprit, au préjudice de ces doctrines, que s'il n'y avoit que Calvin qui les eût désapprouvées.

The vision of ecclesiastical history, implicit in the *Pensées diverses*, as a conflict between two traditions, in which truth is maintained against the inroads of error and by a cohort of *testes veritatis*,[194] men of God, critical and opposed to the degeneration of the Church, becomes explicit for the first time. The *grands hommes* devoted to verity of whom Calvin is the heir and the voice, are unnamed: the *Dictionnaire* will identify and compose their biographies (see above, p.31ff.). This deflection of the Jesuit's position conceals a further barb. Not only is Rome on the side of error and Geneva on the side of truth, the presence of witnesses to verity throughout the ages, crowned in the Reformation, intimates the ineradicable nature of Catholic superstition: 'puis qu'on a été contraint de

192. Cf. *CP*, II, 5, *OD*, ii.411a-b.
193. *CG*, letter XI, §7, *OD*, ii.49b; Maimbourg, *Histoire du calvinisme*, p.66-70, 75.
194. Polman, p.215-34; above, ch.1, n.81.

prêcher dans le XVI siecle contre les mêmes corruptions, & les mêmes erreurs qui lui avoient été reprochées tant de fois'.[195] That is to say, *opiniâtreté*, or stubborn persistence in error, a traditional sign of heresy,[196] is characteristic not of Calvinism but of Rome who, as the case of Agreda illustrates, can suffer neither her ills nor their remedies (above, p.26).

Finally, to heresy, schism and *opiniâtreté* is added, for the first time, explicitly, in Bayle's ecclesiastical historiography, the accusation of Machiavellianism.[197] Maimbourg may see the majesty of Catholic ceremonial as a sign of perpetuity and universality but, to Bayle, the opposition between Rome and primitive Christianity indicates that pomp and ceremony are inventions of ecclesiastical statecraft. 'Vérité' and 'Vertu', he muses, need no ornament but 'leur simplicité, leur nudité', while 'erreur' and 'vice' require that 'on les farde, & on les embellit de tous les ornemens dont on se peut aviser'.[198] The changes made to the practice of the early Church – attributed in the *Pensées diverses* to 'prudence Chretienne' and evangelistic zeal[199] – are now the fruit of a 'prudence humaine', learnt at the feet of Machiavelli. The Italian theorist teaches, continues Bayle, quoting from the *Prince*, 'qu'il faut inventer à l'exemple de Numa Pompilius, quelque belle Religion, bien ornée, & bien parée de Cérémonies, afin de dominer plus aisément sur les esprits'.[200] The authority of Rome, to which its clerics attribute its 'longue prospérité', is nothing more than a perpetuity of political ruses leading to an authoritarian hold on the consciences of its faithful. The observation is worthy of Gabriel Naudé but its application is more limited than that of Bayle's libertine forebear. False religion and not Christianity at large is its object, as is indicated by the generalisation, now all too familiar, to the plight of the Huguenots:

nous ne nous piquons pas de cette fine prudence, dont Messieurs de l'Eglise Romaine donnent au monde depuis si long-temps de si admirables leçons [...] La seule conduite qu'ils tiennent en France pour nous exterminer, est une production de Politique si fine, si rusée, si artificieuse, qu'elle peut servir de sujet de méditation, vingtans durant, à ceux qui se veulent perfectionner dans l'art des Intrigues. Ces Messieurs se moquent du

195. *CG*, letter XI, §7, *OD*, ii.50a.

196. *CP*, II, I, *OD*, ii.396.

197. The *PD* (1683) alludes to Machiavellian tactics but only in the second edition, published after the *CG* (1682).

198. *CG*, letter XI, §3, *OD*, ii.48a. The position is consistent with the ideal of unmediated discourse; see above, p.82ff.

199. Passage quoted p.124 above.

200. Letter XI, §3, *OD*, ii.48a; Bayle refers to the *Prince*, ch.11, p.81-84, which does in fact allude to the efficacy of religion as a tool in power struggles. However, the attribution of Numa Pompilius's success to his clever invention of a religion occurs in Machiavelli's *Discourses on the first decade of Livy's History*, I, 11, p.170-74. The usefulness of religion to statecraft is one of the major themes of Naudé's *Science des princes*, i.111ff., ii.27ff.

monde quand ils nous disent, que l'assistance particuliere de l'Esprit de Dieu se reconnoît manifestement à cette longue prospérité, dont leur Eglise jouït; car de la maniere qu'ils se sont fortifiez de tous les avantages temporels, qui peuvent faire subsister un Etat, il ne leur faut qu'une Providence très-générale pour durer éternellement. Il n'y a que des miracles, & que des coups redoublez d'une Providence particuliere, qui puissent ruïner leur Eglise.[201]

Bayle's masterly irony is here at its most biting: the signs of the divine origin of Roman Catholicism are presented as indications of a 'Dieu absent'. Temporal prosperity, oppressive orthodoxy and the persecution of the Protestants are manifestations of a Church who has driven the Divinity from her midst. Anticipating his contention that Machiavellianism is inimical to 'la Morale de l'Evangile' (above, p.201ff.), Bayle opposes the Spirit of God to the spirit of intrigue evident in the Church of Rome. The true Church may be preserved from the hounds of hell[202] but all the powers of an omnipotent Deity could neither destroy nor prevail upon the Church of Rome, fortified *against* providential intervention by its 'Intrigues', its domination of the French Church and the Church universal. In a word, the causes of the *grandeur* and majesty of Rome are anthropocentric and not theocentric. The scene is set for the enunciation in the *Commentaire philosophique* of a reversal of the signs of the true Church.

The triumphalism of contemporary Catholic historiography, its use of St Augustine to prove the legitimacy and continuity of constraint with the practices of the early Church and its confusion of superiority of numbers and temporal success with truth, are neatly reversed in Bayle's passionate defence of toleration. The importance of the *Commentaire philosophique* for Bayle's ecclesiology resides in its vision of an ecclesiastical tradition of *douceur*, emanating from the founder of Christianity, Jesus Christ. In the first place, echoing Erasmus, the *philosophe* of Rotterdam contrasts 'les infamies [...] pratiquées [en France] par les Dragons',[203] with 'le principal caractere de Jesus-Christ, & la qualité, pour ainsi dire de sa personne,' namely 'l'humilité, la patience, la débonnaireté'.[204] Far from advising persecution, Christ commands his disciples to flee from it, and his ideal for humanity is that of forgiveness not hatred. Moreover, drawing on Isaiah's image of the Messiah, Bayle presents Christ not as the type of the

---

201. *CG*, letter XI, §4, *OD*, ii.48a-b. Bayle does not make the naive error, however, of limiting his recognition of Machiavellianism to Catholicism; those ministers who co-operated with the plans for re-unification either in the sixteenth or seventeenth centuries are also criticised for their corruption.
202. 'Xenophanes', footnote E, questions, however, the divine oversight of the Church: see below, p.226ff.
203. *CP*, *OD*, ii.361a.
204. *CP*, I, 3, *OD*, ii.373b.

persecutor but as the archetype of the persecuted: 'il est comparé à un agneau qui a été mené à la tuerie sans se plaindre [...] Quand on lui a dit des outrages, il n'en rendoit point, mais se remettoit à celui qui juge justement'.[205] That is to say, in the strong terms employed in the work, the Church of Rome, 'bien-loin d'être [l'] Epouse de Jesus-Christ', is proven by her recourse to persecution to be 'une infame Prostituée' who, having seized the house of the Lord by force, 'en a chassé le pere, la mere, & les enfans [... &] a égorgé [...] ces enfans le plus qu'elle a pû' (*CP, OD*, ii.359b). In the second place, prostitution of the Spirit of Christ is accompanied by deviation from the 'Apôtres & de leurs premiers Disciples, les plus sûrs Dépositaires de la Tradition'.[206] The fidelity of the Apostles to their Master's example is noted. At the Ascension, Christ commanded 'de ne convertir les nations qu'en les enseignant, les endoctrinant, & les baptisant' and 'ses Apôtres ont suivi l'exemple de sa débonnaireté, & nous ont enjoint d'être les imitateurs d'eux & de leur maître'.[207] The early Fathers, moreover, eschewed constraint and continued to emphasise that conversion is to be effected by persuasion and instruction.[208] In a word, persecution is a sign not of the continuity of Roman Catholicism and primitive Christianity but of schism with the teaching and practices of the early Church. Finally, the opposition of the Pharisees to Christ and the persecution of the early Christians by the pagans is generalised into a typology of the true Church, in stark contrast to the image vaunted by Rome:

tous les discours de Jésus-Christ & de ses Apôtres nous préparent à être haîs du monde, dans la tribulation, dans les croix, dans l'exercice continuel de la patience, au milieu des persécuteurs de la verité. Si bien qu'il est naturel de croire à une bonne ame, & qui ne veut se déterminer que selon la crainte de Dieu, que la verité se rencontre du côté des maux temporels, & non pas du côté qui nous menace, qui nous afflige, si nous persévérons dans notre Foi, & qui nous promet mille avantages terrestres, si nous allons à lui. [...] cela même qu'on menace [les gens] de persécution leur servira de preuve, ou de préjugé, qu'ils suivent cette verité Evangelique, que l'Ecriture a prédit qui seroit mal voulüe du monde, & persécutée sur la terre.[209]

The statement represents a shift in the conception of the *testes veritatis*, a shift later forcefully utilised in the article 'Nestorius' and so many others where Bayle takes the part of persecuted minorities. The *notae* of the true Church become persecution and affliction, while the use of violent constraint and temporal

205. *CP*, I, 3, *OD*, ii.373b; Isaiah liii.7;.
206. *CP*, I, 8, *OD*, ii.387a-88a.
207. *CP*, I, 3, *OD*, ii.374a.
208. *CP*, I, 8, *OD*, ii.387a-88a.
209. *CP*, II, 1, *OD*, ii.394b. Some of the persecuted sects in the sixteenth century looked upon persecution as a sign of the true Church. Cf. Joseph Lecler, *Histoire de la tolérance* (Paris 1955), i.185, and Labrousse, *Pierre Bayle*, ii.451, n.10.

success are the distinctive marks of schismatic and degenerate groups of false believers. The perpetuity of verity is a perpetuity of persecution. Christ, the Apostles, the early Christians and the Protestants share a common experience: the affliction imposed upon them by a Church whose Machiavellian power, politics permit an authoritarian control of ecclesiastical history. The crisis of French Protestantism in the Revocation era finds a voice in the shifting historical vision of Pierre Bayle who, 'seeking to remain alive to the conflicts of his time',[210] revitalises and re-orientates some of the long-standing tenets of his communion. The decade following the Revocation and the *Commentaire philosophique* witnesses, however, a further politico-religious conflict, this time from within.[211] The writings of Pierre Jurieu, together with Bayle's broader reading, lead to an extension of the *notae* of the true and the marks of the false Church, on the one hand to certain trends within Catholicism and, on the other, to aspects of Calvinism. Consequently, the distinctly denominational guise of truth and error in the early works, while continuing, also yields to a trans-confessional conception of verity and superstition, a conception not without difficulties for the detection of the Divinity in the theatre of ecclesiastical history.

The extravagances of Agreda and the more philosophical notions of Nestorius reveal in the 1690s that the gulf between the dogma and praxis of Rome and those of Geneva remains one of degenerate Christianity and primitive verity, as unbridgeable a divide as at the time of the Reformation. However, as a result, perhaps of Bossuet's *Histoire des variations* and certainly of Bayle's acceptance of a cyclical philosophy of history, the concept of religious truth as the fruit of a *retour aux sources* is transformed into the dynamics of ecclesiastical history.[212] The bishop of Meaux may argue that, on the one hand, 'variations' are a 'marque de fausseté' and, on the other, 'la vérité [...] a un langage toujours uniforme',[213] but to the *philosophe* of Rotterdam the consistency and perpetuity of the transmission of certain positions are proof positive of error. The argument is based on his pessimistic anthropology. It is a fact of history and human experience that moral or doctrinal reforms do not last, a sorry condition explained by the aphorism 'nullum violentum durabile, un état violent ne peut être de durée' ('Nestorius', footnote N). By a violent state is understood 'un état contraire aux inclinations de la nature' and nature to Bayle, as to so many Augustinians of the day, is always corrupt and fallen.[214] No sooner has a reformation of morality or doctrine been introduced than 'les passions, que la nature a données au

210. Rex, *Essays*, p.xiii.
211. Cf. above, ch.3, n.74; Rex, *Essays*, p.197ff.
212. On this and the Protestant reaction, see Rébelliau, *passim*.
213. Bossuet, *Histoire des variations des Eglises protestantes*, in *Œuvres*, xix.4.
214. 'Nestorius', footnote N, and above, p.81ff.

genre humain [...] sont un poids qui ramene bientôt les hommes à leur prémiere condition si quelque retour de zêle, si quelque réforme les a élancez vers le ciel' ('Nestorius', footnote N). Given that post-lapsarian human nature is inimical both to *probité* and to *vérité*, their irregular appearances on the stage of history ('Manichéens', footnote D) are attributed to constantly reiterated programmes of reform. The reflection leads to an analogy with, on the one hand, the success of popular devotion to the Virgin and, on the other, the 'bonnes mœurs' typical both of early Christians and of sixteenth-century Calvinists ('Nestorius', footnote N):

La vie humaine n'est qu'un théatre de changement, mais malgré cette inconstance il y a certaines choses, qui, étant une fois introduites, croissent à vue d'œil, & durent pendant plusieurs siecles avec des progrès continuels. C'est ce qu'on ne peut pas dire des innovations qui tendent à réformer les abus publics, & à corriger les mauvaises mœurs. [...] Les réformations de Religion s'établissent quelquefois à durer longtems par raport aux dogmes spéculatifs, mais quant à la Morale pratique, elles parviennent promptement à leur perfection, & au plus haut point de leur crue, & à cela succede un relâchement très rapide, & un état corrompu qui demanderoient une nouvelle réformation.

The unstinted growth of those *erreurs populaires* prevalent in pagano-Catholicism is an exception to the rule of history seen as 'un théâtre de changement'. Necessarily, the domination of superstition in the Church Universal results from its flattery of depraved instincts. Had it challenged human nature, like all violent states, it could never have lasted. Error rather than truth speaks 'un langage toujours uniforme'. In opposition comes the Reformation, whose verity, quite apart from the stock parallel Calvinism/early Church, is proven *by its variations*. Its challenge to depraved instincts – a sign of divine vocation – is evident in the later decline of its severe morality. That is to say, ecclesiastical orthodoxy, verity and moral rigorism – the marks of the true Church – are now the property of those willing to admit error and depravity and thence to instigate 'une nouvelle réformation'. Far from being a token of schism, variations, inasmuch as they express a desire to reinstate the standards of primitive Christianity in each new age, represent a conformity to the cyclical movement of history, in turn the instrument of a divine Providence concerned to check the ravages of total depravity.[215] Calvinist theological method and Calvinist historiography fuse: both challenge the linear degeneration of Catholicism. The *retour aux origines* is the foundation of the call to reform and of an alternative reading of ecclesiastical history.

The linear development of superstition and vice is not only the fruit of depraved instincts, it is also facilitated by the unparalleled and progressive

215. 'Esope', footnote I; see below, p.231.

control of ecclesiastical affairs by the papacy. The typology of the Machiavellian prince in the biographies of kings here reappears in the lives of the popes[216] and is now wholly iconoclastic in its intentions (below, p.234-35). The ambivalence to Machiavelli's principle of the two moralities – one proper to religion, the other to politics – is transformed into an incisive irony directed against the leaders of the Church of Rome. Their 'ruses', 'intrigues' and 'finesses' are proof not only of a divine absence but also, by means of opposed images of good to Machiavellian popes,[217] of the dictum that 'les Papes qui n'ont que Dieu pour eux, font pitié'.[218] The fourteen articles in question display certain similarities with the Machiavellian analysis of the lives of Alexander and the two Louis, notably in the choice of sources. Guicciardini and Sarpi, both influenced by Machiavelli, are indicative of a selection of perspective: the two authors had either been placed on the Index or censured by their co-religionaries for their cynical analysis of the rise of the Roman See to the status of a universal monarchy.[219] Bayle, moreover, frequently has recourse to Protestant histories of the papacy, either the celebrated *Mystère d'iniquité* by Du Plessis Mornay, or the more recent *Historia Papatus* by Heidegger.[220] The selection reveals a profound ideological accord: the first, an Augustinian reading of ecclesiastical history, records the progress of the papacy and the opposition to its rise by the *testes veritatis* of all ages; the second draws its iconoclasm from Guicciardini (Dompnier, 'L'histoire religieuse'). Mindful, however, of the sensibilities of his Catholic readers,[221] Bayle vaunts his use of the histories of the ex-Jesuit Maimbourg, 'un homme qui a vécu long tems parmi les Jésuites, & qui n'est rien moins que disposé à favoriser les non-Catholiques'.[222] The choice is parallel to the astute use of Du Pin in the article 'Nestorius' (above, p.52): as a Gallican, Maimbourg, for all his former affiliations with the Society of Jesus, is less than sympathetic to Roman aspirations to universal sovereignty.[223] Moreover, as in that entry, the distorted image of the

---

216. See Appendix III, for a list of the articles on popes.

217. Only two of the fourteen popes are good (Hadrien VI and Innocent XI) inasmuch as they either lived virtuous lives or attempted reforms of the Church. The articles on the good popes (like those on the good kings) reveal, however, that virtue is a poor match for the wily corruption of the Vatican and that reforms are vigorously resisted and finally defeated ('Hadrien VI', article and footnotes Q and R; 'Innocent XI', article and footnote G).

218. The dictum occurs in *CG*, letter XI, §5, *OD*, ii.49a, where it is attributed to Pallavicino.

219. Fueter, p.84-95, 337-40; Hubert Jedin, *A history of the Council of Trent*, trans. Dom Ernest Graf (London 1957, 1961), ii.7ff. They are often used by the Protestants because of their mutual hostility to the papacy.

220. For full references, see above, ch.1, n.81.

221. 'Sixte IV', footnote C; 'Paul II', footnote C.

222. 'Leon I', footnote C; 'Gregoire VII', footnote F; Guicciardini and Sarpi are also Catholic sources, a fact which Bayle does not fail to exploit on occasion.

223. For Gallicanism, see above, ch.2, notes 47, 48.

papacy is forcefully opposed to the doctrine and practices of the early Church.

The glory of Rome and its apostolic See becomes, by the technique of the *démolition du héros*,[224] the scene of depravity and vice. Twelve of the fourteen popes considered are distinguished by the infamy of their lifestyles. Taken collectively, the papacy is arraigned before the tribunal of history for its extravagance and luxury, its sexual incontinence and voluptuousness, its drunkenness, nepotism, simony, persecution and bellicose ways.[225] Here, however, private vice does not contribute to the public weal: the theological perspective appears. Such practices may have contributed to Catholic wealth but extravagance, debauchery and nepotism all led to an institutionalisation of vice in the form of simony and the sale of indulgences.[226] All these practices, moreover, are tokens of lives 'peu convenable[s] aux successeurs des Apôtres' ('Leon X'), all precipitated the sixteenth-century Protestant Reformation. Piety is evinced by some but, as the case of Chigi illustrates, is only a Machiavellian 'grimace' or 'finesse', assumed in order the better to rise to power ('Chigi', *in corp.*). Indeed, power politics is the fundamental trait of the papacy and only those versed in 'le manége de la politique' ('Innocent XI', footnote G) succeed in turning 'l'esprit des Princes en faveur des intérêts temporels & spirituels de la Religion' ('Gregoire I'). The notion is common to all Bayle's sources, as is the perception of Gregory VII as a key figure in 'la domination sur le temporel' acquired by the Church of Rome.[227]

Curiously, while Protestant polemicists are wont, according to Gabriel Naudé, to present pope Gregory VII as 'le plus sale & vilain monstre qui fut jamais revestu de nature humaine' (*Apologie*, p.578), the author of the *Dictionnaire*, a Machiavellian realist, maintains that 'on ne lui sauroit contester les qualitez d'un grand homme, non plus qu'à certains Conquérans qui sont d'ailleurs tout couverts de crimes' ('Gregoire VII', *in corp.*). That is to say, Gregory VII's prohibition, under pain of excommunication, of the lay investiture of clergy and prelates and his subsequent excommunication of the emperor Hildebrand[228] are seen as courageous and wily extensions of 'la puissance Pontificale', compar-

---

224. Above, p.208-209, and Bénichou, p.155-80.

225. 'Leon X', article and footnote C; 'Paul II'; 'Innocent VIII', article and footnote D; 'Jules II', footnote L; 'Paul II', footnote B; 'Paul II' and footnote D; 'Chigi (Fabio)', footnotes C and D; 'Ottoboni', footnote A; 'Sixte IV', footnote A; 'Sixte IV', footnote L; 'Gregoire I', footnote E; 'Paul II', footnote A; 'Sixte IV'; 'Eugene IV', and footnote D; 'Jules II', footnotes D and E; 'Leon X'; 'Ottoboni'.

226. 'Leon X' and footnote M; 'Ottoboni' and footnote A.

227. *NRL*, May 1684, cat.vi, *OD*, i.61a; Arquillière, p.22-23, and *passim*, maintains that Gregory VII did in fact formulate most clearly the jurisdiction of spiritual over temporal power. Pope Gregory is also commonly perceived, in Protestant historiography, as a precipitator of the degeneration of the Church (Snoeks, p.43 and *passim*).

228. See Arquillière, *passim*.

able in their effect to the conquests of Alexander and Caesar.[229] The ambivalence to Machiavellianism evident in the entries on these two monarchs now reappears in the form of a theological opposition between Roman conquests – military and ecclesiastical – and 'le véritable esprit de la Religion, qui est d'éclairer & sanctifier l'ame [...] sans empiéter sur la politique' ('Gregoire VII', footnote S).

Je me sers d'autant plus hardiment de cette Comparaison, que je suis persuadé que la conquête de l'Eglise a été un Ouvrage où il n'a pas falu moins de cœur & moins d'adresse, qu'il en faut pour la conquête d'un Empire. [...] On ne sauroit considérer sans étonnement qu'une Eglise, qui n'a, dit-elle, que les armes spirituelles de la parole de Dieu, & qui ne peut fonder ses droits que sur l'Evangile, où tout prêche l'humilité & la pauvreté, ait eu la hardiesse d'aspirer à une domination absolue sur tous les Rois de la terre: mais il est encore plus étonnant que ce dessein chimérique lui ait si bien réüssi [...] C'est [... un] sujet de surprise, quand on voit la nouvelle Rome, ne se piquant que du Ministere Apostolique, aquérir une autorité sous laquelle les plus grans Monarques ont été contraints de plier [...].[230]

The criticism of Rome continues in the reiteration of Bayle's reversal of the signs of the true Church. Her 'domination absolue' is typical of a Church in schism with apostolic tradition and the true Church, known by its *humilité* and *pauvreté*.[231] None the less, a new note of bewilderment is sounded and revealed in the recurring lexis *étonnement, surprise, étonnant*, together with the later cross-reference to the article 'Xenophanes'.[232] Entrenched in his view of Roman Catholicism as an institutionalised form of error, superstition and vice and faithful to his ideal, indeed mythical notion of early Christianity, Bayle is pained to see the former triumph at the expense of the latter. The position, present in the earlier works, now fuses with a bitterness to which 'Xenophanes' forcefully gives voice. If Machiavelli and Rome are contrary to 'la Religion de Jesus-Christ', if superstition is the antithesis of verity, if the Devil is the sworn enemy of God, then why does the Almighty, with all his omnipotence, fail to quell the spiritual prostitution of the Church, the machinations of Hell and the obfuscation of truth by error?[233] The conclusion necessary from our author's vision of Rome

229. 'Gregoire VII', article and footnote B; cf. footnote A.
230. 'Gregoire VII', footnote B.
231. Above, p.221-22, and 'Gregoire VII', footnote S.
232. The cross-reference appears for the first time in 1702; the shared perspective of the two articles evidently appeared to Bayle when revising the *magnum opus*.
233. Cf. 'Gregoire VII', footnote S; 'Xenophanes', footnote E; discussions with Richard Popkin in 1981 convinced me that behind the intellectual heterodoxy of the Manichean articles in the *Dictionnaire* lies an emotional and psychological bitterness, one to which this paragraph attempts to give voice. That is to say, Bayle's philosophical difficulties with the problem of evil may also read as a diatribe against a Divinity who seems to stand idly by, allowing evil to triumph. This is not to argue that Bayle ends up in a position of unbelief. On the contrary, fideism is the final stronghold of a beleaguered faith. Cf. Labrousse, *Bayle* (Past Masters), p.66-67, for a similar interpretation.

as the majority, if erroneous, Church is that God is defeated in the 'guerre (sans paix ni treve) que le Démon fait à Dieu' ('Xenophanes', footnote E). In a word, the earlier polemical demonstration of Catholicism as the Church of the 'Dieu absent' is on the verge of becoming a historiographical vision in which 'le théâtre du monde' is the scene of the humiliation of the Divinity.[234]

The puzzlement over the unchecked rise of the papacy – one more aspect of Bayle's perplexity with the problem of evil – is part of the wider problem experienced in his later years, of identifying the hand of Providence in ecclesiastical history. While, on the one hand, the links between Calvinism, the early Church, and verity, and those between Catholicism, paganism and superstition persist, on the other, truth is no longer held to be the property of one confession. This trans-confessionalisation of truth is already implicit in the early works (Launoi and the Gallicanism he represents are both accepted as witnesses to the truth) but the *Dictionnaire* reveals a deliberate break with the conceptions of that Reformed historiography which informed and continues to inform Bayle's depiction of Church history. The cracks appear in his attitude towards sixteenth-century evangelical Catholics: among others, John Barnes, Cassander, Erasmus, Mondrevius, Paolo Sarpi and Wicelius,[235] all annexed to the Reformed conception of the *testes veritatis*. The annexation is not, however, unproblematic. Many (Erasmus and Castellan are foremost among them) refused to break with Rome. Bayle's reflection on their refusal is ambivalent, as is indicated by the following quotations. The first is a comment on Erasmus, the second a rejection of Protestant historians' presentation of Castellan's ignominious death as a divine punishment for his persistence within Roman Catholicism:

Il n'est pas ici question d'éxaminer si la conduite qu'Erasme a tenue par raport à la Religion est bonne: je dirai seulement qu'il a été, ce me semble, un de ces témoins de la vérité qui soupiroient après la Réformation de l'Eglise, mais qui ne croioient pas qu'il y falut parvenir par l'érection d'une autre société, qui s'apuiât d'abord sur des ligues, & qui passât promptement *à verbis ad verbera*. Il se faisoit une notion trop bornée de la Providence de Dieu, & ne considéroit pas assez qu'elle nous conduit au même but, tantôt par une route, tantôt par une autre. Ainsi avec son *non amo veritatem seditiosam*, il demeura dans le bourbier, & s'imagina faussement qu'il n'étoit que de se tenir au gros de l'arbre; puis que la maniere dont Luther écrivoit, & les guerres qui accompagnoient sa Réformation, étoient un préjugé que le temps de la délivrance n'étoit pas encore venu.

Calvin, Beze & plusieurs autres, se persuadérent que tous ceux qui avoient d'abord favorisé la Réformation, soit en tâchant d'adoucir l'esprit des persécuteurs, soit en témoignant un desir extrême de voir cesser les maux de l'Eglise, étoient autant d'apostats, & autant de traîtres à leur conscience, s'ils demeuroient dans la Communion Romaine, & s'ils changeoient de conduite à l'égard des Réformez. Je dis que c'étoit juger trop vite.

234. 'Xenophanes', footnote E, and 'Pericles', footnote L; cf. Labrousse, *Pierre Bayle*, ii.458-59.
235. These are all listed by Bayle as evangelical Catholics in 'Barnes (Jean)'.

Croire que l'Eglise a besoin de réformation & aprouver une certaine maniere de la réformer, sont deux choses bien différents. Blâmer la conduite de ceux qui s'oposent à une réformation, & desaprouver la conduite de ceux qui réforment, sont deux choses très compatibles. On peut donc imiter Erasme, sans être apostat ni perfide, sans pécher contre le Saint Esprit, sans trahir les lumieres de sa conscience; & c'est ce que Theodore de Beze ne paroit pas avoir compris; il s'imaginoit que tous ceux, qui tomboient d'accord que Calvin & que Luther avoient raison en plusieurs choses, étoient dès-là pleinement persuadez qu'il faloit rompre avec l'Eglise Romaine, & dresser autel contre autel, briser & renverser les images, & ne s'arrêter pas à la vue même des torrens de sang que l'on alloit faire répandre. C'est une illusion: il y eut sans doute bien des gens qui crurent que puis que la Réformation rencontroit de si grans obstacles qui mettoient l'Europe dans la derniere désolation, Dieu témoignoit que le tems de réformer n'étoit point encore venu.[236]

While the first of the quotations is milder in tone, it is nearer in spirit to the summary of Protestant attitudes to Erasmus and Castellan provided in the second. That is to say, anticipating the position added later to the article 'Nestorius', Bayle holds to a belief in the Reformation as a providential corrective to the 'bourbier' of Roman Catholicism. Erasmus may not be presented as an apostate but he is perceived as a witness to the truth whose conception of divine intervention was too limited to appreciate the hand of God at work in a schism necessary to the spiritual welfare of the Church. None the less, the hint in the first of a certain disapproval, on Bayle's part, of the violence of Luther and the Reformation ('qui s'apuiât [...] sur des Ligues') almost becomes a passionate denunciation in the second passage of that confession to which Bayle sacrificed homeland and family ties. Looking at the Reformation with Erasmian eyes and sharing the pacifist inclinations of his predecessor in Rotterdam,[237] Bayle appreciates in turn the heart-rending consequences of a schism which precipitated social upheaval, the shedding of far too much innocent blood and the desolation of Europe. The bewilderment evident in the view of the rise of the papacy is implicit in the horror felt at the aftermath of a reform designed to reinstate the primitive purity of the early Church. Now well versed in the history of his communion, Bayle notes its recourse to arms (for example 'Beaumont' – the early Christians were submissive in the face of persecution), its schisms[238] (the early Church was faithful to apostolic doctrine), its blood-letting[239] (the early Christians, like the Messiah, were as lambs led to slaughter), its Machiavellianism and corrupt morality, so contrary to 'la Morale de l'Evangile' (e.g. 'Milletiere, 'Rotan'). The apparent similarity between the two concluding re-

236. 'Erasme', footnote T; 'Castellan', footnote Q, respectively.
237. Vivanti, *passim*; above, p.165ff; Laplanche, 'L'Ecriture', i.61ff.
238. 'Mammilaires'; the article devoted to Arminius is a good example of Bayle's hostility to Protestant sectarianism.
239. 'Macon', and 'Beaumont'.

marks masks a profound divergence of tone. The first does not perceive violence as a 'préjugé légitime' against the divine vocation of the Reformation; the second, on the contrary, betrays a doubt lest '[les] torrens de sang' be a sign of divine reprobation[240] of a Reform in which, albeit in its ideal profile, the *philosophe* of Rotterdam never ceases to believe. The disillusionment of the later years, not unrelated to the ideological conflicts in the *Refuge*,[241] yields to a cynicism with respect to all institutionalised religion. Truth and purity, signs of 'le doigt de Dieu' in the early Church and, at times, in the Reformation, become the property of a mystical Church in the *Continuation des Pensées diverses* (1704): 'les Chrétiens parfaits ou tendans à la perfection ne font point de corps, ils sont répandus en petit nombre dans des Sociétez qui savent très-bien attaquer & se défendre de même'.[242] In a word, the opposition between minority, verity, purity on the one hand and majority, error, immorality on the other continues but the respective groups no longer don confessional garments: the hand of God in ecclesiastical history has ceased to be perceptible.

Ethics, politics and religion, three areas which, to our author, betray the ideological affiliations of the historian, not only reveal the presence of Augustinian, Machiavellian and Calvinist reading-grids in the *Dictionnaire*, they also testify to an attenuation of the divine presence in the 'théâtre du monde', bringing Bayle closer in spirit to Voltaire and the eighteenth century than to sixteenth-century political or religious precursors, the inspiration of his thought. None the less, for all the apparent similarities, the crisis of the European conscience, of which Bayle is the herald and the voice, must be read not as a knowing subversion of traditional values but as the *cri de cœur*, perhaps even the swan-song, of an age at variance with itself. The conflict between anthropocentric and theocentric causation, the attribution of the cycles of history now to God, now to man, are the fruits not of a generation determined to efface the Almighty from history but of a group of writers and intellectuals in search of the divine footsteps in the sands of time.[243] The quest for the Divinity is particularly acute in Bayle's case: commitment to the Reformed communion, in his early years seen to represent the truth he so ardently pursues, precipitated the death of his brother, the rout of his co-religionaries at the Revocation and his own exile. Later, to his chagrin, that self-same confession, in the person of Jurieu and his supporters, upheld positions Bayle so abhors in Catholicism. The rise and fall of the Reformed religion in France, the *grandeur* and *décadence* of

240. 'Melanchthon', footnote I, where Bayle attributes a similar doubt to his hero.
241. Cf. Howells, p.57ff.; Labrousse, *Bayle* (Past Masters), p.25.
242. *CPD*, §cxxv, *OD*, iii.362b.
243. Jehasse makes a similar point for the sixteenth-century *fin de siècle* generation, who had also lived through troubled times (p.499).

empires and political régimes, the cycles of reform and immorality in public and private ethics inevitably provoke the question: *à quoi bon?* The Manichean entries in the *Dictionnaire* are penetrated with a divine silence on the issue. The article 'Esope' gives the only adequate human reply to this metaphysical hush:

Le monde est un véritable jeu de bascule; tour à tour on y monte & on y descend. On doit admirer dans ce jeu-là les profondeurs d'une sage Providence, & l'activité de nos passions. [...] Si l'homme n'étoit pas un animal indiscriplinable, ne se seroit-il pas corrigé de son orgueil, aprés tant de preuves de la Maxime d'Esope réïtérées en chaque païs, & en chaque siecle? D'ici à deux mille ans, si le monde dure autant, les réïterations continuelles de la bascule n'auront rien gagné sur le cœur humain. Pourquoi donc les réïtérer sans fin & sans cesse? Il faut mettre le doigt sur la bouche, & adorer humblement la sagesse du Conducteur de cet Univers [...].[244]

Not only is progress absent from the historical tapestry (a position at variance with eighteenth-century attitudes),[245] the meaning of the cycles of history, here the result of a co-operation between the passions and Providence, has also absconded in the face of Bayle's pessimism. The humiliation of the Divinity in the theatre of history, so bitterly evoked in 'Xenophanes', yields to a renunciation of any sense in the course of human history. Depravity seems everywhere to prevail, but mystery and its counterpart fideism replace the erstwhile analysis of historical causation. Not only is man not the final arbiter of his destiny, the historian, too, is not the ultimate judge of human actions. In the final analysis, both cede the stage to the majesty and inscrutability of the Hidden God.

Looking back, towards the end of his life, over the years spent in the company of books, Bayle traces for his critics the cause of the ambivalences we note in his thought. The statement reiterates the opposition between *vérité* and *erreur* and the self-identification of the author of the *Dictionnaire* with those who are not ashamed 'de reconoître le besoin qu'ils auroient eu de vieillir pour discerner une vérité' (*CPD*, §xxxix, *OD*, iii.241b):

Il y a des doctrines qui me paroissent aujourd'hui très-incertaines, dont je ne croïois pas autrefois que l'on pût douter sans extravagance; & je trouve beaucoup de probabilité pour le moins dans des opinions, qui me sembloient si absurdes il y a quelques années, que je ne comprenois pas qu'on osât les soûtenir. Vingt ans d'étude peuvent produire de grands changemens dans une tête, & font bien voir du païs.

Yesterday's creeds are today's credulities. Reading necessarily brings evolution in those, unlike the 'Docteurs opiniâtres', whose pusuit of truth is equivalent to a refusal '[de] s'enraciner de plus en plus dans leurs préjugez'. Evolution, however, as the case of Melanchthon, another historical hero,[246] reveals, can

---

244. 'Esope' (1st article), footnote I; cf. 'Pericles', footnote K; 'Lucrece (Titus)', footnote H.
245. Jean Ehrard, *L'Idée de nature en France à l'aube des lumières* (Paris 1970), p.387ff.
246. Labrousse, *Bayle* (Past Masters), p.34.

bring the charge of Pyrrhonism against one whose 'sens froid [...] laissoit agir son génie sur le pour & sur le contre' ('Melanchthon', footnote I). But, as if defending himself in advance against the eighteenth-century image of his work, Bayle notes his hero's reasons for remaining with a Reformation and retaining a theology whose weaknesses were evident to his penetrating judgement. 'Où voulez-vous qu'il allât? [...] N'eut-il pas rencontré dans la Communion Romaine beaucoup plus de choses à condamner, plus d'emportement, plus d'opression de conscience?'[247] The question is pressed with all the vehemence of personal conviction. Bayle, libertine, Cartesian or Calvinist? His humanist curiosity has transformed him into a 'protestant malgré lui'. Only by forgetting 'le contexte huguenot qui a présidé à sa formation et [...] celui du Refuge au sein duquel s'est épanouie sa maturité'[248] can the ambivalences of his thought be read as the self-conscious heralds of the dawning Enlightened age.

247. 'Melanchthon', footnote I; cf. *RQP*, II, clxxxii, *OD*, iii.891a.
248. Above, p.13, and ch.1, n.22.

# 8. 'Le rire des honnêtes gens': historical iconoclasm: conclusion

L'ardeur de se montrer, et non pas de médire,
Arma la Verité du vers de la Satire.
Lucile le premier osa la faire voir:
Aux vices des Romains presenta le miroir:
Vengea l'humble Vertu, de la Richesse altiere,
Et l'honneste Homme à pié, du Faquin en litiere.
Horace à cette aigreur mesla son enjoûment.
On ne fut plus ni fat ni sot impunément:
Et malheur à tout nom, qui propre à la censure,
Put entrer dans un vers, sans rompre la mesure.

Boileau, *L'Art poétique*, chant II[1]

En vérité, mes Pères, il y a bien de la différence entre rire de la religion, et rire de ceux qui la profanent par leurs opinions extravagantes. Ce serait une impiété de manquer de respect pour les vérités que l'esprit de Dieu a révélées: mais ce serait une autre impiété de manquer de mépris pour les faussetés que l'esprit de l'homme leur oppose.

Pascal, *Les Provinciales*, letter XI[2]

PIERRE Bayle, to his contemporaries a writer 'de grande littérature, d'une profonde littérature',[3] has become in modern times an author of forbidding erudition. 'What treasures are to be found in Bayle,' observes Mossner, 'but what an effort to dig them up! Proper source for a twenty-one-year-old burning with intellectual curiosity, Bayle is definitely to be avoided by the middle-aged who have little spare time on their hands.'[4] The effort, both physical and mental, required to follow the *philosophe* of Rotterdam on his voyage through the vast historical and intellectual pageant recreated in his *Dictionnaire* and miscellaneous works may blind the modern critic to two of the salient features, recognised by contemporaries, of this monument of learning. The first, the subject of this study, is the unmistakable religious and ideological convictions, albeit convictions in a state of crisis, on which the *magnum opus* reposes. The fact did not escape Bayle's eighteenth-century Catholic critics, who decry his 'passion partisane en faveur de Luther, Calvin, de Beze'.[5] It is an opinion, for all its lack of nuance,

1. Boileau, *L'Art poétique*, chant II, in *Œuvres complètes* (Paris 1979), p.166.
2. Pascal, *Les Provinciales*, letter XI, p.195.
3. Above, p.1 and n.3.
4. Quoted by Popkin, in *Historical and critical dictionary, selections*, p.xiii.
5. Rétat, *Le Dictionnaire de Bayle*, p.149.

pinpointing none the less an oft-neglected aspect of the *érudit* of Rotterdam: the apparent impartiality of the multiple footnotes conceals a committed writer at work. The second, the theme of this conclusion, is Bayle's frank delight in and consummate mastery of the satiric mode. 'Vous ne haïssez point la raillerie', he muses to his fictitious correspondent in 1685, 'ni moi non-plus.'[6] As the articles 'Agreda' and those of the lives of the patriarchs (above, p.6ff, 168ff.), among others, indicate, erudition, conviction and satire fuse on many occasions to create a historical iconoclasm, lethal in its effect. The intentions may be in deadly earnest but the medium is laughter. The gaiety of Bayle's learning exposed him in his lifetime to the charge of impiety (above, p.173). In the twentieth century, misguidedly proud of its so-called 'relentless progression toward truth [and] objectivity'[7] in the historical sciences, comedy and conviction open him to the charge of bad faith. If Bayle as a critic of Maimbourg opposes the rhetoric of sources and the asceticism of the *savant* to the self-indulgent and vicious satirical histories of the Jesuit, then how, in all conscience, can the author of the *Dictionnaire* be seen to yield to the temptation he so ardently censures in others? The answer, implicit in this study, lies in a theory of satire which reconciles verity and source with conviction and laughter, a theory, moreover, learnt by Bayle not only through reading but also by experience.

The problem of historical composition, to one born into a minority persecuted with the sword and the pen, is that the majority controls both the corridors of power and the printing presses. The espousal of the cause of persecuted minorities in so many instances in the *magnum opus*, reposes on the belief that the 'historien équitable' has as his task the reversal of the historical record, too long dominated by an ideological authoritarianism exclusive of the opinions of the ever-oppressed minority.[8] The case of Nestorius would be clearer, observes Bayle ('Nestorius', footnote E):

L'on verroit plus clair dans cette affaire si l'on avoit les Relations des Nestoriens, & celles des autres Sectes; mais nous ne savons gueres ces choses que sur le raport du Parti victorieux, & nous en savons néanmoins assez, pour pouvoir juger que la Puissance Impériale a eu toûjours trop de part aux Décisions.

The remark provides the key to the bias evident in Bayle's selection of sources. Libertine, Protestant, Gallican and Machiavellian analysts are chosen because all share a common distrust of traditions and authorities whose positions are right because they are founded on might.[9] The resulting iconoclasm is destructive only

6. Above, p.113.
7. Kelley, p.9. See above, p.184, n.11.
8. Bodin, *Methodus*, p.296 and 312, holds a similar position.
9. It is necessary to distinguish between Machiavelli and writers like Guicciardini and Sarpi who use, as Bayle will later, Machiavellian concepts to demystify power-politics.

in its initial phase. The undoubtedly biased source, judiciously selected (a testimony to Bayle's remarkable scholarly judgement), is the crucible from which an alternative history emerges. In the case of Nestorius, Du Pin's Gallican reading exposes the power-politics behind the so-called heretic's condemnation (above, p.52). No biography of the heresiarch survives but it may be reconstructed from sources subversive of oppressive historiography. Faithful to his humanist heroes, Bayle's iconoclasm is a signpost on the path to the rediscovery of 'la plus authentique tradition de la vérité'.[10]

History as subversion functions as a *retournement de la médaille*. The case of Nestorius, for all the complexity of the *Dictionnaire* entry, is relatively simple: alternative sources exist capable of providing an alternative image. The case of superstition and, particularly, Catholic superstition (although in later years Jurieu becomes a similar object of ridicule) is more problematic. The alternative histories are recent and Protestant and subject to the charge of prejudice. The hold of hagiography is to be undermined by more subtle means. A significant remark is made on the polemical warfare concerning the life of St Francis of Assisi. The Franciscans published *Les Conformitez de la vie de St François à la vie de Jesus-Christ*, a work full of exaggerated hagiographical *topoi*, to which sixteenth-century Protestants opposed l'*Alcoran des Cordeliers*, wherein 'ils ne firent que publier les Extraits de cet Ouvrage, avec quelques notes' (François (d'Assise)', footnote F):

Aparemment les Franciscains auroient été un peu plus sages, s'ils avoient prévu ce qui arriva par le moien de Luther & de Calvin. Mais il y avoit si long-tems que tous ceux qui osoient crier contre l'Eglise Romaine étoient écrasez par la force du bras séculier, que l'on se persuadoit aisément que tous leurs imitateurs auroient la même destinée. On fut trompé. Il s'éleva un grand corps d'Eglise avant le milieu du XVI siecle. Ce grand corps se maintint, & subsiste encore aujourd'hui fort en état de se faire redouter. Il a eu de toutes sortes de plumes en abondance, desorte qu'il a falu boire toutes les sotises qu'on avoit faites. On avoit eu l'imprudence de permettre l'impression du Livre des Conformitez, & il a falu en porter la peine. Ce n'est pas une plaie qui ne fasse que passer, comme lors que l'on extermine toute une Secte avec ses Livres. Ceux qui ont fait cette plaie ont des Auteurs à foison, & une infinité de Bibliothèques & d'Imprimeries.

The symbiosis of theology and scholarship appears again as the author links the Reformation to the institution of an alternative *corps* of writers, fully equipped ('une infinité de Bibliothèques & d'Imprimeries') to meet authoritarian historiography head on. Confessional conflict becomes a battle of books. The battle, however, is won only by the employment of a certain method: the enemy is thrown into disarray. That is to say, the success of the *Alcoran* is attributed to its apparently innocent *quotation* of positions publicly maintained by the

---

10. See above, p.119ff.

Franciscans: error is condemned from its own mouth. The 'imprudence' of *Les Conformitez*, like that of Agreda's *La Mystique Cité*, is held up to the public gaze and the Catholic opponent is made to 'boire toutes les sotises qu'on avoit faites'. The satirist cannot be accused of bias or *mauvaise foi* for, like Pascal, '[il n'a] pris sujet de rire que de ce qu'il y a de ridicule dans [les] livres'.[11] Erudition is the *agent provocateur* of laughter.

Humanism and classicism combine in the annexation of comedy to erudition in the 'Chasse aux Fautes', the object of that foil to human error, the *Dictionnaire* (above, p.120-21). In an observation added, like so many others on the function of laughter, to the second edition, perhaps an *apologia pro historia sua* (above, p.173), the author points to the corrective, even the cathartic role of erudite laughter. The Protestant controversist Philippe de Marnix, with whom 'Agreda' is explicitly linked (above, p.19), filled his *Alvearium Romanum* and *Tableau des differens de la religion* with 'Contes burlesques':

Ce Livre rempli de Contes burlesques fut reçu du peuple avec un aplaudissement incroiable, & fit plus de tort à la Communion de Rome que n'auroit fait un Livre sérieux & sçavant. On veut même qu'il ait donné occasion à plusieurs personnes de méditer profondement sur les Controverses, & de se desabuser. Les Colloques d'Erasme avoient produit le même effet. [...] la maniere la plus funeste d'attaquer une doctrine est celle de la tourner en ridicule.[12]

The critical methodology which tracks superstition and debunks *erreurs populaires* up and down the footnotes of the *magnum opus* adopts comedy as its ally. As history is the mirror of the past (above, p.101), so satire (and here Bayle joins hands with Boileau) is the mirror in which vice and error are recognised and rejected. The author of the *Art poétique*, however, extends his counsel to writers of verse, accepting the counsel, Bayle, a writer of prose, turns for a model to Erasmus, the master of humanist and ironical verve. That 'témoin de la vérité', who sighed over the corruption of human nature and the degeneration of the Church (above, p.228-29), inspires his seventeenth-century counterpart in a parallel campaign. Cathartic laughter is the defender of truth and the shield of 'l'innocence opprimée'.

The satire of 'Agreda', the reversal of the history of Nestorius are inseparable from a conception of irony wherein truth, comedy and the source operate together in the war against error and superstition in all their forms. The columns of the *Dictionnaire* testify, however, to a second kind of satire exemplified by Maimbourg and later Jurieu (a faithful imitator of earlier Reformed satirical controversy). Despite the undoubtedly Protestant tones in which Bayle censures

11. Pascal, *Les Provinciales*, letter XI, p.195.
12. 'Sainte-Aldegonde', footnote G; cf. 'Viret', footnote C.

the depravity and superstition of the papacy, his critique of Maimbourg-like *Protestant* polemics earned him a warning from the Consistory of Rotterdam.[13] The remarks on laughter and *l'art de médire* which pepper the second edition of the *magnum opus* constitute a reply and a self-defence. Three rules are noted:

C'est une chose remarquable, qu'y aiant une infinité de personnes possédées d'une démangeaison insurmontable de publier des Satires, il y en ait si peu qui sachent l'art de les bien empoisonner. La plûpart de ceux qui s'en mêlent ignorent, que pour y bien réüssir, c'est-à-dire pour faire qu'elles portent coup, il faut se mettre en possession de ces deux choses, & les observer religieusement: l'une est de n'avancer rien dont on ne puisse donner des preuves, & sur tout de s'abstenir des accusations qui peuvent être facilement réfutées; l'autre est de ne point s'opiniâtrer à soutenir un fait réfuté. J'oubliois un troisieme avis: c'est qu'il faut cacher soigneusement sa passion, & fuir les aparences d'emportement. J'avoue qu'en faisant tout le contraire de ces choses on ne trouve que trop de gens de son Parti qui avalent doux comme du lait tout ce qu'on débite: mais, c'est cela même qui fait un grand préjudice à la cause; parce que l'autre Parti s'indigne, & regarde comme un corps destitué de raison, d'équité, & de l'assistance de la grace, celui d'où partent tant de Satires si avidement avalées.[14]

The remark picks up and applies to the satirist some of the guidelines given to the good historian (above, p.87ff.). The latter serves the truth of the past, the former the truth of his convictions, but both are subject to certain scholarly exigencies. Firstly, the *servitude de la citation*, characteristic of the good historian (above, p.101-103), must also typify the good satirist. The lessons of the *Provinciales* are not lost on Bayle,[15] for whom irony without proof (as the cases of Garasse, Maimbourg and Jurieu indicate) is nothing less than calumny. To the decadent rhetoric of history and invective is opposed *la rhétorique des sources*, synonymous with veridical eloquence (above, p.90ff.). Secondly, the satirist is to join the *témoins de la vérité*, inasmuch as comedy is not to be achieved by the propagation of error. Credulity is eschewed in favour of that judicious discernment required of the Hercules of letters (above, p.93ff.): the hydra of error is to be beaten not joined. Thirdly, persuasion is the object of a satirical mode consecrated to the service of verity. Consequently, *passion* and *emportement*

---

13. 'Le consistoire l'exhorte à prendre garde en sixième lieu à ne pas réfuter légèrement ce que nos théologiens ont dit de certains papes vicieux, puisque, s'il peut alléguer quelques conjectures pour la défense de ces papes sur certains faits, on peut lui opposer de fortes raisons pour leur condamnation, et qu'il est injuste de prendre sans nécessité le parti des séducteurs qui ont fait tant de mal à l'Eglise et de vouloir faire passer nos auteurs pour des accusateurs téméraires' (7 December 1698), *Actes du Consistoire*, in *Dictionnaire*, ed. Beuchot, xvi.299-300.

14. 'Bellarmin', footnote E; cf. 'Gregoire VII', footnotes P and S; 'Annat', footnote B; 'Loyola', footnote R.

15. The eleventh *Lettre provinciale* elaborates a distinction between two kinds of ridicule, one impious inasmuch as it ridicules religious truth, the other legitimate insofar as it ridicules error – to be found in printed and publicly acknowledged sources – in order to lead men to the truth (p.193ff.). The distinction is also made by Bayle in 'Periers', footnote B.

are to be avoided, for their presence in an ironic discourse rouses the indignation of the opponent, clouds his judgement and, given the influence of the *passions de l'âme*, closes his mind to the truth being defended (above, p.107ff.). In a word, 'dead-pan' irony is not only more commendable, it is also more effective. The theory is consistent with the practice in 'Agreda' and similar articles. Sources are scrupulously cited. Conviction, not absent, is muted. The historian / satirist concerned to serve the truth alerts his reader to his bias, proves the reality of the grounds for satire via his source, leaves his position open to verification and allows the reader to decide for himself by conscientious citation. In the words of Labrousse, 'chez qui l'emploie, l'ironie atteste une confiance dans l'intelligence et la bonne foi de l'interlocuteur, qui est la condition préalable, mais bien rarement remplie, de toute discussion honnête' (*Pierre Bayle*, i.209). The charge of impiety, to which this is the indirect reply, is reversed by an analysis placing the invective polemics defended by the Rotterdam Consistory on the side of the saboteurs of truth.[16] Like Pascal before him Bayle distinguishes 'entre rire de la religion' and ridicule of 'les faussetés [de] l'esprit de l'homme'. Ethical and erudite satire is a legitimate and truthful way of winning to 'la cause' 'le rire des honnêtes gens'.

As is indicated by an examination of Bayle's correspondence in those years of crisis preceding the Revocation, the theory of laughter devised in his mature years is the fruit of bitter personal experience. Exiled from family and fatherland in Rotterdam, the author of the *Nouvelles de la République des lettres* frequently uses his reviews of Catholic *apologia* of oppression as a vehicle to express indignation.[17] This impassioned defence of the oppressed at a time when, in the words of his correspondent François Janiçon, 'l'on prend occasion de tout de nuire',[18] draws in 1683 a firm if respectful rebuke from the latter. Conviction, he writes, is commendable but 'Je suis persuadé qu'il n'y a rien, qui ne se peut dire quand on veut bien se donner la peine de le mettre d'une maniere honeste et modérée, sans y mesler trop de chaleur ou de passion.' The reflections on the 'style modéré' which Bayle will publish two years later (above, p.107ff.) are already in gestation. Verity must don the robes of moderation. For to Janiçon 'douceur' and 'modération' are more suitable 'à la pieté, à la reformation et à l'estat où nous nous trouvons' (24 December 1683). Not only that, gentle irony is more effective, 'le principal est qu'il fasse l'effet qu'on veut faire, qu'il gagne

16. The procedure is consistent with the position taken *vis-à-vis* a certain kind of exegesis deemed subversive of truth (above, p.168ff.).
17. Elisabeth Labrousse, 'Les coulisses', p.106.
18. Janiçon, 24 December 1683, in Labrousse, *Inventaire*, no 216. I am most grateful to Mme Labrousse, who provided me with copies of her transcripts of this and other relevant letters in the epistolary exchange with Janiçon.

ou qu'il adoucisse les esprits, et qu'on n'en puisse faire qu'un bon usage'. A letter in the following year returns to the subject, proferring the advice later turned to effect in the *Dictionnaire*. The *Nouvelles*, to Janiçon's mind, adopt an unnecessary and even harmful polemical tone:

C'est que vous y tournés un peu trop les choses en controverses et en disputes lors que l'occasion s'en presente: au lieu qu'il seroit bien mieux, et de plus d'effet de les rapporter plus simplement, et seulement par recit et historiquement, vous contentant d'indiquer les choses, et d'en dire un mot en passant, laissant au lecteur à tirer les consequences. [...] Vous vous rendriés trop suspect aux Cath[oliques] Rom[ains] sur tout dans ses [*sic*] commencemens, ou vous devez vous établir d'abord en simple historien, et retenir vostre zele. Je ne voudrois pas pourtant vous obliger à supprimer tout entierement, parce que ce seroit trahir la verité et vostre conscience, et qu'il est toujours bien sceant qu'un Protestant parle protestant, mais seulement encore paroitre plus modéré que vous n'etes, et presque plus indifferent [...].[19]

Conviction is allowed but the defence of the oppressed must choose as its medium the naked communication of mind with mind (above, p.112-13). Erudition, the impartial display of the facts, is to suffice, the reader to be respected and permitted to draw 'les consequences' (above, p.100f.). Classical theory, religious belief, communication of the truth and resistance to oppression all fuse in a remark which might have come from the pen of the later Bayle. Janiçon's letters seem to have remained unanswered.[20] The journalist to whom they are addressed may echo their counsel in the *Nouvelles lettres critiques* on Maimbourg's history (above, p.107ff.) but the author of the *Commentaire philosophique* is as yet too horrified to write in anything but indignant tones. The nervous breakdown which followed this period of intense literary activity[21] was precipitated, however, not only by an excess of work but also by the guilt experienced at the news of his brother Jacob's death. In 1685 Janiçon writes again, this time to inform his correspondent that in the imprisonment of Jacob the authorities thought to strike a blow at that defender of the Reformed faith, the author of the *Critique générale*. The silent years between the *Commentaire philosophique* and the *Dictionnaire* – years in which Bayle himself became a victim of invective and power-politics[22] – were undoubtedly ones of bitter reflection. The new tone of urbanity in the *magnum opus* reveals its author's mature conviction that oppression and error are combated not with impassioned

19. Janiçon, 11 August 1684, Labrousse, *Inventaire*, no 285.
20. Bayle's replies may have been lost. For a list of the letters in the exchange, see Labrousse, *Inventaire*, p.363-65.
21. Labrousse, *Pierre Bayle*, i.198-99; Rex, *Essays*, p.126.
22. It must be admitted that, in the polemical warfare with Jurieu, Bayle gave as good as he received and most decidedly failed to live up to his own ideals.

discourse – an 'Historien passioné n'est guere croyable' (above, p.61) – but with impeccable and apparently impartial erudition.

The charge of bad faith, then, is both ill founded and misguided. The one, given Bayle's submission of irony, laughter and conviction to truth, erudition and the source; the other because, despite his unceasing pursuit of ideal history and unmediated discourse, with the humility of the true scholar, he is the first to admit the impossibility of complete impartiality (above, p.183-84). The service of truth to which he deemed himself called and the corresponding eradication of error inevitably involve the composition of history from the perspective of his upbringing and convictions. The urbanity of his scrupulous erudition, together with the conviction it conceals, testify to the profit he drew from Janiçon's criticisms. Unable to 'trahir la vérité et sa conscience', he learnt instead to 'paroistre plus modéré [...] et presque plus indifferent'. His moderation and apparent indifference may have earned him a reputation for Pyrrhonism but, to Bayle and his correspondent, it is but the proof 'qu'il est toujours bien sceant qu'un Protestant parle protestant'. Like Horace of old this writer of committed prose embraces gaiety as a friend to verity.

# Appendices

# Appendix I
## Nestorius: the background

THE scandal involving the patriarch of Constantinople Nestorius occurred at a time when the Church was still in quest of a conception of Christ capable of simultaneously embracing his deity and humanity, while maintaining both their unity and distinction. Two schools of thought existed, different more in emphasis than in christological doctrine. On the one hand, the Antiochene school concentrated on the humanity of Christ: acknowledging the unity of natures, they none the less emphasised the duality – Christ was both human and divine. On the other, the theologians of Alexandria fixed their attention on the divine nature of Christ and, while confessing his duality, asserted in the strongest terms the dominance of divinity over humanity in the incarnation. Nestorius, enthroned as patriarch of Constantinople on 10 April 428, was an Antiochene in christology and his exposition of the implications of that school's position initiated the controversy.

Towards the end of the year 428, his chaplain Anastasius protested in one of his sermons to the people against the title *theotokos* given to the mother of Christ. The shock both to the laity and to the clergy of the imperial city was intense, as the term had long been in use in the tradition of the church. Nestorius, however, defended his chaplain, employing expressions offensive to those who differed from him. Concerned lest the incarnation be thought to involve the impassible Word in any change or suffering, Nestorius affirmed the impossibility of ascribing a mother to the eternal God. The position seemed to imply that the Christ borne by Mary later *became* the vehicle of Divinity. Like all Antiochenes, however, Nestorius, starting with the unity of the two natures, wished to stress their distinction: each nature preserved its own properties and acts. To his contemporaries, the argument appeared to indicate a shift from the dual nature of Christ to a stress on the two persons in the Christ. These implications were repeatedly denied by the patriarch, struggling in good faith to understand and define the incarnation.

None the less, his position challenged the doctrine of hypostatic union, whereby the immutable Word appropriates a human nature which becomes *im*personal, allowing the Word to be incarnate or 'enfleshed'. To Nestorius this implied a confusion of the two natures and he preferred the term *sunapheia* (conjunction), which allows both for the continuing impassibility of God and for the spontaneity of action of the man. Hence the Word and the man each brought to the union his own personality, drawn together by gracious condescension, on the one hand, and a loving obedience on the other. The union between the two natures, from this point of view, is *moral* but, while each retains his individuality, the result is one person, the Christ. A second stage denies the absolute continuity between the Word before and the Christ after the incarnation. To Nestorius the Christ was not God but *theophoros* (God-bearing), in whom the Divinity dwelt in a similar if more intense way to the indwelling of the prophets. He is, then, to be worshipped not *as God* but because God was in him. The position safeguards the impassibility of the Divinity for it was the Christ and not the Word who suffered and died. For similar reasons, the notion of Mary as *theotokos* becomes untenable. The mother must be consubstantial with the son; Mary was a creature, could she then have borne God? The fruit of her womb is the Christ, later united to the Divinity. As an alternative Nestorius suggested the terms *theodokos* (God-receiving) or that of *Christotokos* (Christ-bearing). The term *theotokos* was only to be received if understood to refer to the God-man. The explanation, like the doctrine, did not go unopposed.

Cyril, patriarch of Alexandria, informed of the disturbances resulting from the preaching of Anastasius and Nestorius, intervened with a pastoral epistle for Easter 429 and a special letter *Ad monachos Ægypti* to explain the incarnation and the *theotokos*. Given his Alexandrian background, he stressed the unity of Christ's divinity and humanity by positing two *stages* in the existence of the Logos, one before and the other after the incarnation. At the incarnation, while continuing to exist as God, the Word took the form of a servant. Consequently, after the incarnation he was the same person, unchanged in his essential deity: he who had existed 'outside the flesh' had now become 'enfleshed'. The unity of the person of Christ is, then, presupposed from the start; Emmanuel neither laid aside his divinity nor appropriated an independent humanity. The conclusions to be drawn were radically different from those of Nestorius. From the soteriological point of view, all the actions and passions of his humanity could be ascribed to the Word: Jesus is the divine Word, living, dying and rising again for men. From the point of view of the *theotokos* the Word, Son of God by nature, is also *naturally* Mary's son: he appropriated humanity in Mary's womb. To his mind, then, Mary did bring forth a God, she is *theotokos*. These subtle doctrinal differences in the patriarchs' understanding were, however, complicated further by a confusion in terminology.

Cyril uses the term *physis* (nature) to describe the unity of divinity and humanity in Christ and takes the term to mean concrete, individual or independent existence. Unfortunately, to the Antiochenes it connoted the humanity or divinity conceived as an assemblage of characteristics or attributes. Thus, when

Cyril stressed the unity of the *two* natures in Christ, his use of the term *physis* suggested to his opponents such a confusion of the two natures as to imply but one nature in the Christ. The terminological misunderstandings hardly facilitated reconciliation between two schools of thought which differed over this very issue: the manner in which the two natures in Christ may be understood to be united. Nestorius's resistance and refusal to submit to Cyril arise from the conviction, then, that the patriarch of Alexandria was in imminent danger of revitalising the Apollinarian heresy.

Cyril sent two letters to Nestorius, expounding his christology and bidding the latter to end disturbances by asserting the *theotokos*. Nestorius, acknowledging receipt of the first, replied to the second with an exposition of his own interpretation and a discreet condemnation of Cyril's position. The latter reacted with his *De recta fide ad Theodosium* and his *De recta fide ad reginas libri II*, both designed to gain imperial support, and towards the middle of 430 he wrote to the Holy See, stating the controversy and including a dossier of extracts from Nestorius's sermons. The latter had already written two letters to pope Celestine to make inquiries about the Pelagians at Constantinople and complaining about the abuse of the term *theotokos* by some new Arians and Apollinarians. He had used the opportunity to expound his own doctrine and plead for papal support. In a synod held in Rome in August 430, however, pope Celestine upheld the Alexandrians and the *theotokos* and sent four letters publishing the decision to Nestorius, the clergy and laity of Constantinople, the leading bishops of the East and Cyril. Nestorius was threatened with excommunication if he failed to retract within ten days of receipt of the letter, and Cyril, invested with the authority to act for Celestine, was commissioned to supervise the proceedings. With ill-advised zeal, he convoked a synod at Alexandria which issued a lengthy epistle in two parts, written by Cyril. The first part expounds the Alexandrian christology and summarising it in the second come twelve provocative anathematisms to which the patriarch of Constantinople was asked to subscribe. Twelve counter-anathematisms from the latter condemned in turn the apparent Apollinarian leanings of Cyril's position. John of Antioch and other Antiochenes who had first advised Nestorius to submit changed their minds on reading Cyril's anathematisms. Criticism and counter-criticism followed and at the beginning of 431 the affair remained unsettled. Theodosius II convoked a general council to be held at Ephesus at Pentecost, 431.

On the day appointed, Nestorius was at Ephesus with sixteen bishops, Cyril with fifty, Memnon (bishop of Ephesus) with forty. Neither the papal legates nor John of Antioch's party had arrived and the assembled prelates waited fourteen days. Finally, following a request from a number of the bishops, Cyril, mindful of the hardships inseparable from further delay, opened the council on

22 June. The legitimacy of the measure is questionable. The previous evening sixty-eight bishops and count Candidian (in the Emperor's name) are said to have protested against opening the council before the arrival of all the delegates. Moreover, Cyril was Nestorius's prosecutor and had not been specifically designated by Celestine to preside. The acts of the council indicate, however, that John of Antioch had sent two bishops ahead asking Cyril to proceed, and the latter is consistently referred to therein as the archbishop of Rome's designated replacement. Thus, while the council had been convoked by the Emperor, Cyril, seeing it as a continuation of Celestine's wishes, prolonged his supervision of the affair. Some historians maintain, however, that the two bishops said to have come from John of Antioch are also listed among the protesters against the opening of the council. Not only that, Cyril could not have been unaware of the political advantage of his presidency of the council, and the precipitate opening forestalled the procedural changes inevitable with the arrival of the legates.

The council opened with a three-fold summons to Nestorius, who declined to appear, denounced the injustice of the measures taken against him and declared his willingness to appear at the arrival of the Orientals. The council addressed itself to the doctrinal issues, read the Nicene creed, Cyril's second letter to Nestorius, his letter to the Egyptian monks, the letter of Celestine and, lastly, a dossier on the incarnation compiled from Nestorius's writings and extracts from the Fathers. Nestorius's doctrine being deemed heretical, he was condemned and anathematised in his absence by 198 bishops. The prelates worked late into the night to complete the business and their decision met with rejoicing in Ephesus. Four days later, John of Antioch and a party of oriental bishops arrived, hastily held a clandestine meeting, deposed Cyril and Memnon for violence and heresy and excommunicated the bishops who had sat with them in the council. The sentence was communicated to the imperial court and the clergy and laity of Constantinople. Meanwhile the papal legates arrived (10 July) with a resolute letter from Celestine stating his opposition to a re-trial: the decision of the Roman synod held and was to be ratified and promulgated at Ephesus. The following day, however, when they had read the official minutes of Cyril's council, they upheld its measures and sent a letter to the Emperor with an account and a request that the bishops might return home. The Emperor responded by suspending both councils until the cause of the disturbances had been clarified.

He received deputations from both parties: Cyril sent three bishops and the Oriental count Irenaeus to explain their respective positions and win imperial support. Cabals and bribery are alleged to have been rife. Cyrillian bishops gained the first advantage, reversed by the arrival of the count. The Emperor's doctor redirected the decision, however, with the result that Theodosius finally decided to uphold the depositions of Nestorius, Memnon and Cyril. His decision was communicated to both parties, ordered to reassemble quietly once the three bishops had been expelled. John of Antioch's party acquiesced but the other, convinced of its orthodoxy, protested and disturbances were renewed. The Emperor received further deputations, this time at Chalcedon. Initially the Orientals, who spoke against Cyril and his apparent subversion of divine impassibility, were favoured. None the less, the imperial judgement was again reversed and Theodosius, bidding the Orientals to be reconciled with Cyril and Memnon, refused to countenance appeals on behalf of Nestorius. The *volte-face* has been attributed to bribes judiciously distributed. Whatever the cause, Nestorius was never rehabilitated and the christological statements in the Nicene creed and Cyril's second letter to the 'heretic' were received as enshrining orthodoxy.

# Appendix II
## Biblical articles in the *Dictionnaire*

| 1697 | 1702 | 1720 |
|------|------|------|
| 1. Aaron | Aaron* | Aaron |
| 2. Abel | Abel† | Abel |
| 3. Abimelech | Abimelech | Abimelech |
| 4. Abraham | Abraham* | Abraham |
| 5. Adam | Adam* | Adam |
| 6. Agar | Agar* | Agar |
| 7. Anne | Anne | Anne |
| 8. Caïn | Caïn† | Caïn |
| 9. Cham | Cham† | Cham |
| 10. David | David** | David |
| 11. Elie | Elie† | Elie |
| 12. Elisée | Elisée | Elisée |
| 13. Esechiel | Esechiel | Esechiel |
| 14. Eve | Eve** | Eve |
| 15. Jean | Jean | Jean |
| 16. Job | Job† | Job |
| 17. — | Jonas | Jonas |
| 18. Judith | Judith | Judith |
| 19. Lamech | Lamech† | Lamech |
| 20. Lamech | Lamech† | Lamech |
| 21. — | Marie | Marie |
| 22. Samson | Samson | Samson |
| 23. Sara | Sara* | Sara |

† Slight additions.

\* Additions (that is, footnotes, or extra remarks designed to reply to the controversies caused by the first edition).

\*\* Substantial changes/additions.

# Appendix III
# The lives of the popes

| 1697 | 1702 | 1720 |
|---|---|---|
| 1. Chigi | Chigi | Chigi |
| 2. — | Eugène IV | Eugène IV |
| 3. Grégoire I | Grégoire I* | Grégoire I |
| 4. Grégoire VII | Grégoire VII* | Grégoire VII |
| 5. Hadrien VI‡ | Hadrien VI*‡ | Hadrien VI‡ |
| 6. — | Innocent VIII | Innocent VIII |
| 7. Innocent XI‡ | Innocent XI*‡ | Innocent XI‡ |
| 8. Jules II | Jules II* | Jules II |
| 9. Jules III | Jules III | Jules III |
| 10. Léon I | Léon I | Léon I |
| 11. Léon X | Léon X* | Léon X† |
| 12. Ottoboni | Ottoboni | Ottoboni† |
| 13. — | — | Paul II |
| 14. Sixte IV | Sixte IV* | Sixte IV† |

\* Additions
† Slight additions
‡ Good popes

# Bibliography

The bibliography gives references to: i. all works cited in the text; ii. all works on Bayle consulted, whether cited or not in the text; iii. all editions of the same work, where more than one edition is cited.

*Actes du Consistoire de l'Eglise wallonne de Rotterdam, concernant le Dictionnaire historique et critique de M. Bayle*, in *Dictionnaire historique et critique*, ed. Beuchot, xvi.287-300

Agreda, Marie d', *La Mystique cité de Dieu*, trans. Thomas Croset, Marseille 1695

Armogathe, J.-R., 'Les vies de Calvin aux XVIe et XVIIe siècles', in *Historiographie de la réforme*, ed. Joutard, Paris, Neuchâtel, Montréal 1977, p.45-59

– 'De l'art de penser comme art de persuader', in *La Conversion au XVIIe siècle*, Actes du Colloque du Centre méridional de rencontres sur le XVIIe siècle 12 (1983), p.29-41

Arnauld, Antoine, *Œuvres*, ed. Bellegarde and Hautefage, Paris, Lausanne 1775-1782

Arnauld and Nicole, *Défense de la traduction du Nouveau Testament imprimé à Mons, contre les Sermons du P. Meinbourg jésuite*, Cologne 1668

– *La Logique ou l'art de penser*, Paris 1970

Aron, Raymond, *Introduction à la philosophie de l'histoire, Essai sur les limites de l'objectivité historique*, Paris 1981

Arquillière, H. X., *L'Augustinisme politique: essai sur la formation des théories politiques du moyen âge*, Paris 1955

Augustine, St, *Opera*, Antwerpiae 1576-1577

Auvray, Paul, 'Richard Simon et Spinoza', in *Religion, érudition et critique à la fin du XVIIe siècle et au début du XVIIIe*, Paris 1968, p.201-14

– *Richard Simon*, Paris 1974

[Baillet, Adrien,] *Jugemens des sçavans sur les principaux ouvrages des auteurs*, Paris 1685-1686

– *De la Devotion à la sainte vierge et du culte qui lui est dû*, Paris 1696 (nouvelle édition)

Balzac, Jean-Louis-Guez de, *Les Œuvres de monsieur de Balzac*, Paris 1665

Barber, W. H., 'Bayle: faith and reason', in *The French mind: studies in honour of Gustave Rudler*, ed. Will Moore *et al.*, Oxford 1952, p.109-25

Baron, H.-M., S. J., 'Le P. Jean Crasset (1618-1692), le jansénisme et la dévotion à la Sainte-Vierge', in *Bulletin de la Société française d'études mariales* (1937), p.137-67

– 'L'offensive janséniste contre Crasset', in *BSFEM* (1938), p.175-82

Barr, James, *Fundamentalism*, London 1977

Basnage de Beauval, Henri, *Histoire des ouvrages des savants*, septembre 1687-juin 1709, Rotterdam

Basnage, Jacques, *Histoire de l'Eglise, depuis Jésus-Christ jusqu'à présent*, Rotterdam 1699

Bayle, Pierre, *Dictionnaire historique et critique*, Rotterdam 1720

– *Œuvres diverses*, La Haye 1737

– *Dictionnaire historique et critique*, ed. Beuchot, Paris 1820

– *Pierre Bayle, Choix de textes*, ed. Marcel Raymond, Paris 1948

– *Historical and critical dictionary, selections*, trans. R. H. Popkin, Indianapolis, New York, Kansas City 1965

– *Dictionnaire historique et critique* (Selections), ed. Alain Niderst, Paris 1974

– *Ecrits sur Spinoza*, ed. Françoise Charles-Daubert and Pierre-François Moreau, Paris 1983

– *Pensées diverses sur la comète* (1912), ed. A. Prat nouvelle édition, Pierre Rétat (Société des Textes français modernes, Nos 81, 82), Paris 1984

Beaujot, Jean-Pierre, 'Du syntagme "erreur populaire" et de ses ambiguïtés chez Pierre Bayle', in *Beiträge zur Analyse des sozialen Wortschatzes*, ed. Ulrich Ricken, Halle 1975/1977, p.59-70.

Beaujot, Jean-Pierre, and Marie-Françoise Mortureux, 'Genèse et fonctionnement du discours: les *Pensées diverses sur la comète* de Bayle, et les *Entretiens sur la pluralité des mondes* de Fontenelle', in *Langue française* 15 (1972), p.56-78

Bell, Millicent, 'Pierre Bayle and *Moby Dick*', *PMLA* 66 (1951), p.626-48

Bénichou, Paul, *Morales du grand siècle* (1948), Paris 1983

Benoist, Elie, *Histoire de l'Edit de Nantes*, Delft 1693-1695

Benrekassa, Georges, 'Les enfants de Melchisédech', *Littérature* 13 (1974), p.75-91

Bernus, A., *Richard Simon et son Histoire critique du Vieux Testament*, Lausanne 1869

Blondel, David, *Familier esclaircissement de la question si une femme a esté assise au siege papal de Rome entre Leon IV, & Benoist III*, Amsterdam 1647

Bodin, Jean, *Methodus ad facilem historiarum cognitionem*, Parisiis 1566; nouvelle édition et traduction par Pierre Mesnard, in Bodin, Jean, *Œuvres philosophiques*, Corpus général des philosophes v, 3, Paris 1951.

Boileau, Nicolas, *Œuvres complètes*, ed. A. Adam and F. Escal, Paris 1979

Bolgar, R. (ed.), *Classical influences on European culture (1500-1700)*, Cambridge 1975

– *Classical influences on Western thought (1650-1870)*, Cambridge, London, New York, Melbourne 1979

Bossuet, J.-G., *Œuvres*, Versailles 1815-1819

Bourlon, I., *Entre cousins germains: controverse entre les jansénistes et les protestants*, Arras, Paris n.d.

Brown, Harcourt, 'Pierre Bayle and natural science', *Romanic review* 25 (1934), p.361-67

Brunetière, Ferdinand, *Etudes critiques sur l'histoire de la littérature française*, Paris 1888-1907

Brush, Craig B., *Montaigne and Bayle: variations on the theme of skepticism*, The Hague 1966

Busson, Henri, *La Pensée religieuse française de Charron à Pascal*, Paris 1933

– *La Religion des classiques*, Paris 1948

Butler, Philip, *Classicisme et baroque dans l'œuvre de Racine*, Paris 1959

Calvin, Jean, *Commentaires de M. Jean Calvin, sur les cinq livres de Moyse*, Genève 1564

– *Institution de la religion chrestienne*, Paris 1859

Cantelli, Gianfranco, *Teologia e ateismo: saggio sul pensiero filosofico e religioso di Pierre Bayle*, Firenze 1969

– *Vico e Bayle: premesse per un confronto*, Napoli 1971

Carr, E. H., *What is history?*, Harmondsworth 1980

Cassirer, Ernst, *The Philosophy of the Enlightenment* (1932), trans. Fritz C. A. Koelln and James P. Pettegrove, Boston 1966

Cazès, Albert, *Pierre Bayle, sa vie, ses idées, son influence, son œuvre*, Paris 1905

Chadwick, Henry, *The Early Church* (1967), Harmondsworth 1978

Chalmers, Alexander, *General biographical dictionary*, London 1812-1817

Chantalat, Claude, 'Les idées littéraires de Pierre Bayle dans le *Dictionnaire historique et critique*', thèse complémentaire, Université de Paris IV (Sorbonne), 1983

Chauffepié, Jacques-Georges de, *Nouveau dictionnaire historique et critique pour servir* de supplément ou de continuation au Dictionnaire historique et critique de M. Pierre Bayle, Amsterdam, La Haye 1750-1756

Cherel, Albert, La Pensée de Machiavel en France, Paris 1935

Claude, Jean, La Défense de la Réformation contre le livre [de Nicole] intitulé: 'Préjugez légitimes contre les calvinistes', Quevilly, Rouen 1673

– L'Examen de soy-mesme pour bien se preparer à la communion (1682), La Haye 1693

Compagnon, Antoine, La Seconde main ou le travail de la citation, Paris 1979

Congar, Y. M.-J. (O.P.), La Tradition et les traditions: essai historique, Paris 1960

La Conversion au XVIIe siècle, Actes du XIIe colloque du Centre méridional de rencontres sur le XVIIe siècle 12 (1983)

Courtines, Léo Pierre, 'Some notes on the dissemination of Bayle's thought in Europe', Revue de littérature comparée 68 (1937), p.700-705

– Bayle's relations with England and the English, New York 1938

Cowdrick, Ruth Elizabeth, The Early reading of Pierre Bayle, New York 1939

Crasset, Jean (S. J.), La Veritable devotion envers la S. Vierge establie et defendue, Paris 1679

Crousaz, Jean Pierre de, Examen du pyrrhonisme ancien & moderne, La Haye 1733

Curtis, D. E., 'Pierre Bayle and the expansion of time', Australian journal of French studies 13 (1976), p.197-212

Daillé, Jean, Traicté de l'employ des saincts peres, pour le jugement des differends, qui sont aujourd'huy en la religion, Genève 1632

[Daniel, le R. P. Gabriel], Réponse aux Lettres provinciales de L. de Montalte ou Entretiens de Cléandre et et d'Eudoxe, Cologne 1696

Declercq, Gilles, 'Un adepte de l'histoire éloquente, le père Maimbourg, S. J.', XVIIe siècle 143 (1984), p.118-32

Delvolvé, Jean, Religion, critique et philosophie positive chez Pierre Bayle, Paris 1906

Demoris, René, 'Saint-Réal et l'histoire ou l'envers de la médaille', in Saint-Réal, De l'usage de l'histoire, p.43-55.

Denis, Paul, 'Lettres inédites de Pierre Bayle', RhlF 19 (1912), p.422-53

Descartes, René, Les Passions de l'âme, ed. Geneviève Rodis-Lewis, Paris 1970

Deschamps, Arsène, La Genèse du scepticisme érudit chez Pierre Bayle, Liège 1878

Dibon, Paul (ed.), Pierre Bayle, le philosophe de Rotterdam, Paris 1959

Dodge, Guy Howard, The Political theory of the Huguenots of the dispersion, with special reference to the thought and influence of Pierre Jurieu, New York 1947

Dompnier, Bernard, 'L'histoire religieuse chez les controversistes réformés du début du XVIIe siècle: l'apport de Du Plessis Mornay et Rivet', in Historiographie de la réforme, ed. Joutard, Paris, Neuchâtel, Montréal 1977, p.16-36

Doucin, Louis (S. J.), Histoire du nestorianisme, La Haye 1698

Dray, William, Perspectives on history, London 1980

Drelincourt, Charles, Replique aux Responses de monsieur Camus evesque de Belley, Charenton 1645

– Neuf dialogues contre les missionnaires sur le service des Eglises réformées, Genève 1655

Dubois, Claude-Gilbert, La Conception de l'histoire en France au XVIe siècle (1560-1610), Paris 1977

Dumoulin, Pierre, Nouveauté du papisme, opposée à l'antiquité du vrai christianisme: contre le livre de monsieur le cardinal Du Perron, Sedan 1627

– Des Traditions et de la perfection et suffisance de l'Escriture saincte, Sedan 1631

– Anatomie de la messe, Genève 1636

– Deuxième partie de l'Anatomie de la messe, Sedan 1639

Du Pin, Louis-Ellies, Nouvelle bibliotheque des auteurs ecclesiastiques, vols 1-3, Paris 1686-1689; vols 3-6, Mons 1691-1692

– *Bibliotheque des auteurs ecclesiastiques du dix-septième siecle*, Paris 1708

Du Rondel, Jacques, *Réflexions sur un chapitre de Théophraste*, Amsterdam 1686

Ehrard, Jean, *L'Idée de nature en France à l'aube des Lumières*, Paris 1970

Evans, Wilfred Hugo, *L'Historien Mézeray et la conception de l'histoire en France au XVIIe siècle*, Paris 1930

Faguet, Emile, *Dix-huitième siècle: études littéraires*, Paris 1890

Faret, Nicolas, *L'Honneste homme ou l'art de plaire à la court* (1630), ed. Magendie, Paris 1925

Ferreyrolles, Gérard, 'Augustinisme et conception de l'histoire', *XVIIe siècle* 135 (1982), p.216-41

Flint, Robert, *History of the philosophy of history*, Edinburgh, London 1893

Foucault, Michel, *Les Mots et les choses*, Paris 1966

France, Peter, *Rhetoric and truth in France*, Oxford 1972

Fueter, Edouard, *Histoire de l'historiographie moderne*, trans. Emile Jeanmaire, Paris 1914

Fumaroli, Marc, 'Aux origines de la connaissance historique du Moyen Age: humanisme, réforme et gallicanisme au XVIe siècle', *XVIIe siècle* 114-115, (1977), p.5-29

– *L'Age de l'éloquence: rhétorique et 'res literaria' de la Renaissance au seuil de l'époque classique*, Genève 1980

Furetière, Antoine, *Dictionnaire universel*, La Haye, Rotterdam, 1690

Gazier, Augustin, *Histoire générale du mouvement janséniste, depuis ses origines jusqu'à nos jours*, Paris 1922

Geddes, Michael, *The Life of Maria of Jesus of Agreda, a late famous Spanish nun*, in *Miscellaneous tracts*, London 1705-1709

Gerberon, G., *Histoire generale du jansenisme*, Amsterdam 1700

Goldmann, Lucien, *Le Dieu caché*, Paris 1959

Gouhier, Henri, *La Philosophie de Malebranche et son expérience religieuse*, Paris 1926

– *La Pensée métaphysique de Descartes*, Paris 1962

Goyet, Thérèse, *L'Humanisme de Bossuet*, Paris 1965

[Graverol, Jean,] *L'Eglise protestante justifiée par l'Eglise romaine sur quelques points de controverse*, Genève 1682

– *Instructions pour les nicodémites*, Amsterdam 1700

Haag, Eugène and Emile, *La France protestante*, Paris, Genève 1846-1859

Harlay, François de, *The Condemnation of monsieur Dupin, his History of ecclesiastical authors, by the archbishop of Paris; as also his own retractation. Translated out of French*. London 1696

Haxo, H. E., 'Pierre Bayle and his biographers', *Modern language notes* 37 (1922), p.55-56

– 'Pierre Bayle and his literary taste', *PMLA* 38 (1923), p.823-58

– 'Pierre Bayle et Voltaire avant les *Lettres Philosophiques*', *PMLA* 46 (1931), p.461-97

Hazard, Paul, *La Crise de la conscience européenne (1680-1715)*, Paris 1935

– *The European mind (1680-1715)*, Harmondsworth 1973

Hazewinkel, H. C., 'Pierre Bayle à Rotterdam', in *Pierre Bayle le philosophe de Rotterdam*, ed. Paul Dibon, Paris 1959, p.20-47

Heidegger, J.-H., *Historia papatus, novissimo historiae Lutheranismi et Calvinismi, fabro [...] reposita acc. Fr. Guicciardini Historia papatus*, Amstelodami 1684

Hepp, Noemi, 'Quelques aspects de l'antiquité grecque dans la pensée française du XVIIe siècle', *XVIIe siècle* 131 (1981), p.117-33

Hermant, Godefroi, *Mémoires*, ed. A. Gazier, Paris 1905-1910

Heyd, Michael, 'A disguised atheist or a sincere christian? The enigma of Pierre Bayle', *Bibliothèque d'humanisme et de renaissance* 39 (1977), p.157-65

Hobbes, Thomas, *Leviathan*, London 1651

Hodge, Charles, *Systematic theology*, Michigan 1979

Hoffer, Paul, *La Dévotion à Marie au déclin du XVIIe siècle: autour du jansénisme et des 'Avis salutaires de la B.V. Marie à ses dévots indiscrets'*, Paris 1938

Honders, Huibert Jacob, *Andreas Rivetus als invloedrijk gereformeerd theolog in Holland's bloeitijd*, 's-Gravenhage 1930

Howells, R. J., *Pierre Jurieu: antinomian radical*, Durham 1983

Huppert, George, *The Idea of perfect history: historical erudition and historical philosophy in renaissance France*, Urbana, Chicago, London 1970


James, E. D., 'Scepticism and fideism in Bayle's *Dictionnaire*', *French studies* 16 (1962), p.307-23

– 'Scepticism and religious belief: Pascal, Bayle and Hume', in *Classical influences on Western thought, 1650-1870* ed. Bolgar, Cambridge, London, New York, Melbourne 1979, p.93-104

Jauss, H., *Pour une esthétique de la réception*, trans. Claude Maillard and Jean Starobinski, Paris 1978

Jeanmaire, Emile, *Essai sur la critique religieuse de Pierre Bayle*, Strasbourg 1862

Jedin, Hubert, *A history of the Council of Trent*, trans. Dom Ernest Graf, London 1957, 1961.

Jehasse, Jean, *La Renaissance de la critique*, Saint-Etienne 1976

Jossua, Jean-Pierre, *Pierre Bayle ou l'obsession du mal*, Paris 1977

*Journal des savants*, Paris 1665-1759

Joutard, Philippe (ed.), *Historiographie de la réforme*, Paris, Neuchâtel, Montréal 1977

Julien-Eymard D'Angers, *Recherches sur le stoïcisme au XVIe et XVIIe siècles*, ed. L. Antoine, Hildesheim, New York 1976

Jurieu, Pierre, *La Politique du clergé de France*, Cologne 1681

– *Preservatif contre le changement de religion*, La Haye [1682]

– *Abbregé de l'Histoire du concile de Trente*, Genève 1682

– *Examen de l'eucharistie de l'Eglise romaine*, Rotterdam 1683

– *Le Janseniste convaincu de vaine sophistiquerie*, Amsterdam 1683

– *L'Esprit de Mr Arnaud*, Deventer 1684

– *Prejugez legitimes contre le papisme*, Amsterdam 1685

– *Lettres pastorales*, quatrième édition, Rotterdam 1687-1688

– *La Religion du latitudinaire*, Rotterdam 1696

– *Le Philosophe de Rotterdam accusé, atteint et convaincu*, Amsterdam 1706


Kelley, Donald R., *Foundations of modern historical scholarship*, New York, London 1970

Knetsch, F. R., 'Le jugement de Bayle sur Comenius', *Bulletin de la commission de l'histoire des églises wallonnes* 6 (1969-1971), p.83-96

– 'Jurieu, Bayle et Paets', *BSHP* 117 (1971), p.38-61

Kolakowski, Leszek, 'Pierre Bayle, critique de la métaphysique spinoziste de la substance', in *Pierre Bayle le philosophe de Rotterdam*, ed. Paul Dibon, Paris 1959, p.66-80

– *Chrétiens sans églises, la conscience religieuse et le lien confessionel au XVIIe siècle*, Paris 1969


[La Bastide, Marc Antoine de], *Réponse au livre de monsieur l'evesque de Condom qui a pour titre Exposition de la doctrine de l'Eglise catholique sur les matieres de controverse*, Rouen 1672

– *Seconde réponse à monsieur de Condom*, n.p. 1680

– *Considerations sur les Lettres circulaires de*

*l'Assemblée du Clergé de France de 1682.* n.p. [1683?]

– *Réponse apologetique à messieurs du Clergé de France,* n.p. 1683

Labrousse, Elisabeth, 'La méthode critique chez Pierre Bayle et l'histoire', *Revue internationale de philosophie de Bruxelles* 11 (1957), p.450-66

– 'Les coulisses du journal de Bayle', in *Pierre Bayle le philosophe de Rotterdam,* ed. Paul Dibon, Paris 1959, p.97-141

– 'Documents relatifs à l'offre d'une chaire à Bayle à l'université de Franeker au printemps de 1684', in *idem,* p.219-37

– *Inventaire critique de la correspondance de Pierre Bayle,* Paris 1961

– 'Obscurantisme et lumières chez Pierre Bayle', *Studies on Voltaire* 26 (1963), p.1037-48

– *Pierre Bayle,* vol.i: *Du pays de Foix à la cité d'Erasme;* vol.ii: *Hétérodoxie et rigorisme,* La Haye 1963-1964

– 'Pierre Bayle et ses correspondants genevois', *Bulletin de la Société d'histoire et d'archéologie de Genève* 14 (1969), p.139-59

– 'Le paradoxe de l'érudit cartésien, Pierre Bayle', in *Religion, érudition et critique à la fin du XVIIe siècle et au début du XVIIIe,* Paris 1968, p.53-70

– 'Quelques sources réformées des *Pensées diverses',* in *Mélanges offerts à René Pintard,* Strasbourg 1975, p.443-49

– 'Les guerres de religion vues par les huguenots du XVIIe siècle', in *Historiographie de la réforme,* ed. Philippe Joutard, Paris, Neuchâtel, Montréal 1977, p.37-44

– 'Pierre Bayle et les deux antiquités', unpublished paper given at the Warburg Institute, 2 February 1979

– 'The political ideas of the Huguenots of the diaspora (Bayle and Jurieu)', in *Church, State and society under the Bourbon kings of France,* ed. Richard M. Golden, Lawrence, Kansas, 1982, p.222-83

– *Bayle* (Past Masters), London, New York 1983

Lacoste, Edmond, *Bayle nouvelliste et critique littéraire,* Paris 1929

La Mothe Le Vayer, F., *Œuvres,* Paris 1656

– *Œuvres,* Paris 1669

Lamy, le père Bernard, *De l'art de parler,* Paris 1676

La Penna, A., 'Vivere sotto i tiranni: un tema tacitiano da Guicciardini', *Classical influences on European culture 1500-1700,* ed. Bolgar, London, New York, Melbourne 1975, p.295-303

Lapide, Cornelius à, *Commentaria in Pentateuchum Mosis,* Antverpiae 1671

Laplanche, François, *L'Evidence du Dieu chrétien,* Strasbourg 1983

– 'L'Ecriture, le sacré et l'histoire, le protestantisme français devant la Bible dans la première moitié du XVIIe siècle', thèse d'état, Université de Paris IV (Sorbonne), 1983, published by APA-Holland in 1986

Launoy, Jean de, *De auctoritate negantis argumenti dissertatio,* Paris 1662

Le Brun, Jacques, *La Spiritualité de Bossuet,* Paris 1972

– 'Critique des abus et signifiance des pratiques (la controverse Leibniz-Bossuet)', in *Theoria cum praxi,* Akten des III internationalen Leibnizkongresses, 1977), Wiesbaden 1980, p.247-57

– 'Sens et portée du retour aux origines dans l'œuvre de Richard Simon', *XVIIe siècle* 131 (1981), p.185-98

Lecler, Joseph, *Histoire de la tolérance,* Paris 1955

Leclerc, Jean, *Bibliothèque universelle et historique, 1686-1693,* Amsterdam 1686-1718

– *Parrhasiana, ou pensées diverses sur des matiéres de critique, de morale et de politique,* Amsterdam 1699-1701

Lemoyne, Pierre, *La Galerie des femmes fortes* (1647), Leiden, Paris 1660

Lenient, C. F., *Etude sur Bayle,* Paris 1855

Lennon, Thomas M., *et al.* (ed.), *Problems of Cartesianism,* Kingston, Montreal 1982

Lenoble, Robert, *Mersenne ou la naissance du mécanisme*, Paris 1971

*Lettre au R. P. Annat, jésuite: sur ses remèdes contre les scrupules*, n.p. [1664]

Levi, Anthony, 'La psychologie de la conversion au XVIIe siècle: de François de Sales à Nicole', in *La Conversion au XVIIe siècle*, Actes du Colloque du Centre méridional de rencontres sur le XVIIe siècle 12 (1983), p.19-28

Leydecker, Melchior, *Historia Jansenismi*, Utrecht 1695

Lucian, *How to write history*, London 1959, vi.1-73

Machiavelli, Niccolò, *Le Prince*, trans. Amelot de La Houssaye, Amsterdam 1686

– *The Prince and other political writings*, trans. Bruce Penman, London, Melbourne, Toronto 1981

Magné, Bernard, *Crise de la littérature française sous Louis XIV: humanisme et nationalisme*, Lille 1976

Maimbourg, Louis, *Sermons pour le Caresme où toutes les parties de chaque Evangile sont comprises et rapportées à un point principal*, Paris 1672

– *Histoire de l'heresie des iconoclastes et de la translation de l'Empire aux François*, Paris 1679 (2nd edition)

– *Histoire du calvinisme*, Paris 1682

Malebranche, Nicolas, *De la recherche de la vérité*, ed. Geneviève Rodis-Lewis, Paris 1965

Mandrou, Robert, *Des humanistes aux hommes de science*, Paris 1973

– *From humanism to science*, trans. Brian Pierce, Harmondsworth 1978

Manuel, Frank E., *The Eighteenth century confronts the gods*, Cambridge, Massachusetts 1959

Margival, Henri, *Essai sur Richard Simon et la critique biblique au XVIIe siècle*, in *Revue d'histoire et de littérature religieuses*, vols i-v, 1896-1900

Martimort, Aimé-Georges, *Le Gallicanisme de Bossuet*, Paris 1953

– *Le Gallicanisme*, Paris 1973

Martin, Henri-Jean, *Livre, pouvoirs et société à Paris au XVIIe siècle (1598-1701)*, Genève 1969

Mason, H. T., *Pierre Bayle and Voltaire*, London 1963

– 'Pierre Bayle's religious views', *French studies* 17 (1963), p.205-17

McKenna, Anthony, 'Pascal et Epicure: l'intervention de Pierre Bayle dans la controverse entre Antoine Arnauld et Malebranche', *XVIIe siècle* 137 (1982), p.421-28

Meinecke, Friedrich, *L'Idée de la raison d'état dans l'histoire des temps modernes*, trans. Maurice Chevallier, Genève 1973

Mesnard, Pierre, 'Le commerce epistolaire comme expression sociale de l'individualisme humaniste', in *Individu et société à la Renaissance*, Bruxelles 1965

Meurillon, Christian, 'Saint-Réal et Pascal', in Saint-Réal, *De l'usage de l'histoire*, p.57-71

Michel, J., 'Bibliographies et instruments de travail au XVIIe siècle, aperçus sur l'éveil d'un monde moderne offrant à tous des commodités pour la recherche et l'étude', *Mélanges de sciences religieuses* 17 (1960), p.131-42

Momigliano, A. D., *Studies in historiography*, London 1966

Monod, Albert, *De Pascal à Chateaubriand: les défenseurs français du christianisme de 1670 à 1802* (1916), Genève 1970

Montaigne, Michel de, *Œuvres complètes*, ed. A. Thibaudet and M. Rat, Paris 1962

Moore, Will, *et al.*, *The French mind: studies in honour of Gustave Rudler*, Oxford 1952

Moréri, Louis, *Le Grand dictionnaire historique*, Paris 1759

Mornay, Philippe Du Plessis, *Le Mystère d'iniquité, c'est à dire l'histoire de la papauté, par quels progrez elle est montée à ce comble, & quelles oppositions les gens de bien lui ont faict de temps en temps*, Saumur 1611

Naudé, Gabriel, *Instruction à la France sur*

*la verité de l'histoire des freres de la Roze-Croix*, Paris 1623

– *Apologie pour tous les grands personnages qui ont esté faussement soupçonnez de magie*, Paris 1625

– *Science des princes, ou considérations politiques sur les coups d'état, avec les réflexions historiques, morales, chrétiennes, & politiques, de L.D.M.C.S.D.S.E.D.M.* [Louis de May], n.p. 1752

Nedergaard, Leif, 'Manuscrits de Pierre Bayle', *Modern language notes* (Baltimore) 78 (1958), p.36-39

Neveu, Bruno, *Un historien à l'école de Port-Royal: Sébastien le Nain de Tillemont 1637-1698*, The Hague 1966

– 'Sébastien le Nain de Tillemont (1637-1698) et l'érudition ecclésiastique de son temps', in *Religion, érudition, et critique à la fin du XVIIe siècle et au début du XVIIIe*, Paris 1968, p.21-32

Nicéron, le R.P., *Mémoires pour servir à l'histoire des hommes illustres dans la république des lettres avec un catalogue raisonné de leurs ouvrages*, Paris 1727-1745

Nicole, Pierre, *L'Heresie imaginaire*, 3 February 1665 (5th letter) (pamphlet)

– *Prejugez legitimes contre les calvinistes*, Paris 1671

– *La Perpétuité de la foy de l'Eglise catholique touchant l'eucharistie*, Paris 1669-1674

– *Essais de morale, contenus en divers traittez sur plusieurs devoirs importans*, vol.i, Paris 1671

Nisbey, H. B., 'Lessing and Pierre Bayle', in *Tradition and creation: essays in honour of E. M. Wilkinson*, ed. C. P. Magill *et al.*, Leeds 1978, p.13-29


O'Cathasaigh, Sean, 'A study of certain of the *Œuvres diverses* of Pierre Bayle', Ph.D., Cambridge (Sydney Sussex College) 1980

Orcibal, Jean, *Louis XIV et les protestants*, Paris 1951


Paganini, Gianni, *Analisi della fede e critica della ragione, nella filosofia di Pierre Bayle*, Firenze 1980

Pascal, Blaise, *Pensées*, ed. Philippe Sellier, Paris 1976

– *Les Provinciales*, ed. Louis Cognet, Paris 1983

Perry, Elisabeth Israels, *From theology to history: French religious controversy and the revocation of the edict of Nantes*, The Hague 1973

Pezron, le R.P. Paul, *L'Antiquité des tems rétabli et défenduë contre les juifs & les nouveaux chronologistes*, Paris 1687

– *Défense de l'antiquité des tems, ou l'on soûtient la tradition des peres & des eglises, contre celle du Talmud; et où l'on fait voir la corruption de l'hebreu des juifs*, Paris 1691

Picard, Raymond, *La Carrière de Jean Racine*, Paris 1961

Pintard, René, *Le Libertinage érudit dans la première moitié du XVIIe siècle*, Paris 1943

– 'Les problèmes de l'histoire du libertinage: notes et réflexions', in *XVIIe siècle* 127 (1980), p.131-61

Pittion, Jean-Paul, 'Intellectual life in the Académie of Saumur (1633-1685): a study of the Bouhéreau Collection', Ph.D., University of Dublin (Trinity College), 1970

Plutarque, *Les Vies des hommes illustres*, trans. Amyot, ed. Gérard Walter, Paris 1977

Polman, Pontien, *L'Elément historique dans la controverse religieuse du XVIe siècle*, Universitas catholica lovaniensis, series II, tome 23, Louvain 1932

Popkin, Richard H., 'Pierre Bayle's place in 17th-century scepticism', in *Pierre Bayle le philosophe de Rotterdam*, ed. Paul Dibon, Paris 1959, p.1-19

– 'Pierre Bayle', in *The Encyclopedia of Philosophy*, New York, London 1967

– 'The development of religious scepticism and the influence of Isaac La Peyrère's pre-Adamism and Bible criticism', in *Classical influences on European culture*

*(1500-1700)*, ed. Bolgar, Cambridge 1975, p.271-80

– *The History of scepticism from Erasmus to Spinoza*, Berkeley, Los Angeles, London 1979

Racine, Jean, *Œuvres complètes*, ed. Raymond Picard, Paris 1980

Randolph, Mary Claire, 'Pierre Bayle's case against satire and satirists', *Notes and queries* 181 (1941), p.310-11

Rapin, le père René (S. J.), *Œuvres*, Paris 1725

Rébelliau, Alfred, *Bossuet, historien du protestantisme: étude sur l'"Histoire des variations" et sur la controverse au dix-septième siècle*, Paris 1903

*Religion, érudition et critique à la fin du XVIIe siècle et au début du XVIIIe*, Paris 1968

Reesink, Hendrika Johanna, *L'Angleterre et la littérature anglaise dans les trois plus anciens périodiques français de Hollande de 1684 à 1709*, Zutphen 1931

Rétat, Pierre, *Le Dictionnaire de Bayle et la lutte philosophique au XVIIIe siècle*, Paris 1971

– 'Libertinage et hétérodoxie: Pierre Bayle', *XVIIe siècle* 127 (1980), p.197-211

– 'Logique et rhétorique: la *Réponse aux questions d'un provincial* de Bayle', in *Mélanges offerts à Georges Couton*, Lyon 1981, p.455-69

Rex, Walter, 'Pierre Bayle, Louis Tronchin et la querelle des donatistes', *BSHP* 105 (1959), p.97-121

– *Essays on Pierre Bayle and religious controversy*, The Hague 1965

– 'Bayle, Jurieu and the politics of philosophy: a reply to Professor Popkin', in *Problems of Cartesianism*, ed. T. M. Lennon *et al.*, Kingston, Montreal 1982, p.83-94

Rice, E. F., Jr., 'The humanist idea of Christian antiquity and the impact of Greek patristic work on sixteenth-century thought', in *Classical influences on European culture (1500-1700)*, ed. Bolgar, Cambridge 1975, p.199-203

Rivet, André, *Operum theologicorum quae Latinè edidit*, Roterodami 1651-1660

Robinet, André, 'L'aphilosophie de P. Bayle devant les philosophies de Malebranche et de Leibniz', in *Pierre Bayle le philosophe de Rotterdam*, ed. Paul Dibon, Paris 1959, p.48-65

Robinson, Howard, 'Bayle's profanation of sacred history', in *Essays in intellectual history*, New York 1929, p.147-62

– *Bayle the sceptic*, Columbia 1931

Rousset, Jean, *La Littérature de l'âge baroque en France*, Paris 1953

Sacy, Le Maistre de, *Les Enluminures du fameux almanach des PP. jesuites intitulé, La Déroute et la confusion des jansénistes ou Triomphe de Molina jésuite sur S. Augustin* (1654?)

Sainte-Beuve, C. A., 'Du génie critique et de Bayle', in *Portraits littéraires*, Paris 1862-1864, i.364-88

Saint-Réal, César Vichard, abbé de, *Œuvres*, Amsterdam 1730

– *De l'usage de l'histoire* (1671), ed. René Demoris and Christian Meurillon, Lille 1980

Sallengre, Albert Henri de, *Mémoires de littérature*, La Haye 1715-1717

Sandberg, Karl C., *At the crossroads of faith and reason: an essay on Pierre Bayle*, Tucson 1966

Saurin, Elie, *Apologie pour le sieur Saurin [...] contre les les accusations de M. Jurieu*, Utrecht 1692

– *Examen de la théologie de M. Jurieu*, La Haye 1694

Schlossberg, Herbert, 'Pierre Bayle and the politics of the Huguenot diaspora', Ph.D., University of Minnesota, 1965

Scholberg, Kenneth R., *Pierre Bayle and Spain*, Chapel Hill 1958

Schwarzbach, Bertram E., *Voltaire's Old Testament criticism*, Genève 1971

Screech, M. A., *Rabelais*, London 1979

Sellier, Philippe, *Pascal et saint Augustin*, Paris 1970

Senofonte, Ciro, *Pierre Bayle dal calvinismo all'illuminismo*, Napoli 1978

Serrurier, Cornelia, *Pierre Bayle en Hollande: étude historique et critique*, Apeldoorn 1912

Shackleton, R., 'Bayle and Montesquieu', in *Pierre Bayle le philosophe de Rotterdam*, ed. Paul Dibon, Paris 1959, p.142-49

Simon, Richard, *Histoire critique du Vieux Testament*, Rotterdam 1685

– *Histoire critique des versions du Nouveau Testament*, Rotterdam 1690

– *Histoire critique des principaux commentateurs du Nouveau Testament depuis le commencement du christianisme jusques à nôtre tems*, Rotterdam 1693

Simon, Richard, *Le Dictionnaire de la Bible*, Lyon 1693

Skinner, Quentin, *Machiavelli* (Past Masters), London, Melbourne, Toronto 1981

Smith, Horatio E., 'Bayle and his biographers', *Modern language notes* 27 (1912), p.158-59

– *The Literary criticism of Pierre Bayle*, New York 1912

Snoeks, Rémi, *L'Argument de tradition dans la controverse eucharistique entre catholiques et réformés français au XVIIe siècle*, Louvain 1951

Solé, Jacques, 'Religion et méthode critique dans le *Dictionnaire* de Bayle', in *Religion, érudition, et critique à la fin du XVIIIe*, Paris 1968, p.71-117

– 'Religion et vision historiographique dans le *Dictionnaire* de Bayle', in *Religion, érudition, et critique à la fin du XVIIIe*, Paris 1968, p.119-200

– 'Religion et conception du monde dans le *Dictionnaire* de Bayle', in *BSHP* 117 (1971), p.545-81

– 'Religion et conception du monde dans le *Dictionnaire* de Bayle', in *BSHP* 118 (1972), p.483-509

– *Bayle polémiste: extraits du Dictionnaire historique et critique*, Paris 1972

– 'Pierre Bayle, historien de la réforme', in *Historiographie de la réforme*, ed. Philippe Joutard, Paris, Neuchâtel, Montréal 1977, p.71-80

– 'Rationalisme chrétien et foi réformée à Genève autour de 1700: les derniers sermons de Louis Tronchin', *BSHP* 128 (1982), p.29-43

Spinoza, Benedict de, *A theologico-political treatise and a political treatise*, trans. R.H.M.E. Elwes, New York 1951

Steinmann, Jean, *Richard Simon et les origines de l'exégèse biblique*, Paris 1960

Thiers, Jean Baptiste, *Traité des superstitions selon l'Ecriture sainte, les decrets des conciles, et les sentimens des saints peres, et des theologiens*, Paris 1679

Thijssen-Schoute, C.-L., 'La diffusion européenne des idées de Bayle', in *Pierre Bayle le philosophe de Rotterdam*, ed. Paul Dibon, Paris 1959, p.152-70

Thils, Gustave, *Les Notes de l'église dans l'apologétique catholique depuis la réforme*, Gembloux 1937

Thomassin, Louis, *Traité de l'unité de l'Eglise*, Paris 1686-1688

Thuau, Etienne, *Raison d'état et pensée politique à l'époque de Richelieu*, Athènes, Paris 1966

Tietz, Manfred, 'Saint-Louis roi chrétien: un mythe de la mission intérieure du XVIIe siècle', in *La Conversion au XVIIe siècle*, Actes du Colloque du Centre méridional de rencontres sur le XVIIe siècle 12 (1983), p.59-69

Tocanne, Bernard, *L'Idée de nature en France dans la seconde moitié du XVIIe siècle*, Paris 1978

Tyvaert, Michel, 'L'image du roi: légitimité et moralité royales dans les histoires de France au XVIIe siècle', *Revue d'histoire moderne et contemporaine* 21 (1974), p.521-47

Vacant, A. and Mangenot, E. (ed.) *Dictionnaire de théologie catholique*, Paris 1903-1950

Vancourt, Raymond, 'La religion de Bayle', *Critique* (1960), p.879-92

Vernière, Paul, *Spinoza et la pensée française avant la Révolution*, Paris 1954

Vigoureux, F., *Dictionnaire de la Bible*, Paris 1926-1928

Viguerie, Jean de, 'Le miracle dans la France du XVIIe siècle', *XVIIe siècle* 140 (1983), p.313-31

Vischer, Wilhelm, 'Calvin, exégète de l'Ancien Testament', *Etudes théologiques et religieuses* (Montpellier) 40 (1965), p.213-31

Vivanti, Corrado, *Lotta politica e pace religiosa in Francia fra cinque e seicento*, Torino 1974

Voeltzel, René, *Vraie et fausse Eglise selon les théologiens protestants français du XVIIe siècle*, Paris 1956

– 'Jean Le Clerc (1657-1736) et la critique biblique', in *Religion, érudition, et critique à la fin du XVIIe siècle et au début du XVIIIe*, Paris 1968, p.33-52

Voltaire, F.-M. A. de, *Dictionnaire philosophique*, ed. Julien Benda, Paris 1961


[Wake, William,] *An exposition of the doctrine of the Church of England, in the several articles proposed by Monsieur de Meaux*, London 1686

Weibel, Luc, *Le Savoir et le corps: essai sur Pierre Bayle*, Lausanne 1975

Wendel, François, *Calvin*, trans. Philip Mairet, London 1963

Whelan, Ruth, 'Le *Dictionnaire* de Bayle: un cénacle livresque?' *Littérales* 1 (1986), p.37-51.

– 'La Religion à l'envers: Bayle et l'histoire du paganisme antique', in *Les Religions du paganisme antique dans l'Europe chrétienne XVI-XVIIIe s.*, Paris 1987, p.115-28

– 'The wages of sin is orthodoxy: the *Confessions* of Saint Augustine in Bayle's *Dictionnaire*', *Journal of the history of philosophy* 26 (1988), p.195-207

Whitfield, J. H., 'Livy ⟩ Tacitus', in *Classical influences on European culture (1500-1700)*, Cambridge 1975, p.281-93

Whitmore, P. J. S., 'Bayle's criticism of Locke', in *Pierre Bayle le philosophe de Rotterdam*, ed. Paul Dibon, Paris 1959, p.81-96

[Widenfeldt, Adam,] *Monita salutaria B. V. Mariae ad cultores suos indiscretos*, in Leydecker, *Historia Jansenismi*, Utrecht 1695, p.631-40


Yardeni, Miriam, 'New concepts of post-Commonwealth Jewish history in the early Enlightenment: Bayle and Basnage', *European studies review* 7 (1977), p.245-58


Zuber, Roger, 'Guez de Balzac et les deux Antiquités', *XVIIe siècle* 131 (1981), p.135-48

# Index

*Addition aux Pensées diverses, see* Bayle

Agreda, Marie d', biography and ideas 14-16; controversy and contemporary attitudes 16-18; Bayle's theological critique of 3, 18-21; affair of 21-23; and popular devotion 26-30, 96-97; *see also* Bayle, *Dictionnaire*

Alexander the Great, 201-202, 205, 206-209, 212, 225, 227

Amelot de La Houssaye, Abraham Nicolas, 204

anthropology, *see* Augustinianism, Cartesianism, Fall, Machiavellianism, Pascal

Arnauld, Antoine, and Bayle 28n; *Défense de la traduction de Mons*, 62, 63-64, 65, 66n; *Logique de Port-Royal* 59, 84, 107n, 112n, 128, 132n, 134, 178; and Nestorianism 48, 53n, 54n; and *question de fait et de droit* 46-47, 48; *Renversement*, 108, 112n, 189; *Réponse à la lettre d'une personne de condition*, 110; *Seconde lettre* [...] *à un duc et pair de France* 48; *see also* Jansenism

Augustine, St, *Adversus Faustum Manichaeum* 170n; and Bayle 187, 194, 206; and biblical exegesis 155n, 158, 159n, 169n, 170-71; *De civitate Dei* 85n, 172, 187n, 192, 197-98, 214n, 216n; and philosophy of history 186n; *De Sermone Domine in Monte* 170n

Augustinianism, 19, 79, 178; anthropology 63, 68, 82, 84, 85n, 166-67n, 223; cosmogony 177; doctrine of Fall 157; ethics 191-201; exegesis 159n, 174n; and *humaniores litterae* 144; original sin 176-77; philosophy of history 186n, 187, 188, 190, 213, 225, 230; politics 202, 208, 211

*Avis important aux refugiez, see* Bayle

Baillet, Adrien, 27, 37n, 101n

Balzac, Guez de, 192n, 197, 200

Barber, W. H., 12

Basnage de Beauval, Henri, 18; *Histoire des ouvrages des savants* 15n, 17, 18, 22n, 27n, 40n, 41n, 44n, 51n, 87, 203n

Basnage, Jacques, 20, 136n, 140

Bayle, Pierre, *Addition aux Pensées diverses* (*APD*) 62n, 67n, 128, 143-44; *Avis important aux refugiez* 80n, 111n; *Critique générale* (*CG*) 36, 49, 50, 59, 61, 62, 63, 65, 66, 68, 69, 70n, 72n, 74, 75, 76, 77, 78, 80, 81, 90n, 93, 99, 112, 125, 143, 161n, 183, 188, 218, 219, 220, 221, 225n; *Commentaire philosophique* (*CP*) 27n, 74n, 112, 143, 151, 165, 167, 168, 171, 184, 187, 188, 194-96, 218, 219, 220, 221-23, 239; *Continuation des Pensées diverses* (*CPD*) 9n, 21n, 66-67, 75, 84n, 85, 90n, 96, 97, 98n, 128n, 129, 134, 136n, 138, 142n, 143n, 146, 178n, 188, 201, 206, 230, 231; *Dictionnaire*: conception of 120, 121, 184-86; and conception of history 186-87; *Préface* 102-103, 105n, 106n, 121, 155n, 185; articles cited (in the order used in *Dictionnaire*): 'Aaron' 156n; 'Abel' 150n, 152n, 155n, 160n; 'Abelli (Antoine)' 114n; 'Abelly (Louïs)' 25; 'Abimelech' 150n, 152n, 155n, 158, 160n, 168, 171; 'Abrabanel' 149n; 'Abraham' 150, 152n, 155n, 160n, 168; 'Accarisi (François)' 77n; 'Acindynus (Septimus)' 168, 170; 'Acosta' 179n; 'Adam' 156n; 'Adriani' 90n; 'Agar' 152n, 155n, 168, 172; 'Agreda' 14-28, 30n, 37, 61, 71, 86, 103, 113, 139, 140, 141, 188, 219, 234, 236, 238; 'Agrippa' 98; 'Akiba' 146n; 'Alciat (André)' 77n, 105; 'Alciat (Jean-Paul)' 91, 111n, 122n; 'Alegambe' 90n, 98, 101n; 'Amphiaraüs' 112; 'Anabaptistes' 170n; 'Anacreon' 138; 'Anaxagoras' 77n; 'Andronicus' (1st article) 99n; 'Annat' 237n; 'Antonio' 122n; 'Arimanius' 150n; 'Aristandre' 208; 'Aristote' (1st article) 102n; 'Arminius' 177n, 179n, 229n; 'Arsinöé' (2nd article) 99; 'Augustin' 158n; 'Baius' 77n; 'Barnes (Jean)' 228n; 'Basta (George)' 99; 'Baudoüin' 99, 106; 'Beaulieu' 121n; 'Beaumont' 229; 'Bellarmin' 237; 'Bezanites' 30n, 65, 79n, 141n; 'Beze' 91n, 92, 108; 'Blondel (David)' 142; 'Bochart' (2nd article) 122n; 'Bolsec' 86n, 91n; 'Bonfadius' 103n; 'Borri' 19n; 'Botero' 98; 'Brachmanes' 136n; 'Brasavolus' 137; 'Brun (Antoine le)' 77n; 'Buchanan' 99n; 'Bunel (Pierre)' 106; 'Caïn' 146n, 155n, 156n, 159; 'Calvin' 29n, 91n, 151n, 197n; 'Camden' 90n, 107; 'Capriata' 73n, 104; 'Castellan' 229n; 'Cassius Longinus' (3rd article) 98n; 'Catius' 88, 114n; 'Cattho' 136n; 'Cavalcante' 102n; 'Caussin' 101; 'Cesar' 207; 'Cham' 150n, 155, 160n; 'Charron' 177; 'Chigi (Fabio)' 77n, 226; 'Cimon' 68n; 'Constance' 97n; 'Daillé' 110n; 'David' 155n, 162, 168n, 174n, 175n; 'Decius' 77n; 'Elie' 168n; 'Elisée' 158n; 'Emile' 107n; 'Epicure' 197; 'Erasme' 27n, 67, 102n, 111n, 229; 'Ermite' 107n; 'Esechiel' 156n; 'Esope' (1st article) 136, 187, 231; 'Eve' 150n, 155, 156n, 157, 158n, 159n, 161n; 'Eugene IV' 226n; 'François (d'Assise)' 22, 91, 143n, 235; 'Garasse' 79n, 86n; 'Geldenhaur' 77n; 'Goulu (Jean)' 131; 'Gregoire I' 91n, 226; 'Gregoire VII' 186n, 225n, 226, 227, 237n; 'Grotius (Hugo)' 83; 'Guebriant' 93n, 98; 'Guicciardin' 205; 'Hadrien VI' 29n, 225n; 'Haillan' 77n, 103-104, 105n; 'Hall (Joseph)' 105n; 'Hall (Richard)' 90n; 'Helene' 83n; 'Henichius' 114; 'Hercule' 89, 90n, 122n; 'Hyperius' 136n; 'Hobbes' 205, 206; 'Hoffman (Daniel)' 178n; 'Hosius' 102n; 'Jansenius' 49; 'Jean, St.' 152n, 156n; 'Innocent XI' 225n, 226; 'Job' 160n; 'Jodelle' 138; 'Jonas' (1st article) 97n; 'Jove' 77n; 'Judith' 168n; 'Jules II' 226n; 'Junon' 96n; 'Lamech' (1st article) 163, 172; 'Launoi (Jean de)' 59n, 105n,

113n, 139-41, 143; 'Laurentio' 183n; 'Leon I' 225n; 'Leon X' 226; 'Loyola' 92, 237n; 'Louis VII' 210; 'Louis XI' 100, 210, 211, 212; 'Lucrece' 197-200; 'Lucrece (Titus)' 187n, 231; 'Luther' 45n, 100, 110n, 143n, 178n; 'Macedoine' 207-11; 'Machiavel' 204-205, 209; 'Macon' 229; 'Mahomet' 51, 52, 100, 217; 'Mahomet II' 62n, 212n; 'Maimbourg' 66n, 107n; 'Mammilaires' 229n; 'Manichéens' 54n, 100n, 176-77, 224; 'Mariana' 64n, 95n, 103n; 'Marie' 150n, 156, 158n; 'Marillac (Louis)' (2nd article) 78n, 92, 102n; 'Melanchthon' 230, 232; 'Milletière' 27n, 229; 'Musurus' 95; 'Nestorius' 19n, 20, 23n, 26n, 29, 30, 32-40, 41, 45, 51, 52, 53-54, 61, 69, 71, 74, 76, 78-79, 86, 91n, 103, 113, 132, 141, 187, 188, 197n, 208, 214, 217, 222, 223, 224, 225, 234, 235, 236; 'Nicolle' 130n; 'Orose' 100; 'Ottoboni' 226n; 'Ovide' 83n, 103, 152n; 'Papesse' 74, 135-38, 141; 'Patin' 98; 'Paul II' 225n, 226; 'Pauliciens' 177n; 'Peyere' 146n; 'Peiresc' 105n; 'Pellisson' 130n; 'Pericles' 89n, 187n, 228n, 231n; 'Perriers' 237n; 'Pyrrhon' 36n, 175-77; 'Pythagoras' 122n; 'Polonus' 114n, 137; 'Poquelin' 185; 'Porcius' 211; 'Reinesius' 121; 'Remond' 1, 5n, 73n, 82, 86n, 89, 104, 107n, 183, 184; 'Rimini' 161n; 'Rodon' 55; 'Roseo' 74n; 'Rotan' 27n, 229; 'Sabellicus' 77n, 98; 'Sainte-Aldegonde' 19n, 236; 'Samson' 160; 'Sara' 155n, 159, 163n, 168, 169, 172, 173-74; 'Sforce' 100; 'Simonides' 178; 'Sixte IV' 225n, 226n; 'Sophronie' 168, 198n; 'Spinoza' 107n, 179n, 197; 'Sponde' 91; 'Suetone' (2nd article) 114n, 205n; 'Tacite' 206n; 'Theopompe' 106n, 107; 'Timoleon' 188, 212-13; 'Viret' 19n, 236n; 'Usson' 82, 89, 120, 184; 'Weidnerus' 91n; 'Xenophanes' 227, 228, 231; 'Zenon (l'Epicure)' 178n; 'Zia' 198n; 'Zoroastre' 146n; 'Zuerius' 136n, 186n; *Dissertation sur les libelles diffamatoires* 79n, 111n, 114n, 120; *Eclaircissemens: sur les athées* 197; *sur les*

*Pyrrhoniens* 179; *Nouvelles lettres de l'auteur de la Critique générale* (*NLC*) 66n, 67n, 70n, 74n, 78n, 108n, 109-12, 113, 239; *Nouvelles de la République des lettres* (*NRL*) 40n, 51n, 60n, 66n, 87, 101n, 102n, 107, 147, 148-49, 152n, 153, 154, 155n, 157n, 158, 160n, 161, 164, 199, 204, 226, 238; *Pensées diverses* (*PD*) 5, 26, 70, 71, 76, 79, 110n, 111n, 122-24, 126-30, 134n, 185, 189-95, 199, 202-203, 211, 214, 215-17, 220; *Projet et fragments d'un dictionnaire critique* (*Projet*) 10n, 114, 119, 120, 121n; *Réponse aux questions d'un provincial* (*RQP*) 69n, 70n, 137n, 160n, 192, 232
Benedict III, 134, 135
Bible, *see* Scripture
*Bibliothèque universelle*, *see* Le Clerc, Jean
Blondel, David, and Bayle 122, 132n, 134, 137, 138, 139, 140, 141, 142, 143, 144; *Familier esclaircissement* 135, 136n, 137n, 138n, 142, 144n
Bodin, Jean, *Methodus* 59, 62n, 66, 68n, 69, 73, 81, 87, 88, 89, 93, 95, 100, 101, 107
Boileau, Nicolas, 208, 233
Bossuet, Jacques-Bénigne, and Agreda affair 16-17, 20n, 21, 28; and Bayle 13, 22; and Du Pin 31, 32, 40-43; *Discours sur l'histoire universelle* 26, 149n, 183n, 213n, 214-15; *Exposition* 24; *Histoire des variations* 214, 219, 223; and popular devotion 23, 27n, 28
Brantôme, Pierre de Bourdeille, seigneur de, 205

Caesar, Julius, 201n
Calvin, Jean, and Bayle 169n, 170, 173n, 197; and Catholicism 125; and cosmogony 177; denigration of 91, 92; exegesis 151, 155n, 159n, 162-63n, 170n, 171n, 172-73, 174n; and Fall 84-85
Calvinism, and authoritarianism 141-42; and Bayle 12, 13; Calvinist methodology 122, 125-26, 144; image of 60-62, 72; and Jansenism 49-50, 76; and notion of elect 113-14, 127, 140, 143; *see also* methodology, Scripture

Camden, William, 90-91
Cantelli, Gianfranco, 12
Cappel, Louis, 148n, 152
Cartesianism: anthropology 68, 82, 84, 85n, 105, 195; and Bayle 13, 178; and christology 35-36; cosmogony 177; and history 82, 102, 131, 133n, 213; materialism 21; and methodology 122, 131, 132n, 133-34, 144; and *passions de l'âme* 195, ambition 77-88, *prévention* 63, 72-75, vanity 193, vengeance 76-77, physiological and psychological 81; and transubstantiation 36-37, 133; and superstition 123
Cassirer, Ernst, 2
Charron, Pierre, 190, 200
Chrysostom, St, 110, 155n
Claude, Jean, and Bayle 13; *Défense de la Réformation* 22, 60n, 108, 109, 125, 215n; *Examen de soy-mesme* 189n
Comynes, Philippe de, 212
*Commentaire philosophique*, *see* Bayle
*Continuation des Pensées diverses*, *see* Bayle
Coronel, Maria de, *see* Agreda
Crasset, Jean, 23-24, 25, 26
*Critique générale*, *see* Bayle
Croset, Thomas, 16, 21
Cyril of Alexandria, background 243-47; and Bossuet 41; christology 32, 33-35; and council of Ephesus 37-40; and eucharist 36; image and typology of 44, 52, 53-55, 81, 216, 219

Daillé, Jean, *Traicté de l'employ des saincts pères*, 110n, 130n, 158-59
Daniel, Gabriel, 169n
Davila, Enrico Caterino, 205
Descartes, René, and *consentement universel* 132n; *Discours de la méthode* 144; and Hobbes 206; and mathematics 121n; *Passions de l'âme* 63, 68n, 81, 105
devotion, popular: attitudes to: of Bayle 27, of Catholics 25-26, of intellectuals 18, 28-29, 155, of Jansenists 23-25; development of 19, 23, 29, 224; and Scripture and Early Church 20; and supernatural in history 70, 95-97; and theology

218-19; to Virgin 15-16, 19, 22, 23-25;
*see also* superstition
*Dictionnaire historique et critique, see* Bayle
Drelincourt, Charles, 36n, 84n
Doucin, Louis, 31n, 45, 47n, 48, 54
Du Moulin, Pierre, 14n, 141n
Du Pin, Louis-Ellies, accused of Nestorianism 32, 41; and alternative history 143,
225, 234; and Bayle 33-39, 52-53, 54-
55; *Nouvelle bibliothèque* 37-42, 139n;
and Protestant historiography 43; and
rehabilitation of Nestorius 31, 33-37,
140; *see also* Bossuet
Du Rondel, Jacques, 199

ecclesiology: Early Church: 20, 42, signs
of 52, 60, 123-24, 215-16, myth of 123-
24, 227, 229, 230, and Calvinism, 125,
218-19, 224, and Catholicism 140, 219,
222, 223, 224, 226; signs of true church
in *PD* 214-18, in *CG* 218-21, in *CP* 221-
23, in *Dictionnaire* 223-30; *testes veritatis*,
52-53, 140, 188, 216, 219, 222, 228,
236; *see also* Illyricus, methodology
Enlightenment, and Bayle 10, 11, 12, 28-
29, 54, 86, 144, 175, 195, 200, 232
Ephesus, council of, 27-40, 41, 42, 243-
47
epistemology, of child, 85n; and devotional
theology 218; and *multitudo* 128-29;
postlapsarian 85, 107, 167-68, 171; and
revelation 166-67; and satire 109-10
Erasmus, Desiderius, 132, 168n, 190, 221,
228, 229, 236
exegesis: Calvinist 151, 158, 161; crisis of
146-49; and ethics 150-51, 165, 171;
Judeo-patristic 149, 150-51, 157, 158,
159, 160, 173, 174, 194-95; 'liberal'
148, 150, 163; and humanism 149, 150,
159; literal sense 160, 161, 165, 168;
and *lumière naturelle* 165, 167, 168, 172,
196; modes: allegorical, tropological and
typological 155, 160

Fall, and anthropology 63, 68, 205; biblical
account of 157-58, 160-61, 164; consequences of 4, 10, 29, 83-84, 201; and
devotional theology 218; 'ethics' of 175-

77; and history 82-86; and revelation
166-67, 179; *see also* Augustinianism,
Cartesianism
Faret, Nicolas, 90n, 105n
fideism 151-52, 165, 168n, 178, 188, 214,
231
Furetière, Antoine, 1

Gallicanism, and Agreda 21; and Bossuet
42; and methodology 135, 139; superstit-
ion 140, 225, 228, 234
Garasse, François, 79, 83, 107, 108, 115n
Graverol, Jean, 60n, 108-109
Grotius, Hugo, 1, 83, 200
Guicciardini, Francesco, 95n, 205, 225,
235n

Hardouin, Jean, 156n
Harlay, François de, 32n
Hazard, Paul 11, 179
Heideggerus, Johannes Henricus, 152n,
225
*Histoire des ouvrages des savants, see* Basnage
de Beauval, Henri
Hobbes, Thomas, 147, 188n, 206
Hottingerus, Johannes Henricus, 152n
Huet, Pierre-Daniel, 146n
humanism, and authentic tradition 121-
22, 126; and Dark Age 99; and ideal of
perfect scholarship 115, 183; and methodology 62, 134, 135, 138-39, 144;
model for *Dictionnaire* 121; and moral
instruction in history 100-101; and rhetoric of sources 97-98; and Republic of
Letters 4, 87, 92, 183; and politics 201n,
209; and satire 236-38; *see also* Lucretia

Illyricus, Flaccius, 22-23n, 140

Janiçon, François, 238-40
Jansenius, Cornelius, 46, 190n
Jansenism, and Agreda 16n; and Calvinism
49-51, 64, 76; and ethics 192, 193; and
Mons translation 63, 64, 65, 66, 75; and
*multitudo* 128; and Nestorius 45n; and
Nestorianism 45n, 46-47n, 48; and po-
pular devotion 23-24; and satire 107-

11; and *question de fait et de droit* 45, 46-47

Joan, Pope, 122, 134-36, 139

*Journal des savants*, 15n, 16n, 17n, 18, 20-21n, 22, 51n, 141n

Jurieu, Pierre, *Abbrégé de l'histoire du Concile de Trente* 24n; and Bayle 5n, 14, 39, 67-68, 82, 86n, 143-44, 145, 168n, 174n, 223, 230, 235, 236, 239; *Esprit de Mr Arnauld* 82; *Examen de l'eucharistie* 21n; and history 73, 97; *Le Janséniste* 24n, 25n; *Lettres pastorales* 24n, 26, 43-44; and Nestorius 43-44, 45; and Nestorianism 31; *Le Philosophe de Rotterdam* 3, 9, 11n, 173; *La Politique* 24n, 25n; *Préjugez légitimes* 124n; *Préservatif* 24n, 25n; *La Religion du latitudinaire* 32n; and satire 237, 240; and Saurin, 32, 53-54

La Bastide, Marc Antoine de, 25n, 217n

Labrousse, Elisabeth, 12-13, 29, 82, 131, 174, 186, 238

Lamy, Bernard, 94, 95

La Peyrère, Isaac, 146n, 147

Lapide, Cornelius à, 150n, 161, 169n, 170n, 171n

Launoy, Jean de, model for Bayle 9n, 28n, 122, 129, 134, 136n, 139-41, 143, 228

Le Clerc, Jean, and Bayle 91-92n, 179; *Bibliothèque universelle* 25n, 26, 40n, 45n; *Parrhasiana* 92n, 100n, 101-102, 103, 104n; and Scripture 163n, 164n

Lemoyne, Pierre, 199

Leo IV, 134, 135

Le Vayer, François La Mothe, and Bayle 62n, 63, 192, 199; *De la connaissance* 81n; *Discours de l'histoire* 61n, 70, 73n, 84, 85, 89, 96, 103; *Jugement sur les historiens* 71n; *Du peu de certitude* 59n, 73n, 89n, 100n, 120n; *La promenade* 81n; *De la vertu* 190-91

*libertins érudits* 3, 11, 105n, 113n, 115, 122, 131, 133, 134, 144, 188-89, 190, 191, 234; *see also* Le Vayer, Naudé

*Logique de Port-Royal*, see Arnauld, Nicole

Louis VII, 209-10, 225

Louis XI, 202-203, 209, 210-12, 225

Louis XIV, 203, 208

Lucian, 103

Lucretia, 191-92, 198-200

Machiavelli, Niccolò, *The Prince* 203, 204, 206, 207, 208, 210, 212n, 220; *Discourses* 220

Machiavellianism, and anthropology 188, 207, 208; and church 220, 221, 223, 225, 226, 227, 229; and history 144, 203, 204, 205, 206, 230, 234, 234n; and politics 202, 204, 205, 208, 209, 210, 211, 212

Maimbourg, Louis, Bayle's critique of 4, 61-63, 66, 149, 236-37; education 72; and Gallicanism 225; *Histoire du calvinisme* 72, 82n, 218, 219; *Histoire des iconoclastes* 74; and historical style 68-69; as preacher 63-66, 77; his *prévention* 72-75; and satire 237; as type of historian 69-70; and scepticism 70; his venality 77-78; his vengeance 76-77

Malebranche, Nicolas, 131n, 166n, 177, 190, 195

Manicheism, 151, 175-77, 216, 227, 231

Marnix, Philippe de, sieur du Mont Sainte-Aldegonde, 18n, 236

Matthieu, Pierre, 203

methodology, and *antiquitas* 123-25; and *l'argument négatif* 136, 139, 140-41, 142; and *ars critica, ars historica*, 119-22, 139, 141, 143, 149, 150, 156; and *auctoritas* 130; and critique of superstition in *PD* 122-30; historical and theological 125-27, 129; and Launoy 139-41; and *multitudo* 127-29, 132, 137; and pessimism 141-45; and Pope Joan controversy 134-39; *see also* Calvinism, Cartesianism, ecclesiology, Naudé

Mézerai, François Eudes de, 90n, 91-92

Momigliano, A.D., 138

Montaigne, Michel de, 10n, 92, 121n, 130, 132, 200, 205, 206

Moréri, Louis, 63n, 72n, 86n

Mornay, Philippe Du Plessis, 22n, 225

natural law, 151, 167, 168, 171, 172, 173, 175n, 176, 177, 195, 196, 200, 201

Naudé, Gabriel, *Apologie* 31, 55, 68n, 74n,

77n, 91n, 120n, 121n, 131-33, 141n,
226; and Bayle 133, 135, 206, 207;
*Instruction sur les frères de la Roze-Croix*
119, 131, 144n, 146; *Science des princes*
29n, 39, 144n, 201, 202, 203, 204, 205,
207, 208, 220
Nestorius, 19; background 243-47; his
christology 31, 32-37; and council of
Ephesus 37-40; and Jansenism 46-50;
and Protestantism 43-45; and Thomassin 50-51; typology of 3, 216, 219, 223;
*see also* Bayle, *Dictionnaire*
Nicole, Pierre, *Défense de la traduction de
Mons* 62, 63-64, 65, 66n; *Essais de morale*
114n; *Logique de Port-Royal* 59, 84,
107n, 112n, 128, 132n, 134, 178; *Perpétuité* 108; *Préjugez légitimes* 60, 107, 108
*Nouvelles lettres de l'auteur de la Critique
générale, see* Bayle
*Nouvelles de la République des lettres, see*
Bayle

Paganini, Gianni, 12
papacy, 224-28, 249
Pascal, Blaise, 178, 179n; and *contrariété*
83, 193, 209; *Provinciales* 107, 108, 110, .
169, 199, 233, 236, 238; *question de fait
et de droit* 46n
patriarchs, lives of, *see* Scripture
*Pensées diverses sur la comète, see* Bayle
Pétau, Denis, 156n
Pezron, Paul, 146n
philosophy of history, conceptual reconstruction of the past 183-84; cyclical
186-87, 223, 224, 231; and ethics 187,
189-201, religion 188, 214-30; politics
187-88, 201-14; *see also* Augustinianism, ecclesiology, Lucretia, Machiavelli, Naudé, Stoicism
Pintard, René, 11
Plutarch, 200, 201, 206, 207n
*Projet et fragments d'un dictionnaire critique,
see* Bayle
Providence, 12, 14; *Dieu caché* 194, 231;
and historical causation 183n, 187, 188,
200-201, 202, 212, 213, 214, 224, 228,
231; and original sin 176-77

*Querelle des anciens et des modernes* 101-102,
158

Racine, Jean, 179n, 207
Rapin, René, 94-95, 100, 104n, 106-107
Rébelliau, Alfred, 60
Reformation, 60, 142, 223, 226, 229, 230,
232, 235-36
*Réponse aux questions d'un provinicial, see*
Bayle
Republic of Letters, 4, 185; and art of
correction 111, 114-15; and asceticism
104-105; attitude to and authority of
source 92-94, 98-103; and Christian
Stoicism 105-106; and cyclical philosophy of history 186-87; dialectic in 63,
86, 119; and diligence 90-91; and elect
or élite 113-14; and *jugement* 91-93;
and religious commitment 115-16; and
rhetoric 95-98; and style 106-113; and
toleration 112-13
Rétat, Pierre, 11
Rex, Walter, 13, 123, 133, 151, 167, 189,
200
rhetoric, and alternative history 234-36;
and hagiography 69, 71, 171, 174; and
harangues 94-95; and history 66-68, 71-
72, 77, 120, 126-27; and panegyrics 69;
and Scripture 156; of sources 97-98;
and style 106-107; *see also* Janiçon, satire
Rivet, André, and Bayle 151, 158, 169n,
170, 171, 172, 173; *Exercitationes in Genesin* 150n, 161, 163n, 168n, 170n, 171,
172n, 198n; *Isagoge* 158, 161n, 171-72
Robinson, Howard, 11, 170n

Sainte-Beuve, Charles-Augustin, 12
Saint-Réal, César Vichard, abbé de, *De la
critique* 114n; *De l'usage de l'histoire* 183,
188n, 202, 205n, 208, 209, 212
Saldenus, G. A., 152n
Salian, Jacques, 156
Sallengre, Albert Henri de, 19n, 119
Sarpi, Fra Paolo, 43, 205, 225, 228, 235n
satire, 69; and alternative history 234-36;
as immoral 79-80, 83; as persecution
80-81; as plague of history 78; *la raillerie*

*chrétienne* 107-11; rules for 237-40; and toleration 112-13

Saurin, Elie, accused of Nestorianism 31n, 32, 53-54; rehabilitation of Nestorius 31, 38n, 40, 44; and transubstantiation 36n

Scaliger, Jules-César, 1, 121, 132

scepticism, 11, 12, 13, 62, 82, 178, 196; historical 59, 61, 73, 83, 120, 185; and Maimbourg 70; and critique of popular ideas 133

Scripture, and Agreda 27, 28, 29; articles in *Dictionnaire* 248; and *ars critica* 149, 150, 156; authority of 12, 130, 133-34, 153, 162, 178, 195, 215; Calvinist theology of 4, 150-51, 152, 157, 159, 160-63, 164, 174, 177; chronology of 146n, 149-50; hermeneutics 151, 157-58, 159-60, 167-68; inspiration of 147, 150, 153, 163, 164; lives of patriarchs 151, 163n, 168-73, 234; and Mosaic authorship 146-47, 150; profanation of 155n, 170n, 175; quotations and allusions: Gen. xii.12ff., xvi.1-15, xx.1ff., xxi.8-21, 162n, 168n; – Deut. xii.12ff., 168n; – 1 Sam.xvi. 20, xvii.55, xxiv, xxvi, 162n; – Prov. viii.14ff., 15; viii.15, 20-21n; – Jer. xvii.9, 83n; – Mt. v.31-32, 170n; xxvii.5, 153n; – Lk. xiv.15, 165n; – Jn. viii.22, 153n; – Acts i.18, 153n; – 1 Cor. vii.4, 170n, 172n; – Gal. v.22, 64; – Heb. xi.4, 159; – Apoc. xii.1ff, xxi.1ff., 15n; as source, 152, 153, 154, 156, 157; style of 164; text and translations of: Hebrew 146n, 152, 160, Greek 152, Genevan 152, 160, Marot 152n, Mons 63, 64, 65, 75, 152, 178n, Septuagint 146n, 152, Vulgate 152, 160; theory of 165-66; and truths essential and inessential to salvation 154, 157, 163; variant readings of 152; *see also* exegesis

Selden, William, 102

Seneca, Lucius Annaeus, 1, 2

Senofonte, Ciro, 12

Serrurier, Cornelia, 12

Simon, Richard, exegete, and Bayle, 4,

28n, 147-50, 153-54, 158, 162, 164n; *Histoire critique des versions du Nouveau Testament* 63n, 64n, 65; *Histoire critique des principaux commentateurs du Nouveau Testament* 64; *Histoire critique du Vieux Testament* 147, 154n, 155n, 158, 161n, 162n

Simon, Richard, *Dictionnaire de la Bible* 148n, 155n

Sirmond, Jacques, 156n

Solé, Jacques, 13

Spinoza, Benedict de, 147, 148, 193, 197

Stoicism, 4, 63, 81, 82, 90, 105, 113, 115, 193, 197; and ethics 198, 200; and history 184, 187

Suetonius Tranquillus, Gaius, 205

superstition, Catholic 26, 42, 45, 49, 124, 189, 215, 224, 227, 228, 235; and Protestants 9n, 22, 50, 235; and history 30, 70-71, 81, 84, 85, 126-27, 187; critique of 3, 9n, 14, 21, 27, 37, 145; in *PD* 122-30; and Launoy 139-41; and Scripture 174; and total depravity 224-25; *see also* devotion

Tacitus, Cornelius, 69, 206n

Tertullian, Quintus Septimus Florens, 110

Thiers, Jean-Baptiste, 9, 27n, 28n

Thomassin, Louis, 50-52

Thou, Jacques Auguste de, 73, 74, 90n

toleration, and Bayle 49-53; and ethics 194-95; hermeneutics 168; and historical style 112-13; and Jansenists 46-47n, 48

Tronchin, Louis, 133-34, 195

Turrettini, François, 201

Vanini, Giulio Cesare, 191-92, 193, 196

Varillas, Antoine, 86n

Vernière, Paul, 148

Voltaire, François-Marie Arouet, and Bayle 2, 10, 11, 14, 55, 175, 179; *Dictionnaire philosophique* 163n, 164n

Wake, William, 26n

Widenfeldt, Adam, 23-24, 27